Action without Hope

Action without Hope

VICTORIAN LITERATURE AFTER CLIMATE COLLAPSE

Nathan K. Hensley

The University of Chicago Press CHICAGO AND LONDON

The University of Chicago Press, Chicago 60637
The University of Chicago Press, Ltd., London
© 2025 by The University of Chicago
All rights reserved. No part of this book may be used or reproduced in any manner whatsoever without written permission, except in the case of brief quotations in critical articles and reviews. For more information, contact the University of Chicago Press, 1427 East 60th Street, Chicago, IL 60637.
Published 2025
Printed in the United States of America

34 33 32 31 30 29 28 27 26 25   1 2 3 4 5

ISBN-13: 978-0-226-83805-2 (cloth)
ISBN-13: 978-0-226-83806-9 (paper)
ISBN-13: 978-0-226-83807-6 (e-book)
DOI: https://doi.org/10.7208/chicago/9780226838076.001.0001

The University of Chicago Press gratefully acknowledges the generous support of the Lafferty Family Endowed Fund for English and the Virginia Graham Healey Fund for Excellence in English, both at Georgetown University, toward the publication of this book.

Library of Congress Cataloging-in-Publication Data

Names: Hensley, Nathan K., author.
Title: Action without hope : Victorian literature after climate collapse / Nathan K. Hensley.
Description: Chicago : The University of Chicago Press, 2025. | Includes bibliographical references and index.
Identifiers: LCCN 2024030261 | ISBN 9780226838052 (cloth) | ISBN 9780226838069 (paperback) | ISBN 9780226838076 (ebook)
Subjects: LCSH: English literature—19th century—History and criticism. | Ecology in literature. | Environmental psychology in literature. | Hope in literature. | LCGFT: Literary criticism.
Classification: LCC PR468.E34 H46 2025 | DDC 823/.80936—dc23/eng/20240723
LC record available at https://lccn.loc.gov/2024030261

♾ This paper meets the requirements of ANSI/NISO Z39.48-1992 (Permanence of Paper).

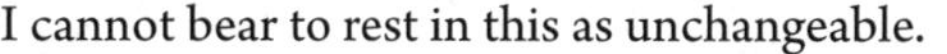

I cannot bear to rest in this as unchangeable.
—Dorothea Brooke, in *Middlemarch* (1871–1872)

Contents

Illustrations

Plates (gallery follows page 174)

Figures

INTRODUCTION
The European Game Has Ended

It's so overwhelming to even just think about it.

—Anonymous participant, Focus Group 2, 2012, asked to discuss "current coastal threats, coastal hazards, personal and governmental hazard mitigation efforts, expectations of future threats, and climate change impacts" (quoted in Moser 295)

I did not expect to escape.

—J. M. W. Turner, on being tied to the mast of a steamship during a storm (apocryphal)

The Abyss

Who saw ecocide more fully than J. M. W. Turner? Among nineteenth-century observers at least, who knew more intimately the visual repertoire—the changed landscapes, the poisoned air, the uncannily reworked light effects—of the world as transformed by human action? "Of all the British landscape artists of the Romantic period," we are told, "Turner was the most fascinated by modernity." That is what the Yale Center for British Art tells us, anyway (Forrester 283), in its curatorial writeup of *Leeds* (1816), only one of Turner's more conventional, because early, depictions of the fossil-fueled lifeworld taking shape around him. The painting deploys the idiom of the nineteenth-century picturesque to frame for middle-class viewers an industrializing Leeds at safe remove: smoke from just-built factories coils gently into the sky in the distance; human figures arrange themselves on the grassy hillside in attitudes of work or leisure. There is a dog.

As is now well known, Turner's later works turn this somewhat orthodox thematic interest in extraction's emergent aesthetic language into new dilemmas for painterly form. Early exercises in the fossil picturesque like *Leeds* become frantically nonlinear vortex compositions, such as *The Angel Standing in the Sun* (1846) or *Rockets and Blue Lights (Close at Hand) to Warn Steamboats of Shoal Water* (1840) (figure 1). These and other of Turner's famed "gyroscope" compositions, tornadoes of color and motion, were overlaid, increasingly, with scumbles of pigment, color on top of color, whose figures—wrecked ships, agonized figures, human witnesses—become subordinated to the rain, steam, and speed of a rapidly carbonizing economy. The inferno Turner saw gathering around him is where we now live.

This book describes what it feels like to live in a world that is coming undone. Its central presumption is that the advance of catastrophe in our post-natural moment produces an intuition, arrived at by embodied hunch or straightforward analysis of the facts, that nothing can be done to stop, or even meaningfully to slow, the interlinked biochemical processes habitually arranged under the heading "climate change." As I will discuss in the coming pages, these processes accelerated massively in the

FIGURE 1. Joseph Mallord William Turner, *Rockets and Blue Lights (Close at Hand) to Warn Steamboats of Shoal Water* (1840). Oil on canvas. Clark Art Institute, Williamstown, MA (1955.37). Photograph: Clark Art Institute.

same mid-twentieth-century period that gave birth to the scholarly field of Victorian studies. Yet they were first set into motion, centuries ago, by the very smoke Turner watched coiling above Leeds. Andreas Malm refers to this as "the warming condition": the curious scenario by which the present is saturated with the concrete physical residue of almost infinite prior acts of capture, combustion, and emission, the future effectively dictated by this ineradicable chemical inheritance. "The air," Malm writes, "is heavy with time" (*Progress* 5).

Escape from this legacy is effectively impossible; transcendence is not an option. Any procedure for creating a livable world will come not from without but from within this inherited past. In 1856 George Eliot used the phrase "incarnate history" to describe the material accumulation of the past in the present ("Natural History" 287). Yet as she might have observed, the trailing aftermath of the nineteenth century is not only material but conceptual too: a matter not just of physical chemistry but epistemological disposition, or knowledge. Eliot evoked the lingering quality of this intellectual architecture by describing "the internal conditions" of human beings immersed in the "external conditions which society has inherited from the past" ("Natural History" 287). Eliot's formulation explains that what lives on from the nineteenth century is not only a set of concrete physical facts like atmospheric carbon or wrecked landscapes but the very conceptual structures we use to understand those things.

To recover the saturated interplay of exterior and interior conditions—of knowledge and fact, extractive practice and intellectual performance—*Action without Hope* analyzes individual creative acts from across the period of fossil capitalism's emergence. In so doing it uncovers a prehistory of what I claim is a deeply contemporary sense of powerlessness; it goes further to suggest how intimacy with artifacts of the nineteenth-century British system might paradoxically clear space for comprehending a world beyond the one to which Turner's anguished spectators bore witness. The British Empire helped universalize the extractive modern paradigm whose aftermath we inhabit now. But it also produced accounts of that catastrophe from within, firsthand reports from inside a society beginning to eat itself alive. Each of the five chapters to follow traces with sometimes hyperbolic care the contours of a given nineteenth-century aesthetic object or set of objects. Taken together, these exhibits can be said to track a handful of exceptionally perceptive writers and artists as they used aesthetic form to come to terms with the early phases of an extractive modern order they correctly understood, with Turner, to be suicidal.

Evoked in the context of socially scaled processes reaching back centuries, the term *suicidal*, like *catastrophe* above it, will sound polemical to readers trained on the euphemisms and circumlocutions of official climate discourse. Yet the self-harming qualities of the extractive paradigm—its crisis tendencies and movement toward its own undermining—are evident to even casual observers today. Poison and cure fold together, such that global climate conferences become business opportunities for oil conglomerates; sustainability initiatives advance continent-sized strategies of new enclosure; and the green rubrics of corporate solutionists have not slowed, but instead accelerated, emissions and the breakdown effects they sponsor (Rowlatt; Adebayo and Bhalla; National Oceanic). But to some particularly acute observers, the autodestructive tendencies of the extractive paradigm were evident from the first. From canonical figures like Emily Brontë, Christina Rossetti, and Eliot to the obscure watercolorist William Berryman, the thinkers I treat here grasped in different ways that their modernizing world was best understood not as continually improving, progressively enlightening, or providing increased comfort for ever more people. Instead they saw themselves as part of a slow-motion calamity: an expanding regime of resource capture and wealth accumulation, fueled by incinerated carbon, whose inevitable failure, it seemed, no single person could do anything to avert.

The terminal crisis of this nineteenth-century world gathers while you read these words. It is legible in, for example, serialized superstorms, clear-cut hillsides, and mass extinction—along with the human suffering those tropes of the climate breakdown story still too often obscure. In this specific material sense, *Action without Hope* documents a nineteenth century that is in fact profoundly contemporary. Yet perhaps paradoxically, given this broad claim for the persistence of the past into the present, the analyses at the core of the book are narrow: focused on small-scaled gestures and seemingly only aesthetic improvisations. These minute adjustments in the given elude the procedures of apprehension and capture in which we have been trained by a world outfitted for total use. They slip past regular habits of mind, evade the practices of attention incentivized by management consultants and the educational apparatuses co-opted by them. Instead of major themes or overarching summaries, then, the arguments to follow are built around local acts of intimate elaboration, sometimes just a brushstroke. The concrete outcome of these gestures in the world, I will seek to explain, is solidarity with others across bounds of difference.

Often these tiny alterations in the structure of the world can seem insignificant: out of scale and unrelated, it would seem, to the higher-order problems that are the ostensible reason for my describing them here. Turner's use of the scumbling technique, for example, in which he would use a knife, brush handle, or thumbnail to scrape one pigment over another in a kind of semitransparent glaze, is from one angle merely a straightforward painterly technique, a thing you do with a tool. But seen in another light, the practice becomes legible as only one instance of how focused attention on the details of aesthetic practice might touch up to problems at a social scale. In this case, Turner's technique can be seen to productively short-circuit long-standing literary-critical and pictorial categories like *surface* and *depth*, and perhaps, with them, the entire apparatus of ideology critique as such. That is because here the concept of *surface* is more a problem than a solution, as one figure creates the ground for another, while each "level" of the aesthetic object remains visible through the next. Rather than latent and manifest, hidden truth and its disclosure, we have walls of incomplete opacity: screens of mediation that separate bare canvas from the eye.

In a note from one of his Louvre sketchbooks, Turner referred to this effect as "crumbling layers" (Townsend, *Techniques*, 52), but a better metaphor might be *archive*, or *ensemble*, since the technique understands gestures at one moment of composition to be recuperable, even amplifiable, in the movements of brush or blade at a later moment. One layer does not supersede the other in a progressive accumulation building toward the present. Instead of overcoding or burial, then, we have an aesthetic mechanism by which a prior movement of the hand might be brought into dynamic relation with a temporally later one, the first act and the second turning now into a single, nonlinear ensemble with no evident priority between them. As my own metaphoric description might have already hinted, Turner's scraping physical engagement with knives and paint, discussed further at the end of this introduction, provides a model for the historical practice of this book, which will draw into relation artifacts from a nineteenth century we have not yet outlived and the collapsing conjuncture of the present.

The steamship at the center-right of *Rockets* (plate 2) can stand as one emblem for Turner's career-long obsession with the extractive regime emerging into dominance across his lifetime. Coal-burning technology figured in his work as early as 1832, and, as one critic notes, "he had sketched and drawn steamships . . . almost from their introduction in England" (Smiles 144). It is important to say, however, that the notion of Turner's exemplary status as a witness to and ambiguous documentarian of a process we used to call "modernity"—the argument with which I opened this book—is uncontroversial. It is, in fact, a cliché, the plot more or less of a 2014 Turner biopic by Mike Leigh ("Heartwarming," "imaginative," and "beautiful," the internet judges [Eve; Uglow[1]]) and the theme of any number of exhibits and shows outfitting this modern painter for an omnivorous culture industry that now finds itself piqued by, and willing to pay for, compelling new content on the topics of "energy," "pollution," and even "climate change."

Turner is a star of this newly concerned milieu. Yet the painter's oft-cited interest in *modernity* and *industrialization* can be more sharply redescribed as a sustained investigation of gathering ecocide and the accelerating processes of enclosure, the capture of nature, and the transformation—in a single lifetime (1775–1851) or one long painting career—of a society fueled by biomass, water, and wind, into one at first unevenly and then almost fully powered by Turner's signal subject matter, steam. I will have more to say across these pages about the intersection of contemporary culture industries, including academic ones, and the material processes of despoliation to which they seem only tangentially related. Here I will repeat something I alluded to above, to be explored more fully in chapters to come, which is that while this book deploys any number of system-level abstractions (*ecocide, capitalism, enclosure*) and advances a broad storyline linking socially scaled activity across centuries, its attention will fall on single things: remaindered instances and particular moments that fall through the cracks of our usual languages for describing global processes.

The point is that no system can be construed but through its individual forms of appearance, no general process felt but in its momentary instantiation in specific places, at human scale—in the flesh. And just as no totality can be grasped in full, so no historical process can be contained entirely by the instances that would evoke it or the conceptual units that would purport to name it. What follows from this basic description of dialectical method is that a properly materialist procedure will resist the closure of high-order labeling and wrestle instead with the impossible dilemma of multitiered or split analysis. The result, for this book at least, is an oscillating double vision, an approach that aims to honor the idiosyncratic detail while keeping sight of the abstract systems of which they are always but a partial evocation. One goal of this book is to depart from conventional ways of framing "environmental" issues by cordoning them from questions of social form and intellectual practice; another is to insist that instances of creative expression constitute theoretical-material interventions into the world, however small they might be and insignificant they first appear.

In light of this point about embodiment and oblique apprehension, it is worth saying directly that Turner's unusually long career spanned the early and then mature phase of England's extractive economy, from his first paintings of sea- and landscapes in the 1790s to his final, almost figureless watercolor sketches from the year of his death, 1851, also the year of the Great Exhibition. The infrastructural transformations of fossil modernity that interested Turner—railroads, causeways, viaducts, steamships—were only part of a process of progressive enclosure and privatization all but universalized during Turner's lifetime. He witnessed the historical victory of a growth-based extractive economy that was definitionally self-defeating, since it not only depended on the sustained, even accelerating consumption of finite stocks of archived sunlight (that is, fossil energy in the shape of coal) but also required expansion to sustain its equilibrium. The conversion of free land to private property, to pick just one part of this omnivorous expansionary process, had essentially concluded by the time of Turner's maturity, given that (as J. M. Neeson notes in *Commoners*) "much of England was still open in 1700; but most of it was enclosed by 1840" (Neeson 5, quoted in Fruit 673; cf. Lesjak 18–30).

Turner's marine scenes tell the story of a society's shift toward total enclosure and full extraction in miniature. Early sea paintings, in the Dutch style, show harbors full of sailing vessels and a chaotic portside mercantilism. A midcareer canvas like *Keelmen Heaving In Coals by Moonlight* (1835) is transitional: it depicts masted sailing vessels in harbor but also working bodies "heaving" fossilized carbon, the scene lit by an inferno. His late ocean scenes, darker and more somber, focus sometimes eerily on the infrastructure of an advanced extractive system: railway trestles, "burning blubber," and always steamboats, these last appearing like ghosts in altered worlds, often "leaving" (figure 2).[2] As the melancholy curls suggest, loss is a central motif, even if the tenor of their wraithlike figures is anything but unambiguous. They are charged with emotion—but it is hard to say exactly which.[3]

The curious feeling of inhabiting a failing world is the subject of this book's first section. But to comprehend how infinitely tiny gestures might scale up to concrete political activity (the focus of the final section), it is necessary to answer what I suggest, in the middle one, is the key historical problem of the late carbon era: How did we come to inhabit this suicide world? In dialogue with recent work on fossil capitalism and the history of extraction by scholars like Malm, Elizabeth Miller, and others, I explain that nineteenth-century observers as different as Karl Marx, William Stanley Jevons, and John Stuart Mill all understood that the bourgeois system metastasizing over their lifetimes was premised on the concept of growth. The centrality of the growth-concept to the rising bourgeois order meant that the system's very stability—its capacity to maintain equilibrium in the present and endure into the future—depended on a ceaselessly expanding energy base and the continued conversion of "natural resources"

FIGURE 2. Joseph Mallord William Turner, "A Steamer Leaving Harbour," from *The Whalers Sketchbook* [Finberg CCCLIII] (ca. 1845). Chalk and watercolor on paper. Tate Gallery, London (D35244). Photograph: © Tate Gallery.

into value. But the world, it emerged, is finite. This constitutive paradox of extractive accumulation meant that crisis was baked into the imperial system from the outset, catastrophe written into the script from the start.[4]

Malm has influentially told the early history of this formation using the phrase "fossil capitalism," while Miller, focusing on literary texts, tells the story of the nineteenth century's intensifying mastery of the earth by centering the idea of *extraction*. This term, crucial for my analysis here, names the "nonreciprocal, dominance based" relation to the land, in Naomi Klein's words (quoted in E. Miller, *Extraction Ecologies*, 7), whose concrete form of appearance is the withdrawal of material from the earth in ways that are nonrenewable on human timescales. As Klein and others have defined it, extractivism in this sense is the opposite of regeneration: in extractive processes, the drive to convert nature into value requires disaggregating ecological systems into isolable units via "forced removal" (Mezzadra and Neilson 2, quoted in E. Miller, "Extraction," 404) or what Jared Hickel simply calls "theft" (76). Its fundamental logic, as Jason Moore notes, is the frontier: a "boundary between commodified and uncommodified life" whose permanent extension is required for the system to maintain stability (222). It is true, as Imre Szeman and Jennifer Wenzel have warned, that the "conceptual creep" of the term *extractive* has converted an analytical tool for describing material exploitation into an all-purpose metaphor for bad behavior and a meme in contemporary moral economies of censure (511). The target of their critique is the too-easy circuitry, in current environmental humanities discourse, between the material and ideological domains, or what Eliot called external and internal conditions: a canonical dilemma in dual-systems Marxism I discuss later in this introduction.

Extraction is a relation to the earth predicated on exploitation. But to exploit means both "to take advantage of in an unfair or unethical manner; to utilize for one's own ends," and "to make full use of; to derive benefit from."[5] It therefore names not just a material practice of *rapio*, seizure, and the conversion of world into value, but an epistemology or orientation toward the world: a grammar of understanding organized around the priority of utility, or use "for one's own ends." How this grammar of understanding becomes actual in material practice, and how these circuits of ideological expression might be rerouted, is the question of mediation that lies at the heart of this book. The density of interplay between material and ideological domains, extraction's internal and external dimensions, is what leads Miller to explain how the coal-fired nineteenth century witnessed an even broader transformation than can be described in the language of "industrialization" or even "fossil capitalism." That is because those processes were only "part of a larger social transformation" across this period, a shift into what Miller calls "an extraction-based life" (*Extraction Ecologies* 6).

As Miller shows in gorgeous detail, and as contemporary discourse on degrowth confirms, the new depletionary paradigm could only ever end one way. For their part, Marx and Engels noted in 1848 that the rising machinery of coal-fired capitalism was self-annihilating in the simple sense that it required permanent expansion, but the world had limits. Marx's favorite target of satire, Mill, had himself already glimpsed the outcome of the very processes of capitalist progress he was otherwise so invested in celebrating. It is a testament to his rigor that in 1848, the bourgeois economist too saw into the future of growth, and, like Marx, warned of a world

> with nothing left to the spontaneous activity of nature; with every rood of land brought into cultivation, . . . ; every flowery waste or natural pasture ploughed up, all quadrupeds or birds which are not domesticated for man's use exterminated as his rivals for food, every hedgerow or superfluous tree rooted out, and scarcely a place left where a wild

> shrub or flower could grow without being eradicated as a weed in the name of improved agriculture. (*Principles* 750, quoted in Mason, *Christina Rossetti,* 10)

Mill's striking picture of a world de-wilded and reorganized for profit was written and revised as the mid-Victorian Acts of Enclosure carved the open world into ever-tinier salable parcels. This timing means that from one angle, anyway, his nightmare had already come to be.

Of course, as Carolyn Lesjak has recently shown, enclosure "continues apace today" and is therefore best understood as ongoing or durational, an "attritional catastrophe" rather than an evental one (7). Given that ever-intensifying processes of privatization and capture extend now to potable water, seafloors, and the surface of the moon, it seems clear enough that the impulse to convert raw material to value will not end of its own accord. Obvious consequences follow: as one official explained in 2019, summarizing a report on biodiversity collapse, "we are currently, in a systematic manner, exterminating all non-human living beings" ("World Missing All Targets"). This analysis isn't precisely right, since the now-universalized practice of factory farming means that the bones from industrially raised chickens have been proposed as one possible marker for a new geological era (Wong), a thin band of processed animal remains to mark our moment in the rock. Human beings, meanwhile, emerge in the total extractive economy rechristened as frontiers for rent-seeking or, if no surplus can be extracted, disposable waste. A logic of generalized enclosure means that one is either a human resource to be turned to account or an instance of "remaindered life" cast to the midden-heaps, refugee camps, and e-waste dump sites of the now-planetary marketplace (Tadiar).

I return to such contemporary scenes of subjection in the conclusion of this book. Now I will note that, for certain nineteenth-century observers at least, the crisis tendencies of the carbon era's rising common sense meant that fantasies of endless advance were always just that; that modern life, as Emily Brontë observed in a school essay, "exists on a principle of destruction" ("Butterfly" 176); and that—in Jevons's italicized warning from *The Coal Question*, 1865—"*we cannot long maintain our present rate of increase of consumption*" (274, emphasis in original). These writers and others saw as if by X-ray through the ideologies of growth still structuring everyday thought and recognized, if just dimly, that the extractive modern project was always conjuring the storms that would eventually wipe it away. The apparent contradiction by which clear analysis and dim apprehension oscillate and trade places with one another follows from my effort to describe historical actors who experienced thought outside available languages, generating knowledge via intuitions that did not yet have names. The question of how writers and artists approached this numinous middle-world of thought, an epistemology of the inexpressible, organizes the readings I unfold in the pages to come.

What is evident here is that the constitutive paradoxes of extraction-based life could only gather intensity as cheap nature became scarcer and the "need" for expansion, in Marx and Engels's words from 1848, "chase[d] the bourgeoisie over the entire surface of the globe" (Manifesto). The violence of this chase would always be felt by those nearest to being caught. Martinican writer Frantz Fanon, for instance, observed the crisis tendencies of the bourgeois system in 1961, when at the conclusion of *The Wretched of the Earth*, he shifts mode to address readers directly. "Come, then, comrades," Fanon writes.

> The European game has finally ended; we must find something different. We today can do everything, so long as we do not imitate Europe. . . . Europe now lives at such a mad, reckless pace that she has shaken off all guidance and all reason, and she is running headlong into the abyss[.] (312)[6]

Having scanned the physical and cognitive wreckage of the Algerian War (1954–1962), Fanon saw around himself a fully colonized world, a global plantation.

In this zone of universal domination, capture had been raised to a kind of religion. Here, he writes in a famous sentence, "they are never done talking of Man, yet murder men everywhere they find them" (*Wretched of the Earth* 311). As Fanon appreciated through the prism of the Cold War, the catastrophe of "Europe" he dates to the early 1960s had its roots in the Enlightenment philosophies of man and the nineteenth-century imperialisms that set those ideas to work: this crisis was system-wide and total, not only human but ecological too—a matter of the earth.[7] Fanon's anticolonial critique is in this sense usefully viewed alongside Samuel Beckett's *Endgame* (1957), whose frozen sociality transpires in a "pollute[d]" world from which even rats have been "exterminated" (3, 54); or Rachel Carson's *Silent Spring*, published a year after Fanon's account (1962), which saw mass toxicity and bodily contamination as the outcomes of the new postwar conglomerates' profit motive. All three writers, despite vast differences of approach and commitment, diagnosed the self-undermining tendencies of a thoroughly modern world, made barren by chemicals and ringed with the concertina wire of total enclosure.[8]

It bears stating directly, however, that in no way is the final demise of the extractive order guaranteed. Against the confident teleologies of the nineteenth-century Marxisms that inspired Fanon, for example, capitalism is in no way certain to collapse, at least in the near term. It is in no way certain that we are in an endgame. To the contrary, the present shows in vivid terms how nimble the current system can be, as it identifies new frontiers of capture, fresh domains of extractive possibility, ever deeper trenches in the ocean to scrape clean of life. The innovations of tar-sands extraction under the banner of "tight oil," for instance, shows that no zone of what Moore calls cheap nature can be cordoned from exploitation forever; the pings and buzzes of our phones confirm that not even sleep is safe from enclosure's desire to engulf and turn to profit whatever spaces of as-yet-uncommodified life remain on earth (Crary 24/7). The work of overturning this relentlessly acquisitive and definitionally ruinous paradigm—or, as I explain, the work of preparing to overturn it—is the ultimate focus of the pages to come.

After Hope

It has become habitual to frame possible responses to this generalized and seemingly irreversible crisis in terms of affective disposition: Hope or despair? Between this suitable pair of affective alternatives an entire subgenre of climate writing now oscillates, as the culture industry offers for well-intentioned readers the privatized emotional registers that are understood to be either "enabling" or "disenabling" for "action." In her moving account of scientists facing down the transformation of the earth in their daily work on coral, for example, Irus Braverman aims to apply what she calls "the hope-despair polarity" to the field interviews she conducted with those who study dying coral reefs every day (250). Against the book's own framing, however, what emerges is that these alternatives cannot be adequate to the scenario at hand, as scientists labor to shape into language the profoundly tangled feelings that arise when something you love bleaches white and dies when your job was to save it.

And Rebecca Solnit, in an updated preface to *Hope in the Dark* focused on climate change (2016), finds that to preserve the hope of her title, the term must be redefined. Hope is not, Solnit writes, "the belief that everything was, is, or will be fine." Instead, "the hope I'm interested in is about broad perspectives with specific possibilities, ones that invite or demand that we act." It is not, she says, "a sunny everything-is-getting-better narrative, though it may be a counter to the everything-is-getting worse narrative. You could call it an account of complexities and uncertainties, with openings" (xiii–xiv). There is much to recommend this diagnosis of a field of uncertainty characterized by openings, as I will myself explain in the following pages, in dialogue with the Italian Marxist Antonio Gramsci's idea of the war of position: the low-intensity and small-scaled operations that prepare the ground for more total confrontations to come.

It is worth observing that Solnit's committed account reworks key insights from Ernst Bloch's *The Principle of Hope* (1954–1959), whose cryptic and idiosyncratic Marxism gives shape to her call for clear-eyed analysis of the present with an eye for tactical intervention (see Solnit, *Hope in the Dark*, 19–23). In the opening chapter of his three-volume project, Bloch distinguishes between cheapened forms of hope that work to sustain existing social arrangements and the orientation toward an improved future without which no human project can proceed. Facile versions of hope, he notes, are "preached from every pulpit," but limited to "mere inwardness or to empty promises of the other world" (I, 5). This degraded hope, Bloch says, common to religious and bourgeois mythologies alike, effectively shunts possibility to the domains of the private or transcendental while silently affirming that the actual world is unavailable for alteration at all. Hope in this false sense becomes the flipside to the nihilistic *refusal to do* that is the bourgeois world's other ideological means of preserving itself. Against the toxic pairing of an evacuated "hope" that leaves the social order unchanged and inert passivity in the face of the status quo, Bloch arranges a reimagined hope that emphasizes the anticipatory impulse: an orientation toward the future informed by an unflinching diagnosis of the present and the commitment to a livable world. It is, Bloch writes, an "intention towards possibility that has still not become" (I, 7).

Bloch is clear that the anticipatory impulses he works to describe do not presume they will achieve fruition, in whole or even partial terms. Victory is in no sense to be expected. Instead such impulses are conditioned by defeat: inchoate strivings to alter the given must be informed, he says, by detailed understanding of the balance of forces in the present and "warm[ed]," too, by "love for the victims, [and] hatred of exploiters" (I, 272). This warmth will be kindled in the chapters to come. But hope in its more usual senses presumes that a given outcome can be achieved, that fulfillment is at least theoretically possible. Conventionally deployed, the hope-concept presumes that the anticipation constitutive of this term might conceivably be met with results to match its forward-looking orientation. It is the "expectation of something desired; desire combined with expectation."[9]

For this reason and others I will elaborate across these pages, the hope-concept in its bourgeois form is desperately mismatched to the catastrophe of the present. That is because the current configuration of the extractive system into what Gramsci called the organic basis of society, the nestling of extraction into the very foundations of life, means that a total overhaul or "fix" is not possible. Victory in a war of maneuver, or frontal assault on a given order, is in no sense achievable. The material processes are too baked in, the police powers of the extractive common sense too entrenched, to allow for resolution in this full sense. Instead: imperfect operations of alteration, minute movements, "*directing act[s] of a cognitive kind*" aimed at reworking from within a given world whose fundamental structures are as entrenched as they are unlivable (Bloch, I, 12, italics original). Coral scientist Terry Hughes, having surveyed the dying Great Barrier Reef by airplane in 2017—the largest living structure on earth—reported that he "showed the results of aerial surveys of bleaching . . . to my students, and then we wept" (quoted in Braverman 87).

As Bloch's account accurately predicted, journalistic frameworks that recycle orthodox sustainability doctrine and corporate greenwashing continue to offer hope and despair as alternative private dispositions to be calibrated toward the ideal outcome of "action." In such formulas this last term, *action*, is habitually understood on the bourgeois template as private, voluntaristic decision in a field of possibility defined by its capacity to be modified, if not entirely reshaped, by individual deeds. This notion of action is itself an artifact of the period of extractive domination that is the topic of this study. As Frances Ferguson has shown, the view of action developed and slowly naturalized across the course of the nineteenth century understands the term to name a discrete and measurable input that can be construed operationally on a binary model: something either is an action or isn't one. The test for this, Ferguson explains, is visibility: to be an action it must be visible, countable, and calculable on a balance sheet of inputs and outputs that define the utilitarian approach (4–5).

On this emergent (in the nineteenth century) and now established understanding, action comes to describe a discernible and at least theoretically quantifiable input to a calculus of likewise measurable factors in an input-output spreadsheet of multifactorial accounting.[10] The action model bequeathed to bourgeois thought from the nineteenth century is economic, then, insofar as it operates on a finally quantitative, on-off model of digital evaluation amenable to actuarial representation and financial capture; it is managerial in that it presumes any antagonism can at least theoretically be solved by the proper or technologically optimized balance of input and output within the system.

Extending Ferguson's account, Daniel Stout has described liberalism's inability to escape the entanglements of the real world in exactly these terms. Stout refers to the "singularly countable action" as the chit of liberalism's metaphysics of causality and describes the forms of collective life and mutual being that have shadowed this fantasy of liberal action since its earliest days (173). The philosophical incoherence of the liberal-bourgeois model has generated infinite elaboration and near-constant conceptual attention, Stout shows, often in forms, like literary texts, whose capacities for analog representation and ability to contain apparent contradiction enable more sophisticated accounts of how change actually comes to be. Like Stout, Jennifer Fleissner has recently defined liberalism's sacred figures of *will* and *action* not as settled ideas to be defended or critiqued but as domains of contestation and creative exploration within a conceptual-philosophical tradition we cannot in any case escape: "enduring dilemmas," Fleissner calls them, wound at the core of the modernity story itself (xii). Fleissner's account helps underscore a key premise of this book, which is that the internal and external conditions of an inherited past cannot be approached with any expectation of transcendence, but must be worked on immanently, from within.

Action without Hope shares with these scholars the sense that the conceptual inheritance of the Enlightenment is not so easily discarded as the neoromantic gestures of some ecocritics might today suggest. Anne-Lise François has referred to "overly narrow definitions of action as production and articulation" that are, she says, "associated with Western modernity's ideology of improvement" (33). But as François further argues, the disablement of these heroic modes, in strategies of *désouvrement* and suspension offered by figures like Maurice Blanchot or—in contemporary ecocriticism—new materialist claims of relational matter or posthuman assemblage, are themselves easily recuperated into a (masculine) heroic mode, albeit now in the key of a romanticized renunciation that is suspiciously like an ideology of escape. Such recuperated romanticisms would reclaim heroic mastery in the act of negating it or pretend to transcend the world by opening up domains of emancipation in the mind (see also Bloch, I, 5). Against such fictions I describe how the ideological infrastructure of freedom persists into our broken world as an injury that will not heal. The task becomes to survey the fragmentary remains of the modern concept-world and to salvage from the ruins of the bourgeois project the materials by which alterations in the structure of the given might be effected.

In this sense and others, the present undertaking is an exercise in historical epistemology, since it aims to track the conditions for knowing across a dynamic historical arc and to generate an account of how categories for accessing and comprehending reality emerged alongside a material condition—extractive capitalism—that was their social condition of possibility. And while I have so far set up a historical model of persistence and simple identity, claiming that the nineteenth century "lives on" in the present, in fact the storyline to be advanced here is more complex than that. My suggestion is that an epistemology of extraction, predicated on use and the domination of the object world, developed over a timeline whose looping course I chart across four moments of intensity or semi-discrete phases: the early experiments in slave-based monoculture on the British sugar islands, the emergent fossil capitalism of the nineteenth century, the mid-twentieth-century Great Acceleration, and, roughly speaking, the present.[11]

This periodizing claim will not take shape here as a linear story or vectored historical line; still less will it become recognizable as a unified *genealogy of extraction* or *history of capitalism*, though it draws on several such accounts. Instead these moments of intensity will rotate, swap places, and inform one another in a storyline I understand to be both continuous and, in each moment of its configuration and deployment, singular.[12] The periodizing model I rely on thus understands itself as figural in the sense that it constellates crucially distinct but, I argue, related moments into an itinerary of material causal relation that it nevertheless does not propose on the model of teleological sequence. And while the narrative of gathering enclosure and material unraveling to which I have alluded rests on what seems to be a sequence of beginnings, middles, and ends, it is crucial to my claims here that at no point was the outcome of this story set in stone. The idea that historical processes can be altered is the core principle of this book.

One point that follows from this claim for the nondeterministic nature of the "fossil capitalism" and "imperialism" stories is that the past itself cannot be understood as sealed in a wax museum of things, dead and fixed. Against what Bloch calls the "seclusion of the preterite," in which prior knowledges are hypostasized into false grammatical fixity by the simple past tense (I, 284), I understand the nineteenth century and its uneven records as an archive of possibility available for poetic redeployment and committed rearticulation in the present: a participial, rather than preterite, ensemble. This approach aims to resist the temptation to moralize backward on a neutralized past even as it construes the scene of its own writing as (in Martin Jay's words) "itself a contingent historical context, which generates unexamined assumptions"—presumptions that are, I add, themselves implicated in the story of fossil modernity unevenly told across this book's long arc (16). My approach to periodization is "poetic," then, at least in the sense Theodor Adorno meant when, in an essay on Hölderlin given first as a talk in 1963, he explained that "the logic of tightly-bounded periods, each moving rigorously on to the next, is characterized by precisely that compulsive and violent quality for which poetry is to provide healing" ("Parataxis," 135). For Fanon writing the year before, the universalizing system of extractive domination moved at a mad, reckless pace, pushing always toward an abyss. That abyss is our present.

In such a conjuncture, I suggest, the notion of action itself must be rebuilt. As I show in chapter 4, the vestigially cybernetic presumption that systems can be brought to equilibrium by the expert management of inputs is an artifact of the neo-Victorian projects of the early Cold War. Here I will observe that the impoverished and self-evidently contradictory concept of action proffered by the bourgeois voluntarisms of the eighteenth and nineteenth centuries—base code for the contemporary capitalist cognition whose emergence I chart in these chapters—finds any number of shapes in contemporary climate discourse. The cartoon models of action driving these techno-managerial approaches are perversely evident in efforts, for example, to quantify the added value of natural scenery; to price out air pollution on unit terms; or to measure the human benefit-effects of wildlife, say, or potable water, so that both can be integrated into actuarial representations of the costs and benefits of an analytical field called "the world." Ones and zeros, everywhere.

The extractive order's action model is materialized yet more vividly in corporate efforts to measure the unit-price of student protests, say; cost out the possibility of labor strikes; or forecast possible "impacts" of organized insubordination against the fossil system so as to work around these externalities and keep the machine churning at full efficiency. For the Emirati carbon-capture firm that purchased some 20 percent of Zimbabwe's publicly owned forests for the purposes of converting them to offset plantations in late 2023, for example—along with parts of Angola, Zambia, Tanzania, Liberia, and the Bahamas—such calculations helped underwrite a strategy by which tiny chits of salable action, *carbon credits,* could be accumulated and then sold on a global exchange. Given that the purpose of Blue Carbon is to sell these chits back to the UAE's state oil company, ADNOC, whose president also chaired the COP28 climate summit (Adebayo and Bhalla), it is clear enough that the primary purpose of any market in so-called offsets is to enable the extractive system to continue as before and ideally accelerate its operations. As Blue Carbon's website observed: "Climate strategies must include tangible actions and local and international collaboration to faster [*sic*] low carbon transitions."[13]

The hiccup between *faster* and *foster* on the petrostate's greenwashing website is poetic insofar as it betrays that one purpose of contemporary action-jargon is to accelerate processes already in place rather than open space for interrupting them. (The glitch has since been corrected.) In a yet more degraded idiom, the fairy-tale worlds of "tangible action" and naïve voluntarity find shape in the helpful charts and instructive graphs that now circulate smoothly through the circuitry of contemporary common sense. Lacquered in the visual Esperanto of corporate design, these approved messages urge us to reduce meat consumption or recycle, *taking responsibility* and *doing your part* and *reducing your carbon footprint* in ways perfectly consonant with the predictions of the Ogilvy and Mather public-relations campaign that invented the carbon footprint concept for BP in 2004 (Kaufman). Such refurbished individualisms are in no sense adequate to a scenario defined by the terrible dizziness of actual unwinding.[14] Interviewing California residents in 2012—an early and comparatively halcyon moment in the unfolding of the current crisis—one researcher found that while some of the most engaged residents were willing to speak freely about the alterations to their lifeworlds, "others found the topic so emotionally distressing that they did not volunteer their fatalistic views until invited to speak to them" (Moser 294). The unnamed focus-group participant cited in the epigraph above could not answer the prompt at all, instead noting: "It's so overwhelming to even just think about it" (quoted in Moser 295).

Such aphasic affective withdrawals cannot be counted in unit terms. In the popular press, however, tropes like "climate grief" and "environmental despair" labor to domesticate such alien states of suspension into already existing grammars or shape the old ones to new purpose. The need to grid out and manage unproductive states of feeling ensures that diagnostic terms like *ecoanxiety* have emerged alongside efforts to develop therapies and even, perhaps, cures for this emergent new disorder (Belkin).[15] The curative aspirations of such therapies aim to outfit human beings for continued optimal performance in a world that is functionally broken, drowned by superpowered rainstorms and scorched by the fires of a total burning. The well-meaning efforts of the psychologists just referenced, then, work alongside the previously noted complaints about climate "doomism" to repackage bourgeois thought and Victorian-era myths of progress for the era of structural collapse (see plate 1).

The complicities of this intellectual tradition with the dynamics it aims to redress mean that other bodies of thought, outside the therapeutic rhetorics of climate journalism, the vestigial voluntarisms of neoliberal management-speak, and the normative neoromanticisms of flat ontology in the environmental humanities, are required. These other vocabularies help illuminate what is most daring about the counter-bourgeois experiments I recover in these pages. In chapter 1, I describe the woozy and unstructured affective states that arise from the failure of "world" understood in the phenomenological sense as stable background for experience. In chapter 2, I track the long unfolding of an extractive episteme in the greatest and most difficult novel of the period, *Wuthering Heights*. Chapter 3 turns to poetry and begins to sketch how, in Emily Brontë's cryptic and nearly illegible poetic fragments, the grammar of an obscene common sense might be rewired. Chapter 4 addresses Eliot's astonishing novel of interconnection, *Middlemarch* (1872), to show how its notions of feedback and systemic entwinement relay across discrete moments in the extractive system's long itinerary. Chapter 5 returns to poetry to show how Christina Rossetti's icy and withholding verse positions solidarity among the dispossessed not as a solution, but as a strategy for endurance in the ruins of a world carved up for profit.

A conclusion comes back to painting. William Berryman's tiny watercolors of an extraction-scarred Jamaica, circa 1811, show how the wobbling and inevitably erroneous notation of daily practices among the dominated—improvised life—might disclose new political forms emerging from within the grid of total enclosure. Across these arguments I labor with inevitable failure to maintain contact with the lifeworlds and ways of knowing overrun by the progress of our modern storm. This attempt necessitates a broad bibliography: Black studies, feminist theory, and postcolonial studies, for example, have long been concerned to understand the world-making powers of subjects conscripted into systems whose terms they did not choose. For these reasons, I draw on theorists of minoritized life who have helped recover modes of effectivity and elaboration that take shape when the concepts of *will* and *consent* are brutally inadequate to the situation. One contribution of *Action without Hope* is to show what theories of subaltern capacity might teach us about hope under climate change.

But as the title suggests, this book goes further to argue against the presumption that hope in its everyday sense is necessary for action in today's burning world at all. Like the uncompromising poetry of Brontë and Rossetti I discuss in chapters 3 and 5, the traditions of anticolonial and revolutionary thought teach us that collective practices need not have any anticipation of positive outcome to sustain commitment in a struggle. By reanimating the figure of a collective action without expectation, scaled up from tiny gestures, this book reverses the scholarly focus on the bourgeois individualism and progress stories long associated with the Victorian period.

It also recalibrates world-scaled analyses of "the Anthropocene" down to gestures and details, specific objects and performances, and (most importantly) the human beings who practice these modes of intervening in the world. These elaborative, downscaled idioms of making and doing reconfigure the common sense of their age and ours; in its place they propose a vernacular theory of minor activity that is premised not on autonomous decision or completed projects but on solidarity and the performance of mutual aid in a world that has been programmed to destroy itself. This program can be rewritten. But that rewriting will always be partial; it will transpire from within, not outside, the degraded grammars in which the modernity story has unfolded so far. Seen with the restorative practice of historical attention I describe in the coming chapters, the acts of recoding to follow open spaces for effecting change from within a system of aspirationally universal capture.

Shipwreck, with Storm

As I've indicated, this system took shape across the jagged unfolding of a nineteenth century that saw depletionary life, in Elizabeth Miller's term, emerge, coalesce, and become dominant. When Joseph Conrad told this story, he figured the tale of fossil modernity's arrival as straight decline, manifesting a conservative nostalgia for a purer age of sail in novels like *Typhoon* (1902) and *Nostromo* (1904). Turner, by contrast, documented the slow universalization of extraction with important ambiguity. His depictions of the whaling industry in canvases like *Whalers* (1845) and *Whalers (Boiling Blubber) Entangled in Flaw Ice, Endeavouring to Extricate Themselves* (1846) show what looks to me like smeared death, but were painted on speculation to please a whaling magnate. Hyper-canonical studies of railways and toxic air like *Rain, Steam, Speed* (1844)—stars of faculty PowerPoints on the horrors of industrialization—were repulsive to the otherwise fawning Ruskin, since, in his mind, they "celebrated the man-made modernity that [Ruskin] deplored" (D. B. Brown, "Born Again," 34). But the same painting whose alleged cheerleading made Ruskin ill was, for Théophile Gaultier, "a real cataclysm. . . . You would have said it was the setting for the end of the world" (quoted in Gage 190).[16]

Turner's later works hover yet more restlessly in this crucial space of irresolution. They resist subsequent viewers' desire to script them into

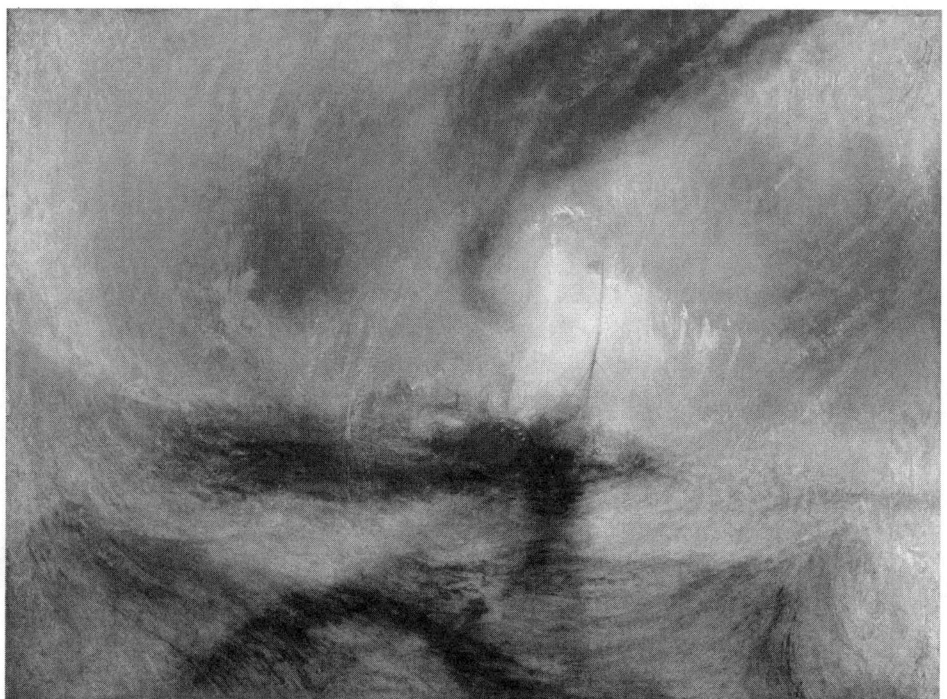

FIGURE 3. Joseph Mallord William Turner, *Snow Storm—Steam-Boat off a Harbour's Mouth* (exhibited 1842). Oil on canvas. Tate Gallery, London (N00530). Photograph: © Tate Gallery.

the shape of either fawning national epic or critical account of early-phase climatic change. To see, today, Turner's smeared and darkened vortex compositions like *Snow Storm—Steam-Boat off a Harbour's Mouth* (1842) (figure 3), or to view privately, as I did before the pandemic, the late-career watercolor sketchbooks of shipwrecks and fires held in the Tate's Turner Bequest, is to watch someone in the process of reckoning with a catastrophe whose full character is not yet fully apprehensible to him. The historian Bernard Bailyn differentiates between manifest historical processes, which were evident to the actors who lived through them, and latent historical processes, which were unknown to contemporary participants but become legible, later, from historical remove. Turner's acts of witness escape this distinction, since they model an incipient, as-yet-unformed knowledge of a system predicated on destruction.

Turner's interest in shipwreck was fundamental to this aesthetic practice of slanted or performed historical knowledge. I use the phrase *performed historical knowledge* to describe a non- or paracognitive mode of apprehension that transpires in physical enactment and somatic motion and is, by virtue of that embodiment, nonfungible: available for reproduction, transmission, and capture—even in my own accounts here—only at a loss. It is true that, like seascapes and sailing generally, shipwreck was a canonical theme for easel painters in this period. But Turner was more drawn to maritime tragedy than most.[17] Ruskin felt the sea played to Turner's strengths, since they let him juxtapose "Terror and Repose" (quoted in Riding 11). The critic was fond of bloviating upon Turner's handling of the sea, but he also saw in the sea and wreckage works a crystal of the painter's interest in the devolution of established forms, a "wild, unwearied, reckless incoherency" manifest also in his treatment of sky (quoted in Concannon 211).[18] (Ruskin later said the paintings were evidence of mental derangement.) Criticism has long seen how shipwrecks "aestheticiz[e] rupture," since they turn the breakdown of established order into spectacle and narratological event (Mentz xxvi). For Steve Mentz, the shipwreck story is a "thoroughly antipastoral view of the human relationship with its environment" (xxxi), since it shows not harmony or continuity but breakdown, unwinding, and ruin. The important twist, for Turner, is that he is part of the story.

When Hans Blumenberg describes shipwrecks as paradigmatic of the modernity experience, he understands shipwreck as a kind of ultimate experience in the sublime: we witness disaster from a position of safety, and emergency becomes, in one gloss, a "public spectacle" insofar as the wreck "places the spectator . . . in an ethical and aesthetic relationship with the disaster's victims" (Taylor, "Going Down," 145). For Kant as for Burke, of course, the key to the sublime was precisely this remove of the spectator from the scene of danger, or (in conceptual terms) his transcendence with respect to the threatening event. All three thinkers—Kant, Burke, and Blumenberg—understand "us" to be outside the wreck. We are subjects and it the object.

But the collapse of form in Turner's shipwreck paintings, their program of disabling normal figure-ground relations and implicating the viewer in scenes of dissolution, model something else, a kind of counter-sublime by which we are not separate from but immanent within, indeed living inside the disaster.[19] It is important, given the mix-up of subject and object characterizing Turner's late-career mode, that to make *Snow Storm,* he did not imagine the scene from a distance nor view the scene from the safety of shore.

According to the canonical biographical episode, he was at the center of the vortex. As his biographer reports and any number of gallery websites repeat, Turner (in his own words) "got the sailors to lash me to the mast to observe it; I was lashed for four hours, and I did not expect to escape, but I felt bound to record it if I did" (quoted in Finberg 390). I recount this detail, which is almost certainly embellished if not completely false, because it concretizes a point about Turner's work that is relevant to the procedure of this book. Turner made art from inside the soot-dark core of an extractive modernity, taking as central subject a process in which he was also a participant. His ambiguous testimonials translated the embodied experience of world-historical transition into the aesthetic idioms of color, figure, and gesture; these formal languages thus give material form to systemic movements far larger than any single act of notation could ever contain.

Bound at the center of a storm unfolding around him, positioned within a disaster he then labors to evoke as though from outside, Turner and his work help frame linked problems for thought in the era of earth systems collapse. These are: (1) how an individual cultural producer or artifact might be understood to bear witness to a historical process whose full shape is not yet cognizable at its own moment of creation (this is a problem of historical position in a still-unfolding nineteenth century); and (2) how the inchoate, because emergent, effect thus witnessed might be understood not as an object outside its viewer, not as a thing an artist or critic could "represent" or "depict" according to the subject-object protocols of instrumental reason, but as a process in which the viewer-author participates, and even, by his own act of documentation, modifies, if only at vanishingly tiny scale. This question is one of immanent critique: how an aesthetics of wreckage, or the analysis of it, might understand its own procedures not as separate from, but immanent within a systemic disaster that is also the subject of the artwork itself.

Market-tested arguments continue to offer private optimism as an antidote to structural crises. Against such accounts I track a handful of nineteenth-century writers and artists as they developed nonstandard languages from within the bourgeois voluntarisms and orthodox grammars that continue to structure how we think about action in failing systems today. A key thread of the book is that no effort to survey, diagnose, or even ascertain the contours of the contemporary crisis can unfold as though from beyond it. We speak the dialect of this disaster; it shapes our thought and forms our patterns of mind. Often these shaping mechanisms are strikingly explicit, as when fossil fuel companies pay off universities, petrostates privatize mangrove swamps, or extractive conglomerates fund research on climate science and the environmental humanities.

In these obvious cases the links between culture and materialism are unnervingly direct, if uncertain in their final meaning. As I note in chapter

1, Ian Hacking's classic study of probability thinking in the seventeenth and eighteenth centuries, *The Taming of Chance,* a foundational text for humanistic studies of the relationship of science and literature, was published with support of the Exxon Corporation (Hacking, front matter). Tedious memoranda and everyday budget documents at Cambridge University Press list costs charged to "EXXON FUND" and refer to $50,000 transferred from the oil company to the press in 1984. Day-to-day correspondence also alludes to newly commissioned books on, for example, voluntarism.[20] In the mid-1980s, Exxon also funded James C. Scott's research into the subhistorical strategies of resistance that I draw on in chapter 4 (*Domination* xvi). It is by now well known that during this period Exxon was conducting internal research on climate change while developing a coordinated, multimillion-dollar public strategy of deferral and obfuscation, a process made famous in the "Exxon Knew" campaign.

It is no accident that academics were conscripted, however unknowingly, into this broad project. A critical tactic for "heavily regulated industries," as one guidebook for corporate strategy specified in 1978, is to shape the intellectual conditions in which they operate. The how-to guide explains that

> regulatory policy is increasingly made with the participation of experts, especially academics. A regulated firm or industry should be prepared whenever possible to coopt these experts. This is most effectively done by identifying the leading experts in each relevant field and hiring them as consultants or advisors, or giving them research grants and the like. This activity requires a modicum of finesse; it must not be too blatant, for *the experts themselves must not recognize that they have lost their objectivity and freedom of action.* (Owen and Braetigam 7, quoted in Franta 556, emphasis mine)

The guidebook outlines the direct means by which corporate propaganda can be laundered into knowledge via the mediating function of scholarship. These efforts "must not be too blatant," the strategists caution; and "the experts themselves must not recognize" that they have been compromised, that "they have lost their . . . freedom of action." The authors of *The Regulation Game* are discussing the tactical capture of scientific experts rather than highly mediated sponsorships of Cambridge book series (Hacking) or anthropology postdocs at MIT (J. Scott). Still it is useful to recall here that Turner had no problem painting a theme to please a patron or conjuring an incident to wow academy judges. He, too, was co-opted by the system to which he bore witness; he too was part of the broken world he depicted. The title of the Exxon-funded Cambridge series is "Ideas in Context."

Commissions from extraction magnates, like oil company names on book frontispieces, are obvious. More often the filaments of co-optation are subtler; the sinews of involvement are, to use Eliot's term, more gossamer. Across these chapters, my suggestion will be that no one has "freedom of action" in the sense imagined by the industry strategists cited above: we are all tied to the mast in storms we did not initiate. In such a situation the task becomes to inventory the material means by which approved grammars and orthodox motifs of thought connect with, and support, the regime of capture they purport to critique—as when sustainability, for example, is deployed as a meme to justify the expansion of politer forms of neoliberal extraction, resilience deployed to normalize disinvestment, or toxicity thresholds put in place to effectively pre-approve "safe" levels of poisoning (Bosworth et al.; Bond 7–8).

In this book at least, the point of such analyses is in no way to produce a moment of disclosure that suggests how apparently critical discourses are in fact co-opted, or that seemingly unencumbered intellectual practices are actually compromised. It is instead to suggest that all critical discourses are co-opted in some sense, "compromised" insofar as they are necessarily immanent to a total material order whose fundamental architecture is defined by extraction and use. When rationality itself has been shaped to fit the contours of existing social and political arrangements, and when those arrangements are predicated on destruction, it is plain enough that the circuitry of reason must be rewired.[21] Thus, a further goal of this book is to show that small-scaled acts of reconfiguration can torque a fallen idiom from the inside, interrupting the smooth functionality of a world whose obscenity is coded into the very structures of everyday thought and speech. These small acts of sabotage can then help create lines of filiation by which other, equally unfree speakers of our broken language might find solidarity in struggle.

As I've already repeated, the variations of scale between the tiny details I describe and the vastness of these topics will seem dizzying. Yet as I show in the chapters on poetry in particular, such scalar tricks are these writers' own method and practice: Christina Rossetti approaches the cosmic scales of universal time in poems as short as four lines long. Like Rossetti, Brontë engages vast metaphysical dynamics—"infinite immensit[ies]," she calls them—with poetic performances written on scraps that, in the hand, feel no bigger than Post-It notes. Her efforts go smaller still, in subsyntactical features that alter at almost illegible scale the gathering bourgeois common sense these verse fragments take as their target. Brontë systematically misspelled some of the key terms of the narcissistic lyric tradition she inherited and sought to rework, giving *despair*, for example, as *dispair*. Her microstylistic innovation warps the internal structure of this conventional Romantic mood to emphasize severing or de-wholing, dis-pair, against the privatizing mythos of a self-consolidating sadness. A list of Brontë's habitually misspelled words also includes *griv* (grieve), *hopless* (hopeless), and *whreched* (wretched) (E. Brontë, *Poems*, ed. Roper and Chitham, 279).

Seen with the restorative attention I model across these pages, Brontë's seemingly erroneous slip of the pen—corrected by every editor ever to have worked on the poetry—becomes legible not as a mistake at all. Instead it is a tiny aberration from a language whose relationship to a gathering catastrophe was, for Brontë, readily apparent. Her immensely small gesture disrupts the frictionless circulation of an extractive common sense and at least one of its approved genres. What such glitchy instants of disfluency open up are tiny spaces of elaboration within the otherwise total confines of a European Game that was emergent in Brontë's day, regnant in Carson, Beckett, and Fanon's, and materially collapsing in our own. In these small gaps can develop what Gramsci called wars of position: downscaled, localized struggles that do not themselves overturn a given order but prepare the way for the changes in the organic basis of society so that a more total war might emerge in the future.

As I've suggested, one aim of this book is to evoke the historical pileup by which a nineteenth-century past is not really past at all. Instead it lives on, in the material infrastructures and chemical aftereffects of a world that is coming undone. But it lives too in the systems of thinking we bring to bear in knowing those things: in the cognitive structures and mental grammars inherited over the long unfolding of the bourgeois experiment. Such a double account as I have just given would seem to pit material facts against mental ones, in this way tracking along the well-worn grooves of what Marxist theory refers to as the base-superstructure dynamic or, in the materialist feminism of Lise Vogel and recent work by Nancy Fraser for example, dual-systems theory. In this enduringly alluring analytical model, material processes sit on one side of an analytical divide, and cognitive or mental processes ("culture," "ideology," or "identity") sit on the other.

But when Eliot referred to the historical interplay of "external" and "internal" conditions she drew attention to the relations of mediation that connect the physical world and the cognitive structures we use to conceive it. In positioning mediation as a site of material possibility, I part from the resilient dualisms of orthodox materialism to focus on how ideation becomes actual in physical gestures, often tiny, that instantiate conceptual movement in the world. We encounter these traces only belatedly, and at removes: through the circuitry of mediating screens and inescapably translational repackaging across gulfs of difference, one layer of paint overlaid upon another. The acts of internal disruption I recover here are separated from us by time, removed from me by situation, knowable only at distance. They are legible only as translations. Yet the wobble of a pen or scrape of a paint-knife, recoded into printed lyric or .jpg on a screen, nevertheless testifies to moments of embodied practice whereby the script of the given has been altered. In this sense, what *Action without Hope* attempts to practice is a kind of salvage analysis: a recuperative relation to past cultural performances that views this archive of prior acts not only as a cognitive prehistory of our present ruin, but also, and in opposition to this prehistory, as a repertoire of concrete possibility based on collective work.

For that reason and others, this book's answer to the key question of the era of climate collapse—what can we do?—will emerge only slowly across these chapters, via the threadwork and detail of an almost fanatically inductive analytic procedure. By this argumentative process, ideation and argument emerge only in tandem with the objects in which those things are instantiated. The purpose of such a wandering style, to be explained in more detail in the pages to come, is to honor the swerve of individual creative acts and model forms of attentiveness that cut against now-universal demands for efficiency and optimization. To invest attention in such overrun instances is, I contend, to maintain fidelity to the details overcoded by just such cognitive habits as Brontë interrupts in her agrammatical practices and allegedly bad spelling. Against the homogenizing demands of thematization and summary, I mean, this book lingers in particularity. Its long chapters and focused readings can be read as formal symptoms of a practice intended to interrupt the reifying tendencies of critical projects that mimic in their own analytic habits the top-down logics of branding, capture, and self-proprietorship that have organized our burning world since the time Brontë first misspelled *despair*.[22] The chapter summaries I gave were only one sentence long.

But no escape is total, no procedure pure. In ways that will become clear across these chapters, it is relevant to my points above that *The Wretched of the Earth* was written in a language I do not really know. The title of this introduction, then, arrives to the English-speaking reader like me only in altered form, via circuits of transmission, recoding, and citation. Each of these translational acts was situated in a particular moment and material scenario that (so I argue here) it is the business of a committed literary criticism imperfectly to reconstruct. Despite having been written in English, every artifact I describe in the coming chapters is foreign in this sense too: produced by physical means in a singular situation that can be comprehended only by analogy and inevitably distorting acts of later recovery. The material infrastructures and concrete scenes that enable such reconstruction are not outside of but within the European game Fanon identifies: Brontë's editors no less than I myself exist inside the dynamics of capture that are the subject of this book. The university that pays my salary takes funding from leveraged buyout specialists to support "global business" (Scarborough). The bill for Fanon's travel to the United States at the end of his life was paid by the CIA (Macey 485–86). Yet the broken world enables new solidarities too. Constance Farrington, the first English translator of *Les Damnés* and thus an effective co-author of the now-canonical Grove edition I cited earlier, was from Cork, Ireland. She reported being drawn to Fanon's work because of similarities she saw between the Algerian War that provided Fanon's context and the freedom struggle in Ireland that was her own.[23] One layer, visible through another.

Like all ideation, then, Fanon's has become material in singular acts of inscription and relay that transpired in overlapping political grids, social timelines, and physical worlds. The processes by which ideation becomes real are characterized by an almost infinitely describable particularity of circumstance, down to places, names, dates, details, strokes of a pen, or (in Fanon's case) spoken words taken down by dictation. Yet such microscopic scenes of relay—the domains of the particular—open out, as in Turner's incomplete sketches or Brontë's tiny fragments, to vistas of analysis larger than can be contained in any empirical recounting of pointillistic details. Fanon dictated the book to his wife Josie or his assistant Marie-Jeanne Manuellan; accounts differ. Both should be considered, with Farrington, further uncredited co-authors of this call for heroic anticolonial militancy (Macey 450; Shatz 298). Any responsible account of "theory" will therefore always be the story of historical activities by often uncredited individuals, often women, even and especially when the full reconstruction of those scenes of collaborative making is, in the end, impossible. The aspiration to capture them will always fail. Josie Fanon's notes do not survive. She died by suicide in 1989, "always reluctant to talk about her private life, especially her life with Fanon" (Macey 132).

It is relevant to my account, too, that while he composed the book Fanon's own body was falling apart. As Fanon's biographer recounts, the period of *Les Damnés*'s creation fell during the "chronic phase" of Fanon's own blood disease. As he formulated his diagnosis of Western imperialism's death drive, Fanon's ultimately fatal illness was in a period of brief remission, his myeloid leukemia temporarily abated, but in no way cured, by tiny white tablets of the drug Myleran. These caused "nausea, vomiting and diarrohoea and a persistent cough," as well as the darkening of the skin (Macey 442, 441). In this way did the crisis tendencies of a world-scaled catastrophe play out, for Fanon at least, in tandem with the terminal phases of a disease affecting a single human body. As Rossetti's case will show in chapter 5, conceptual procedure transpires through the body, and macropolitical storylines play out at the more intimate scales of physical life—for these writers, in private symptoms that could barely be named. Days before he died, having been presented with the first reviews of *The Wretched of the Earth* while lying in a Maryland hospital just miles from the basement where I am writing this introduction, Fanon said: "That won't give me my bone marrow back" (quoted in Macey 484).

Action without Hope arises from the conviction that macrosystemic processes ramify most consequentially at smallest scale. It addresses what Jeremy Davies describes as the "terminal crisis of the Holocene" (14) but locates its central investments in minor gestures and improvised activities, concrete embodiment, and the location of conceptual activity on earth. To do so it reconstructs nineteenth-century languages for imagining new beginnings outside the categories of agency, volition, and action still structuring even the most committed climate writing today. I argue that in order to develop these nonstandard grammars of capacity, nineteenth-century thinkers (a) redefined categories like "will" in light of human beings' densely mutual relations with other worldly phenomena (in Brontë and Eliot); (b) rescaled action from the grandly heroic to the intimate and small (in Eliot and Rossetti); and (c) (in Rossetti especially) reconceptualized personhood itself by locating the universally shared qualities of organic beings not in "freedom" but in common experiences of constraint. Together, these efforts enabled witnesses to an early and then maturing extraction-based life to conceive of possibility outside the limiting categories of bourgeois subjectivity, without losing the commitment to new beginnings out of which collaborative and improvised alterations in the structure of the present might be effected.[24]

To call these new models into being, the artists I treat here needed to think both within and against the bourgeois categories they inherited. This double motion meant that they turned away from the thesis-based presentations, logical proofs, and modes of essayistic argumentation that still give shape to thought in official forms today. Instead they called on the capacities of aesthetic performance. Sonnets and fractured lyrics, watercolor sketches and vast, multiplot novels: these and other artistic technologies, I argue, worked at slant angles and sometimes almost immeasurable frequencies to recast the philosophical and, I claim, aesthetic category of action. The specific tactics I describe range from lyric suspension, passive voice, and networked plot forms to pictorial techniques like Turner's scumbling and the disabled transfer grids I describe in the conclusion.

For Christina Rossetti in chapter 5, the stringent requirements of the sonnet form become a template by which to imagine how restriction might shape subjectivity more than the lyric autonomy romanticized by male predecessors like Wordsworth. The resulting idiolects of possibility aim toward solidarity and collaboration rather than isolable acts of decision available for optimization by managers. They develop from the experiences of minoritized subjects, very often women, whose practices of intervention depended not on direct lines of predication or the dominant syntaxes by which *subjects* do things to *objects*. Rather, they mobilize partial and agrammatical models for doing, lower in frequency than the cymbal-clashing stories of self-sovereign agents still claiming pride of place in the think-tank dreamworlds of climate policy today. Often you can hardly see them. What emerges is a series of translated performances that reframe the post-Enlightenment presumption that effective change must come from willed decision. Instead, these sketches and semi-grammatical presentations open paths forward when the structure of thought is implicated in the disaster.

Turner's Blue

To end I want to take just one final turn into the logic of immanence I am trying to unpack here and discuss something more basic and boring than all that, which is paint—in fact, a specific smear of it. A dab of bright sapphire, vivid and small. Just north of a larger swatch of darker blue, almost black, with which it is semicontinuous (plate 3). The intensity of this tiny blue flash, its vividness and purity of tone, argues for its identification as ultramarine, one of at least eight chemically distinct varieties of blue Turner is known to have used during his career (Townsend, "Pigments," 243). He used ten reds and at least a dozen different versions of the tone for which he became infamous, yellow (Townsend, "Pigments," 243; Gage 19).[25] (Critics said he had "yellow fever," and studies abound of these slurs on Turner's use of color—some made by Thackeray.)

As curator Joyce Townsend has demonstrated, Turner's eagerness to deploy new and often industrially sourced materials was matched by no other British artist: he was an early and enthusiastic adopter of newly discovered and synthesized pigments and paint media, a bannerman for the modern regime of art (Townsend, *Techniques*, 39; Townsend, "Pigments," 231). One of the more controversial new pigments he used first, chrome yellow, owed its startling brilliance to the newly discovered heavy metal chromium, which like other heavy metals and dioxins is also present—via agro-industrial runoff and feedlot effluvients—in the groundwater of my hometown, Fresno, California, and therefore in my own body (EWG Tapwater Database; Pichon; Swift).[26] Other of his new pigments used cadmium, barium sulfate, and zinc. Cobalt blue, present on the Chelsea palette, is, like those metals, a product of globally scaled extraction. Discovered in the late eighteenth century and commercially available only after 1803, it entered Turner's palette in 1806. It's a byproduct of copper mining, mildly radioactive, and, of course, toxic to the miners who extract it. At this moment in Turner's career, it would have come from the scarred and otherworldly copper-mining regions of Cornwall and Wales, zones transformed into wastelands already by the 1790s and now filming locations for movies about Mars. Of the Parys copper mine, in Anglesea, Wales, an 1855 source quotes a Richard Warner, writing in 1799, who calls it "waste, wild, and barren in the extreme." "The bowels of the mountain," he concludes, "are literally torn out" (quoted in Leifchild 220, 221).[27]

Turner liked the paint you could get from such tearing, but also used the old favorites. His ochres, like all of them, derived from pulverized earth roasted in ovens until the ferric oxide shifted from brown to orange to red; his vermillions came from the powdered mineral cinnabar, mercury sulfide—originally mined in Spain, then Australia and South America; his madders from the smashed roots of the plant *rubia tintorium*; his burnt siennas from the excavated and then heat-treated hillsides surrounding the Italian city of that name. Turner's artworks, I'm saying, are like all cultural objects a material record of an infinitely detailed combination of human act and material scene: in particular, his paintings crystallize processes of rare-earth and heavy-metal extraction that were, by the mid-nineteenth century and already before, fully global in scale. When Constable said Turner's canvases were colored "with tinted steam" (quoted in Rees 257), he said more than he meant to: Turner's canvases embody in brute material form the regime of extraction and capture they depict as theme and topic.[28]

In addition to examining nearly all of Turner's works in the Tate Gallery, Townsend has used photochemical analysis to identify the paints on Turner's palette, known as the "Chelsea" palette after the neighborhood Turner was staying in when he died. This microscaled materialism discovered that at least four of Turner's eight blues are represented on the Chelsea palette—synthetic ultramarine, smalt (a cobalt-based powdered glass), Prussian blue, and his favorite, natural ultramarine. As Townsend shows, Turner is known to have preferred actual ultramarine to its artificially synthesized (but chemically identical) facsimile. The original stuff, the most important blue in the history of art, beloved of Giotto but too expensive for Michelangelo (Mangla n.p.), cost, in Turner's day, nearly 150 times the price of the synthetic (invented in 1826). It was more expensive than gold. But despite the dramatic cost difference Turner continued to use organically sourced ultramarine for his exhibition paintings and even some sketches, preferring the natural to the synthetic likely because (as Ravi Mangla writes) "ground assiduously by hand, [natural ultramarine] is riddled with odd minerals: calcite, pyrite, augite, mica. These deposits cause the light to be refracted and transmitted in subtly different ways" (n.p.) (plate 4).[29]

But the dancing blue of Turner's most hopeful passages of sky could be extracted only from a single subregion of what is now Afghanistan, hand-carted in rock form by peasant and animal down unpassable mountains to be powdered, again by peasants, then exported via the Silk Road to Naples, where it entered circulation to the West, only later to spangle Turner's canvases about heaving coal. Preservation scientist Joyce Plesters describes the history of acquiring this valuable powder as a series of "improved method[s] of extraction" and explains how the method required "at least three separate extractions, by this means collecting several grades of pigment of diminishing quality" (63). She says nothing of the human beings performing these tasks, at least some of whom, according to one mid-nineteenth-century observer, were enslaved—"labour in the mine being compulsory" (Wood 171). It remains clear that like nearly every material Turner used, ultramarine was made by almost comically exploitative processes of capture, a triple extraction linked to global supply chains coercive in their basic architecture, whose disastrous effects constitute the subjects those paintings seemingly only depict. "Every fiber of our being," Donna Haraway notes, "is interlaced, even complicit, in the webs of processes that must somehow be engaged and repatterned" (35). There is almost certainly chromium in my organs as I type these sentences (cf. Suljević et al.; Ray).

The point is that Turner's *depictions of* extractive modernity are part of that subject too, the result being a kind of enacted theory of involvement in catastrophe. This position of immersion or intimacy is in no way unique to Turner. Instead it is defined by the curious but entirely common scenario—also our own—by which someone might be both witness to a disaster, a critic of it, and perhaps even its victim, as well as its partial author. All I've done here is redescribe the findings of curators and preservationists in light of long-durational environmental harm and a definition of immanent critique borrowed from dialectical philosophy. But one thing this recasting might do is help attune us to the wreckage we inhabit and that accumulates even in our efforts to comprehend or critique it. The processes to which Turner bore witness live on in sacrifice zones, dead reefs, and carbonized air, I mean, but also as episteme: in oil company strategy sessions and petroleum-powered daily life, yes, but also the think-tank rhetorics and neoliberal voluntarisms favored by corporate universities and their authorized environmental initiatives.

The extractive fossil system and the conceptual apparatus proper to it comprise a single totality that must be unwound from within and threaded into new shape. Decades before Turner's most ambitious studies of the emergent fossil regime, long before the extractive lifeworld had come to feel natural, he painted a genre-piece called *Thomson's Aeolian Harp*, now at the Manchester Art Gallery (1807) (figure 4). It is nothing special. The canvas shows no trace of the emergent fossil economy that would later suffocate *Snow Storm* in a grimy darkness or make *Rain, Steam, and Speed* (1844) into a study of smoke and motion. Instead there is stillness: "a feathery tree," as the museum's description explains, a bending river, lithe figures near classical ruins, and "trees . . . in full dark green foliage."[30] Four women in sheer dress are allegories of the seasons, emblems for the eternal order of nature and the "enamelled world" long understood as the ideological upshot of the pastoral mode (R. Williams, *Country and the City*, 18). The painting is itself a translation: as the title indicates, it reworks James Thomson's equally forgettable ode (1748), which dilates in rhymed quatrains on the image that would later give Coleridge, Shelley, Emerson, and others a trope for interactive creativity, "Aeolus's Harp."

It was the gilt-wood frame of this painting to which climate activists glued themselves, in the summer of 2022, in an act of protest calling for an end to the capture and combustion of fossil-based fuel. "It is the third time this week," the *Guardian* reported, "that supporters of the group, which is calling for a government-imposed moratorium on new oil and gas extraction projects, have glued themselves to major works in UK galleries" (Gayle). The Just Stop Oil action in Manchester was merely one in a series of interventions that summer aimed, activists said, at shifting public understanding of the climate crisis by torquing the domain of the thinkable and helping make direct action conceivable for a public disinclined to entertain postures of open refusal. The physical encounter of two students with one of Turner's lesser-known works was a small event, barely noticeable: it was overshadowed by the more famous actions where soup was poured on a Van Gogh, for example, or paint sprayed on buildings, and anyway was forgotten soon afterward. And it was intimate: skin touching frame, two bodies linked to an artwork by the chemical bond of cheap glue. The group explained later that protesters involved in these activities

FIGURE 4. Joseph Mallord William Turner, *Thomson's Aeolian Harp* (1809). Oil on canvas. Manchester Art Gallery, UK. Photograph: © Manchester Art Gallery / Bridgeman Images.

tend to remain joined to the frame for only between one and two hours; acetone or baby oil removes the glue (Ali). It was temporary. It was not a revolution. The bond dissolved.

Like the intimate act of disruption in which young people touched *Thomson's Aeolian Harp* for two hours and then stopped, the practices of internal reordering described in the coming pages are unfailingly small, often disconcertingly so in relation to the ecocidal processes I argue they can be seen to address. But they are real. Said one participant in the minor act at Manchester: "The youth of the world have literally nothing to lose anymore, we are a generation sacrificed" (quoted in Gayle). There will be no escape from this sacrificial moment, no solution to hope for. But thought and practice can be rewired from the inside, old languages turned to new purpose. As the coming chapters will show, disaster can generate possibility; seemingly total enclosure opens space for elaboration at small scale, often just gestures. The results will not be total. Improvisation is required.

PART I

Melting Worlds

1

Grew, Shivered, and Passed Away

THE EXPERIENCE OF UNWINDING

Every single achievement of every human society on Earth occurred under a climate that no longer exists.

—Simon Lewis, cited by Fiona Harvey in the *Guardian* (2021)

Long have I sigh'd for calm.

—Tennyson's unnamed speaker, in *Maud: A Monodrama* (1855)

Melting and Flowing under My Eyes: On Background

Experience happens when a subject uses its capacities for sensation to register objects in a world. In nearly every existing account of the phenomenological encounter, this world is presumed to be stable, in the sense that it persists across successive perceptual acts and can be counted on to behave similarly from one moment to another. In this way, the term *world* names the background state that enables the subject to have experience as such: to apprehend *what it is like to be*.[1] For Maurice Merleau-Ponty in *Phenomenology of Perception* (1945), "the world" is "the natural milieu of the field of all my thoughts and of all my explicit perceptions" (lxxiv).

Sarah Ahmed describes the limits of this canonical account by pointing out that any supposedly natural background state will always include features that might, in a more critical phenomenology, become objects of perception, rather than the background for it: the fact of the quiet room that enables the male phenomenologist to think in the first place, for example ("Orientations" 546). For Frantz Fanon, meanwhile, the "genuine dialectic between my body and the world" (*Black Skin, White Masks* 91) happens only with the proviso that *world* names a place constructed to feel normal to some subjects but not others. Any allegedly natural or preontological world is in this sense also a mechanism for hiding the violence and exclusion on which such orders of normalcy necessarily depend. "The white man is all around me," Fanon writes; "the earth crunches under my feet and sings white, white" (*Black Skin, White Masks* 94).

These and related accounts show how background orders of regularity are ideological insofar as they reflect social features as natural and encourage the flourishing of certain subjects but not all of them.[2] Another point is important too: in critical and orthodox phenomenological accounts alike, *world* is durational insofar as it persists across discrete perceptual acts and effectively stabilizes experience as such, even if it does so, as in Fanon, negatively. World is in all these accounts ongoing, reliably present, and almost physical in its durability, this permanency being critical to its capacity to ground perception in the first place. It is "pre-objective," in Merleau-Ponty's words (lxxxii), crunching metaphorically underfoot. Like other forms of processing the object world that I will suggest bear relation to it—statistical inference and inductive extrapolation in particular—the phenomenological encounter depends on an organized background state whose past behavior can be counted upon to have predictive value for the future. But what if the ground for experience cannot be counted on? What if the world is moving?

For reasons that hardly need rehearsing—though I'll allude to them below—this feeling will be familiar to readers of this book. The phrase "global weirding" has emerged to describe the heightened uncertainty, veering extremes, and serially disrupted sense of stability in our altered present. In these "postnormal times," as one climate writer notes, "things we take for granted become uncertain . . . and longstanding norms, if not the very idea of normalcy itself, break down before our very eyes" (Sweeney 204). This ambient sense of breakdown is a signal affect of the late carbon era. But the nineteenth century provides ample testimony that this kind of destabilized or melted experience is at least as old as the regime of carbon-fueled imperialist expansion that has made the world bend and shift for us today. When the Time Traveller punches the gas on his machine in H. G. Wells's 1895 novel, for example, he describes what it feels like when what was once solid begins to melt away—when world, in the sense of experiential background, begins to fall apart. In so doing he diagnoses what I will suggest is a material condition that, across time, we share with him.

"I drew a breath, set my teeth, gripped the starting lever with both hands, and went off with a thud" (18), he says. As days become minutes and time begins to blur, the Traveller feels what he calls the "peculiar sensations" that flow from a widening mismatch between the observer's expectation of stability and what he actually encounters (19). Time and space, since Kant the paradigmatic pre-experiential intuitions, begin to wobble. Weird sensations follow, as perceptual capacities fitted to one context or lifeworld are made now to address an entirely different, geohistorical one, a context in motion, where seasons pass like dreams and days stretch to the "thousands of millions" (81).[3] As he witnesses phase shift into phase, world melt into world, the Traveller experiences in sickeningly serialized form the process of creative destruction by which one sociohistorical order breaks apart and another coalesces to replace it.

Ursula Heise, Aaron Rosenberg, and others have described Wells's novel as the prototypical story of scale shift, and for the Traveller the result of this mismatch between human and geological registers is a kind of internal crisis. The disorientation that eventuates from the subject's unmooring from its milieu finds expression for the Traveller in a variety of ambiguous physical symptoms: "new sensations," he calls them. These include "sickness and confusion," a "hysterical exhilaration" (20, 81, 20). "I'm afraid," he says,

> I cannot convey the peculiar sensations of time travelling. They are excessively unpleasant. There is a feeling exactly like that one has upon a switchback—of a helpless headlong motion! I felt the same horrible anticipation, too, of an imminent smash. As I put on pace, night followed day like the flapping of a black wing. . . . The slowest snail that ever crawled dashed by too fast for me. The twinkling succession of darkness and light was excessively painful to the eye. Then, in the intermittent darknesses, I saw the moon spinning swiftly through her quarters from new to full, and had a faint glimpse of the circling stars. Presently, as I went on, still gaining velocity, the palpitation of night and day merged into one continuous greyness; the sky took on a wonderful deepness of blue, a splendid luminous colour like that of early twilight; the jerking sun became a streak of fire, a brilliant arch, in space; the moon a fainter fluctuating band; and I could see nothing of the stars, save now and then a brighter circle flickering in the blue. (19)

What the Traveller evokes here is what we might call a minimally organized affective response. It is organized, because he feels these sensations and tries—in fact is compelled by the narrative structure of his framed first-person report—to put those feelings into words. But minimally so, since his "peculiar sensations" respond only unevenly to his efforts to name them.

The sensations "cannot be conveyed," he says, but his elaborate lyrical evocations nevertheless seek to do just that. This displacement of affective state into rhetorical performance is common, I will suggest, for efforts to formalize the experience of world-failure. To read such performances is to work backward from representational and linguistic malfunctions—glitchy utterances and broken syntaxes—to the embodied apprehensions that produced them; these embodied apprehensions or somatized knowledges in turn give ambiguous testimony to historical crisis, mediating melting worlds into a sort of broken poetry.

Recall that the Traveller tries, but fails, to put a name to the response this multisensory show evokes in him. It is at once "excessively unpleasant" and "splendid": an ambiguously valued, synesthetic trance state, where all perceptual capacities are engaged but little is possible to represent nominally, in the language of concepts. "An eddying murmur filled [his] ears" (19), he says, sensation now fully replacing cognition as his bodily system aims unsuccessfully to establish perceptual stability in a world that is in fact a whole sequence of them in succession, or none at all—a "dim elusive world," he says, "that raced and fluctuated before my eyes" (20). I open this chapter with the Time Traveller's famous moment of literary nausea because it pinpoints the perceptual and affective crises that arise when the ground for experience has withdrawn and another order has yet to stabilize in its place. Diagnosed by nineteenth-century observers of the metastasizing carbon economy like Wells, this dilemma of intersystem experience is now doubly acute in the twilight hour of that system, as mass extinction, biodiversity collapse, and the degeneration of the cryosphere, among other morbid symptoms, all fill the present with a sense of what the Traveller calls "helpless headlong motion."

In terms developed by Sianne Ngai, such chaotic emotional conditions as the Traveller hesitatingly conjures are particularly sensitive at assessing not just moments of perceptual flux but scenarios "marked by blocked or thwarted actions" (27). In these moments, the capacity to alter the shape of social life feels withdrawn. If this observation is true, then aesthetic evocations of unorganized mood have a doubly diagnostic capacity, since they perform by literary means not just what it feels like to inhabit a failing world but what it feels like to know that nothing you do can stop it—that your "agency," in Ngai's words, is "obstructed" (32). Min Hyoung Song's 2022 *Climate Lyricism* is only one of many recent accounts that attend variously to the worry, deep concern, and host of other feelings that follow from the intuition of full and effectively unstoppable climate breakdown. In so doing Song's text illustrates Ngai's point that unresolved affects arise in conjunctures when altering the course of systemic historical processes no longer feels possible. "I feel powerless," Song writes in his first paragraphs. "Maybe you feel this way too" (1).

Later chapters will address this crisis of contemporary action head on, and revisit, too, the I-thou rhetorical scenario so often presumed to be stable in contemporary engagements with this topic.[4] To set the stage for those analyses, this chapter reads three literary dispatches written from inside what I will now treat as a single moment in the longer unfolding of a historical system whose terminal crisis gathers while you read these words. Within the bracketed moment analyzed here, "the late nineteenth century," this chapter rolls back the clock from 1885 to 1865 and 1855 to show how literary texts conditioned by a consolidating fossil capitalism give voice to the sickening disorientation of experience during historical phase transition. These experiences will always register unevenly, striated across the social field in ways the I-thou circuitry of academic prose can only ever strain to comprehend. Relaying the self-reports of middle-class residents in the world's first fossil-fueled empire, the three stories about unmoored experience treated below—*The Time Machine* (1895), *Alice's Adventures in Wonderland* (1865), and *Maud* (1855)—offer oblique testimony to the vertiginous lack of background stability that now characterizes life even for those lucky enough to read books in today's burning world.

Wells and Carroll give literary shape to the physical nausea and cognitive confusions of experience without a ground but conclude by affirming the lie that bourgeois life and its appropriate genres, from the bildungsroman and the marriage plot to the concerned monograph about climate change, can cure this condition. The mellow glow of the Traveller's study and Alice's return to tea confirm their novels' final investment in the suicidal normal of extractive accumulation and the forms of expression proper to it. *Maud* is weirder: in the uneven poetic stanzas and variable verse forms that befuddled contemporary readers, Tennyson's "monodrama" models via poetic performance the intermittently exhilarating and nauseating predicament of experience without stability to ground it—a combination of disorientation and powerlessness, unspecifiable in any single term, familiar to anyone scrolling news today. In this sense Tennyson's gem-crusted and unstable experiment shows how disorientation might come to stand as a perverse new kind of normal, albeit when that term no longer means anything at all.

Phase Shift in Theory and Practice

Periods of creative destruction between stable systems are interstitial (from *interstitium*, "gap" or "interval") insofar as they are characterized by both breakdown and emergence, as one order of systemic organization falls apart and another gathers lurchingly in its place. As Antonio Gramsci

FIGURE 5. Kashmere Gardens, Houston (September 2017). Photograph by the author.

is often quoted as saying, it is a time of monsters.[5] Ecologist Marten Scheffer uses the term *regime shift* to describe what ecological biologists call a "relatively fast transition from one persistent dynamic regime to another" (n.p.). In the language of ecological biology standardized in the post–World War II period, the phrase "persistent dynamic regime" names an established and relatively consistent, albeit internally dynamic, order of operation in a given biotic system or set of them. For the cybernetic theorists of action I discuss later in the book, this paradoxically static dynamism was also known as a "stable state." Scheffer's overview of ecological phase shift at the scale of a given biotic system cites the canonical example of a shallow lake, familiar from ecology textbooks of the Cold War that I treat in chapter 4. This example helps him underscore for students that the determination of whether any systemic state is "stable" will always be a matter of perspective.

The perception of stability, that is, depends on the scale at which the system is viewed. What from one vantage looks stable is, from another, dynamic. A shallow lake whose nitrogen load has not yet tipped it into eutrophication, for example, might be considered steady when viewed as its own self-enclosed system. Look more closely, however, and we might see that any number of subsystems within the lake—its chemical cycles or species interactions, even clusters of cells within an organism—could be dynamic, in the sense of tending toward crisis or change. In the reverse direction, a lake undergoing local crisis might be seen, at larger scale, to be but one subsystem in a watershed that is operating in regular fashion when viewed as a larger unit. What seems steady at one scale of systemic organization, in other words, appears unsteady at another, and vice versa. As one high school textbook put it in 1953: "the entire biosphere may be one vast ecosystem with numerous more or less circular systems within it" (quoted in Kingsland 190). Gaia was the name Cold War earth systems scientists gave to this planetary-scaled arrangement, the "biosphere" now construed as the largest Russian doll of so many smaller and interlocking ones inside it. This relatively obvious point about the scalar quality of "stability" helps highlight a related principle at work in the concept of time, with consequences for the notion of experience I am tracking here. Any point on a line can always be broken down into a yet smaller-scaled line, or the reverse: any narrative line (the sequence of events in a given year, or minute, or decade) can be frozen into a point ("the 1850s," "fall 2017," "now").

This quality of narrative reversibility by which the synchronic event can always be viewed (at another scale) as durational, while any duration can always be condensed into a point, is a basic principle of structuralist narratology. It is something Lauren Berlant underlines when they explain how ongoing "environmental" phenomena—states of being that are durational, rather than punctual, diachronic rather than synchronic—can be made apprehensible through the rhetoric of crisis. The figure of "crisis" turns durable background states or slow violence into an event you can see and experience, effectively crystallizing a diachronic process into an evental instant (Berlant 101), a line into a point. Using the "moment's monument" of the sonnet (as her brother Dante put it), Christina Rossetti will toy with this dialectical quality of all periodization to astonishing effect in the final chapter of this book. For now I want to note only that a phase transition that is "relatively fast" (in Scheffer's words) from the perspective of a given ecosystem or even the earth system itself—a lake turning to a dead zone, the Holocene turning into whatever will follow it—can be a matter of brutally painful, enduring duration for the organisms locked into the shorter timescales of their own experience.

This point has consequences for how we understand what counts as the present. Surveying in 2010 the earth systems changes then newly being packaged under the label "Anthropocene," Mike Davis summarized that "our old world, the one that we have inhabited for the last 12,000 years, has ended." But as Davis explains, the withdrawal of that world will be followed not so much by any new era, he says, but by what he calls "radical instability" (30, 31). Six years later, Donna Haraway observed similarly that "the Anthropocene is more a boundary event than an epoch" (100): not so much a new era as a hinge between periods, less like the Pleistocene, say, and more like the K-Pg boundary event, when a meteor severed the Cretaceous from the Paleogene and restarted the clock of evolution.[6] These accounts are themselves dispatches from another era, the 2010s, when Anthropocene-talk and fresh attention to the ecological made "environmental humanities" into a brand name.[7] This microperiod can now be seen as its own instant in the unfolding of a geophysical transition that has effectively become an ongoing, if continually degrading, durational state.

As a crisis point or boundary event, "the Anthropocene," Haraway noted in 2016, "marks severe discontinuities; what comes after will not be like what came before" (100). Since the time of Haraway's observation, the unraveling of earth systems has accelerated at nonlinear rates, misery compounding on misery, the sense of "discontinuity" becoming more "severe" with every passing storm or fire season. Seen this way, the floods and heatwaves of quotidian experience now are the chaotic durational experience of what would appear, on the line of geological time, as a point of transition. "Clearly," writes Fredric Jameson in an assessment of his own ongoing work on periodization, "the great structuralist issue of diachrony and synchrony is still with us" ("Criticism and Categories" 564). While leaving blank the phenomenological problem of *what it is like* to live through it, then, theorists of narrative and historical change help disclose that the withdrawal of the usual that characterizes contemporary experience for even rich and well-protected individuals today severs the relation between self and world central to the dynamic of experience. In so doing, it triggers a suite of inchoate affective responses that I am suggesting become legible at the level of aesthetic structure.

The erosion of experiential ground in late-stage Holocene life became clear to me in the early fall of 2017, when I was beginning work on this book—a moment of climatological distress that has since been dwarfed by yet more surreal disasters. The newspapers tried to comprehend what was happening. "Harvey is a 1,000-year flood event unprecedented in scale," noted the *Washington Post* on August 31, 2017. The *Post* added that "what constitutes different return frequencies (100-year, 500-year, 1,000-year and so forth) is probably changing" (Samenow). Two days prior, the same paper had asked: "Houston is experiencing its third '500' year flood in three years. How is that possible?" (Ingraham). *Ars Technica* confirmed the new meaninglessness of these statistical markers by saying that "yesterday's 100-year storm is today's 30-year storm" (S. Johnson). "Is Harvey a 500-year storm or a 1,000-year storm?" inquired the *Arizona Republic*. "What does that even mean?" (W. Johnson). The *New York Times* stepped in to clarify, pointing out that such estimates do not reflect one thousand years of recorded data (which does not exist), but rather the results of a probabilistic model based on what is usually around one hundred years of observed information: this dataset constitutes the frame of reference from which a regime of expectation can be extended (Popovich and O'Neill). The stochastic or chance-based model so derived can then be extended into a theoretically infinite future, chance now tamed into a regular succession of algorithmically predictable future events.[8]

Just two weeks after Harvey's sixty inches of rainfall triggered these journalistic forays into statistical analysis, I traveled to Houston for the first time. I was there for an academic meeting, arrived to discuss the relationship between Victorian literature and climate change. My university would reimburse the expenses. As I taxied past still-operating petrochemical infrastructure to the conference hotel, trains heaved on tracks, smudged high-water marks were visible on underpasses, and wreckage from the storm lay on the streets in piles. In the majority-Black neighborhood of Kashmere Gardens, just a few miles away from the hotel brunches and name-badges, houses had been gutted to prevent mold. People were still living in the stripped-out homes. Ruined furniture sat outside, bleaching in wan sunlight (figure 5).[9]

The relationship between scholarly procedure and climate catastrophe that took shape for me in Houston as grotesque contradiction—and that I have set up as such here, by relaying the scene of the post-Harvey academic symposium—is better seen as laying bare a fact that should animate any instance of the "environmental humanities" today: namely that the apparently highly mediated domain of intellectual activity and concrete scenes of material disaster are not separate spheres at all but in fact belong in the same world. As Raymond Williams among others have noted, the "basic dualism" (*Marxism and Literature* 99) that would cleave the sphere of cultural and intellectual production from the world of the material is a fantasy. Culture is material too: and in policing the supposed separation of base and superstructure, material and ideal, dualist analyses obscure the fact that (in Williams's words) "language and signification" act as "indissoluble elements of the material social process itself, involved all the time both in production and reproduction" (*Marxism and Literature* 99).

In this sense will any act of thought today participate somehow, and in some material way—however mutedly—in the concrete social processes of an extractive capitalism whose more vividly observable forms of appearance include catastrophic scenes of environmental racism such as Harvey in 2017 and those following whatever storms transpired in the year you are reading these words. There is no position outside these processes. The question is what posture intellectual activity will take in relation to this ecocidal common sense: Will it run smoothly through the circuitry of its official channels and approved idioms, knitting ever more tightly together the consensus of its institutional languages? Will it adopt falsely romantic outsides that confirm by negation the immutable qualities of the order they pretend to refuse or transcend? Or might thought instead try to work immanently within these established languages, rewiring the extractive order's self-maintaining circuitries on the model of adaptive salvage? Understanding emergent culture, Williams notes, "depends crucially on finding new forms or adaptations of form," since "what we have to observe is in effect a *pre-emergence*, active and pressing but not yet fully articulated" (*Marxism and Literature* 126, emphasis original).

The distillation of anecdote and its transformation into the coin of academic circulation is therefore only one way that the apparently highly differentiated domains of analytic procedure and material disaster might connect. This move is not what I intend here. It is crucial to recall that conceptual and material domains are not twins, and as Imre Szeman and Jennifer Wenzel observe, supposedly "extractive" intellectual practices are not isomorphic with material activities of despoliation. Allegory will not do. Instead, dense relations of mediation connect the scenes of intellectual performance and concrete disaster—filigrees of relation, infinitely tiny traceries of connection linking what we do and say to the petrochemical refinery complexes swamped in Houston, the cancer fields surrounding them, the offshore drilling platforms only temporarily knocked offline by the storm.

In addition to emblematizing the entwinement, rather than the partition, of intellectual production and material process, tableaux like the one I've relayed here also provide occasion for rehearsing Saidiya Hartman's warning, in *Scenes of Subjection* (1997), about the varieties of reward that accompany even apparently critical recountings of racialized disaster (3–4). For Hartman as for Williams, this relationship of immanence within a functionally catastrophic material social process is not the end point of an argument but its starting point. The challenge then becomes to "give expression to these outrages," in Hartman's phrase, without (a) "exacerbating the indifference to suffering" that is the pedagogical outcome of routinized spectacle, or (b) accelerating the "narcissistic identification" that "obliterates the other" by presuming that I, you, and them are one and the same (*Scenes* 4). Framed this way, Hartman's injunction for experimental modes of halfway disclosure and sideways evocation—"not yet fully articulated," Williams said—defeats conventional distinctions between base and superstructure and exposes the obscenity of ecocritical brand building in the context of an unwinding present.

The scenes of destruction I only glimpsed in Houston had been shaped by processes of internal colonization and abandonment in place for decades and in fact centuries. In short: the land on which the city now sits was annexed by force from the Karankawa people in the 1820s; the early city housed the enslaved who worked sugar and cotton plantations just outside it until the Civil War; the Jim Crow era brought restrictive zoning and racial segregation, partitioning the city into white and Black zones; and migrants from the countryside after World War II expanded the city's Black population, even as more than 90 percent of them remained contained in "mostly black areas" as late as 1970 (Bullard 249). The sacrifice zone of Kashmere Gardens had been purpose-built, in one of these areas, on a floodplain: placed in harm's way for all the reasons structurally excluded populations in the US and elsewhere have been cordoned off and exposed to the full violence of an extractive racial capitalism. Before Harvey, the Kashmere Gardens area had already been designated a "100-Year floodplain" (Purser n.p.).

It is relevant to the argument I've set in place here about regularity, expectation, and the intimacy between social abandonment and academic production that, as I noted in the introduction, Ian Hacking's classic study of probabilistic reason, *The Taming of Chance* (1990), was sponsored by the Exxon Corporation. Hacking's study appeared in the Cambridge University Press (CUP) "Ideas in Context" series, "published with the support of the Exxon Education Foundation" (Hacking front matter)—a series that also included monumental works in the history of ideas like J. G. A. Pocock's *Virtue, Commerce, and History* (1985) and studies of liberal choice like *Hobbes and Voluntarism* (2000), among many other key investigations into the origins of bourgeois society. A CUP memo of August 21, 1984, archived as a photocopy, explains it all in plain terms:

> We are receiving from Exxon $50000 over five years, towards the costs of the Ideas in Context series. It will mainly be put towards manufacturing costs and extending the publicity for the series.
>
> A separate account for the money has been set up. Could we adopt the following accounting procedures:

> I or RJM make requisitions to the Fund (at the request of PAM, CJW or FSS where appropriate); my requisitions to be countersigned by RJM, CLD or AW; and all requisitions to be sent on to RS to keep a running total.
>
> I will prepare an annual report on the utilization of the funds at the beginning of each year. JS-W.[10]

The note is banal: it reads like any other internal memo about inputs and outputs on a balance sheet, which is the point I am making about it. The taming of chance into repetitive journalistic articles about the return-rate frequencies of hurricanes, for instance, was itself an intellectual output, at some highly mediated level, of the material processes that generated those storms in the first place, the intellectual machinery and the petrochemical infrastructure connected in some way, somehow.

Relevant too is that Exxon's Houston campus, "constructed to the highest standards of energy efficiency and environmental stewardship" sits on "385 wooded acres" some forty minutes by car from Kashmere Gardens.[11] "Sustainability touches all aspects of" it, Exxon says, and the LEED Gold–Certified facility only confirms again that rhetorics of corporate sustainability are designed, most of all, to keep the apparatus churning: sustainability language is meant to "allow any organization to act as if they are addressing environmental concerns while leaving core business operations intact, . . . disavowing their role in creating climate change and refusing responsibility for more transformative environmental action" (Bosworth et al. 4). Also relevant is that two of Exxon's Houston refineries, closer to Kashmere, released into the air some twelve thousand pounds of benzene, carbon monoxide, and sulfur dioxide after Harvey knocked them offline (Akpan), particulated aftereffects to be metabolized into the bodies of Kashmere residents only slowly—long after I'd flown away and begun to research probability.

The anecdote of the Houston conference, like Exxon's sponsorship of Hacking's text, discloses with special clarity that the production of academic knowledge about "climate" transpires not outside of or at removes from the mechanics of extraction and catastrophe but from within them. And while this book's focus falls on often highly mediated artifacts of an incipiently disastrous nineteenth-century England, its ethical and political focus remains on the human lives who absorb the shock of that extractive order, and whose experiences should stand as the final sphere of consequence for any minimally responsible "environmental humanities" now.[12]

In Houston, after Harvey, even mainstream journalists came slowly to comprehend that no amount of past data could help understand what was happening in this strange new present, at the far end of "all those historical fires, of the cumulative emissions, the pulses of CO_2 stacked on top of each other" (Malm, *Progress,* 5). In the event, horizons of expectation had torqued such that a thousand-year storm could gather, as happened in the fall of 2017, three times in the span of roughly a month: Harvey, Irma, and Maria, all in a row, a millennium's worth of superstorm condensed into thirty days. ("Every minute mark[ed] a day," the Time Traveller says [Wells 19].) Such statistical confusions are now the stuff of everyday life. A dramatic leap in the frequency of extreme fire events, for example, means that timelines have condensed and temporality itself has become subject to bizarre torsion: extreme fires "currently estimated to occur only once every 1,000 years, would occur roughly every 5 to 10 years," a 2021 study said ("Western North American Extreme Heat"). But the careful conditional tense in the scientists' attempted prediction, extreme fires *would occur,* discloses that even the most carefully qualified projections are finally speculative: models that are by definition built on past observation or "priors" can no longer ground future prognoses. Describing the historically novel episode of total waterlessness in Cape Town in summer 2018, Bill McKibben noted that "of course the phrase 'based on past history' no longer makes sense, because that history took place on what was essentially a different planet with a different atmospheric chemistry" (*Falter* 24).

The problem of world-withdrawal is an aesthetic dilemma, too. If genre and scale both name domains of more or less stable cognitive operation or perceptual fitness, they function as aesthetic corollaries to the concept of *lifeworld* in the phenomenological sense discussed above. We can follow John Frow, then, to see genre as a set of socially enforced conventions that enable and constrain the production of meaning (10), genre constituting a loose contract between reader and text that secures in that encounter a common ontological structure or world. Genre can be understood as a "relatively stable ontological domain" dependent on what Frow calls "background knowledges," or implicit horizons of expectation that shape a given field of possibility (10). "To speak of genre," he goes on, "is to speak of what need not be said because it is already so forcefully presupposed" (93). Subjects like those at the center of Fanon's "The Lived Experience of the Black Man" (*Black Skin, White Masks* 89–119) or Ahmed's *Queer Phenomenology* experience the disorienting misfit between their own bodies and the world constructed as universally valid around them: in this sense, as we will see, they resemble Alice, whose experience of unfitness in a world constructed for others produces disorientations at the level of her own body and generates a suite of feelings she cannot name.

The ugly feelings of world-shift arise, I am arguing, when periods of sociohistorical stability erode and the individually scaled category of subjective experience transpires in what are, at larger scale, hinge points or pivots. Evidence for the nineteenth-century version of this dynamic will come in readings of texts that perform stylistically the experiential derangement of phase transition. In the contemporary setting, the affectively swirling feelings of phase shift are, I assume, already known to you. Today a search for *climate anxiety* returns some 128,000,000 results, but other words work too—*despair, worry, depression* all spin the internet searcher into studies, articles, and scholarly and popular overviews of how changes in earth systems have produced powerful but ill-defined affective states, mostly negative. A 2021 survey of children in ten countries found "nearly 60% saying they felt 'very worried' or 'extremely worried' about climate change," and, as *Nature* summarized, "many associated negative emotions with climate change—the most commonly chosen were 'sad,' 'afraid,' 'anxious,' 'angry' and 'powerless'" (Thompson; cf. Hickman et al.).

This overlapping and incomplete inventory of contemporary affects ("sad," 68 percent; "anxious," 63 percent; "guilty," 51 percent) betrays the scientists' faith that the emotional response to climate disaster will be highly organized and can be gathered into terminological coherence by the subjects themselves. But no taxonomy of terms or drop-down menu of named responses can exhaust or describe without remainder the eddy of only relatively organized affective states that follow from inhabiting a world coming apart. Ngai refers to "the dysphoric affect of affective disorientation—of being lost on one's own 'cognitive map' of available affects," as a paradigmatic modern mood (14). As Alice and Tennyson's speaker in *Maud* will help us see, "indifferent" and "sad" can coexist with "angry," and "afraid" not infrequently travels with "guilty." So too can "powerless" move perhaps surprisingly alongside "optimistic"—something we will see more fully in this book's second half. Survey results show that young people undergoing climatic shift report "difficult thoughts, emotions, and functional impairment." The structure of these difficult feelings can only ever be approximated in the pseudo-clinical vocabulary of named emotion. And anyway, "the construct of 'climate anxiety' itself is new and complex, with varying definitions across the literature" (Hickman et al. e871).

If phenomenology is a way of putting language to the encounter between subject and object in a stable world they share, then no narratable state of feeling can take certain shape when the world is in flux or failing. It follows that any minimally perceptive description of *what it feels like to be* in an intersystemic moment will itself fall apart, as the nominalizing aspirations of linguistic capture give way to literary evocation, slantwise performance, and figural displacement. (The Time Traveller used apophasis, saying something by claiming not to: "I cannot convey . . .") A central claim of this chapter is that historical periods of disorganization and reorganization between socio-biophysical stable states generate correspondingly inchoate affective complexes: negatively charged, ambient feelings something like anxiety, tinged with fear and haunted by sadness but also containing an odd, entirely unjustifiable exhilaration. Such tumbled-together emotional conditions defeat the hypostasizing aspirations of representational language. Instead they find shape only at angles: not in documentary reporting, one-to-one naming, or perhaps in representation at all, but in what I will describe as moments of performative enactment.

You will have noted that this observation rests on the idea that episodes of systemic breakdown share a kind of kinship across time: that the vertigoes of early fossil capitalism can be recognized as an experiential dress rehearsal for the late paroxysms of that order, today. To make this claim is to presume both (a) that aesthetic works have diagnostic power beyond that of explicit thematization in "theory," and (b) that moments of crisis, transition, or breakdown share structural features across historical time. In this case, it means that the emergent and early-dominant moments of fossil capitalism in the nineteenth century, when, as Andreas Malm and others have shown, the contemporary fossil system began slowly to feel natural—these moments can be read as "anticipatory" in the concrete sense that its aesthetic evocations help describe experience during the terminal crisis of that system, now. In 1895 the Traveller felt the "horrible anticipation" of what he called "an imminent smash." Today, the smash is now.

It was 1865 when William Stanley Jevons, in *The Coal Question*, came to realize that any extractive fossil economy was bound to collapse: any system predicated on extraction and dependent on growth would always, eventually, find its limit. Accounts produced during the rise and consolidation of this regime testify to the emergence of both "unraveled life," in Berlant's terms (21), and the unraveling world in which that life might unfold. And if emotions are "unusually knotted or condensed 'interpretations of predicaments'" (Ngai 3), then the unsettled emotions of subjects inhabiting unraveling worlds tell us something about the predicament of an order spinning off its axis. As usual, such effects are felt most acutely not by enriched denizens of the Global North like Wells's Traveller but by those on the edges and underside of the bourgeois system—those with the fewest resources to absorb the shock. For Shirley Paley and her family, for instance, who had lived in Kashmere Gardens since the 1990s by the time Harvey gutted her home, the feelings of living through phase shift were both profoundly negative and hard, in the end, to describe. A year after the storm, Paley reported that her granddaughter, traumatized by the event that had left their house under six inches of standing water, had attempted to take her own life, and, at one point, turned on her own father. "She started fighting him," Paley said, "coming back, stating that the rain was going to get her" (quoted in Betts n.p.).

Holdover Effects: The Time Machine

The objectless violence of Paley's traumatized granddaughter manifests as emotion the structural collapse of social and biophysical systems. It is what Ngai called an unusually knotted interpretation of a predicament. In particular, the predicament it interprets is multicausal and complex, but can be shorthanded, I will maintain, in something like "the crisis phase of extractive capitalism." It is a situation in which the background of life has begun to shift and move, "world" in a phenomenological sense withdrawing and, for the subjects in abandoned places like Kashmere Gardens or the majority-nonwhite rural edges of Fresno, where hexavalent chromium levels are fully twenty times those of the already elevated areas where I grew up, turning even more hostile than it was before.[13] The background stability of an already unlivable order fades; new disasters leap into visibility.

Despite having been invented by an author haunted by an "enduring preoccupation with resource exhaustion" (E. Miller, *Extraction Ecologies,* 184), the Time Traveller inhabits a milieu defined by not by structural abandonment or routinized harm but bourgeois comfort and beefsteaks, rational discourse over sherry. Still he too has become used to his environment. For Wells it is the Traveller's body, and the physical responses of his affect system, that register the consequences of his withdrawing order of regularity. As Wells is at pains to show, the Traveller's bodily apparatus has developed to operate in the *lebenswelt* to which it has become habituated. This is the world of what Darko Suvin calls "complacent bourgeois class consciousness," a general framework the Traveller and his tweedy audience of clubmen share with their presumed readership (quoted in Geduld 13).

In this way does the novel convene a "we" into which the rising professionals of the novel's rhetorical scenario and its extradiegetic audience are presumed collectively to belong. The Traveller's total isomorphism with this bourgeois lifeworld—his perfect synchrony with his fellows and their readers—signals his somatic acclimatization to a normalcy that is effectively imperialist, defined among other things by its instrumentalist relation to the object world. Imperialism is his habitus, extraction his socially conditioned physical state. What this acclimatization means is that, in the future world as in the present one, he loves meat and hates spiders, reads newspapers, knows slang, and likes a glass of champagne or two to quench the thirst (Wells 14). Cigars are smoked; professional achievement respected; comfort enjoyed. The world is secure. "The circumstances in which I . . . set the Time Traveller," Wells noted later, "were all that I could imagine of solid, upper-middle-class comfort" (quoted in James 37).

These circumstances do not go away in the future world of AD 802,701 so much as they linger as background knowledge, as the Traveller continues to project his perceptual habits onto a world whose new objects do not match the ones on which his body has been trained. This misfit or holdover effect between new perceived phenomena and old ways of knowing is the structuring dialectic of all science fiction, as Jameson among others has noted ("Progress"). But the Traveller's mismatched perceptual capacities also disclose something about the body's role in what is often understood as the purely conceptual problem of ideology: it is the Traveller's precognitive template, after all, somatized into an embodied sense-apparatus or affect system, that has been formed in one world but now must encounter objects in a new one.

The "carnal cravings" the Traveller feels when confronted with the Eloi fruit plate (Wells 27) are but one instance of how (in Suvin's words) the "Victorian norms set up in the framework of *The Time Machine* and supplemented by the Time Traveller's reactions" hold over, as embodied, paracognitive "impulse," into the new lifeworld in which he finds himself (335). This holdover effect means that in addition to documenting swirling worlds and withdrawn expectation, *The Time Machine* taxonomizes how "the affective, which is to say emotional and sensory, life of the subject has a dynamic relationship to the structure of society"—even, and perhaps especially, when the structure of that society is changing (Samalin, *Masses*, 14).

For Roland Barthes, describing any background state is pointless in narrative terms because all plot, by definition, happens in front of it. To spend time describing the setting for action—the world or milieu in which events happen—is therefore "a kind of narrative *luxury*, lavish to the point of offering many 'futile' details that do not have a 'function' within the narrative action of the story" (Barthes, "Reality Effect," 141, emphasis in original). Amitav Ghosh updates this presumption of the inert nature of narrative background for the era of climate change when he suggests that under contemporary conditions the background has come alive (*Derangement* 3, 15–24).[14] As critics like John MacNeill Miller and Jayne Hildebrand have recently noted, ecocriticism has tended to focus its critique of the concept of *background* on the anthropocentrism it typically codifies, as the nonhuman backdrop for story becomes "unconsidered, instrumentalized, and unimportant," and "merely the setting or stage on which what is really important, the drama of human life and culture, is played out," in the words Miller cites from Val Plumwood (quoted in J. M. Miller 168). Less often emphasized is the idea that background is conceived as *ground* in the first place: steady, consistent, solidly there. As Daniel Wright puts it in *The Grounds of the Novel* (2024), novels must establish their ontological baselines by figural means, but "in the actual world, the grounds, limits, or edges that support our sense of what existence means . . . are given" (9).

But as we've seen, under climate collapse it is just this space of the given that is shifting. Where experience depends on the subject's habituation to a regime of expectation or world presumed to be stable, the structural unavailability of predictable futurity transforms the phenomenological predicament into a new site of difficulty. Of course, as Wright's analysis of fictional groundings implies, a subject's physical body and material sensorium no less than her "mind" will change shape and acclimate itself, over time, to whatever series of events has proven reliably recurrent in a new horizon of expectation or world. This process of vernacular statistical analysis confirms Walter Benjamin's assertion that experience as such is "a matter of tradition," an inhabited temporal sequence in which past events create "a convergence in memory of accumulated and frequently unconscious data" ("On Some Motifs" 157).[15] Like Benjamin's Baudelaire, who diagnosed the experiential disorientations proper to a rising bourgeois capitalism and "placed the shock experience at the very center of his artistic work" ("On Some Motifs" 163), Wells's novel takes shape as an essay on the problem of bourgeois experience when its proper genre of experience has evaporated.

The Traveller's physiological responses—his allegedly natural or precultural apparatuses of sense and feeling—have been structured by the lifeworld to which these faculties have been acclimated from birth. This baggage includes not only obvious and oft-cited intellectual prejudices against communism, dark bodies, and feebleness, nor yet his unthinking presumptions about gender, but reflexes and other apparently involuntary responses too. (Suvin called them "reactions.") The book's obsessively mentioned appetites and tastes, its "cravings" (Wells 27), document the novel's interest in how sociohistorical background transfers from culture to nature via the affect system. Such moments not only dissolve the surprisingly resilient ideological distinction between those domains; they also confirm that the holdover effects of lifeworld are not merely ideological or cognitive, in the sense of intellectual beliefs or purely mental predispositions. They are physical too, "culture" now somatized and a regime of sociohistorical expectation transpired into the flesh. The success of this acclimatization is measured by the trauma that ensues upon its removal: after too long away from home, the Traveller says, "I began to think of this house of mine, of this fireside, of some of you, and with such thoughts came a longing that was pain" (Wells 77).

As the Traveller's "longing" and "pain" indicate—a literal nostalgia, or painful longing for home—the novel goes out of its way to mark the Traveller's defamiliarizing journey away from the context that produced him in not intellectual but bodily terms. But the Weena subplot perhaps more vividly shows how the Traveller finds even the most allegedly natural aspects of him—his physical urges and sexual drives—structured by generic and social conventions stabilized in a now-withdrawn milieu. These somatized templates he then projects onto scenarios arranging themselves serially around him. In the case of Weena, the generic holdover is the bourgeois marriage plot and the suite of desires appropriate to it. While this apparatus is abruptly abandoned late in the story in favor of other pleasures—the thrill of scientific romancing, the "long[ing]" he feels to kill Morlocks (Wells 67)—the Traveller's storyline in future earth is structured by the "queer friendship" he quickly establishes with the nonhuman creature he unthinkingly writes into the role of woman (Wells 42). The domestic romance plot thus exists as a kind of phenomenologically residual structure that uncannily shapes the Traveller's movements in this foreign future world. Replaying this plot as if by muscle memory, after a "long and tiring" day, the Traveller "returned to the welcome and the caresses of little Weena" (Wells 52).

The Traveller's tilt-a-whirl movement across plural lifeworlds exposed the one in which such embraces came naturally as but one of many possible ones. In this his journey undercuts the myth of bourgeois universality even as it strikes what should be a death blow at the notion of a generally shared common sense that, since Kant, has been presumed to undergird the processing of all judgments. "Corporeal, cognitive, and political," as Kandice Chuh summarizes in a reading of Kant, "the sensus communis links the phenomena of sensation to the operations of reason and the subtending orders and ideologies of a time and place" (23). What Chuh emphasizes is the particularity of allegedly universal sense-processes. The dynamic of acclimating sensation that connects ideology, understood in terms of concepts or ideas, and material bodies could be glossed again using the *habitus* concept of Pierre Bourdieu, where *habitus* indicates the physicalized ideological content of social position, the inscription of culture into the somatic frame. It is in keeping with this point about bodily habituation that a "strange, dumb confusedness" gathers in the Traveller's body as he spins across the eons (Wells 19), the inchoate mechanisms of physical disorientation here measuring his new distance from the bourgeois fireside and the stable order of expectation and sensus communis it emblematized.

The rupture of the Traveller's myth of universality comes as a shock, for sure. But it is axiomatic to bourgeois consciousness that stability must be restored: mastery over the object world reasserted, order reestablished. "The white man," Fanon observes, "discovers he is the predestined master of the world. He enslaves it. His relationship with the world is one of appropriation" (*Black Skin, White Masks* 107). It makes sense, then, that as the lifeworld of Wells's prototypical white man melts away he begins to feel the resulting vertigo as a threat to his capacity to control his environment. Soon it comes to threaten his much more basic power to make sense of what he sees at all, "making sense" being a byword for the bringing-to-stability of unruly phenomena and the forcing of singularities into conformity with concepts you have already prepared for them. The failure of this process of conceptual mastery registers, for the Traveller, as physical crisis: a woozy disorientation that he definitely does not like. In this sense does the Traveller's breakdown play out the consequences of world-withdrawal on the subject's body-mind, even as it suggests the now effectively hardwired reflex of the bourgeois man to, when threatened, restore mastery at all costs.

Or try to. In a deleted chapter preserved in manuscript at the University of Illinois, Urbana-Champaign, Wells described the "confusion & tumult" of the Traveller's bodily condition, a "strange sickness" and "heaping wretchedness that grew to agony." This complex of affects left him, the Traveller says in this canceled scene, so "hurt & weak physically" that "I began to cry like a child" (Geduld 184, 185):

> So conceive [of] me the Time Traveller, the discoverer of futurity, clinging nevertheless to his Time Machine and choking with sobs & with the tears streaming down his face[.] (Geduld 185)

The crisis of stability turns the meat-loving man of the nineteenth century, imperialist even here ("discoverer of futurity"), into a choking, weeping child who must, as though by defensive instinct, insist on his masculinity ("streaming down *his* face").

The Traveller responds to this threatening flux by trying, "instinctively," to quell it. For one habituated into the basic gender templates and impulse to conquer of an extractive bourgeois system, the phobic response to uncontrol has become precognitive, in a process of sociohistorical somatization that cuts against the residual Cartesianism that continues to separate mind from body in orthodox theories of "the subject."[16] Faced with the unfamiliar, the Traveller smashes the dark beings, reveling in the crunch of their (to him) disgusting bodies ("I *longed* very much to kill a Morlock or two" [Wells 67, emphasis added]); he discards Weena; he brags and preens, asserting a misplaced sense of intellectual prowess; and in one of the funnier instances of this will-to-mastery, writes his name on an exhibit in an abandoned museum, "yielding to an irresistible impulse" (Wells 69).

It is no accident, I am suggesting, that this last spasm of masculine self-assertion follows directly from the flash of impotence disclosed when he "confess[es]" to his primary worry that his "seventeen papers on physical optics" are now only rotting paper. The detail mock-heroically links the scene of academic production with civilizational collapse, comparing small things with great, but also—in ways described above—confirms their highly mediated relation (Wells 69, 68). Elizabeth Miller observes that the museum in the palace of green porcelain celebrates mining, a detail that positions "the work of industrial extraction in a historical past that the future will one day leave behind" (*Extraction Ecologies* 178). The Traveller's own vehicle, meanwhile, made of "nickel," "ivory," and parts "sawn out of rock crystal" (quoted in E. Miller, *Extraction Ecologies*, 178) confirms his place in a society defined by a relation to the object world comprehensive in its emphasis on depletion. Of course, all this laughably masculine and imperialist mental infrastructure meets its match at last in the hyper-speed whirlwind that ends the book. Here the Traveller comes up to the inadvertently comic limit of his ability to project the historical ontology he shares with readers onto the new worlds he encounters. When he meets an instance of jellied, quivering posthuman life at the end of the novel, all the Traveller can do, lamely, is analogize it with what he and we already know: it is, he says, "the size of a football perhaps" (Wells 85).

This limp stab at information processing seeks to fit an unruly object into a template that cannot match it. Yet this newest of the Traveller's instinctive efforts to establish his particularity as universal fails too, and for all his attempts at self-assertion, the analogy-maker disappears, in the end, into the liquid world of geological time, his physical body now withdrawing into "transparent" insubstantiality: "The Time Traveller was not there," the narrator explains in the famous scene:

> I seemed to see a ghostly, indistinct figure sitting in a whirling mass of black and brass for a moment—a figure so transparent that the bench behind with its sheets of drawings was absolutely distinct; but this phantasm vanished as I rubbed my eyes. The Time Machine had gone. Save for a subsiding stir of dust, the further end of the laboratory was empty. (Wells 90)

The image of "a whirling mass" turning to a "stir of dust" replays as escape the sickening arrival that opened the novel, albeit now seen from the outside rather than narrated from inside, as experience ("I seemed to see"). But while the Traveller may have dematerialized, the novel itself concludes by reverifying the solidity of the drawing room where it all began.

The voice of the narrator reasserts the continuity of bourgeois life (Wells 91) and ratifies the suite of humanist clichés the novel itself has suggested are better seen as desperate hedges against a temporal vastness that obliterates any delusion of bourgeois universality. Against its own evidence, then, the novel tries to believe that the perverse normal of middle-class experience is somehow universally valid: two flowers stand as symbols, the narrator says, "that . . . gratitude and a mutual tenderness still lived on in the heart of man" (Wells 91). But such platitudes, seized from the genre-world of liberal romance (A. Rosenberg *Scale*), cannot succeed in banishing from memory the flopping, jellied posthuman world the Traveller tried cognitively to tame.

Wells's novel raises the problem of generalized instability or phenomenological worldlessness—what it feels like to inhabit an infinitely plural cycle of background states, where none can stand as normal—only to reinstall bourgeois life at the center again. Building on what she identifies as a "phenomenological turn" in recent criticism (32), Adrienne Ghaly has recently asked what biodiversity loss feels like, noting how prevailing tropes of lack in phenomenological accounts of climate change—"silence, a spotless windshield, a dawning sense of absence" (34)—strategically occlude the causal relation between "our" everyday experience and the ecocide that often seems to disrupt it (35). The everyday, in other words, is itself the problem. Ghaly helps us see that what is experienced as "normal" for bourgeois subjects of the Global North is the smooth running of an extractive capitalist system; the paradox is that this very normalcy is the driver of events that are experienced as "disruptions" to that order now. Put another way, Ghaly's point is that the extractive processes that have guaranteed the smoothly unbroken background of bourgeois life since the Time Traveller's day are precisely what have authored the very cataclysms—superstorms, heat waves, die-offs—now experienced as exceptional to that form of life today.

Suvin's breakdown of the book's structure concludes with section 5, "Framework reestablished" (340). The solid comfort that is reestablished in the *Time Machine*'s closing paragraphs confirms its investment in what Ghaly describes as bourgeois life's definitionally imperialist drive toward ecocide. But the final word of this nested story is not so obvious, and it is important that Wells discloses that the signal mental disposition of its reasserted normal is not any fully vested emotional or intellectual state, but a more disorganized affect closer to what is today known as soft denial (MacDuffie, *Climate of Denial*, 3–14; 107–9). In Wells's novel, the narrator reports in a scandalized tone that for the Time Traveller, progress was a lie, and "the growing pile of civilisation only a foolish heaping that must inevitably fall back upon and destroy its makers in the end" (91).

What the final gesture tells us is that the Traveller has learned something we suspect too: that the bourgeois order, built on the lie of progress and set on a path to crisis, is best viewed not as the progressive story of development but as a Benjaminian pile of debris, bleaching on the streetside: a "foolish heaping" only growing with every year of civilization's supposed advance. Is it true? Shifting back to a coercive first-person plural, the narrator refuses to decide, but says phobically, as if in a kind of psychic recoil, that we had better pretend otherwise. "If that is so," he says, "it remains for us to live as though it were not so" (Wells 91).[17] The clunking repetition (is so / not so) discloses as grammatical hiccup that the psychic mechanism of denial and the grammatical operation of sense-making, neither process ever quite complete, go hand in hand.

* * * * * : *Alice and Intersystem Experience*

Conceived amid the sunshine and soft rain of the moneyed English countryside, written for the rich white children of the Oxford intelligentsia, Lewis Carroll's *Alice's Adventures in Wonderland* (1865) is a dispatch from inside a bubble. Its pastoral framework of "shepherds" and "tinkling sheep-bells" (110) and its tight diegetic enclosure, "all in the golden afternoon" (5), labor to shut out the gathering fossil capitalism whose lethal rapacity was more palpably comprehended beyond the confines of Oxbridge. "BUY an ASS," reads a clue for one of Carroll's word puzzles from 1879. "Get COAL from MINE. / Pay COSTS in PENCE" (Carroll, *Picture Book*, 205). The answer to the second of the June 7 problems, "get coal from mine," takes six moves, where each move can alter only a single letter:

MINE
mint
mist
most
moat
coat
COAL

(Carroll, *Picture Book*, 207)

But diverting acrostics that turn extractive capitalism into word games can only hint at the full shape of the system establishing itself over the middle decades of the nineteenth century. In 1865, fourteen years before COAL was pulled from MINE, and the same year *Alice* was published in red cloth by Macmillan and Company, William Stanley Jevons came to the realization that the material basis for England's modern economy would soon be "exhaust[ed]."

"I draw the conclusion," Jevons emphasized in his own italics, that "*we cannot long maintain our present rate of increase of consumption*": "*the check to our progress must become perceptible from within a century from the present time*" (274, emphasis in original). The "check" to "progress" was coming: but inside the bubble it didn't feel that way, and Carroll's novel bears the traces of its disoriented transitional moment even while seeking to bury or overcode them. In Carroll's text, world-ending in the phenomenological sense can be experienced only in bracketed terms: transformed into a fantasy of escape and rendered in that translation into a mood by turns discomfiting and delightful—an ambiguous affective complex condensed into that powerful but finally withholding description, "curious."

There are no factories in *Alice,* and—despite its organization around a seemingly endless hole—no mines. The Dodo may testify to anthropogenic disaster in the shape of targeted extinction, and the Mock Turtle may be forced to sing, "in a voice choked with sobs," about his own body's transformation into food for others (Carroll, *Alice,* 93), real turtle soup having been rendered too expensive for even the moneyed middle classes by the ravenous capture of green sea turtles to near exhaustion earlier in the century.[18] But if the vortex of the nineteenth-century's maturing extractive economy appears in Carroll's classic children's novel entirely as negation or comic displacement, it is true that the novel is organized around sovereign force and is riven, as Emma Davenport has shown, by imperial themes of "discovery," expropriation, and misogynistically framed physical violence. "First," Alice notices, "came ten soldiers carrying clubs" (Carroll, *Alice,* 70).

But in the terms I am developing here, this bone scan of a consolidating fossil regime goes further than documenting the arbitrary violence of the class system or the monopoly on force held by bourgeois political institutions like the army and the crown. Instead it transforms the phenomenological dilemma of intersystemic experience—what it feels like to inhabit a shifting world—into a representational challenge. How can you think, and what do you feel, when your world splits apart? By transforming systemic dissolution into the finally logical problems of torqued probability and upended expectation—Victorian philosophy called it reasoning from experience—Carroll gives shape to the affective complex proper to a failing world.

As millions of readers know, Alice's adventures unfold at the interface of two mutually exclusive orders of expectation, above ground and below. These worlds each have a kind of crazy internal coherence, an internal regularity only unevenly applicable to the other domain. Carroll's original title, *Alice's Adventures Under Ground*, captures the sense that the phenomenological concept of world is most easily defined spatially—in terms of what Fanon calls "home territory" (*Black Skin, White Masks* 89). It also underscores the importance of the genre concept in construing this dilemma. Any new background state or setting— "under ground," say, rather than "above" it—will bring with it a new set of regulative presumptions about, among other things, cause and effect: it's therefore usefully understood as a genre, in Frow's sense of "pre-given" field of reference. Alice's prior world may be realist, at least insofar as it is structured by bourgeois conventions like book-reading, teatime, and the utilitarian rationality required to determine "whether the pleasure of making a daisy-chain would be worth the trouble of getting up and picking the daisies" (Carroll, *Alice*, 9–10). But the new is a place of "adventure."

"Curious" is the emotionally inconclusive term Carroll uses to name feeling of mismatch between these exclusive lexical, logical, and generic systems. Like the Traveller, Alice is both discomfited and exhilarated by the breakdown of lifeworld, but (again like him) seeks to regain equilibrium however she can, "manag[ing]" novelty and stilling disorder to the best of her ability (Carroll, *Alice*, 73). The uneven results of this will-to-management make Alice "burs[t] out laughing" (73), but also "beg[i]n to feel very uneasy" (74), and the unspecifiable quality of this affective complex—"giddy" (59), ill at ease, thoroughly curious—confirms Barbara Johnson's point that words like *curious* and *strange*, another keyword in Alice's lexicon, signal a kind of open concealment or "marked spot," where further specification is noted as desirable but acknowledged to be impossible. Such words are "an X marking spot where later, perhaps, a poet will be able to say more" ("Euphemism" 104).

I've hinted that Alice's intersystemic affective complex eludes specification on grids of emotional categorization: no effort to describe X feeling or Y emotion can quite get it, and in this regard her peculiar sensations evince the ambient quality Ngai describes as "a state of being vaguely 'unsettled' or 'confused,' or, more precisely, a meta-feeling in which one feels confused about *what* one is feeling" (14, emphasis original). In such moments, straightforward emotional labels such as the ones Silvan Tomkins uses, for example, to name the "basic set of affects" (shame, interest, surprise, joy, anger, fear, distress, disgust, and contempt) cannot be adequate (Sedgwick and Frank 5). No fixed grid or list will do, and Alice's intersystemic predicament only radicalizes the fact that any inventory of named emotions will generate omissions, "blank spots in the table of elements" where other terms "have not yet come into being" (Jameson, *Allegory*, 50). If anything, Alice's feeling of unwinding is better considered a strange alchemy of available emotional elements, with others superadded: not unlike the potion she drinks, when any number of seemingly discrete flavors—"cherry tart, custard, pine-apple, roast turkey, toffy, and hot buttered toast"—add up to what she calls a "sort of mixed flavour" (Carroll, *Alice*, 14, 13). Is it good or bad? She doesn't like it, or doesn't quite—but drinks it anyway.

Alice tells us that navigating her unraveled world generates "melancholy," "despair," and even, in the end, makes her scream, "half of fright and half of anger" (Carroll, *Alice*, 108). This fuzzy repertoire diagnoses a transitional situation: she half-hopes, and half-expects, and "sat down with her face in her hands, wondering if anything would *ever* happen in a natural way again" (Carroll, *Alice*, 92, emphasis original). Despite her best efforts to "plan" and "manage" this unspecifiable predicament (Carroll, *Alice*, 16), one feeling Alice cannot escape is "despair" (Carroll, *Alice*, 26). But even this named emotion cannot capture the suite of feelings that track her, as she flounders between two incompatible definitions of the natural way.

In the context of this chapter's argument about the somatic registration of failing background states, Carroll's much-studied interest in the logical matters of sets, expectation, and probabilistic analysis is only half the story.[19] What the Alice book adds to the seemingly ratiocinative translation of "experience" into the register of math is a focus on the affective consequences of mismatched probability-worlds, the subjective effects of changing sets. The moments when Alice interfaces with novelty make visible the limits of her capacity to use prior knowledge to comprehend what to expect in the future. They also index how the scrambled circuitry between expectation and outcome generates consequences at the level of the body, these disordered somatic results confirming that broken life-worlds register perhaps most indelibly not in "mind" or "body" but in their curious intermixture that is the space of actual life.

For the Time Traveller, what remained constant throughout the spree of altering worlds was the physical body of the subject experiencing these background changes. The Traveller is skinnier when he comes home, and ravenous, but inhabits the same fleshly housing he did before the journey. Carroll's innovation is to put even this ground zero for phenomenological experience—the body—into flux as well. Husserl holds that the body is "the absolute zero-point in the system of coordinates in which each acquires an experience of the world" (Landgrebe 12). Famously, Alice witnesses this supposedly universal term torque and turn until she doesn't even know it's herself anymore: even her allegedly stable seat of experience turns out to be in motion, a destabilization effect again expressed by a breakdown in linguistic order. The best term for describing this effect turns out to be one of Alice's most famous ones, *queer*: "strange, odd, peculiar," but also "not in a normal condition; out of sorts; giddy, faint, or ill."[20] Giddy though she may be, Alice can respond to this ambiguous emotion only with gesture and sobs, her face in her hands. Words fail.[21]

Readers cannot forget the two times in the first chapter when Alice's body changes physical form. It is important to my observations here that the nonverbal graphic marks denoting this breakdown—the book's famous cascades of asterisks—do not represent so much as perform or enact the conversion moment between mutually exclusive generic registers, scalar regimes, or phenomenological states. Beer says that in *Through the Looking Glass*, Alice's "body remains constant": Alice "is adamant" in that later book, Beer writes, "in her bodily stability" (41). In Wonderland, however, this seat of phenomenological experience is set into motion too. The mutation of Alice's bodily frame is "the most profound disturbance of the books," Beer says (42), since it means that even the stabilizing site of experience, the I, cannot be pinned down.

An amateur's foray into book history reveals how differently Carroll's nonverbal signals for this interstitial experience have been handled. With amazing diligence, Bridget Sellers and Amy Ding surveyed some eighty-six editions of *Alice*, each offering a take on the asterisks that instantiate Alice's bodily shifts between perspectival regimes or orders of phenomenal normalcy. Each set of punctuation marks—along with some editions that leave them out entirely—attempts via nonlinguistic notation to give shape to the experience of intersystem embodiment that Carroll himself specified (in the handwritten manuscript) should unfold in the typographic mark of the asterisk: an eleven-asterisk approach, following a four-three-four pattern, in the early Macmillans; an in-line five in the Heinemann of 1907, in a single string across; another five in the 1868 edition pirated by *Haney's Journal of Useful Information*, an American publication. My own Penguin (1998) restores the Macmillan text, but an old Bantam Classic (1988) gives fourteen in three lines, 5-4-5 (see figures 6 and 7).[22] An undated Little and Ives, probably from 1940, has none at all.

This detour into bibliographic particularism matters because Carroll took these marks seriously, and specified in the manuscript and in many subsequent alterations to the text—"fastidious," "fussy," and "priss[y]," a later editor calls them (Carroll, *Alice*, lxx)—that these key transitional moments remain denoted by nonverbal graphic marks (figure 8). Each of Alice's embodied states enables her at least potentially to come into turkey, toffee, and hot buttered toast,) she very soon finished it off.

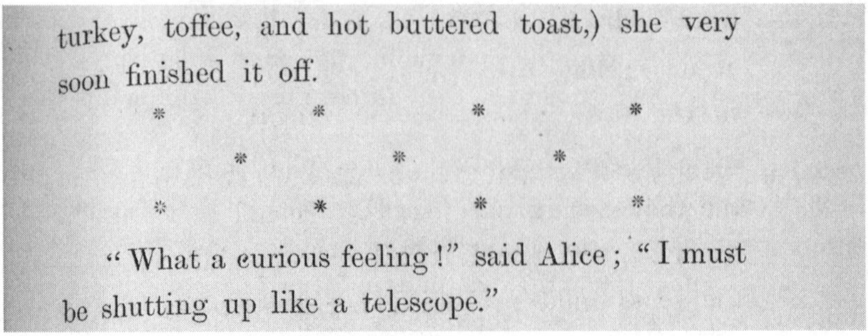

* * * *

* * *

* * * *

"What a curious feeling!" said Alice; "I must be shutting up like a telescope."

FIGURE 6. Lewis Carroll, *Alice's Adventures in Wonderland* (London: Macmillan, 1872). A detail of three rows of asterisks. Booth Family Center for Special Collections, Georgetown University Library, Washington, DC. Photograph: Jay Silvestre, Booth Family Center for Special Collections, Georgetown University Library.

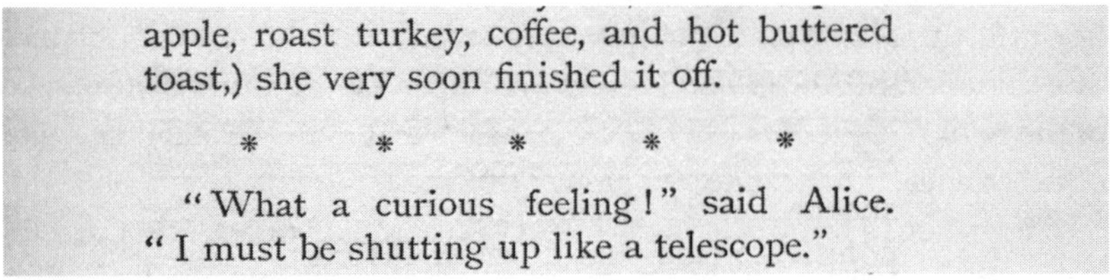

apple, roast turkey, coffee, and hot buttered toast,) she very soon finished it off.

* * * * *

"What a curious feeling!" said Alice. "I must be shutting up like a telescope."

FIGURE 7. Lewis Carroll, *Alice's Adventures in Wonderland* (London: William Heinemann/Doubleday Page and Co., 1907). A detail of one row of asterisks. Booth Family Center for Special Collections, Georgetown University Library, Washington, DC. Photograph: Jay Silvestre, Booth Family Center for Special Collections, Georgetown University Library.

equilibrium with a relatively stable phenomenological world or probabilistic regime, "preconceptual field[s]," in Foucault's words from *The Archaeology of Knowledge* (63) or what Saussure calls *langues*, "system[s] of interdependent terms" that together enable a structure for thought (114). It therefore makes sense that the moment between these states be figured not in any language at all but as performance or evocation. Slantwise or "bodily knowledges," in Sedgwick's words, then: insights felt and inhabited but, because uncounted by any available lexicon, evading capture in linguistic or grammatical form (Sedgwick and Frank 22).[23]

When Alice realizes that nothing will ever happen in a natural way again, she puts her face in her hands, and can only weep. Yet the book's final investment in perpetuating the illusion of bourgeois security—an

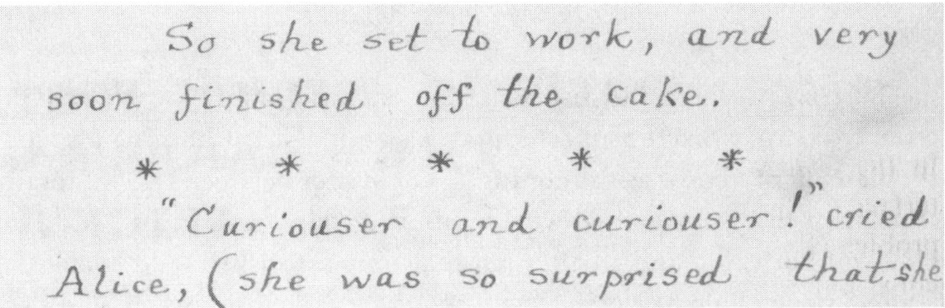
So she set to work, and very soon finished off the cake.

* * * * *

"Curiouser and curiouser!" cried Alice, (she was so surprised that she

FIGURE 8. Lewis Carroll, *Alice's Adventures Under Ground* (1864). Manuscript (Add. 46700, f.7). British Library, London. A detail of one row of asterisks. Photograph: © British Library Board.

illusion shared with *The Time Machine*—means that it cannot end on this aphasic emotional short circuit. Alice's adventure concludes not with suspended regularity or the unnamable sensation of nonterminal change, but at teatime. When Alice is called back to the stable bourgeois-domestic order, her assent to this suicidal normal is entirely noncognitive:

> when she had finished, her sister kissed her, and said, "It *was* a curious dream, dear, certainly; but now run in to your tea: it's getting late." So Alice got up and ran off, thinking while she ran, as well she might, what a wonderful dream it had been. (Carroll, *Alice*, 109)

In the blank space between her sister's command and the word "So" can be discovered a paradigmatic moment of bourgeois interpellation, so seamless it need not be narrated. The world of obedience and gendered subjection is now part of Alice's physical apparatus, the sociocultural form of a functionally ecocidal bourgeois order installed into the body now, as instinct: "So Alice got up and ran off." In this sense does the catastrophic normal of a gathering bourgeois world (in Beer's words) "prevai[l] reassuringly at the close of Wonderland" (Beer, *Alice*, 41), the sentimental clichés of "simple joys," "pleasure," and "happy summer days" along with the whisper of the marriage plot again dispelling threats of escape and closing the book on Carroll's experiment in unraveling worlds. Tennyson's weirdest and most unruly poem will ask what happens when such false closure no longer has the power to console. It ends this chapter by providing a formal model, never more relevant than in a moment of earth systems failure, for what experience feels like when there is no longer a world to ground it.

Or the Madness: Maud *I*

In *The Time Machine,* the disorientation of world-failure arose at the interface of vastly discrepant temporal scales; in *Alice* it became a spatial problem, figured now as the confusing encounter between two internally consistent but mismatched worlds, above ground and below, and two scales of body, big and small, such that only asterisks could evoke the finally unnameable movement between them. To close this chapter's account of experience in melting worlds I turn inward, to the domain of private life and the depletionary relation of subject to object that I will suggest stands as the logical motor for an extractive material order. To move toward *Maud,* however, is to move away from Victorian fantasies of restored stability and reinstated universalism, however internally fractured, and toward a document of the rising carbon economy that refuses the consolation proper to the regimes of bourgeois self-justification I have tracked so far. Published in 1855 alongside "The Charge of the Light Brigade" in *Maud, and Other Poems, Maud: A Monodrama* describes the rising system as a domain of cataclysmic unsteadiness and disorganized affective response. Fueled by theft, animated by lies, and aimed toward collapse while falsely representing its normal operations as "peace," the world of the poem cannot be brought to rest.

It is not for lack of trying. Tennyson positions the narrator's always failing effort at stabilization as both the organizing drama of the poem and, as we will see in readings of its collapsed metrical architecture, its central formal principle. In keeping with Tennyson's Carlylean anti-progressivism, *Maud*'s speaker sees the new normal rising around him as definitionally perverse, organized by a desire for acquisition he repetitively terms "lust": a "lust of gain," "each hand lusting for all that is not its own" (I.1.22–23).[24] As we saw in the introduction, any extractive economy will depend on continued expansion to sustain a rate of profit that enables it to avoid collapse: among other things, the expansionary character of capitalist accumulation means that no moment of arrival or completion is possible except in the domain of fantasy. To the psychic cost of its narrator, *Maud* shows how a system predicated on growth can only ever be a self-annihilating one, even as it arranges for us a series of fantasy-formations and psychic projections intended to pretend, with increasing desperation, that this is not so.

The bits of story that flicker into visibility through the screen of the narrator's delusion plot a disaster and document his repeated and increasingly strained efforts to find fixes for it. (I use "fix" here in David Harvey's sense of a temporary patching-over of a structurally determined crisis tendency in a system [Jessop 146–48]). The major plot points of *Maud* are (1) the gradual dissolution of its speaker's mind, as he narrates misogynistically the suicide of his father and his mother's betrayal of him; (2) his supposedly curative fixation on Maud, a fantasized love object, "faultily faultless" and "splendidly null" (I.2.81); (3) his rivalry with another lover and duel with Maud's brother; (4) his institutionalization in a "mad-house" (quoted in H. Tennyson 341); and (5) his subsequent shipping off to the Crimean war, a quasi-ironized form of closure where the madman at last finds singularity and purpose and imagines himself, wrongly, as part of a coherent system. "And myself have awaked, as it seems, to the better mind / . . . / . . . / I embrace the purpose of God, and the doom assigned" (III.6.55–58).

The idea that one might find security in the "embrace" of "doom" links *Maud*'s speaker to the Nietzschean postures of a certain strand of male climate writing today. It also evokes the nihilistic determinisms that Ernst Bloch, in *The Principle of Hope*, construes as the dialectical twin of bourgeois cheeriness. For Bloch, recall, the belief in "fraudulent hope" (Bloch I, 5) and the hopeless embrace of "the doom assigned" (A. Tennyson, *Maud*, III.6.58) are two sides of the same coin. But here as elsewhere in the poem, Tennyson's canny inclusion of "as it seems" tips us to the deluded nature of our speaker, undercutting his claim to have cured himself by imperial war. Instead Tennyson's verse discloses his speaker's entrapment in the false consolations of fantasy. If *Maud* appears as a "conservative" piece of writing, then—indulging in a neutralizing inertia while recommending war as a cure for psychic and social ills in keeping with the Tory nostalgia it is often mistaken for—it is "a conservative writing wildly out of control" (I. Armstrong 271).

"O let the solid ground / Not fail beneath my feet," pleads the speaker, as he falls into a disorientation occasioned by his father's likely suicide (I.11.398–99). The Oedipal predicament is informed by *Hamlet*, Tennyson said (Ricks 515–16), but is triggered, we learn in the poem's first lines, by the rising extractive economy, as Ella Mershon has noted. The poem begins with the father's leap into the "ghastly pit" (I.1.5) of a quarry or mineshaft after a "vast speculation had failed" (I.1.9). The detail depicts patriarchal authority swallowed up by the holes of a hyperfeminized landscape, in a suicide triggered by market failure: in so doing it positions a gendered struggle for mastery at the degree zero of social crisis and confirms extractive accumulation as the starting point for the poem's simultaneously inner (because psychic) and outward (because historical) scenes of injury. The interior collapse of the poem's fevered speaker is a response, I mean, to both the local context of his private injury and a broader analysis of his present conjuncture, "wretchedest age, since Time began" (II.5.259).

This dual unraveling in turn spins out a catalog of poetic or formal effects that are themselves marked by instability, unevenness, and failure. The unresolved structure of the poem, which swings between generic and metrical registers without a goal or grounding purpose, replicates the oscillations of the narrator's psychic state, as the whole ensemble tends toward what we can for short call breakdown. But in tracking the twinned processes of subjective and social dissolution alongside the speaker's deluded efforts to escape or still them, *Maud* evokes the experiential regime of a devolving extractive-imperial system. This world is coded, over and over again, as modern—the "recklessly speculative age," as Tennyson said, whose "blighting influence" charges the speaker with rage (quoted in Ricks 515). It thus models the shape of experience at the moment of fossil capitalism's chaotic, violent consolidation (the 1850s) even as it holds a mirror to the moment of that order's unwinding today.

Maud was Tennyson's first major poem after *In Memoriam* and has for generations been read as that poem's ironic inversion or cancelation, its "palimpsestic reworking," as Mershon puts it (1). "Probably the most original and highly experimental poem that Tennyson ever wrote" (R. Martin 383), *Maud* was, in James Russell Lowell's contemporary assessment, an "antiphonal voice to *In Memoriam*" (quoted in H. Tennyson 331).[25] *In Memoriam* had secured not just Tennyson's place as poet laureate but as the era's most accomplished poetic processor of trauma, the Victorian state's mourner-in-chief (see Oak Taylor); in the poem the psychic disorganization of loss only slowly coalesces into a forward-moving directionality that might enable the subject to transfer its attachment to a new object. There is no doubt that *In Memoriam*'s working-through takes wandering shape: its 131 sections weave through geology, extinction, and a small library of other topics seemingly unrelated to the poem's ostensible occasion of Arthur Henry Hallam's death.

Dilated though it may be, Tennyson's most enduringly popular poem (a success, readers still say, where *Maud* is a failure) nevertheless models closure at both the macro level of its narrative organization and the micrological scale of its form.[26] The calmingly metronomic time signature of the now-famous "In Memoriam stanza"—iambic tetrameter organized into ABBA quatrains—provides a scale model of this psychic reorganization. Each stanza unit of *In Memoriam* describes a tiny arc of Freudian recovery, the A rhyme returning after a couplet-length delay to secure at the stanza level what Devin Garofalo has described as the "orblike" completion of each of the poem's interlocked scales of organization—line, stanza, section.[27] So even though it was composed across decades, and even while its focus wanders and shifts, the published version of *In Memoriam* becomes the desultory, accumulative record of closure in the specific sense of psychic stabilization. The "successful" processing of ambient or unresolved feeling into the nameable emotion marks the transition from (pathological) melancholy to (healthy) mourning. A journey through interlocking *silva obscura* of distress but culminating in health, *In Memoriam* was intended, so Tennyson said, as a kind "of *Divina Commedia,* ending with happiness" (quoted in Taaffe 123).[28]

In contrast to *In Memoriam*'s elaborately stabilized psychic shock, *Maud* veers and pulls, modeling not the achievement of healthy equilibrium but the fantasy of it. As I will suggest, collapse organizes the poem at both the microscale of metrical scheme and the mesoscale of its structural organization. But *Maud*'s most obvious instability happens on the more basic order of plot. In keeping with Isobel Armstrong and others' accounts of Tennyson as the iconic poet of Tory nostalgia, *Maud*'s plot and rhetorical framing are borrowed from the right-wing anti-progressivism its author absorbed via Carlyle and Charles Kingsley. Through the scrim of its narrator's deluded quest for escape, the poem describes the modern era in terms that could have been lifted from *Past and Present* (1843): the contemporary is a maelstrom of injury populated by beaten women, factory children, and the starving poor. Speculation rules, and Mammon, god of profit, "grins on a pile of children's bones" (I.1.46). In this scene of brutality and accumulation, an appropriative violence has turned social life into a death drive, and "only the ledger lives" (I.1.34).

The diagnostic vision of *Maud* describes the modern economic order, accurately, as a charnel house. On top of the bones, "new-made lord[s]" in "gewgaw castle[s]" (I.10.332, 347) enjoy a splendor whose ultimate source is a constitutively unsustainable violence. At the ultimate source of this money, Tennyson specifies, is "a gutted mine" (I.10.338). "Coal," the speaker says, is "all turned to gold" (I.10.340). With these lines in mind, Mershon observes how the poem makes "the systems and infrastructure of fossil-fueled industry visible," and in drawing attention not just to the exploitation of the earth but of those doing the work, shows how "both the miners and the earth are stripped, naked and gutted, so that their labor can turn coal into gold" (3). The alchemical work of this system is to sublate brutality into surplus, turning lumps of archived sunlight into "gold" by the magic of human misery. In summarizing the nouveau-riche world of gewgaw and paste jewel built atop this catastrophe, the speaker observes that "these are the days of advance" (I.1.25). The irony singes, since *advance* here names not any progressive accumulation or forward-driving process but a "barbarous opulence" (as he says of his rival, an emblem of this order), "jewel-thick," whose "essences turn the live air sick" (I.8.455, 454). In all this *Maud* unfolds a diagnostic vision of a modern world predicated on extraction and programmed to crisis, where, as the narrator observes early on, "the spirit of murder works in the very means of life" (I.1.40).

The speaker's efforts ideologically to fix this spinning crisis-world—to still its movements and arrest its diverse violences—are exposed, over and over again, to be wish-fulfilling illusions, and empty ones: "childish escapes" (I.1.69), he says elsewhere. Escape, dream, illusion, gardens with walls to shut out the world: these and related figures, along with the love relation itself, stand for the speaker's efforts to consolidate stability and flee the dynamics of disaster around him. "And it was a dream," he says in the poem's weirdly truncated final part,

> yet it yielded a dear delight
> To have looked, though but in a dream, upon eyes so fair,
> That had been in a weary world my one thing bright[.]
>
> (III.6.15)

Such open fantasizing and undercut escapism signal *Maud*'s investment in the ultimately destabilizing mode of irony—"deeply ambiguous," Isobel Armstrong notes (271). But the perspectival irony and resulting epistemological insecurity that defines the dramatic monologue as a form is here repurposed. Not only an experiment in voice or testing-ground for characterological elaboration, it is now a diagnostic device for understanding the relation between one hypersensitive mind and a total sociohistorical situation: a fossil capitalism defined by pits and hollows and an ultimately suicidal quest for profit, functionally inescapable. "Were it not wise," our speaker asks early in the poem, "if I fled from the place and the pit and the fear?" (I.1.64) Sure: but how? (plate 5).

Insofar as *Maud* describes from the inside the psychic regime proper to a gathering fossil economy, it makes sense that its primary mood is what critics have long described simply as psychosis. Tennyson originally planned to subtitle it "Or the Madness" (H. Tennyson, *Memoir* 339) and as Herbert Tucker and others have explained, the poem is often construed as emblematic of what William Edmondstoune Aytoun in 1854 called the spasmodic school of poetry, with *spasmodicism* being the byword, in the 1840s and 1850s, for a physical and mental volatility associated with "nervous disease" (Dransfield 280).[29] Isobel Armstrong narrates Tennyson's career from *In Memoriam* to *Maud* as the move "from geology to pathology" (252) and explains how "*Maud* or 'Mad' negotiates political stakes in the definition of madness" (253). But the speaker's allegedly unhinged internal condition—his rudderless or properly disorganized psychic state—can be described as insane or diseased, in the habitual terms of readers then and now, only in the sense that "sanity" is still construed to describe the subject's seamless psychic accommodation to a world built on capitalist extraction. Tennyson's narrator has not successfully adjusted to this pathological normal.

If a sane mind will accommodate itself to its milieu, "fitting" with its world in ways that complete the circuitry between expectation and outcome, *Maud* shows a subject in the process of dissociation from a world that cannot provide the comfort of equilibrium. The *lebenswelt* of a rising extractive capitalism may seem placidly beautiful to those for whom its machinery feels natural: its conventional landscapes and comfortable lawns might instill, as they do in *Alice,* a sense of pleasing calm for those who make daisy chains in front of mansions. Like the sweet and blue-frocked Alice, "Maud" (says the speaker) "has a garden of roses / And lilies fair on a lawn" (I.14.489–90. But he sees things otherwise, and starts the poem this way:

> I hate the dreadful hollow behind the little wood,
> Its lips in the field above are dabbled with blood-red heath,
> The red-ribbed ledges drip with a silent horror of blood,
> And Echo there, whatever is asked her, answers "Death."
>
> (I.1.1–4)

As Raymond Williams explains, the pastoral conventions framing *Alice's Adventures* that Tennyson so economically evokes here—with "little woods," "field," and "heath," in just three lines—are defined primarily by their function as a laundering device or mechanism of psychic escape. Conventionally deployed, pastoral protocols transform extractive accumulation into something like beauty, as scenes of lacquered calm and serene bucolic order naturalize exploitation and make dispossession look charming.[30] Pastoral is in this sense an aesthetic technology of denial—denial, of course, being the function Allen MacDuffie among others has identified as the core psychic posture of fossil imperialism, one of the ways by which an "externalization society," as Kohei Saito puts it, accomplishes its necessary "forgetting" (MacDuffie *Climate of Denial*; Saito, *Slow Down,* 10). *Maud* inverts the escape-hatch function of pastoral codes by visualizing the crimes those tropes were invented to hide. Its opening lines hiss with the cruelty that gardens and lawns occlude: illusions of steady beauty and managed nature become a bloodbath of eroticized harm, spangled with the "silent horror of blood" and punching with a spondee to start—"I hate."

Named here as "hatred," the speaker's negative affect toward the object world mirrors the violent arrangements of the modernity that disgusts him: his "hatred" is both a response to a world that is defined by "rapine" (I.4.123) and an image of that very violence. (Mirroring, as the allusion to Echo and Narcissus in line 4 suggests, is a thematic throughline of the poem.) Transformed into the genre-template of love poetry and its conventionalized erotic relations between male subject and female object, the rage toward the world that is fundamental to the extractive system—"a world of plunder and prey" [I.4.125], the narrator calls it—takes shape in the speaker's narcissistic fixation on a love object that turns out to be a projection of himself.

Everywhere he looks is a mirror. Christopher Ricks writes that in *Maud,* Tennyson shows how "a morbid self-consciousness precludes the consciousness of others' selves" (Ricks 250). It is in keeping with this narcissistic projection of subject onto world that the speaker's depictions of Maud are not really depictions of Maud at all but of an idealized, fantasized vision of her. Splendidly null, as the speaker calls her, Maud is not a subject but a screen for her observer's projection: on object he soon makes part of himself. What Tennyson's biographer calls "the deep and neurotic self-absorption of the narrator" (R. Martin 386) means that, while the poem is titled after Maud, it is not about her at all, except insofar as that name becomes a kind of rack on which clichés and ready-made romantic images can be draped—"stars, flowers, and especially gems," Tucker notes (*Doom* 416).

When in a famous moment the narrator says "I kissed her slender hand, / She took the kiss sedately, / Maud is not seventeen, / But she is tall and stately" (I.12.424–27; quoted in Tucker, *Doom,* 417), he effectively overcodes any sensual particularity of the object—what Maud really might be like—with preset idiomatic figures borrowed from poetic cliché, figures Tennyson reveals *as* figures in the dopey rhymes (sedately / stately) and flattening adjectivalism (slender, tall, stately), which despite excess verbosity show nothing. This is, says one reader, "a world of literary convention where rapture is to be expressed either in genteel clichés . . . or in gushing outbursts" (Drew 126). What we see is "not her," as Tucker summarizes, "not her, but a poise, a prize, a place" (*Doom* 417). For Ricks, "the thing which [the speaker] cannot bear about Maud is precisely the dread of her as a unique person" (*Tennyson* 252). Since Maud has been stripped of any particularity that might render her idiosyncratically herself, she becomes a chattel or item of landscape, available like any other object for instrumental use by the subjects with the power to observe or describe those things. This becoming-object via a dehumanizing deletion of particularity renders the poem's title woman available for what Szeman and Wenzel describe as the extractive relation, "a human instrumentalisation of nonhuman nature: the use of nature only as a means toward human ends" (511).

As I observed in the introduction, the entire point of Szeman and Wenzel's intervention is to avoid moving the term *extraction* too easily from material to immaterial domains, using it to describe, say, both the stripping of minerals from the earth and the hypostasization of a human other into an object for your own use via poetic device. Used in this promiscuous sense, they point out,

> one of the perils of extractivism is that it tends to flatten the ground, collapsing historical, geographical, and cultural distinctions that should be important to fully understanding the specific operations of extraction, including the ideologies and imaginaries that surround it at any given time and in any given space. (514–15)

The crucial point is specificity, and how criticism flattens it. False equivalences between cultural operations and material processes ("mining coal, drilling for oil, harvesting timber," in their partial list [515]) erase qualitative distinctions among those procedures by reducing them into fungible terms, each replaceable with the next. Yet it is precisely this operation of cognitive instrumentalization—flattening, collapsing, and turning particularities into false equivalents—that Tennyson's poem shows unfolding in broken verse, as the practices of ecocidal reason echo through both its material and cognitive realms, the instrumentality at the core of material life (mines, accumulation, murder) now ramifying at the levels of psychic process and poetic device.[31]

At minimum, the speaker's commitment to converting Maud into a set of clichés that might cure him helps us see that the stakes for the poem's lyric involution or primary narcissism extend beyond habitual scholarly questions about Tennyson's real political beliefs or his supposed identification or disidentification with the speaker's Carlylean social analysis. Instead those clichés help us recognize the aesthetic and conceptual correlates to the extractive paradigm we inhabit still. The following chapter will unfold this claim about the epistemology of extraction in more detail, as it tracks the mental habits and conceptual grammars that developed to shore up a relation to the world based on use. Here we can see that *Maud* dramatizes as lyric scenario the violent projection of the subject onto the object and in so doing lays bare the modern cognitive apparatus whose rewiring from the inside is the true subject of this book. "Even the insubstantiality of Maud herself as a character," Robert Martin writes, "is the result of his never seeing her directly, only in the mirror of his own egotism" (386). In *Negative Dialectics,* Theodor Adorno describes the subject's "rage" (*Wut*) toward the object world as the constitutive orientation of a capitalist total system that seems bound to destroy itself. A hunger or "impulse" toward subsumption of the not-I is the avaricious philosophical appetite at the core of what Adorno, like Tennyson, represents as a catastrophic modern paradigm (*Negative* 22–24).[32]

There will be other chances, across the pages of this book, for engaging with and historicizing Adorno's account by locating it within the postwar expansion of environmental calamity known as the Great Acceleration. Here, the account of a world-devouring lyric narcissism helps make sense of why, in *Maud,* the language of eroticized subjection becomes master trope for a broader logic of other-abolishing mastery the poem codes as a particularly contemporary delusion. It is the fever dream of a speaker whose situation is unthinkable without coal mines, finance capital, or foreign war, and who is never more modern than when he criticizes the murderous capture whose machinery is replicated in his own mental habits. For the speaker of Tennyson's poem, wandering among pits and hollows, Maud is "my bride to be, my evermore delight, / My own heart's heart, my ownest own" (I.18.671–72).

The repetition of the possessive *my* underscores the logic of acquisition here, confirming that the object called "Maud" is no longer herself, whatever that may be, but an aspect of the poet's own mind, now secreted within him and thus made part of the subject in a psychic process that confirms how (in Jacques Derrida's words for describing introjection) "incorporation is a kind of theft" ("Foreword" xvii).[33] Tennyson's frantically repetitive pun on *own* again shows how the erotic relation that would make Maud the speaker's *own* in an erotic sense is a species of the same extractive violence by which property is acquired. The self-consciously infantile rhetorical device, I mean, positions an inherently violent erotic relation (the subject subsuming its desired object) as microcosm for a political relation of extractive instrumentalization whose core dynamic (at its "heart") is the property relation itself: "my ownest own."

I am suggesting that *Maud* operates as both diagnosis and dramatization of extractive capitalism's other-abolishing, expansionary tendencies, even as it offers "disease" and "imbalance" as mental states proper to the orientation that can see the exterior object world as nothing so much as an instrument for use: "Dead perfection, no more" (I.2.83). In this sense

Tennyson's weirdest poem provides an ambiguously critical inventory of the mental grammar of an extractive paradigm. Hypercharged on coal, transcendentally homeless, sick with a self-absorbed instrumentalism, the modern subject uses up the world and makes it part of himself, and, in so doing, confirms its own internal wiring for suicide. If I have used "suicide" and "suicidal" as tropes for the crisis tendencies of an extractive capitalist system, here those figures are grotesquely literalized: "What!" he screams, "am I raging alone as my father raged in his mood? / Must I too creep to the hollow and dash myself down and die[?]" (I.1.53–54). Another of the poem's purposefully juvenile puns seals the doomed homology between interpersonal domination and extractive accumulation. The speaker fantasizes that an arranged marriage negotiated between his father and Maud's had "Sealed her *mine* from her first sweet breath": "Mine, mine by a right, from birth till death. / Mine, mine—" (I.19.724–26, emphasis added). In the trauma repetition of the lines, the *mine* of erotic ownership and the *mine* of father-killing extraction merge poetically into the same thing.

O That't Were Possible: Maud *II*

Bloody hollows and deadly pits structure the poem's plot while the mine—at once a site of extraction and shorthand for eroticized possession—forms its central figure. All this, combined with the speaker's narcissistic self-delusion, mean that *Maud*'s collapsing motion radicalizes a certain form of lyric inwardness to its logical endpoint of omnivorous world-destruction, what I polemically called, in the introduction, the bourgeois world's suicide pact. Secondhand images of roses and gardens are the delusions that cannot fully banish this organizing violence. But these repeated figures from the well-thumbed playbook of erotic verse signal not the satisfaction of love or any reciprocal relation between subject and object—a relation based on "stewardship," not exploitation (quoted in E. Miller, *Extraction Ecologies*, 7)—but the speaker's unregulated desire for those things. Across registers, then, what the poem documents are the crisis tendencies of a then-rising modern paradigm.

Tennyson's compositional process shows how the question of whether an extractive disposition might ever come to stability organized the poem from the beginning. Built from individual lyrics Tennyson had composed separately (Ricks, headnote, 511), and as early as 1833–1834, the poem also includes other freestanding lyrics Tennyson added later, over a period of years; the whole poem was "written, as it were, *backwards*" (H. Tennyson 319, emphasis original), in an associative, desultory process that among other things counters the progressive linear sequences proper to developmentalist paradigms. The section Tennyson wrote first formed the original core of the poem. Titled "O That't Were Possible," this short lyric would wind up buried at the formal center of the finished poem (part II, section 4), its grand subjunctive question thus turned, via the psychoanalytic process of encryption or secreting-inside, into a kind of guiding conceptual-thematic impasse, the electric pulse at the heart of the thunderstorm. "O, that't were possible," the speaker muses at this introjected moment,

> After long grief and pain
> To find the arms of my true love
> Round me once again!
>
> (II.4.141–44)

Will reconciliation be achieved? Is stability an option? The speaker hopes so: he yearns for a concluding union, the healing of an original separation that would take form, here, in the physical closure of erotic embrace: "the arms of my true love / Round me." This literal form of completion would effect for the speaker, he says, a perfect moment of healing: an exclamation-marked antidote to "long grief and pain."

But the rhyming of *pain* with that key term of melancholic repetition, *again*, along with the gutting subjunctive mood of the verse—would that it *were* possible—shadows this image of conciliation and circularized stability with an undercurrent of what the poem calls doom. *Alice's Adventures* (1865) and Matthew Arnold's "Stanzas from the Grand Chartreuse," which like *Maud* was published 1855, both depict characters caught between two worlds—as Arnold writes, one dying, and the other powerless to be born (l. 85–86). Like those other split-world texts, Tennyson's diagnoses its transitional moment by describing a hiatus between mutually exclusive worlds, one in which stability *were possible*, one in which it's not. But *Maud* suggests repeatedly, and never more vividly than when it pretends otherwise, that in a rising extractive system, all is crisis, no arrival.[34]

I have emphasized so far the structural restlessness of the poem, its fundamental ironic construction and its inversion of bourgeois figural repertoires stolen from love poetry and the pastoral. This unresolved quality is diagnostic, I am suggesting, of a consolidating economic order whose aftermath is visible in the weather as you read this book. But *Maud*'s historically diagnostic structural instability is legible at smaller scale too. The poem's oddly recursive, nonlinear compositional process mirrors the irregularity of its versification, a fact that shows how unevenness and breakdown organize even the internal wiring or microscaled infrastructure of this poetic performance, its syncopation at the level of the line. *Maud* takes shape as a mashup of poetic structures: its stanza forms, line lengths, and even generic signals mix and switch with increasingly frantic disjunction.[35]

In these ways does poetic form operate as a baseline level of instability in a poem that is about instability at the social and personal scales: this veering, shuddering verse gives shape, I mean, to a disorganized affective state that criticism continues to gather into false coherence as "lunacy" or "madness." In the context of this uncanny capacity of *Maud* to tempt readers into the fixity of simplifying diagnosis—the comfort of conclusion—it is important to note that the poem holds out the possibility of regularization only to undercut that promise each time. Rather than unfolding in "free verse" or prose poetry, each subsection of this broken poetic effort is rigorously metrical: each of *Maud*'s internally mismatched poetic registers, in other words, is itself internally consistent, each generic or formal idiom constituting its own internal tempo or microclimate of regularity, albeit one that's inevitably switched out for another at rates that never allow the reader to (as the Caterpillar told Alice) get used to it in time.[36]

For Barbara Herrnstein-Smith, poetic structure is a kind of probabilistic mechanism, since form itself is "an inference we draw from the evidence of a series events," the first parts of a poem effectively becoming a baseline from which to project tentatively a possible future (13). *Maud* does not enable any suborder of regularity to allow sound inferences to be made. Such ruptured probabilistic contracts create what Herrnstein-Smith describes as a low-grade emotional turmoil: a muted, aesthetic simulacrum of anxiety. In reading poetic patterns that have been disrupted in this way, she notes, "we might feel annoyed, or flustered, or perhaps 'threatened,' for the order we had begun to assume would be destroyed and (because no new order would yet have emerged) we would be at the edge of a very minor chaos" (13).

Maud radicalizes this minor chaos, serializes it, and establishes the resulting mixed affective catalog as the supervening mood-complex of the poem. The fact that it is divided into three parts might seem to suggest an overarching design or order, even perhaps the Aristotelian one. But the apparently steadying progression through beginning, middle, and end was retrospectively imposed (Ricks, headnote, 513), and like other aspects of the poem is openly false, given that it does not describe the motion of the poem's action at all. The three sections become shorter as they proceed: part I runs 923 lines, part II 342 lines, and part III—when the speaker ships off to Crimea and "cures" himself—just 59, less than a tenth of part I.[37] Each of these parts is itself subdivided into uneven numbers of sections, while these subsections themselves comprise unmatched numbers of individual stanzas—each of these running varying lengths. Stanzas take the form of unbroken blocks of up to thirty-five lines at the top end (II.1.1–35) to tiny freestanding couplets on the page all by themselves (I.19.684–85). Within these nested but uneven scales of unit division, lines themselves oscillate with similar unregulation, ranging from seventeen syllables (I.4.125) to just two (II.5.240) and every length in between. This agitated structural logic means that no single temporal-formal signature has a chance to become normal.

The poem's "potpourri of verse styles" and "striking variations in meter and rhyme" (Berglund 45) give aesthetic shape, I am suggesting, to an unregulated affective scenario or ugly feeling that is disorganized, in the specific clinical sense of failing to come to rest in a categorization that would respond to nominal capture. No nameable mood gains prominence, no single tempo has a chance to establish itself as right. This "spasmodic" patterning and disoriented feeling diagnoses as affective performance a rising modern order whose apparent advances and seeming improvements are premised, says the speaker, on "death."

Given the importance of denying this fact to the smooth operation of bourgeois consciousness, it is perhaps no surprise that multiple generations of readers have responded to the poem with what Lisa Berglund summarizes as "discomfort" (46). Hallam Tennyson reported that because of its "novelty," *Maud*'s "meaning and drift were widely misunderstood even by educated readers" (H. Tennyson 331).[38] It generated loathing in George Eliot and, in Walter Bagehot, "proper unease" (Ricks, *Tennyson*, 255). William Gladstone asked early on "whether this poem has . . . full moral equilibrium" (H. Tennyson 337, quoted in Ricks 516), no doubt realizing that it does not.[39] To middle-class audiences whose own psychic organization depends, then as now, on the false premise that extractive economies can guarantee peaceful growth and steady states, that *world* in the phenomenological sense will hold still, such frenzy can appear only as madness.

The Time Machine and *Alice* both suggested how the minimally organized and perhaps unspecifiable feeling of living in a broken world cannot be captured in the documentary idiom of representational language. No surprise, then, that the idea of performance is so crucial to *Maud*'s diagnostic project. The poem was meant to be read aloud. Tennyson's performances of the poem became legendary in his lifetime and *Maud* was, according to his son, his favorite poem to perform by voice (H. Tennyson 324). This point matters because it is in recitation or embodied performance that the representational aspiration of language—the nominalizing and objectifying function that defines language's communicative function—is transformed into something like total gesture (figure 9).

The great poet's performances of *Maud* were famous and extended throughout his life even if, according to some accounts, they were often undesired by their audiences. According to Tucker the famous readings were, in a word, awkward, landing on the bourgeois ear with an

FIGURE 9. Dante Gabriel Rossetti, *Tennyson Reading "Maud"* (1855). Brown pen and wash over black ink on paper. Rossetti Collection, Birmingham Museums and Art Gallery, UK (CC0). Photograph: Birmingham Museums and Art Gallery.

unpleasant dissonance and upending the drawing room-expectation of smooth and stately recitation of liberal-humanist idées reçues (*Doom*). In the fall of 1855, Tennyson reported reading *Maud* "to five or six people at the Brownings'" (H. Tennyson 328), while Elizabeth Barrett Browning described Tennyson as "crying out 'Maud' to us, and helping the effect of the poem by the personality" (quoted in H. Tennyson 328–29). Christina Rossetti attended too: a connection that will return in this book's final chapter.

Hallam recalled that these performances, however upsetting to the polite-minded members of the intelligentsia, nonetheless achieved a kind of goal: "Nothing perhaps justified what has been said of my father," he recalled, "that had he not been a poet, he might have been remarkable as an actor, than his reading of 'Maud,' with all its complex contrasts of motive and action" (H. Tennyson 334). One imagines how such performances would have shuttled audiences in and out of emotional registers with surely disorienting speed. Hallam remembered that his father would read *Maud* with the "exultation of love," a

> blessedness . . . so intense that it borders on sadness, and my father's voice would break down when he came to
>
> I have led her home, my love, my only friend.
> There is none like her, none.
>
> (H. Tennyson 335)

Blessedness, sadness, breakdown: I am making a case for the unmoored affective and formal organization of *Maud*, its efforts to construe rudderless experience as a technical problem for versification no less than as a dilemma to be performed, but never named, in bodily motion. If Tennyson's confusing recitations veered among seemingly mismatched registers, they also failed to take the shape of "concept[s] that can be rigorously grasped and transmitted"—thus slipping, just for a moment, the trap of universal capture by which singular instances are outfitted for "linguistic exchange" (Derrida, "Signature," 309). Instead: a performance, translated into other media (a watercolor, a memoir, a monograph) and available for our later reconstruction only at a loss.

For Kant, the human faculty of reason is defined by its ability to move beyond immediate sense experience toward a priori claims, valid outside the confines of one's own body. Paradoxically, however, this process begins with the body, since it depends on what Kant describes as orientation, or finding one's position within a given landscape or world. As Kant says in an essay cited by Sarah Ahmed, "if I see the sun in the sky and know it is now midday, then I know how to find south, west, north and east" (Kant 4; see Ahmed, *Queer*, 6–7). This fundamental act of alignment depends, he explains, on knowing right from left—and this knowledge "comes naturally," or rather "it is a faculty implanted by nature but *made habitual through frequent practice*" (Kant 5, emphasis added). To close this chapter on the derangement of experience in our burning world, and to emphasize the force of nineteenth-century aesthetic thought in helping formalize that profoundly contemporary sense of affective drift, I will reproduce the part of *Maud* readers hated the most. It "has not fared well with critics," Tucker reports (*Doom* 419).

It's a section of self-consciously "infantile language" and "cloying babble" (Berglund 46) that is only the most extreme of the poem's self-ironizing lyric interludes. It comes after a seven-line stanza and a four-line one. But the singsong palliative that arrives to steady things is no cure at all, but performs in five-beat lines what it feels like to be inside a system falling apart, where red, code for rage and love together, is now also a racial signature: "the red man" "dances" with his "red man's babe," in a delusional, repetitive notation that references the "blood-red heath" of the first stanza while alluding to genocides beyond the edges of the speaker's ability to know. Thus, "red" functions now not merely as a racist marker for indigenous people but describes them bathed in gore. The militaristic nationalism that seems to bring the poem into final stability, then—"the hero's defection into lobotomized jingoism," as Tucker calls it, as he ships off to war in the East (*Doom* 429)—turns now to America, which has, since Locke, served as the prime scene for testing the modern subject's capacity to convert nature to property, as I explain in the next chapter.

In Tennyson's hands, this martial fix is exposed as merely one delusional cure among others. Something, anyway, feels off:

Rosy is the West,
        Rosy is the South,
Roses are her cheeks,
        And a rose her mouth.
When the happy Yes
        Falters from her lips,
Pass and blush the news
        Over glowing ships;
Over blowing seas,
        Over seas at rest,
Pass the happy news,
        Blush it through the West;

Till the red man dance
    By his red cedar-tree,
And the red man's babe
    Leap, beyond the sea.

(I.17.575–90)

In the passage, "West" and "South" begin the song as simple substantives, part of "a system of coordinates that must . . . be absolute," in Ahmed's words (*Queer* 12), since they denote cardinal directions presumed to exist for all. And Tennyson's equational use of the simple copula here—Rosy *is* the West—underscores the effort on the narrator's part to secure some notion of ontological fixity or a common world by virtue of these coordinates.

But this effort to fix a system in crisis runs off the rails almost instantly: tempo gathers pace and a singsong cadence of babylike repetition bounces us through increasingly vivid images of a now explicitly imperialist world system. We pass, pass, pass and leap, then blush, and blush (the speaker tells us),

Till the West is East,
    Blush it thro' the West
Rosy is the West,
    Rosy is the South,
Roses are her cheeks,
    And a rose her mouth.

(I.7.593–98)

By the end of this spree "West" becomes "East," and even Kant's world-establishing universal, the sense of direction that grounds all experience, has unraveled, as the reasonable civilization of "the West" turns into its dancing red other, and vice versa. This folding-together plays out as poetic performance Adorno's observation, to be explored further in the next chapter, that bourgeois reason and its supposedly irrational opposites, "violence" and "passion," share a common drive to annihilation.[40] Tennyson goes further: by referencing frontiers of accumulation "over seas" and "beyond the seas," the moment evokes the far-flung genocides that subtend extractive accumulation at home. "His fantasies of erotic domination," Tucker observes of *Maud*'s speaker, "are imperial fantasies as well" (*Doom* 419). In this way does the "*silent* horror of blood" of the poem's first stanza (I.1.3, emphasis added) sublate now into a broken music, as the passage revolves through pseudo-joyous images of devolution and violence, red, red, red, until orientation collapses and only a fevered confusion stands in its place.

Wells's Time Traveller looked out onto the sky millions of years after the decline of humankind, saw the sun, and chose red as the governing figure for the threat to bourgeois universalism: the sun was "a deep Indian red and starless, and south-eastward it grew brighter to a glowing scarlet where, cut by the horizon, lay the huge hull of the sun, red and motionless" (Wells 82; quoted in Cole 170). Such visions of civilizational threat, infected with Orientalist fantasies of decadence and primitive return, disclose, with *Maud*, the genocide at the heart of the bourgeois experiment. If the endgame of this experiment was coded into its program from the beginning, *Maud* helps us see how the structural crises of bourgeois life manifest in the confused emotions and tumbled-up affects of subjects coming apart.

When the Kids Go to Bed

I noted earlier that *Maud* was written backward, and I now want to explain that this chapter was too. We began in 1895, when the fossil imperialism of the nineteenth century was fully in place and England was extracting and burning some two hundred million tons of coal per annum; atmospheric carbon stood at 294.8 ppm. We moved backward to 1865 (287.1 ppm) and landed at a moment, 1855, when the fossil economy's gewgaw surpluses and catastrophic human costs still felt new enough to notice and even, perhaps, to critique (285.1 ppm).[41] By rolling back the tape this way, I've emphasized how the affective and cognitive repertoire of a functionally diseased fossil economy came to take shape: how it felt to inhabit a transitional moment between stable orders and how the "ambient affects" or "weakly intentional feelings" (Ngai 27) proper to such moments in turn diagnose scenes in which the possibility of consequential action feels withdrawn. The relatively disorganized affective states I've tracked took shape in the folds and splinters of a gathering extractive system. But it is the experience of that system's late-phase crises, today, that forms the contemporary occasion for this book.

A year after Hurricane Harvey, a Houston reporter asked Shirley Paley to describe the "changes to [the] living routine" that had followed the ten-thousand-year flood event she had survived only twelve months before. Paley and her family had lived for some time, she explained, in a car parked in the driveway of their swamped house. Now she was struggling to make payments on the federal relief loans that had, nevertheless, not met the cost of the mitigation measures the government had mandated for her demolished home. These and other shifts in background stability prompted negative feelings that were hard to name and took shape most sharply in physical symptoms. For Paley's autistic grandson, the alterations to their regular world were "fraught"; for her granddaughter, they "triggered a visceral trauma response: emotional rages and profound depression." When asked how she herself was coping with multiple and overlapping crises in the long aftermath of the storm, Paley said: "When the kids go to bed, I weep into a towel" (quoted in Purser).

Phenomenology, or *what it feels like to be,* is the science of the subject. In this sense it is the bourgeois intellectual practice par excellence. Restricted to the individual, the study of experience replicates the narcissism of liberal ideology by partitioning subject from world and, as Ahmed and Fanon's accounts attest, presuming as universally valid the contingent and supposedly stable lifeworlds of figures like Husserl or Alice, for whom braiding flowers on the lawn or writing academic books might or might not be worth the effort. Like the highly mediated accounts of ruptured life whose nineteenth-century itineraries I've tracked—framed stories and ironized monologues—Shirley Paley's testimony helps expose the false universalism of lyric phenomenology even as it confirms any individual's self-report to be but the partial evocation of a total material system that in any case cannot be grasped in full. I have therefore used the category of "experience" as a diagnostic device or entry point for a materialist inquiry into historical structure. Experience, on this reading, is the subjective shape of an objective reality that is now fraying at the seams. How did the cognitive and material framework of this modern deathworld come into being? Where did it come from? *Wuthering Heights* knows.

PART II

Capture as Total System

2

The Mental Grammar of Atlantic Extraction

WUTHERING HEIGHTS

> The not merely theoretical but practical tendency toward self-destruction has been inherent in rationality from the first.
>
> —Adorno and Horkheimer, *Dialectic of Enlightenment* (1944)

> We don't in general take to foreigners here, Mr. Lockwood.
>
> —Nelly, in E. Brontë, *Wuthering Heights* (1847)

Faded Hieroglyphics

The previous chapter arranged a set of canonical texts that are recognizably Victorian in the sense that this adjective continues to describe the affairs of white residents of the British Isles between 1837 and 1901. The chapter's aim was to recover what it felt like for members of the polite middle class of the world's first fossil-fueled imperial society—people like Alice or the Time Traveller, the tea-sippers and hearth-sitters—to experience at last the world endings that had long defined life for those on modernity's receiving end.

From this angle, fictional Victorians like the ones whose stories opened this book can appear not as the paradigmatic modern subjects their authors and later critics take them to be, but as members of a class whose very lives depended on energy surpluses impossible without programs of despoliation and capture unequaled before that point in human history. The scenes of this damage were located always, from the point of view of those enriched by them, elsewhere: in scarred hillsides, coalpits, and hinterland sacrifice zones where "uncapitalized nature" still beckoned (Moore 17). The resource frontiers and cheap natures sustaining this "externalization society" (Saito, *Slow Down*, 10) included the sugar islands and spice colonies that long stood as exotic to the metropolitan mind, but also such comparatively proximate scenes as Cornish copperworks or the "coal-district" of the West Riding of Yorkshire (E. Brontë, *Wuthering*, 273). Such spaces of interior colonization, as Emily Brontë will specify for us shortly, are properly unseeable from within the bourgeois mental apparatuses whose equilibrium can be maintained only by rewriting or ignoring entirely the catastrophes that make the steady life-plots of some seem possible. "Rough weather!" Lockwood exclaims, on his first day at the Heights (7).

Recent criticism has shown how despite this structuring blindness, even those at the center of the nineteenth century's extractive system nevertheless had some intuition that the boom was secretly also a bust, that surplus would run dry, that the modern order was, in truth, a suicide pact.[1] This insight was, on the one hand, a revelation about material finitude and the physical limits to growth outlined in works like William Stanley Jevons's *The Coal Question* (1865). But for Adorno and Horkheimer in *Dialectic of Enlightenment* (1944), a similar insight produced a cognitive and theoretical, and in many ways poetic, project. The task was to understand how modernity's self-undermining material system was also a cognitive one, a mental grammar; and further, how even from within the confines of this seemingly total mental architecture, space for possibility might yet be cleared. In this way did Adorno and Horkheimer aim to coordinate the material and conceptual registers of a capitalist world system they did not yet understand as predicated on the extraction and combustion of fossil fuel.

Yet such attention to the domain of the conceptual has been less popular in other circles of avowedly materialist environmental criticism. In a recent polemic against certain forms of theoretical inquiry aiming to address climate change, for example, Andreas Malm spends time dispelling what he styles as the myths of constructivism, a species of idealism he associates with "postmodernism" and other faddish modes allegedly giving priority to "immaterial" matters like discourse or concepts over the real stuff of the world (*Progress* 22–23). "Temperatures are not rising because people have thought about coal or made mental images of highways," he writes; "that is not how environmental degradation happens" (*Progress* 27). The comment sidesteps the canonical problems of ideology and mediation; retreads the habitually misunderstood Marx meme about philosophers only interpreting the world; and asserts the priority of a "material" world held to have no connection at all to the cultural or cognitive one. (This was not Marx's position.)

The investigation I undertake here suggests that the "unreal" "mental images" Malm dismisses (*Progress* 23, 27) are precisely how environmental degradation happens. This claim is true, at least in the sense Raymond

Williams means when he describes the densely reciprocal relationship between conceptual apparatus and concrete activity. Or in terms of what Foucault calls an "episteme": the "fundamental ground" for thought that "defines the conditions of possibility of all knowledge, whether expressed in a theory or silently *invested in a practice*" (*Order* 168, emphasis mine). Foucault and Williams differently account for the mechanisms by which discursive and cultural performances materially instantiate in the world. From this point it follows that the superstorms Malm says are "not a linguistic entity" (*Progress* 27) in fact cipher linguistic and conceptual performances of all sorts, in infinite and infinitely mediated relays between theory and practice, concept and matter, over a period of time reaching from before the onset of the regime of fossil capital to its terminal crisis in the present. "What we must grasp," Foucault writes in *The Order of Things*, "are the modifications that affected knowledge itself, at that archaic level which makes possible both knowledge itself and the mode of being of what is to be known" (54). It is in this sense that the emergence of fossil capitalism becomes a problem for thought.

This chapter suggests that the work of Brontë's enduringly difficult novel is to document the historical advent of a metaphysical or cognitive system proper to a specific phase in the history of capital accumulation by extraction: it charts the coming-into-being of an intellectual repertoire predicated on seizure and organized around the principle of mastery that remains our own. Seen in this light, Brontë's historical novel can be seen to track the ascendancy not just of the bourgeois class (Eagleton, *Myths*), nor of the modern individual (N. Armstrong *Desire*), nor yet even of fossil capitalism itself (Hiday; H. Scott); it traces all these things but understands each of these historical processes, I argue, in terms of an entire vocabulary of thought—one that, while espousing civility, is nevertheless predicated on violence; while favoring calculative rationality and means-ends thinking, is built on an "irrational" impulse toward acquisition; while fetishizing the self-evident fact, is committed to an arrangement of life that is ultimately premised on death.

The first word of *Wuthering Heights* is not a word at all, but a date, followed by a dash: "1801—" (1). Arriving at the dawn of this new century, Lockwood approaches his landlord's gate bearing all these penetrating and aspirationally masterful mental habits as qualities of his own mind. Once installed as a guest in the house he refuses to leave, this genteel imperialist feels "kindled" by "immediate interest for" his "unknown" love object and, reviewing the obscurely scrawled notations on the bedroom wall, "began forthwith to decypher [*sic*] her faded hieroglyphics" (16). Interested he may be, but decipher he cannot; his mind can't speak the language—and neither can we. *Wuthering Heights*'s diagnostic account of extractive epistemology's emergence goes further than mere documentation to set into motion a radicalized form of the subject-object relation whereby any encounter with the object called *Wuthering Heights*, including mine here, says as much about the reader's own conceptual and evaluative apparatus as about any aspect of the object itself. Call it the cognitive grammar of extraction. Can we think outside it?

In what follows I'll suggest that Emily Brontë asked the same question, and used what is still the strangest and most challenging novel of the century of coal as a means to construe the mental infrastructure of the self-undermining modern system she understood correctly to be gathering around her. To make this claim is to hold together a traditional split in approaches to this oddest of nineteenth-century artifacts. As Beth Newman explains, the history of thinking about *Wuthering Heights* is legible as a tension between metaphysical and historical interpretive strategies.

Early metaphysical accounts "denied" the novel's "embeddedness in nineteenth-century life," Newman says (25), an abstracting maneuver repeated by later feminist and poststructuralist critics who viewed the novel in terms of timeless dynamics and universal themes. This tendency to remove the novel from its historical milieu pushed later critics to seek to "rescu[e] *Wuthering Heights* from the transcendentalists" (quoted in B. Newman 25), effectively snatching the novel back from those who viewed it as "a drama of fundamental human passions that transcend time and place" (B. Newman 25). These critics then placed the novel back into *context*, with that term signifying in the New Historicist sense of a bracketed and scaled social milieu conceived as causal with respect to the novel's composition—from the Irish famine and changing property laws to fossil fuel culture itself.[2]

But this false dichotomy between history and metaphysics obscures the novel's most startling work, which is to dramatize how a sweeping history of the extractive system's rise, reaching from sugar plantations of the British Caribbean to the quarry-pocked landscapes of the book's narrative present, plays out as a transformation in mental life as well. "History" and "metaphysics" travel together. The book in this way documents the emergence and naturalization of an extractive epistemology we ourselves turn out to share with the Lockwoods and Edgars of the book's owning class.

What this chapter aims to show is how Brontë diagnosed the emergent bourgeois project of extraction as not just a series of material practices but as an episteme whose contours she anatomized and sought by aesthetic means to disrupt. The resulting counter-logic, or logic in motion, took as its target the circuits of reasonable inference and linear predication that Lockwood and his later avatars in literary criticism still embody, in their efforts to decipher "correspondences" between history and art, for example, or in their reliance on the preset tropes and ready-made clichés of the (instrumentalizing, imperial) Brontë-country picturesque.[3] Brontë's labor is to subject these metropolitan habits of mind to pitiless internal demolition, and, as we will see more fully in the next chapter, to erect in its place a counter-knowledge by which a rescued form of freedom might be imagined.

Haunted World

To start, however, some empirical details—simple facts. The horse-drawn coach that took the Brontë sisters from Haworth to Cowan Bridge, where they attended the Clergy Daughters' School starting in 1824, ran along the Leeds and Kendal Road, passing along the edge of what is now the Yorkshire Dales National Park. "We can fancy the stage-coach journey," wrote J. A. Erskine Stuart in an early entry into the Brontë industrial complex (1888),

> from Keighley by Skipton, past Eshton Hall, where lived Miss Currer, the benefactress of the school, whose surname was afterwards taken as the first part of the *nom de plume* of 'Currer Bell,' past Giggleswick, with its ancient grammar school, and Ingleton, nestling at the foot of gaunt Ingleborough, till the little hamlet of Cowan Bridge is reached, pleasantly situated on the banks of the Leck, a brawling brook, which rattles down a lovely valley to the Lune. (85)

William Sharpe's *Literary Geography* (1904), another guide to the Brontë world, provided cycling directions for the modern tourist, along with a map and, like Stuart's account, an array of empty adjectives meant to convey the charm and beauty of this now-sacred literary ground. For Stuart it is ancient, pleasant, little, lovely; for Sharpe, a "vast and bare," but "pleasant" landscape (119–20).

Almost to Cowan Bridge, the coach carrying the young Brontë sisters would have halted at Thornton-in-Lonsdale, the last stop on the line before their school (Heywood, "Background," 825). There, at the tiny crossroads town, they would have seen through a scrim of trees the great house called Halsteads, also written Hallsteads. Today Halsteads is a ruined shell, full of old records and garbage. The property went on sale in 2016 through the UK House and Heritage Trust, which admitted it was "[a] smaller property than usual and maybe not in the country house category." But "opportunities like this are rare and this was once a very grand building."[4] Before its descent into ruin Halsteads was still *very grand,* if small: an architectural embodiment of the country gentry and its aspirations to permanence, finely appointed and, as grainy archival photographs from the 1970s attest, tastefully detailed in the gothic style, twined with ivy. Like the Facebook-circulated real estate ad, a local historian's snapshot of the lintel of the house shows the stone embossed in Latin script: *ab alio speres, alteri quod feceris* ["Expect to receive from others, what you have done to them"] (Untitled photograph, Thornton-in-Lonsdale).[5]

According to critic Christopher Heywood, Halsteads provided "the topographical model" for that epicenter of civility in *Wuthering Heights,* Thrushcross Grange ("Yorkshire Landscapes" n.p.). Heywood has done more than any critic to uncover the structuring role of the Yorkshire landscape in the Brontës' imaginative world. These analyses are driven by a faith in simple facts. In at least three articles and an introduction to the novel, we are offered originals and prototypes, true references and "matching" connections: stagecoach stations "correspon[d]," caves have "counterpart[s]." As Heywood argues, the landscape of *Wuthering Heights* "echoes" specific locations like Halsteads in ways "far exceeding the likelihood of chance resemblance," these true features and real analogs providing "models" to which the novels "may be assumed to refer" ("Background" 818, 829).[6]

As befits such acts of historical correspondence-making, investigations into the true stories of Brontë country are animated by an "ideal of clarity": the historicist confidence that "the objects under investigation are free of all dynamic qualities that would cause them to elude the gaze that tries to capture and hol[d] them unambiguously" (Adorno, "Skoteinos," 98). This impulse to connect art and life without remainder—to capture and to hold—is in no way confined to Heywood, of course; instead, it is one form of appearance for the general condition of thought under an instrumental material order. But the now-universal push toward equational thinking and its ideal of clarity has shaped empiricist investigations of the Brontës since the earliest days. This point about critical practice only plays out at an almost insignificant plane the historical victory of mental habits whose advent it is the business of *Wuthering Heights* to track. Already by 1890, Lucasta Miller reports, "the fashion for finding 'originals' of every character and place in the Brontës' novels had become such a mania that fact and fiction often became confused" (244).

The curious interplay between object of analysis and our means of analyzing it is confirmed when we observe that the compulsion to find certain references and "glaring symmetr[ies]" (Heywood, "Yorkshire Slavery,"

187) is a quality later critics turn out to share with a main character in the book they analyze. Like the tourist Lockwood, Brontë-industry puffery and empiricist historicism both work within habits of mind that "freez[e] objects into things in themselves so that they can be available to science and praxis as things for others" (Adorno, "Skoteinos," 100). Unruly and oddly shaped individua are by this procedure frozen into the intellectual equivalent of objects—true references, pleasing scenes—in an operation of intellectual reification by which the new outputs, stilled into things, now become available for analytical manipulation or, in the tourist books and real estate ads, actual sales. ("Rare Opportunity," "Historical Significance," as the 2016 property listing for Halsteads says. "Dates from c. 1600.") In *The Principle of Hope*, Bloch describes the reduction of the past into museum pieces, each instance "grasped in isolation" as "a reified Factum" (I, 9), stilled into chits now available for accumulation and, perhaps, backward-facing judgment from an allegedly more enlightened present. That Halsteads provided exact blueprints for Thrushcross Grange seems unlikely given that the Brontës seem never to have entered it. But oblique memories emerge into expression; unarchived experiences find uneven shape in words: and the manor doubtless formed some ghostly input for a novel dedicated to local gentry and the architectural forms giving structure to their tangled intergenerational plots.[7]

Here the point is about conceptual languages, or idioms of thought. The Brexit-era real estate ad and the late nineteenth-century Brontë-industry ad copy, all flat adjectives and local color, conspire with empiricist historicism to dramatize a habit of mind Brontë herself subjects to withering and fundamentally historicizing critique. Despite replicating the picturesque tropes and instrumentalist presumptions ironized by the novel, present-day researches into the historical Brontë world teach us that the sisters would have known, as all residents of the area did, that Halsteads was the seat of the Foxcroft family. The Foxcrofts were legendary profiteers in the slave trade and representatives, along with dozens of other wealthy families in the Lancaster and Liverpool hinterlands, of the Atlantic traffic in human beings whose proceeds were systematically laundered into country houses and refined appointments in the areas the Brontës knew intimately.[8] Life, turned to commodity, turned to built environment, turned to "context."

The patriarch of the house the Brontë children would have glimpsed through the trees was one Thomas Foxcroft, interrelated via marriage and business partnership with other slave-trading families of the area immediately surrounding Haworth and Cowan Bridge. He was sixty years old in 1793, and "had been concerned in 92 African ventures since starting out at the age of 26" (Elder 128). Databases show us that just one of Foxcroft's ships, the *Bloom*, transported some 1,761 individuals from the coast of Africa to the West Indies in a series of seven voyages, unloading cargo at Grenada; Cuba; Dominica; St. John, Antigua; and Kingston, Jamaica, after stunning mortality along the voyage. The historical development of the Atlantic economy in human beings "was associated with several of those processes which have been held to define modernity," Robin Blackburn summarizes, including "the spread of market relations and wage labour" and "the growth of instrumental rationality" (4). Efficiency and improvement were the watchwords. "It is no accident," notes Louis P. Nelson, "that the definitive study of the Royal African Company—that organization that oversaw England's Africa trade until 1750—was written not by a social or political historian but by a historian of business in a series on emergent international capitalism" (12).[9] Thus was the birth of contemporary globalization ciphered into the built structures of a landscape glimpsed by the Brontë children through foliage and windowpanes.

In a kind of empirical rewrite of *Wuthering Heights*'s elaborately confusing plot of inheritance, Catherine Hall and her collaborators have tracked the material persistence of slavery's original crime of commodification across generations. In astonishing detail, the *Legacies of British Slavery* database documents what Hall and her team call the "unexpected resilience of slave-derived wealth" (22), echo-effects whereby the surplus of these early experiments in efficiency "permeated the British elites of the early nineteenth century and helped form the elites of the twentieth century" (2). Wealth from slave ownership and human trafficking, they conclude, "was among the significant forces reshaping British society and culture in the nineteenth century" and beyond—extending, they note, even into the families of MPs and academics today (12). As Zach Samalin has observed in relation to the *Legacies* project, England's slave economy "left behind a tangle of conceptually and historically incoherent legacies that problematizes what it means to think about the past as concluded" ("Introduction" 436).

Acute businessmen, the Foxcrofts of Halsteads were partners in the firm of Welch and Company, among the most important slave-trading organizations in Liverpool: Thomas's sister Agnes married Robert Welch, a "Liverpool merchant," whose second son George was "during the period 1783–92 . . . a leading Liverpool slave merchant." In records his occupation appears as "Gentleman/Esquire."[10] Welch and Company had been founded by the earlier generation of Welches, who owned slaves as well as shipping concerns and resided principally in Leck Hall, named after the "brawling brook" of Stuart's 1880s guide. Now listed in an audit of "The

Transatlantic Slave Economy and England's Built Environment" (Dresser and Wills 128), Leck Hall was positioned directly across the street from the Clergy Daughters' School, where the young Brontës learned arithmetic and writing, pedagogy of a rising order. ("The great Object in View," said the advertisement for the school, "will be their intellectual and religious Improvement; and to give that plain and useful Education, which may fit them to return with Respectability and Advantage" ["School for Clergymen's Daughters," quoted in Barker, *Wild Genius on the Moors,* 137].) The Welch home, with its two-story symmetrical construction, five bay windows, and "tetrastyle Ionic porch," would thus have been visible from the windows of the school Charlotte adapted into Lowood, windows from which Jane "now and then lifted a blind, and looked out" ("Leck Hall"; C. Brontë, *Jane Eyre,* 65; see also Heywood, "Yorkshire Landscapes," 24).[11]

The self-evident details and simple facts I have so far reviewed establish, first, that "numerous families with links in slavery and shipping" lived in proximity to the Brontë children during their most intellectually intensive formative years (Heywood, "Yorkshire Slavery," 193), and, second, that the great houses and family histories of these slavers provided substance for the references to enslavement and bondage littering *Jane Eyre* and *Wuthering Heights,* an entire Atlantic economy ghosted into those pages.[12] For Heywood, *Wuthering Heights* like *Jane Eyre* "present[s] a strongly allegorized" representation of the slave-owning families of the Liverpool hinterlands such as the Foxcrofts ("Yorkshire Slavery" 198). Scholars like Heywood and Maja-Lisa von Sneidern have decoded yet other local connections, all confirming that the "Brontë landscape" was suffused with and sustained by the proceeds of Atlantic accumulation, its entire social world unthinkable without infusions of racial capital from the British sugar islands, where fully half of all newly arrived African captives died within a few years and "the struggle to survive was at the center of enslaved people's experience" (Browne 191, 3).

These are facts: units of information backed by evidence, available to be captured and transferred, or communicated. The names of the people transported on the Foxcroft ships named for new life—the *Bloom,* the *Bud*—have been lost, if they were ever recorded. By April 1790, when the *Bloom* docked at Kingston on its fifth voyage, sales of the enslaved from the decks of ships in harbor had ceased, now moved to intermediary merchant houses onshore, so that newly arrived human beings could be acclimated to the new environment or "seasoned," as the process was called, into what one planter called "really industrious and efficient slave[s]" (quoted in Nelson 32). The architectural forms enabling this optimization process were characterized by barred cellars, reinforced doors, and yards for exercise overlooked by piazzas, "where potential purchasers . . . would have convenient view over the lot" (Nelson 32).

In "Skoteinos, or How to Read Hegel" (1962–1963), written in preparation for *Negative Dialectics*, Adorno gestures toward "[a] philosophical history of clarity," which would, he says, take account of the way "clarity becomes something methodological, a mode of knowledge made absolute" over the course of a secularized modernity's rise to dominance. In a world expunged of ghosts, empirical accuracy is raised to universal principle, positive knowledge elevated into a "fetish for consciousness" (96n), as the knowing subject seeks to exert mastery over his informational objects in ways that replay in cognitive operations the dominance over nature that is the original form, Adorno maintains, of the modernity project as such. The logic of transparency in this way becomes recognizable as the commodity relation transposed to the domain of thought. "Clarity" thus names a "hypostasiz[ing]" relation to the object world that "suppresses the objects" in its effort to enclose and partition it into knowable units ("Skoteinos" 96n).[13]

Adorno's account shows how a homogenizing dedication to the fact flattens the particularity of objects in the very attempt to catch or hold them, *comprehension* now describing an epistemological corollary to the nullification of idiosyncrasy and extirpation of unenclosed nature under imperial capitalism. This relatively familiar account of the domination of nature, developed by Adorno and others in the decades following World War II, describes a modernity uncoupled from more particularized timelines or individuated processes of emergence and naturalization. The critique of instrumental reason typically associated with the Frankfurt School is a macro-level storyline, I mean, an allegory of "modernity" writ large and thus the result of its own sort of hypostasizing operation, as Adorno himself, for example, is well aware. My point is that a newly sharpened language of clarity and exactitude—and the relations of domination it coded into mental syntax—was historically emergent in and around 1801, when *Wuthering Heights* is set; coalesced in 1847, in and around its moment of composition and publication; and is now so fully universalized as to slip beneath notice at all, its phrases breathed into university boardrooms and NGO Zoom calls as the very ether of an ecocidal common sense.

Remember that after the unsettling confusions of Lockwood's dream, in which he is beaten by a swarming collective of fervent believers, the businessman calms himself by counting: "a monotonous occupation," Lockwood says, "calculated to set me asleep" (E. Brontë, *Wuthering*, 22). The modern mind is soothed by such reckoning. Homogeneity relaxes us; simple facts feel natural. Spreadsheets calm. But facts, details, items of information—all these have "expressive character" too (Benjamin, *Arcades,* 460). These individua are the punctual points of contact to the material world, and thus emblematize historical processes for which they can stand only as concrete synecdochal embodiment and, therefore, as figure. "Philosophical thinking crystallizes in the particular," Adorno observes, "in that which is defined in space and time" (*Negative* 138). So while the punctual datum or freestanding instance will always be inadequate as knowledge, it can also, in this fragmentariness, be elevated into a poetic emblem for the total system it is nevertheless definitionally incapable of capturing in full or comprehending.

It is in this sense that "the analysis of the small individual moment" can disclose "the crystal of the total event" (Benjamin, *Arcades,* 461). For Benjamin and Adorno both, the trope of the crystal (*kristall*) offered a usefully materialized image of this jeweled dialectical compression. Crushed by eons of historical pressure or condensed into concentration from a supersaturated medium, the crystal is the gemstone form of its mineral surround. It is made from, and therefore an expression of, the material environment and chemical antecedents from which it is distilled and reconfigured. In just the way that no crystal can be formed but by the condensation of its originating medium, so no factual instance may take shape but as a concentrated expression of the material environment that supplies its inputs and constituent parts. In light of this insight about the expressive but necessarily limited nature of particular instances or facts, it appears that the only way forward will be a self-canceling one: a method of historical analysis that moves between the empirical detail and a critique of the mindset to which the empirical detail stands as knowledge. An oscillating immanent critique, then, a practice of comprehension used against itself. Of his own collection of barely organized instances of nineteenth-century modernity, *The Arcades Project* (begun in 1927), Benjamin says that the goal is "to assemble large scale constructions out of the smallest and most precisely cut components" (Benjamin, *Arcades,* 461).

Only a few more facts, then. The Lascelles family, whose intergenerational sequence of Earls enjoyed their seat at the massive Harewood House outside Leeds, had extensive interests in the Caribbean and did not sell its last plantation there until 1975, a year before I was born. Harewood is now a museum. The Lascelles family remembered there has become infamous entirely separately from any Brontë connection as an exemplar of the laundering process by which "villainous" and "vulgar" slavers (quoted in von Sneidern 175) reinvented themselves as country gentry, trading tainted slave money for clean country property and the titles and social status following from it.[14] An initiative at the University of York is now dedicated to placing Harewood back into the Caribbean networks that made this mansion a "Treasure House of England," with "art collections to rival the finest in Britain."[15]

A monograph tracking these connections views the Lascelles family as metonym for the broader processes of expropriation and transformation that characterize the Atlantic slave economy in general (Smith). In the words of another account, the family is "not a singular instance but a prominent example of a widespread reality" (Nelson 257). It is in this crystallizing sense that, for historian Nicholas Draper, Harewood's rolling lawns and massive park should be seen as a prototypical "expression of the slave economy" in England (22). Its seventy-six mahogany doors can in this sense be seen as material emblems of Caribbean deforestation and also "signal[s]," as one account puts it, of the Lascelles' "West Indian wealth" (Nelson 243–44). The semiotic effect was reinforced by the property's adjacent hothouses, which contained pineapples, aloes, and banana trees, further points of contact with the Lascelles' plantation holdings in "Barbados (Hole Town, Cooper Hill Plantation, Belle Plantation, Kirton Plantation, Thicket Plantation, Fortescue Estate and Bridgetown), Jamaica (Mount Plantation and Williamsfield Plantation), Tobago (Richmond & Goodwood Plantation and Mesopotamia Plantation), and Grenada."[16] Names demand precision in reference, and constitute a "verbal representation of phenomena" that "really yield[s] to the particularity of things" (Buck-Morss 89).

For Heywood, meanwhile, the grounds of the Lascelles' Harewood House "matc[h]" the park at Thrushcross Grange ("Yorkshire Landscapes" n.p.). In *Wuthering Heights,* Nelly calls this park "the finest place in the world" (168). "On the borders of the grounds," Brontë specifies, sits a "plantation" worked by "labourer[s]" (*Wuthering* 170).[17] When Charlotte and Anne in 1836 visited Lascelles Hall, a separate house named after the family, to meet their school friend Amelia Walker, Charlotte found her "monstrously gracious":

> She is taller, thinner, paler and more delicate looking than she used to be—very pretty still, very lady-like and polished, but spoilt utterly spoilt by the most hideous affectation." (Charlotte to Ellen Nussey, July 7, 1836, in Barker, *Life in Letters,* 38)

Charlotte describes these residents of the mansion named for the slaving clan to be "spoilt utterly spoilt," their mannered falseness reflecting a corruption of character she deems—using the same word that in *Jane Eyre* would refer to the Bertha Mason no fewer than six times—"hideous."[18] "To tell me that I had already a wife," Rochester tells Jane in one of those instances, "is empty mockery: you know now that I had but a hideous demon" (C. Brontë, *Jane Eyre*, 363). Written twelve years after this letter, *Jane Eyre* would expunge this spoilt demon from the record, leaving the stain of the plantation complex behind in a pile of charred rubble so as to clear space for heteronormative futurity between white characters, such that (as Jane reports) "perfect concord is the result" (C. Brontë, *Jane Eyre*, 519).[19] "My Edward and I," says Jane in conclusion, "are happy: and the more so, because those we most love are happy likewise" (C. Brontë, *Jane Eyre*, 520).

Emily's view was darker. In a now-famous school essay she composed in Belgium, "The Butterfly" (1842), she wrote that "the universe appeared . . . a vast machine constructed only to produce evil" (178). As the semi-fictionalized speaker of the essay works through this insight, (s)he comes to see in the butterfly an image of how splendid beauty, "lustrous gold and purple," can emerge from pure violence: nature "exists," the narrator says "on a principle of destruction" (E. Brontë, "Butterfly," 176).[20] In Emily's school essay, this principle is imagined as universal, valid in all times and all places.

Wuthering Heights would transform this grim metaphysics into a violent scenario many readers have mistaken for eternal. The tendency toward ruin in the novel appears to be a dynamic outside time. In fact it is rigorously dated, the book's principle of destruction arriving along with its "suitable pair" of central exogamous characters (E. Brontë, *Wuthering*, 1). Heathcliff arrives at Wuthering Heights in 1781, at the height of the Liverpool-based slave economy, and Lockwood arrives in 1801, at the dawn of a new, modern century: twinned advents marked with a slanted chronological specificity I will describe more below. In this way is the auto-demolishing character of accumulation by extraction marked as historically emergent and dynamic across time, the "convergence between progress and decay" structuring the book (Hiday 248) only one modality by which it investigates the intimacy between luster and ruin across the period of an aspirationally universalizing Atlantic capitalism.

Heywood, Draper, Smith, and others have helped describe the *Mansfield Park* effect by which the Liverpool- and Lancaster-area country houses were in fact mediated scenes of slave accumulation.[21] From this angle, the postures of genteel refinement and bastions of culture that Charlotte saw as "hideous," and that her sister would soon ironize in the shape of Thrushcross Grange, are best seen as ghostly emblems of a total process murderous in its fundamental design, a plantation economy transcoded into pictures of beauty. It is important to underscore that this early extractive economy was a fully global one. A will drawn up in 1745 for

George Foxcroft, Thomas's father, specifies that in addition to his country properties and wealth from the slave trade, he owned a "colliery" (Foxcroft "Continuation"). A later Foxcroft will (1795), dated from Singore, India, lists as family property "the Indigo Works at Burdwan," and recommends that "a careful person is sent to superintend" it ("Will of George Foxcroft"). The house called Halsteads can therefore be viewed as the form of appearance or physical emblem for an emergent financial regime—West Indian plantation, English colliery, Indian "works"—with roots in slave-based expropriation and with practices of extraction extending across the world. A crystal.

As Edward Said explains in his iconic reading of Austen's novel, the violent edges of the global extraction economy were visible to nineteenth-century readers most often as silence or absence. These related tropes for inexpression stand to indicate the necessity of "reading-for-the-repressed" scholarship continues to recommend to a Victorian studies organized around white supremacist archives. But to those capable of seeing it, the disaster of modern comfort was always perfectly legible, if in mediated ways: it manifested as habit of mind and cultural style ("hideous") and was evident most of all in small details and throwaway moments: compressed, we could say, at the register of the minor. What appeared, in other words, as the "gentility, sensibility and cultural refinement" of the slave-owning gentry of the Yorkshire countryside is what looks, to Heathcliff at least, like a cloying and dishonestly violent sentimentalism, its values voiced by "idiots" with "vacant blue eyes" that are "full of stupid admiration" (Dresser and Hann 14; E. Brontë, *Wuthering*, 42, 44).

These are the civilized fools who fight over who gets to hold the lapdog and, like Edgar and even Nelly, speak of "common humanity" and "a sense of duty" (E. Brontë, *Wuthering*, 131). But this mannered uprightness is code, Heathcliff knows, for a yet more powerful, if highly mediated violence happening offscreen. It is these blue-eyed humanitarians, after all, who would hire in a minute "half-a-dozen assistants" with "a brace of pistols" to fight battles they are themselves too afraid to fight (103). It is their money, the novel tells us, that comes from the extraction of rent from a repressed landless class. Edgar sees these immiserated peasants, not himself, as "robbers," and imagines that the dispossessed workers stand ready, on "rent-day," to sneak into his mansion "after all were asleep, that they might murder us at their ease" (43). Brontë shows how a foundational war of expropriation against the powerless, legible in Edgar's rack-renting and ciphered in the nameless laborers barely visible at the novel's margins, is no less present for having been transformed into the calmer and more reasonable forms of modern exchange, what Lockwood late in the novel describes as "my business" (274).[22]

"Do you imagine that I shall leave Catherine to his *duty* and *humanity*?" Heathcliff asks Nelly about Edgar (E. Brontë, *Wuthering*, 131, emphasis in original). But the question is rhetorical. The plot Heathcliff devises in response to his insight about the structuring violence of civility will only invert the scenes of subjection that welcome him into the novel. His scheme of revenge, notable for what criticism continues to call its inhuman refusal of pity and its unfeeling focus on achieving its object, centers on the effort to reduce his foes to nonpersons while transforming mysteriously sourced capital into landed property. It is clinical, we could say, efficient and rational: a mirror-image replay of the rise of extractive capitalism I've just rehearsed. But Heathcliff's inverted quest only reverses and radicalizes the harms visited on him in the first place, transforming the "guest" to "the master" as the second generation's action intensifies to the point of obscenity the will-to-mastery characteristic of the first (E. Brontë, *Wuthering*, 165). You have already deduced, then, that the novel's famous structure of repetition and reversal simply bears out the Foxcroft family motto, carved on the Halsteads lintel and sketched in voyages of the *Bloom*, back and forth from Africa's windward coast to Kingston, Trinidad, St. Kitts: Expect to receive from others, what you have done to them (figure 10).

The Lapwing's Feather

A preliminary list of extractive economies alluded to in the novel would include stone quarrying, coal mining, land enclosure, rent collection and, I am suggesting, plantation slavery, extending even to the demand for narrative itself. ("I'll extract wholesome medicines from Mrs. Dean's bitter herbs," Lockwood vows, confirming his plan to correct her story's upsetting bits and turn her raw material to efficient use [E. Brontë, *Wuthering*, 136]). The detail confirms Brontë's effort to construe the extractive paradigm across disparate registers and to assert, with Raymond Williams, the dynamic interplay between the apparently separate domains of the conceptual and the material. Instead of dividing these realms Brontë insists on their mutual reinforcement, as ideas instantiate as practice and historical processes manifest as thought and figure.

It is relevant to Brontë's efforts to articulate extraction as a total system that new game laws, too, transposed the logic of extractive enclosure into another microhistorical domain of practice. Codified in the Night Poaching Acts of 1828 and 1844, and the Game Act of 1831, this new suite of practical enclosures regulated hunting seasons for the first time, establishing landowners' total sovereignty over game on their parcels. The laws

FIGURE 10. “Halsteads” (exterior) (n.d.; ca. 1970s). From the Stan Lawrence Archive, Special Collections and Archives, Lancaster University, UK (SLA/5/2/2). Photograph: Special Collections and Archives, Lancaster University.

drew lines around a new domain for the conversion of life into property during the period of the novel’s action, a fresh frontier at which cheap nature could be captured as value. C. P. Sanger notes that the 1831 Act in particular functions as an important source of dating in *Wuthering Heights*, since it set a seasonal limit for hunting (December 10), a new temporal-political marker that Lockwood acknowledges when he receives "a brace of grouse—the last of the season" from Heathcliff in chapter 10 ([E. Brontë, *Wuthering*, 80).[23]

The details matter, but oblique allusions to the historical fact of newly passed game laws serve best to illustrate the comprehensiveness of Brontë's analysis. Is the novel *about climate change*? Or fossil capitalism? It is about something more: a total system of the commodification of life for use. What the novel shows, I mean, is the emergence of a world outfitted for capture and exchange, a gathering total system whose particular forms of appearance flicker into visibility and recede in echoes of obscure laws or sub-referential murmurs of quarries, plantations, rack-renting. But each subgenre of extraction in the novel can only metonymically evoke a system whose totality cannot be grasped in any one detail. A hunter on open land in the first generation—he refuses to shoot lapwings on Cathy's request but sets a trap over their nests (E. Brontë, *Wuthering*, 108)—Heathcliff in the second becomes the enforcer of the emergent property regime, insisting too on the forms of extraction and control these ownership relations secure. He accuses the second Cathy of poaching, having (in Nelly's words) "caught [her] in the fact of plundering, or, at least, hunting out the nests of the grouse. The Heights were Heathcliff's land," Nelly explains, "and he was reproving the poacher" (E. Brontë, *Wuthering*, 188).

The point is that the novel folds diverse forms of expropriation together to develop a unified theory of extractive accumulation. In this rising system, eminently reasonable, property is violence and the civilizing processes aimed toward wholesome lawfulness cannot be distinguished from the projects of destruction and reformation they presuppose. Eagleton refers to the "neuraesthenically cultivated Lintons" at Thrushcross Grange and "the violence which props them up" (*Hunger* 110), a menace subtending gentility that comes to light, Eagleton says, only when they sic the dogs on Heathcliff and Cathy. As readers have long noticed, it is this house, the Grange, that is positioned to perform the work of culture in the novel, since it transforms Cathy, after her five-week rehab stint, from a "wild and hatless savage" into "a very dignified person, with brown ringlets falling from the cover of a feathered beaver" (E. Brontë, *Wuthering*, 46).

Janet Gezari notes that the feathered hat emblematizes a broader process of social conversion, signaling Cathy's "new alignment with the Lintons and increased social distance from Heathcliff" (*Annotated* 107) since now she's civilized while he remains savage. But in a book so attentive to the lives and deaths of nonhuman animals, the tiny detail—a beaver-felt hat adorned with a bird's feather—also annotates at tiny scale the attenuated violence on which such refinement is predicated.[24] The smallness of the detail enacts the novel's investment in what I describe below as its ethical practice of precise notation and fidelity to the particular waged against the homogenizing logic of theme and summary.

Cathy will later describe with individuating care the species of birds whose feathers now comprise her pillow, "ranging them on the sheet according to their different species" (E. Brontë, *Wuthering*, 108). In this other throwaway moment Brontë's novel pays intricate, if seemingly offhand attention to Cathy's own capacity to see differences among the animals—turkey, wild duck, pigeon, moorcock, and lapwing—that others know only as "birds." Given that Heathcliff later dreams of Cathy "resting her darling head on the same pillow as she did when a child" (257), her careful disassembly of the pillowcase also shows how the tender and individuating engagement with the object world yields awareness of the death that has enabled her own comfort. The world's softest pillows and most gorgeous drawing rooms are in this sense better seen as ciphers of catastrophe, the calm surface of bourgeois life haunted by the specters of the deaths that then and still make this normalcy possible. Heathcliff at least has "a strong faith" in such "ghosts," and expresses what the novel does too: "a conviction that they can, and do exist, among us!" (256)

Cathy's unmaking of her pillow therefore dramatizes the novel's own practice, which is to charge material particularity with ethical and epistemological significance and wage this care for the detail against the standardizing violence of an emergent universal defined by the subject's aspiration to mastery over its objects. Cathy's beaver hat and pillow-work together suggest how a specifying materialist engagement with the world might see vulnerable objects not as conquered by but resistant to both the subjects who view them and the categories into which those subjects must inevitably try to fit them. This downscaling vision is the methodological invitation of the novel itself, I am suggesting, as it posits a practice of intimate attention to the nonstandard and fragile against the masculine blindness to anything but the overt that Lockwood shares with not a few of the book's later readers. The novel also dramatizes the cognitive distance between those who see this way and those who don't. As Cathy arranges the feathers, Nelly speaks for an emergent instrumental rationality by referring to Cathy's "childish devotion." "Lie down and shut your eyes," she says, "you're wandering. There's a mess! The down is flying about like snow" (108).

In contrast to Cathy's individuating care for the remains of these nonhuman animals ("I should know it among a thousand," she says of the lapwing feather [108]), Nelly's mind sees not singular life-forms but their appearance as a commodity, "down." And even this commodity she instantly switches with something else, using the exchange logic of simile to equate Cathy's specific feathers to another thing, "snow." Cathy's intimate taxonomy cuts against the equational processes Nelly sets into motion as if by reflex. Against this abstracting compulsion, Cathy registers care for the specific and refuses the impulse to homogenize particulars under a total category. This form of attention is what the novel documents as a space of counter-bourgeois possibility, a domain of practice beyond the calculable.

Evident across both the minor and major registers of the novel's practice, such moments as Nelly's response here show the conversion process by which "normal" or bourgeois thought transforms life into use and extracts value from it. This process is at once theoretical and material, since the novel has now linked the mental habits of equation-making and the subordination of particulars to material processes of domination and the suppression of physical movement. It is by these related means that the errant world can be stilled for control: "lie down and shut your eyes," Nelly commands; "you're wandering." In disclosing the physical domination on which bourgeois improvement depends—animal bodies turned to feathered hats, savage children into Disney princesses—*Wuthering Heights* draws attention also to the cognitive dispositions for which that violence feels natural.

Dropped babies, beaten wives, and hanged puppies all shock the cultivated mind. These and other moments of spectacular interpersonal violence are what typically stand as evidence of the book's brutality, or what early reviews and readers still—deploying the civilizational jargon of an extractive developmentalism these readers share across time—refer to as the novel's savagery. But not all the world's sources of harm are so startling to the bourgeois mind. And in a novel whose very principles of organization highlight the transformational processes of mediation—its nested frame narratives and interested narrators foregrounding the shaping capacity of intermediaries—it makes sense that the novel's most staggering violence would be mediated too: most visible, in fact, as their seeming opposite, comfort and civility.

In this regard the novel is best seen not as the cartoon opposition between a peaceful modernity and a barbaric feudalism that criticism continues to see. Instead it is a catalog of the harms that persist into a rising social order that congratulates itself most of all on having expunged this cruelty. It shows how the most obvious forms of violence may be felt directly and made evident in spectacular ways—a carving knife in the throat, a tureen of hot applesauce to the face. But catastrophe manifests less directly too: the difference is that these systemic disasters happen offscreen and are felt only by bodies whose personhood the rational mind can scarcely imagine, and whose perspectives, Brontë understands, rarely focalize novels. The *Examiner* lamented that *Wuthering Heights* "drag[s] into the light . . . coarse and loathsome" things a more respectable novel would leave unsaid (Allott 222, quoted in Small viii). But it also hints at other forms of violence, shapes and genres of disaster without which the very liberal values the reviewer espouses—against the *coarse*, resistant to the *loathsome*—would be unthinkable. The novel's work is to limn the edges of a rising order of domination animated equally by cloying sentimentalism and equation-making rationality, and to unwrite the narrative forms that conspire in making the dark groundwork of that reasonable modernity invisible.

Unlisted in von Sneidern's comprehensive account of the notations of slavery in *Wuthering Heights* is the moment when the school-aged Heathcliff and young Catherine, "hav[ing] a ramble at liberty" across the moor, meet the ambiguous image of liberty's involution (41). When the feral children finally arrive at Thrushcross Grange, what they see is not just the emblem of acculturation, civility, or Enlightenment itself still described by the criticism. Instead, or in addition, what they see through the window is the spectacular wealth of the Atlantic economy, shining with "pure white" and smeared, too, with something like blood:

> The light came from thence; they had not put up the shutters, and the curtains were only half closed. Both of us were able to look in by standing on the basement, and clinging to the ledge we saw—ah! It was beautiful—a splendid place carpeted with crimson, and crimson-covered chairs and tables, and a pure white ceiling bordered by gold, a shower of glass-drops hanging in silver chains from the centre, and shimmering with little soft tapers. (41–42)

Von Sneidern suggests that Thrushcross Grange is "isolated from a planter economy" and is only later "contaminated" by the introduction of Heathcliff (von Sneidern 174); in this she repeats the theory of Edgar himself, who says Heathcliff is "a moral poison that would contaminate the most virtuous" (101). But the passage shows instead that contamination is already there. Describing blood-red carpeting and showering gold, Brontë's prose discloses at the minor scale of style that late eighteenth-century wealth in the Liverpool hinterlands is organized by a brutality whose reconfiguration into stained decadence generates physical spaces and mental attitudes that only look like enlightened civility. ("The light came from thence.") In this sense is the novel's most luxuriously "splendid" scene already crimsoned by the murders that made it possible.

"They are called cultural treasures," writes Walter Benjamin as if peeping through the window of Thrushcross Grange, "and a historical materialist views them with cautious detachment. For without exception the cultural treasures he surveys have an origin which he cannot contemplate without horror" ("Theses" 256). Brontë's novel expresses oblique horror at such cultural treasures and alludes to, without resolving, the criminal stories of their origin. Yet as we will see the satisfaction of full exposure is not on offer either, and the novel's project goes beyond the merely critical elaboration of the idea that every document of civilization is also a document of barbarism. In place of the clean satisfaction of exposure, and in lieu of any straightforward celebration of the Kantian beautiful ("ah! It was beautiful"), Brontë positions an investment in the vulnerable and strange whose forms of aesthetic expression are the detail and the unassimilated particular: the minor, raised to conceptual-aesthetic principle.[25]

Later chapters will develop this interest in the trifling, unfinished, and gestural. Now I want to say directly that Brontë's "crimson-covered" scene translates into figure precisely the oblique relationship to catastrophe scholars have located in British country houses of the historical British hinterlands. In their survey of the relationship between slavery and English country houses, Dresser and Hann point out that the "classical motifs," "lavish interiors," and stunning art of these mansions were not separate from the world of Atlantic accumulation, but "were in fact related [to it] and need to be understood as such" (14).[26] In Bristol, Liverpool, and the Yorkshire countryside especially, a rapidly expanding and hugely profitable African and Caribbean trade "played a key role in reshaping the houses" of local elites across the seventeenth and eighteenth centuries (Nelson 257). Brontë discloses at the level of prose how the "pure" and "little soft" things that meet the eye in such spaces as "beautiful!" are also, and at the same time, lavishly corrupt, splashed with "crimson" and improbably sublimated, "shower[ing]" down as liquid and silver, in what Brontë astonishingly represents as shimmering chains.

Before arriving to this tableau of glittering injury, Cathy and Heathcliff understandably seek answers: they want to know what happens inside the enlightened space from which they have been shut out. Heathcliff wonders "whether the Lintons passed their Sunday evenings standing shivering in corners, while their father and mother sat eating and drinking, and singing and laughing, and burning their eyes out before the fire" (41). The outsider's vision of civilized life recodes the hearthside panorama as a primal scene in which luxury cannot be separated from the exclusion it depends upon. Here comfort is defined by its trembling outside, and any singing and laughing requires other bodies to "shiver[] in corners." In

Brontë's bravura reworking of heteronormative tranquility, the light and warmth of the domestic hearth now becomes weapon, endowed with the power to harm through the sheer intensity of its glow. Such finely involuted metaphorics find Brontë experimenting in a literalized dialectic of enlightenment, where the bright energy of civilization itself—product of a coal fire, the book earlier specifies—has the power to blind you.[27] "I'd not exchange, for a thousand lives, my condition here, for Edgar Linton's at Thrushcross Grange," Heathcliff says (42). In the comment, the dark figure refuses not just the partitioned splendor of the drawing room, but the exchange logic and drive toward commodification underpinning it. He "would not exchange."

Is *Wuthering Heights* about slavery?[28] For decades, empirically minded readers have focused the question around the "true identity" of Heathcliff, construing the question of the plantation complex's place in the novel in terms of historical notation and explicit detail, a dilemma isomorphic with the question of Heathcliff's race. Is he Black? A "gypsy"? A lascar? In an essay called "Slavery: *Ideé Fixe* of the Brontës," Humphrey Gawthrop summarizes the now-familiar evidence, listing out the habitually cited references to Heathcliff's "black eyes," his skin "as dark almost as if it came from the devil," his possible status as "a regular black," his mother's possible origins as "an Indian Queen," his having possibly been (in a phantasmic redescription of the middle passage) "kidnapped by wicked sailors and brought to England" (quoted in Gawthrop 284). The list leaves out several instances but hints at how the novel offers an almost obsessively elaborated series of racialized descriptors and puts any number of origin stories into the mouths of its characters while leaving the "real" backstory of its most important character blank. Eagleton, filling in the space, has suggested he must be Irish. But as even Eagleton notes, like so many other aspects of the novel, here the very mass of references constitutes a surplus better seen as lack (*Great Hunger*).

Here as in so much else, I mean, the novel refuses to allow for the solid conclusion it nevertheless has tempted us to formulate. Hillis Miller suggests correctly that any effort to decide on Heathcliff's "real origin" is in effect to fall into a trap the novel has set for us, overcoding uncertainty with misplaced confidence like Lockwood himself. That is because across the novel, "however far inside the reader gets, he finds not presences but only more enigmatic signs, enticing promises of a revelation which never occurs" ("Ellipses" 86). "[T]he secret truth about the novel," as Miller observes in an often-cited line, "is that there is no secret truth" ("Ellipses" 92). On this view, some readers may presume they can unlock the mysteries or perform the "rational reduction to some totally satisfying principle of explanation ("Ellipses" 94), but firm answers elude them. "Is Mr. Heathcliff a man?" readers ask with Isabella. "If so, is he mad? And if not, is he a devil?" (E. Brontë, *Wuthering Heights*, 120) The dots will not connect.

Miller's reading follows Derrida in understanding this mise en abyme as metaphysical in the sense that it describes an epistemological groundlessness understood to transcend time and place: a condition of all writing. His 1980 essay rightly identifies the mechanisms of entrapment by which *Wuthering Heights* implicates its readers, but uses an almost obsessively invoked unspecified phrase, "the reader"—repeated four times in a single paragraph ("Ellipses" 95)—to imagine this figure as a fixed and stable position outside time. The practice follows contemporaneous trends in reader-response criticism to construe the text-reader dynamic as essentially metaphysical, a subject-object relation fundamentally unconditioned by temporality or historical conjuncture. In the much earlier *The Disappearance of God* (1963) however, Miller argues, against this view, that the book describes a "historical process" encompassing "the breakdown and reconstruction of civilization" (210, 208).

In this way does the earlier claim acknowledge that the apparently synchronic deconstructive situation described in 1980 is in fact not only marked by change but fundamentally concerned with it. This tension between two arguments by one of the novel's greatest readers helps frame my point, which is that any question of whether the novel is "about" slavery must be shifted away from the domain of allegedly determining "cultural contexts," away too from factual notations and allegedly equational allusions, and toward the realm of what I earlier called historical metaphysics.

The question, I mean, is about the emergence of a modern epistemology bound to the instrumental reason and utility calculus of plantation slavery as a historical and material configuration.[29] Dedicated to a concept of "improvement" isomorphic with the extraction of profit, the metaphysic consolidating alongside the material innovations of plantation efficiency finds shape, I am suggesting, in an emerging relation between subject and object based on domination. This orientation or episteme is legible in a whole suite of aesthetic procedures and presumptions about language, all of which appear in 2025 as effectively universal and organize even my own analytical performance here. This way of knowing, Brontë suggests, eventuates not only in material disaster but in the very cognitive tools we might use to evaluate or read that very thing. So who is this modern reader? When does he emerge, and where does he come from?

Lockwood, or Enlightenment and Morality

"This is certainly a beautiful country!" Lockwood yells in the novel's second line (1). The loud emptiness of the observation confirms before the novel even starts that our narrator's mental idiom will prove inadequate to the tangled kinship relations, revenants, and violence soon to be staring him in the face.[30] Lockwood's narcissistic insensitivity to others and comically masculine tendency to impose himself onto a foreign object world is physicalized in his tendency to push open gates, barge into rooms, and charge through social cues: "I commenced again," he says after Cathy meets his platitudes about the weather with silence. She rebuffs him again, but "I continued," and "I hemmed once more, and drew closer to the hearth, repeating my comment on the wildness of the evening" (7).

This cliché-structured self-assertion reinforces Lockwood's position as a bourgeois subject in the specific sense described by Adorno, Horkheimer, and other critics of the metaphysics of monopoly-phase capitalism to whom I've alluded so far. Organized internally by the ready-made language of formula, our heavily ironized narrator is distinctive for always trying but failing to subsume the world into himself. "I'm running on too fast," he famously says while describing Heathcliff, "I bestow my own attributes over-liberally on him" (3). However absurdly framed, this rage toward the object world renders Lockwood blind to the concrete specificity of the landscape and human beings he encounters.

Brontë's decision to use Lockwood as a framing device and proxy for the imagined reader demonstrates her understanding that the thought forms proper to the emergent regime ramify across registers—epistemological, temporal, and, I will suggest, grammatical. These forms of thought are finally historical, in that the material social arrangements for which Lockwood's thought stands as normal coalesce only at a specific moment in the history of Atlantic extractive accumulation whose itinerary the novel charts. "My home is not here," he reminds Nellie and us late in the novel, "I'm of the busy world, and to its arms I must return" (226). This clichéd transposition of commerce and eroticism, expressed here in typically secondhand fashion, helps us better understand Lockwood's wish, later, that he had "migrated together" with Catherine "into the stirring atmosphere of the town!" (270), carrying her off like any other object there to be mastered or owned. (Latin *rapio*, to snatch, grab, carry off, abduct, rape, steal.) Like any other modern subject, then, Lockwood even in his apparently reasonable moments is driven by a subconscious and heavily eroticized sense of impulse, "belly turned mind," as Adorno calls it (*Negative* 23). But the drive is for results: for him, "anything which does not conform to the standard of calculability and utility must be viewed with suspicion" (Adorno and Horkheimer 3).

Here as before, the paradigm of utility is matched by a curious warmth for physical domination and a discursive penchant for the ready-made. From within this reifying perspective, weather can be "fine!" or "rough!" and brides can be carried off or "migrated with." What arrives with Lockwood, then, is not only "a notion of sexuality that designates the female as an object of desire" (N. Armstrong, *Desire*, 195), but an entire epistemology of use characterized equally by instrumental calculation, sexual objectification, and the propensity for cliché. It is relevant that the concept of the cliché emerged with industrialized printing to describe the plates or blocks that could repeat speech acts at industrial scale, and satisfying, perhaps, to consider how the first edition of *Wuthering Heights* was littered with errata and misprints. In any case it is clear that Lockwood's secondhand ideas have been pre-distilled into fungible form by commercial process, his mental movements outfitted for easy circulation along grooves established to maximize efficiency in the communicative circuit.

The utilitarian calculus driving Lockwood's mind extends up and down the scale of seeming importance, I am saying, ranging from a gendered domination over feminized objects and actual women all the way down to the seemingly pointless level of vacuous speech. Heathcliff speaks in what Lockwood calls "the laconic style of chipping off his pronouns and auxiliary verbs" (5), but his own language is empty and elaborated, the Continental "*vis-à-vis*" and "*sotto voce*," for example (4, 24) indicating pointless flourish and cultural affectation at once. This pretense mirrors Lockwood's tendency toward prudish self-censorship, as when he refers to "an epithet as harmless as duck or sheep, but generally represented by a dash" (25; see Gezari *Annotated*, 79).[31] All this puts him in opposition to characters like Joseph or Heathcliff, who may drop verbs or "mumbl[e] indistinctly" from the perspective of those who don't understand them (4), but say what they mean and know the world is animated by threatening force.[32] Lockwood says Catherine "waxed lachrymose" but, as Irene Wiltshire points out, his idealist cognitive vocabulary means he "cannot bring himself to speak of anything as palpable as tears" (19).

Marked by clichéd orthodoxy and a fancified idealism that shrinks from the concrete, Lockwood's commodifying rational program is more consequentially evident in the relations it imagines among personhood and property. In the *Second Treatise of Government* (written in 1682, published in 1689), Lockwood's namesake John Locke neatly encapsulated the plantation logic by which *ownership* came to indicate the relation of mastery between a subject and the objects proper to him. A twist was that this emergent conception of property construed the free and owning subject as itself somehow an object too, since every man, Locke wrote, has property in his own person. One key feature of Locke's early bourgeois program, Zach Fruit has reminded us, is that so-called waste lands are open for seizure because they haven't yet been harnessed for extractive production; indigenous residents who've yet to turn the world to use are simply squandering it.[33]

Historians like David Armitage have seen how these famous lines encipher a whole history of colonial plunder and extractive appropriation. Other scholars have observed that the *Second Treatise*'s canonization transpired significantly in the context of Cold War America, where Locke's subject-model and property theory were positioned in curricula as "an antidote to Marx" and "repackaged as inoffensive bourgeois liberalism" (Kidd 14). In this way was a local intervention into the Exclusion Crisis of 1679–1681 translated into a set of ideas about personhood and property supposedly valid outside of time (Kidd 14). This looping chronology links early modern experiments in enclosure and colonial theft with nineteenth century liberalism and the Cold War—a circuit that will return in chapter 4. In the meantime, Armitage has shown how Locke's property theory represents "a crucial link in the historical chain joining liberalism with colonialism" (Armitage 603), since it shows how the more civilized-seeming logics of improvement and modernization work hand in hand with the old smash and grab, new frontiers always beckoning. Locke's work on the *Carolina Constitution* (1669) can be seen alongside the *Second Treatise*'s allusions to indigenous Americans and its turf-cutting "servants," who perform labor but find themselves erased from the capacity thereby to hold property, and therefore to exist as subjects. This Atlantic imaginary helps us see the crucial role that imperial accumulation played in the formation of early liberalism's extractive unconscious.

Locke held shares in the Royal African Company (incorporated in 1772), the slave-trading monopoly whose organizational structure "looked very much like the East India Company"— which itself resembled the Hudson's Bay Company and hundreds of the other joint stock companies driving imperial expansion through to the Victorian years (Stern 111). In the words of historian Philip Stern, these non- or para-state formations constituted a "venture or corporate colonialism" that extracted value from whales, enslaved humans, stripped timber, harvested furs, and other enclosed wastes across the early modern imperium and laid foundations for the state empires that would develop in partnership with them (Stern 11, cf. 1–15). (The East India Company would only be decommissioned in 1858, in response to the Indian Insurrection.) Improvement was the watchword in these early experiments in extractive capitalism, since in the Lockean words of one early director of the East India Company (writing in a posthumous volume of 1664), early corporations added "*Art* to *Nature*, our *labour* to *natural means*" (quoted in Stern 69, emphasis original).[34] I return to several scenes of such catastrophic improvement to close this book.

Now we can observe that it is in keeping with the logic of efficient utility that when Lockwood staggers in from his snowbound walk nearly dead from cold, the servants who have gathered to aid him register as tools for his use. "My human fixture and her satellites," Lockwood reports, "rushed to welcome me" (26).

> I bid them be quiet, now that they saw me returned, and, benumbed to my very heart, I dragged upstairs, whence, after putting on dry clothes, and pacing to and fro for thirty or forty minutes, to restore the animal heat, I am adjourned to my study, feeble as a kitten, almost too much so to enjoy the cheerful fire and smoking coffee which the servant has prepared for my refreshment. (26–27)

Lockwood can see these human fixtures only insofar as they aid or annoy him ("I bid them be quiet"); they are positive or negative inputs to the spreadsheet table of his happiness. His numbed heart, cold in two senses, may be "feeble" in body but retains the power, still, to command, and soon even to "enjoy." Safe in a zone of study for a duration he calculates with near exactitude ("thirty or forty minutes"), he warms to the cheerful refreshment prepared for him by those beings he feels uncompelled to name. But even thus "restore[d]," Brontë suggests, Lockwood remains anesthetized—frozen, in fact, "to [his] very heart."

Edgar Linton might appear, for some readers, as the more appealing version of this rational program, a more sympathetic double to Lockwood's stock buffoon. The genteel but rack-renting landlord is, like Lockwood, a picture of civility: polite where Heathcliff is violent, smooth where his other is hard. Lockwood himself admires Edgar's "soft-featured face" and "long light hair curled slightly on the temples," a picture he judges "sweet" (58). But through the scrim of the businessman's feminizing approval, we glimpse the landed class's fatal susceptibility to the rising order whose dedication to improvement distinguishes them from even the most gorgeous aristocrats they will displace: Edgar is, Lockwood notes, "almost too graceful" (58). But the point is not just about changing class dynamics (Eagleton *Myths*; N. Armstrong *Desire*) but an epistemic procedure for which thinking-as-seizure comes to stand as natural. Organized on the logic of efficient utility and a compulsion to break down barriers, it is this procedure Lockwood uses when he wants to "decypher" the markings he finds on the walls of the Heights (16); when he impulsively "inspect[s] the penetralium" with his "inquiring eye" (2, 3); when he silently revises Nelly's story (137); or when he corrects Cathy before mistaking dead rabbits for a "cushion full of something like cats" (7). It is what unfolds, at smaller scale, in the grammar of his own sentences, which are built, as all sentences are, on logics of vectored predication by which subjects do things to objects.

The categories of this thought form are means and end, use and technics; it is "rationality directed to, and governed toward, its aim" (Moretti 39), where everything has its use; the world exists *for me* and is available at least in potential terms for implementation and deployment toward a goal from which I will profit. In *The Bourgeois* (2013), Franco Moretti describes a coolly dedicated instrumentality as a prevailing mood of bourgeois-capitalist thought, a "calm passion" or numbed heart; he cites Hegel's "crisp summary of the Enlightenment: here, 'everything is *useful*'" (Moretti 31, 35; emphasis original). In "The Antinomies of Bourgeois Thought" (1923), Georg Lukács relatedly describes the central affective register of this knowledge structure as "an unlimited confidence," a serene faith "in the ability of these formal systems to comprehend the 'true' essence of all things" (Lukács 112). An unlimitedly confident man of the world, Lockwood cannot but figure knowledge as capture, and *comprehend* in its original etymological sense of grasping or holding, "To seize, grasp, lay hold of, catch."[35]

I repeat these observations about Brontë's famously ironized narrator because of his key function in what I am suggesting is an epistemic struggle that the novel suggests is a historical and social one too. In all these registers, the problem is mastery, a word whose variants are a leitmotif in the novel, appearing in different forms—*master, mastery, my master, her master, the old master, the young master*—more than two hundred times.[36] The very smallness of scale at which the emergent logic of mastery operates in the novel—visible at the level of sentence and phrase, in its tiniest moments and largest points of plot—confirms Brontë's understanding of the ultimately grammatical relation between subject and object as the hard-wiring or code for an entire suite of material practices, much larger and at the same time more diffuse than any specific reference to coal, quarry, slavery, or "environment." A rising order of extractive common sense, legible at the level of syntax: "the style of the useful" (Moretti 39).

At the start of the novel, as we saw, gates are closed to Lockwood: he leans over them and pushes them in, barging into the penetralia of a place to which he is, as Nelly says, a "foreigner" (39). By the end of the book such limits no longer keep him out, and the metropolitan man now enjoys an access that is, he thinks, universal: "I had neither to climb the gate, nor to knock—it yielded to my hand" (272). Lockwood nowhere sounds more like the ideal subject of Locke's *Second Treatise* than when he marvels that zones once foreign to him now "yiel[d]" to his "hand." "That is an improvement!" he thinks. "And I noticed another [sign], by the aid of my nostrils; a fragrance of stocks and wall flowers, wafted on the air, from amongst the homely fruit trees" (273). Lockwood's nose conveys the pleasant news that wastes have been enclosed, wilds made useful; the sensory input tells him that what had been other to him has now been improved into what he recognizes as *homely*: relating to the home, yes, but also "familiar, well-known."[37] Domestication, then, in a full sense: the cycle by which the "philosophical imperialism" of instrumental thought "annex[es] the alien" now complete (Adorno, *Negative*, 191).

The modern money economy organizes master Lockwood's mind into the shapes of tourist cliché and fantasies of domination masked by a preference for sweetness and light. Yet the novel's work is to show most of all how these metropolitan habits are the intellectual circuitry not of a single villain or fool but of a system: "a modernity whose foundational infrastructures were imperialism, colonization, and plantation-based slavery" (Thomas 1). In this way does Lockwood's initially risible misconception that he and Heathcliff are a "suitable pair" (E. Brontë, *Wuthering Heights*, 1) turn out to encode a critical truth, insofar as his mind and Heathcliff's, both bent on property acquisition and programmed for domination, operate on the same cognitive template. As Adorno notes in describing the similarly unlikely pair of Kant and the Marquis de Sade: the "light-bringing writers" of the Enlightenment may "protec[t] the indissoluble alliance between reason and atrocity, bourgeois society and power," but "bearers of darker messages pitilessly expres[s] the shocking truth" (Adorno and Horkheimer 92).

A Trap Door below the Person

The account of instrumental reason to which I've been alluding is familiar from the Frankfurt School, even if the belief, common to Adorno, Horkheimer, and others, that modern rationality wages a war on nature has been literalized in the moment of climate breakdown. The twist Roberto Esposito adds to this account of administered thought and its relation to the historical triumph of enclosure is something implicit in Locke's formulation that man has property in his own person. Esposito explains that modern reason's objectifying relation to the object world extends within the subject too. Any person can be stripped of this status and become thing or animal, effectively becoming object in a reversal of the becoming-person process that originally granted him priority over the object world in the first place. In this way do the subject-object dynamics of modern thought carry with them a "*dispositif* of the person," in Esposito's words, according to which the subject rests on a "relationship of domination" to the outside world that can always be switched around (*Persons and Things* 6). "It isn't possible," Esposito writes,

> to personalize someone without depersonalizing or reifying others, without pushing someone over into the indefinite space that opens like a trap door below the person. Silhouetted against the moving backdrop of the person looms the inert figure of the thing. ("Dispositif" 24)

Esposito's point about the dialectical quality of personhood is anticipated by Jamaican thinker Sylvia Wynter who, in essays on the plantation slave complex as philosophical system, positions "Man" as the conceptual term purchased, as it were, only at the price of the depersonalization of vast swaths of life now extrojected from that category.[38]

Wynter and Esposito both show how the "trap door below the person" snaps open at the very moment personhood itself is asserted in its guise as mastery and self-consolidating control. Wynter develops this analysis through a historical account of colonialism and enslavement in the British Caribbean. Symptomatically ignoring what is arguably the zero point of this dialectic, Atlantic slavery, Esposito instead reaches to Roman law to explain that, because the enslaved person exists at the ambiguous meeting point of subject and object, "definable both as a living thing and a reified person" (Esposito, *Third Person*, 9), this figure marks a kind of crisis point at the core of bourgeois thought, a short circuit in the grammatical hardwiring of instrumental reason—"as dark almost," Earnshaw says, "as if it came from the devil" (E. Brontë, *Wuthering Heights*, 31).[39]

Yet it is not in this or any other of the novel's endless racial descriptors that Heathcliff becomes recognizable as the site of the novel's efforts to play out the sharpest consequences of extractive thought. Instead it is in his ambiguous relation to personhood. The salvaged child arrives to the Heights after Earnshaw's three-day walk to Liverpool. The Biblically resonant length and shocking duration of this walk—"sixty miles each way" (30)—would also, as Gezari notes, specify to readers in 1848 that Earnshaw's trip predates the area's then-extensive railroad system, given that the Liverpool and Manchester railway that "inaugurated the Railway Age" opened only in 1830, long after the close of the novel's action

(*Annotated* 86). The muscle-powered trip would thus mark to readers that Heathcliff's arrival predates the fossil economy they themselves inhabit, splitting reading subjects and the story they read across two sides of a world-historical divide.[40]

In the novel, the household's human children gather around Earnshaw's souvenir and look down on a form of life whose relationship to personhood remains, for them, elaborately unresolved. In the famous scene,

> [w]e crowded round, and, over Miss Cathy's head, I had a peep at a dirty, ragged, black-haired child; big enough both to walk and talk–indeed, its face looked older than Catherine's—yet when it was set on its feet, it only stared round, and repeated over and over again some gibberish that nobody could understand. (31)

A "child" but also an "it," the being not yet named Heathcliff lives at the borderline of personhood and therefore in the interstices of modern reason. It is for this reason that Heathcliff cannot communicate in the idiom of his hosts; his "gibberish," like Joseph's elsewhere in the novel, produces for Nelly and Mrs. Earnshaw at least—representatives of domestic manners and guardians of the hearth—a phobic response, Nelly "frightened" and Mrs. Earnshaw "ready to fling it out of doors." In fact,

> she did fly up—asking how [Earnshaw] could fashion to bring that gipsy brat into the house, when they had their own bairns to feed and fend for? What he meant to do with it, and whether he were mad? (31)

But the question is never answered, the rationale for Heathcliff's salvage never offered. Was it charity or kidnapping? Selflessness? Or the self's aggrandizement, by capture? Earnshaw can't say: he's too tired and was in a hurry. But the irresolution confirms Brontë's sense of the equivalence of the two alternatives, suggesting that the seemingly opposed projects, in the Lockean world, of improvement and capture, may be one and the same.

What we know is that, like any good student of the *Second Treatise*, Earnshaw was determined not to "leave it as he found it": he ran a cost-benefit analysis regarding the value of his time and evaluated the possibility of finding the "owner" no doubt associated with this lost property. To be sure, Nelly reports, Earnshaw

> inquired for its owner—Not a soul knew to whom it belonged, [Earnshaw] said, and his money and time being both limited, he thought it

> better to take it home with him at once, than run into vain expenses there; because he was determined he would not leave it as he found it.
>
> Well, the conclusion was that my mistress grumbled herself calm; and Mr. Earnshaw told me to wash it, and give it clean things, and let it sleep with the children. (31)

What brings Heathcliff into the world of the novel is the logic of the balance sheet: "money and time" calculated against "vain expenses," alongside a conviction that nothing shall be left as it is found, or wasted. Orlando Patterson describes the fundamental condition of the enslaved human being as being "a genealogical isolate" (5), and like any other goods or chattel, Heathcliff arrives into the Earnshaw family from the entrepôt of the Atlantic slave economy starving, houseless, and as good as dumb—without a personal pronoun, and with no owner "to whom it belonged."

Isabella writes in her letter that the distance between the Heights and the Grange is tantamount to "the Atlantic" (*Wuthering* 122, quoted in von Sneidern 174), and in the stray comment Heathcliff's abused wife unwittingly measures the compass of the novel's world. Her more famous question—Is Heathcliff a man? (120)—resonates in its full amplitude only in light of the novel's concern with the forms of personhood appropriate to the social relations and, I am arguing, metaphysical situation made possible through human commodification and the regime of total extraction it inaugurated. In this sense does the original crime of extractive capitalism function as a dark gravitational center and typological model for the novel's events, a black hole around which galaxies of violence orbitally swirl.

The refusal of personal pronouns in Heathcliff's origin story may be the most spectacular way the novel documents the relationship between property and ruin via the subject-object grammars of instrumental reason. But the terms of the novel's critique of this emergent order are radicalized to the point of near collapse in the irony concluding the book. The novel's final pages dare us to believe, with the guardians of an emergent episteme like Lockwood, that closure has come to the novel's world, heteronormative conciliation achieved, ghosts stilled in "quiet earth" (300). Still persuasive to casual and critical readers alike, it is a conclusion entirely "benign," offering to readers whatever pleasure might accompany the reduction of the novel's spinning, entangled chaos into something like closure:

> I lingered round them, under that benign sky; watched the moths fluttering among the heath, and hare-bells; listened to the soft wind breathing through the grass; and wondered how any one could ever imagine unquiet slumbers for the sleepers in that quiet earth. (300)

It is, as Lockwood said of Edgar, "sweet"; the problem is that it's a lie. The soothing conciliation of sibilants and voiceless fricatives here ("mot*hs* fluttering among the *h*eath, and *h*are-bells," "*s*oft" "gra*ss*" "*s*lumber*s*" "*s*leeper*s*") performs resolution and peace, the prose seeming to agree with Lockwood's reading that ghosts have been stilled and all is quiet.

But on inspection we see hints that this allegedly dead world sleeps without quiet: it is not a bee but a moth, emblem of night, that flutters among the flowers, and the soft wind "breath[es]" because it is charged with the life that the novel's peasants, if not Lockwood, know still to walk the moors. Located in the perspective of an uncomprehending tourist and serial misreader of the territory he visits, this set-piece conclusion becomes legible not as closure but the fantasy of it, albeit a fantasy whose definitive liquidation is, by virtue of the groundless narrative architecture of the novel, finally withheld. Not even negative conclusion comes into focus.

In a sophisticated reading of the ballad forms interlaced within Brontë's novel, Susan Stewart describes the end of the book in terms of an "emergent" or modern form of love based on charity and forgiveness. This companionate bourgeois love relation is "universalized and intelligible to all," Stewart writes, in the marriage plot of Hareton and Cathy II that seems to end the book's sequence in the narrative's near future (193). But the emergent universal of heteronormative pairing positioned at the apparent climax of the novel is countervailed by another form of love, Stewart says, an "old ballad world of a love that destroys the reason" (193).

This alternative to the rising bourgeois episteme is embodied, Stewart observes, in Catherine I and Heathcliff, who, as ghosts, escape to the moors just before this seemingly conciliating finale—unseen and disbelieved by Lockwood and the generations of readers who, with Lockwood, continue to insist that the book achieves its "happy," because conventional, upwardly tending ending. "Idle tales, you'll say," Lockwood notes of the rumors of Heathcliff's posthumous ramblings, uncertainly addressing Nelly or the reader or both, "and so say I" (E. Brontë, *Wuthering Heights*, 299). Readers agreeing with the *you* and *I* of this closed communicative circuit find evidence for their misreading when the second-generation characters start a new year with marriage and set themselves (in Lockwood's hackneyed gloss on Milton) against the forces of darkness, "brav[ing] Satan and all his legions'" (300). While obvious to readers unconsciously identified with Lockwood's habits of mind, this interpretation is ironized and undercut by the form of the book, since as Stewart notes, the conclusion running alongside this falsely tidied end point is no conclusion at all but opens up the narrative's frame, using irony to convert its structure from (closed) mourning to (open) melancholy.

We know *Wuthering Heights* believes in its ghosts, but it is the "respectable character" Lockwood (300) who throws cash at the feet of servants at the end of the book and, "pressing a remembrance into the hand of Mrs. Dean," charges into the kitchen uninvited at the very moment he tries to dream the book into its happy ending. "The sweet ring of a sovereign" at Joseph's feet (300) confirms Brontë's understanding that commodified thought and the falsely consoling plot forms proper to it (reproductive futurity, the marriage plot, "benign" closure itself) all issue from capitalist modernity in its guise as bourgeois mastery, troped in the novel's conclusion as a stupid monetary largesse and pseudo-aristocratic condescension. Gezari explains that the tip of a sovereign, "a gold coin worth about a pound" would have been ostentatious at the time (*Annotated* 431). Earlier in the book an older Heathcliff, well converted into the very idiom of thought he both negates and radicalizes, says Linton's life "is not worth a farthing"—a quarter of a penny (E. Brontë, *Wuthering Heights,* 259; Gezari, *Annotated,* 381). Their valuation strategies may differ, but both men now count life in unit terms.

Part of the novel's work may be to document "the extinction of yeoman strength under the enervating and brutalizing influence of the Caribbean sugar economy" (Heywood, "Background," 819). But it is also to develop a yet more comprehensive critique of the extractive economy's reach, charting the plantation complex's appearance in the cognitive regimes and habits of mind proper to an emergent social system that coalesces across the period Brontë documents. Across the chronological loops of this uncanny historical novel, a ciphered slave economy transforms into an extractive regime built on quarry pits and coal fires and the always advancing capture of nature. (Lockwood's quip that he's been invited "to devastate the moors" (271) resonates well beyond its obvious reference to a hunting party.) This regime of generalized devastation is a total language, I am suggesting, a mental grammar organized, as Brontë put it to her astonished teacher, on a principle of destruction. It is the dark fate of the novel's later readers, even its most sensitive ones, that we think in this language too.

They Think Aw'm *Blind*

Lockwood's *sotto voces* and *vis-à-vises* alerted us to the place of language as a master trope for the novel's divergent mental grammars. Any first reader will recognize instantly that the book is full of nonstandard speeches and bizarre idioms. The text overflows with patterns of expression that carve out the alternative epistemological structures still glossed as "superstitious" or "premodern" by later readers who share our narrator's preference for the reasonable and clear, a fact that testifies to the complexity with which Brontë ensnared her audience into the immanent workings of the book's diagnostic examination. The first reader caught in the novel's trap was Emily's older sister.

In one of Victorian literature's most notorious editorial projects, Charlotte would side against the Josephs and the Heathcliffs to revise her younger sister's novel for its second, posthumous edition by "render[ing] the book more accessible" (in a later editor's words) and introducing "a comparatively 'normative' or conventionalizing view of style'" (Small xxiii). As is now well known, Charlotte's edits to the 1850 edition of the book offered "a simplified, more accessible rendition" of Joseph's Yorkshire dialect, effectively domesticating this alien syntax to protect readers from the "baffled and, intermittently, alarmed fascination" with which Lockwood himself receives this archaic caretaker and the world he represents (Small xxii, xxiv).[41] Other dialect speakers whose language Charlotte corrected include "the herd-boy, the hostler, and the old woman at the Grange" (Wiltshire 27).

In addition to fixing speech, Charlotte's 1850 edition lengthened choppy paragraphs, traded dashes for commas, and domesticated the novel's weirdest phrasings, altering the spelling of idiomatic terms and "sometimes substitut[ing] standard English words for dialect words" (Gezari, *Annotated*, 34). In so doing, Charlotte's new version sought by stylistic means to shift the novel's epistemological and ethical center away from the book's gibberish-speakers and dialect talkers—those whose speech would be plain enough, Charlotte says, "to a Yorkshire ear" (quoted in Barker, *Life in Letters*, 301)—and toward characters with other ears, attuned instead to the newly standardizing grammars of an emergent extractive rationality. Poised against the regional dialect-forms proper to the quarry-marked Yorkshire hinterlands, metropolitan speech thus becomes isomorphic with the bourgeois class position and the episteme rising with it.

Lugs, canty, girn, mensful, scroop, dree, barthen. The lexicon of *Wuthering Heights* will be "in a great measure unintelligible," Charlotte says in her 1850 preface, to readers not already initiated into the world of the West Riding countryside. "And, where intelligible—repulsive" ("Preface" 307). This posthumous framing of her dead sister's novel is mired in preemptive defensiveness and establishes some of the earliest tropes of the Brontë myth (L. Miller 196–204), including that of Emily as untutored rustic, "knotty as a root of heath" and separated entirely from "what is called 'the world'" ("Preface" 307). But Charlotte's preface also helps us see how the above-cited Yorkshire dialect terms, along with some thirty-five other untranslated words in the novel (Wiltshire 28)—words like *pawsed* and *laiking*, *plisky* and *skift*—mark the perimeter of a thought-world to which the novel's readers are presumed to be (as Lockwood is) "foreign." That these instances of alien speech or minor language were suppressed by Charlotte on the grounds that any readers for Emily's novel would find them "unintelligible" tells us as much about *Wuthering Heights* as about the modernizing vortex into which its misprinted and off-putting first edition, published by Thomas Newby, intervened in 1847.[42]

Those on the receiving end of linguistic standardization have long appreciated the force by which such universal grammars are achieved. In an imperial process that was tested most vigorously in the British sugar islands after the importation of polyglot African laborers, rival linguistic orders must be flattened out or expunged so the identity of any dominant language can be secured. In *Poetics of Relation* (1990), Martinican writer Édouard Glissant reflects on this process of internal homogenization by referring to "the totalitarianism of any monolingual intent" (19). Barbadian poet Kamau Braithwaite likewise underscores the relations among linguistic homogeneity, nation-making, and the colonial project. In "Nation Language" (1984) Brathwaite notes that the "conquering peoples" in the Caribbean "did not wish to hear people speaking Ashanti or any of the Congolese languages" since these would of course sound, to them, how Heathcliff's noises sound to the Earnshaws: like gibberish (309). As a result, "there was a submergence of this imported language. Its status became one of inferiority. Similarly, its speakers were slaves. They were conceived of as inferiors—non-human, in fact" (309).

Writing of his own experience learning French as an Algerian Jew, Jacques Derrida reflects on the enforcement of linguistic standardization, observing that the act of separating good language from its degraded opposites, "gibberish" and "dialect," is fundamentally political. Such gestures of linguistic evaluation cleave human from nonhuman, reason from its opposite, and place beings who might "mumble indistinctly" (as Lockwood says Joseph does) in a category alongside those that produce "long, guttural gnarl[s]" (as the dog does, on the same page) (E. Brontë, *Wuthering Heights* 4). For Derrida, any monolingualism operates only "through a sovereignty whose essence is always colonial," and this imperial power of social partition "tends, repressively and irrepressibly, to reduce language to the One, that is, to the hegemony of the homogeneous" (*Monolingualism* 40).[43]

What Derrida calls the "colonial impulse" behind linguistic standardization (*Monolingualism* 40) is thus inseparable from the physical violence of capitalist improvement. Its aim is to flatten the incommensurable and domesticate those internal or external "nation languages" that, Brathwaite suggests, resist the rising language's claim to universality and therefore introduce inefficiencies into the smooth operation of a profit-making order. (On early plantations, indigenous speech was subversive because it was inscrutable to overseers charged with ensuring the continued functionality of the profit-making system.) Summarizing a similar effect, Gilles Deleuze explains that any linguistic order is best viewed as the outcome of a colonial struggle of this type—a war—since "there is no mother tongue, only a power takeover by a dominant language within a political multiplicity" (cited in DeWispelare 15).

Charlotte's phobic and concerned edits intervene in this "power takeover" on the part of what Deleuze calls "the dominant language." At tiny scale, these emendations aim to assert the colonial order of things at the linguistic and epistemological and therefore social levels. Where Charlotte infamously labored to smooth out the book's "wild[est]" features ("Preface" 307), Emily's work is strategically to cleave the social field in two, even while refusing the "concomitant celebration of porousness or boundary breakdown" that academic literary criticism, reiterating a residually poststructuralist ethical program, continues to hold out as a normative good (Baena 108). To say this is by no means to suggest the vanquished and minoritized order has any special relationship to virtue: Joseph's provincial discourse, for example, advances an "extreme dissenting Calvinism" (Mason, "Enthusiastic," n.p.) that treats the physical world as base and unreal, and is therefore its own kind of instrumentalism. And it is possible of course to view Charlotte's editing work, as some feminist scholars have done, as a savvy effort by a woman author to navigate the impossible choices of the misogynist publishing industry in order to make a buck. But as Lucasta Miller explains in *The Brontë Myth*, Charlotte's 1850 preface also betrays the elder sister's embarrassment and concern over the morality of the story, her efforts to standardize dialect and lengthen jerky paragraphs part of a "patronizing desire to correct what [Charlotte] called the 'rude efforts' of her wayward sister's 'unpractised hand'" (201).

However well intended or arguably justified by local material pressures, this "undeniably interventionist" effort by Charlotte (L. Miller 201) is therefore best seen as a translational project, a form of "'transmutation' between conceptual and cultural systems," as Victoria Baena puts it in her own account of this process, citing Roman Jakobson's definition of translation (110). This recoding effort effectively universalizes the uncomprehending perspective of Lockwood, cements the reader's unity with a rising capitalist rationality, and attempts to resolve the novel's antagonism between linguistic and epistemological worlds in the favor of the emergent universal whose contours we have charted so far. This way of knowing finds verbal expression in the "good speech and good writing" that is, in the end, "the language of the master" (Derrida, *Monolingualism*, 42). Thus, terms like *plisky* and *mensful* index the epistemological distance between them and us, where *us* is construed to mean future metropolitan readers of *Wuthering Heights* ("Southern" readers, Charlotte calls them); or their proxy in Lockwood; or you, reading this book now; or me, writing it.

All of us, I am suggesting, inhabit the thought-world of masters Charlotte construes correctly to be in the ascendancy. Its alternative, "something other than a literature of masters" (Deleuze and Guattari, *Kafka*, 17), experiences the death convulsions and haunting persistence it is Emily's work to document in the novel. But it is the metropolitan or bourgeois sociolect of masters, exported to the British sugar islands and enforced by physical and psychological violence against the home nation's internal others, that turns out to be the speech form proper to a rising extractive universalism: no longer *one world among others*, but (in Charlotte's words) "what is called 'the world.'"

This emergent universal is what organized Charlotte's own speech, when, while preparing her edition for Smith, Elder, she wrote to the publishers to outline her proposal for effectively translating it. "It seems to me advisable," Charlotte wrote Charles Smith,

> to modify the orthography of the old servant Joseph's speeches—for though—as it stands—it exactly renders the Yorkshire dialect to a Yorkshire ear—yet I am sure Southerns must find it unintelligible—and thus one of the most graphic characters in the book is lost on them. (Barker, *Life in Letters*, 301; cf. Wiltshire 23)

As it happens, in the peasant sociolects Charlotte and Edgar likewise disdain, *lugs* indicate ears, *canty* means "pleasant or brisk," *girn* is a snarl, *mensful* is proper, *scroop* refers to the back of a book, *dree* is cheerless, and *barthen*, in this novel about rival houses, means shelter (Wiltshire 28). But the presumption of translatability in which I have just indulged is itself a form of equational thinking the novel resists. That is because the book, I am arguing, positions "the poetic economy of the idiom" against the "economic equivalence" of remainderless translation (Derrida, *Monolingualism*, 56). In contrast to the supposed gibberish of the novel's Yorkshire peasants, the language Lockwood thinks with and that you are reading now is marked by "an utmost evenness of manner," Charlotte says ("Preface" 307), this restrained equilibrium being the linguistic insignia for what Terry Eagleton calls the "liberal humanism" of a "civilized present" whose historical victory the novel ambivalently charts (*Myths* 108, 117).[44] The footnoted prose of academic monographs is further testimony to this victory; but like any other language it is both corrupted by power and all one has to use.

The novel's nested layers of irony mean, of course, that any access we have to the mental grammar of the provincials whose lifeworld is in the process of being expunged comes only via moneyed interlopers whose rage toward the object world compulsively subsumes the alien. Yet the novel does not allow this imperialism to happen without a fight, and the novel's canny treatment ensures that the dominant language finds itself in the minor position too. When Isabella asks for a room, for example, preferably a parlor, she receives a chastening rejoinder from Joseph. "*Parlour*!" he says, taunting her. "*Parlour*! Nay, we've noa *parlours*.'" When she asks for a bedroom instead, Joseph scoffs again, this time phoneticizing her speech in "a tone of mockery" and marking her standard speech as, to him, foreign: the gesture provincializes the (emergent) universal and subjects its general rightness to withering counter-examination. "*Bed-rume*!" Joseph exclaims, "Yah's see all *t'bed-rumes* thear is—yon's mine" (125, 126, emphasis original, quoted in Wiltshire 23).

Joseph's sarcastic refusal inverts the universalizing impulse of metropolitan homogenization: his catechism has the function of exposing "standard speech" as but one among any number of sociolects now competing for status as the standard against which others will stand as gibberish. His work helps us appreciate that, while Isabella may complain that Hareton speaks "in a jargon I did not comprehend" (121), this complaint says as much about her as about the object she describes, the book's work again being not to examine the object or the subject in separation but how they interface with one another in a dynamic historical milieu. In this domain of struggle, the nation language of a resistant thought-world is in the process of being exterminated, and the standardizing mental grammar rising in its place is coincident with a money economy and bourgeois metaphysics driven by what Glissant called the totalitarianism of monolingual intent.

All this helps underscore that one innovation of *Wuthering Heights* is to understand that any allegedly residual suite of practices stands in opposition to the dominant and as an alternative to it, even when the dominant, residual, and emergent are always interpenetrated with one another and none of them is in any way pure. This dynamic relation between "rising" and "falling" sociopolitical orders in turn means that the deictic pronomial forms I have used throughout this chapter—us, them, we, they—name the space in which the most crucial work of *Wuthering Heights* transpires. If whole genres of contemporary climate writing unthinkingly hail "you" and "I" into an "us," Brontë's intervention shows how these pronomial terms are in no way stable but instead mark battle lines in an epistemo-political struggle that hinges on our position in relation to a catastrophic Enlightenment. "They think *Aw'm* blind," Joseph says with almost total incomprehensibility (to us). "[B]ut Aw'm noan, nowt ut t' soart!" (77) (table 1).

TABLE 1 Dialect words in *Wuthering Heights*

Word	*Meaning*
barn	"child"
barthen	"shelter"
bide	"stay"/"wait"
brust	"burst"
cant/canty	"pleasant"/"brisk"
chimbley	"chimney"
deaved	"deafened"
dree	"cheerless"
faishion	"make"/"dare"
flaysome	"fearful"
flighted	"frightened"
flitting	"moving house"
frame	"make progress"/"get on with"
gait	"way"/"path"
ganging	"going"
girn	"snarl"/"grimace"
guilp	"scum from porridge"
harried	"robbed"
jocks	"food"
laced	"flogged"
laiking	"playing"
laith	"barn"
lugs	"ears"
meeterly	"moderately"
mells	"interferes"

mensful	"proper"
mun	"must"
neive/nave	"fist"
ortherings	"orderings"
pawsed	"kicked"
plisky	"mischief"/"rage"
quean	"woman"
reaming	"foaming"/"frothy"
riggs	"ridges"
riven	"torn"
scroop	"back of book"
side (out)	"move away"
skift	"move quickly"
sough	"ditch"
thible	"porridge stick"
thrang	"busy"
war	"worse"
wick	"wicked"/"lively"

Source: Adapted from Irene Wiltshire, "Speech in *Wuthering Heights*: Joseph's Dialect and Charlotte's Emendations," *Brontë Studies: Journal of the Brontë Society* 30, no. 1 (2005): 19–29, at 28.

I Cannot Express It

Joseph's doomed exclamation attempts to assert that we are blind and he has insight. In fact it confirms melancholically the opposite: that his "they" are us, and we see the world through Lockwood's eyes, in narrative terms as in philosophical ones. The dilemma hinges on who is the subject, and who the object, in the dynamic readerly situation Brontë sets into play. The stakes of this mechanism of entrapment become more visible when we pan from detail to appreciate how comprehensively the novel positions the subject-object dynamic at the core of its otherwise various thematic and conceptual projects.[45] Against the prophylactic separation of subject and object under the sign of mastery specified by the bourgeois tradition, *Wuthering Heights* performs across its registers a heterodox interpenetration of these positions: its insistence is on the impossibility of any subject's efforts to separate itself from what is not it. This dynamic of interinvolvement or mutuality—I called it entrapment above—becomes central theme and figure in the book, defining its various plots and organizing its physical choreography even as it supplies the governing formal principle of the narrative itself.

A frame tale of infamous complexity, the book's plot is full of passageways and breached barriers, all doors and windows and gates and the always incomplete motion of passing through them. These gothic elements are plot points and aspects of the built environment, but also ciphers for the book's formal design, as nested relations of address emphasize the entanglement of seemingly discrete minds and the positions of narrator and character oscillate without secure resolution, where "multiple narrative envelopes" work "as forms of translation—in many cases illegitimate ones" (Baena 110). What I am suggesting in light of this fact is that the novel's concern with interpenetration, connection, and doubling also marks out its effort, across registers, to offer an immanent critique of an emergent bourgeois program in which subjects can be partitioned from objects and intellectual operations worked on material that stands still for such instrumental usage. Using different terms, Leo Bersani observes that the novel engages in a sustained critique of autonomy: its famous characterological repetitions, two-cycle story-form, and rhymed events all support a structure that also models something like intertwinement. Heathcliff himself, Bersani observes, diffuses across the novel and "is no longer, so to speak, entirely within himself" but instead "'occurs,' in modified versions, elsewhere in the novel" (199). I am suggesting that rather than dissolving into a neoromantic plane of immanence or deconstructive utopia of non-closure, the relational logic of the book spins the subject-object relations at the core of Western thought into unthinkable and contradictory positions, without ever leaving them behind. This dilemma cannot be transcended, Brontë suggests, because it is all there is to think with.

From this perspective, Catherine's most famous speech becomes legible as a manifesto for the internal rewiring of bourgeois thought. The much-excerpted moment aims to describe a form of conceptualization waged against the delusions of a civilization built on capture but can imagine no alternative grammars by which to express it. It is useful to read Cathy's words again, which she addresses to Nelly:

> I cannot express it; but surely you and every body have a notion that there is, or should be, an existence of yours beyond you. What were the

> use of my creation, if I were entirely contained here? My great miseries in this world have been Heathcliff's miseries, and I watched and felt each from the beginning: my great thought in living is himself. If all else perished, and *he* remained, I should still continue to be; and if all else remained, and he were annihilated, the universe would turn to a mighty stranger: I should not seem a part of it. My love for Linton is like the foliage in the woods: time will change it, I'm well aware, as winter changes the trees—my love for Heathcliff resembles the eternal rocks beneath—a source of little visible delight, but necessary.
>
> "Nelly, I *am* Heathcliff—he's always, always in my mind—not as a pleasure, any more than I am always a pleasure to myself—but as my own being—so, don't talk of our separation again—it's impracticable; and—"
>
> She paused, and hid her face in the folds of my gown; but I jerked it forcibly away. I was out of patience with her folly! (72–73)

The speech is often quoted as a moment of high romance and, in miniature ("Nelly, I *am* Heathcliff!"), even excerpted onto the back cover of the Oxford edition, transformed against its own purpose into advertising copy. But this seemingly commodifiable moment of neoromantic transcendence on inspection contains a scandal for normal minds. The central notion here resists the containment of object-based thinking and as a result, Brontë specifies, evades formalization into syntax as such ("I cannot express it").[46]

Again it is Nelly who recognizes the force of Catherine's heretical encounter with the agrammatical. This loyal servant is put "out of patience" with Catherine's refusal to individuate herself. Nelly cannot let the heresy stand, and resorts to police power, "jerk[ing]" the gown away from Catherine "forcibly" to expose the feature of her young charge—the face—most able to secure her singular personhood.[47] The servant's capacity for violence is deployed to enforce the conventions of bourgeois thought and the subject-object distinction that is its fundamental conceptual motor. In scenes like this we see why Nelly is (as Q. D. Leavis said) "most carefully, consistently, and convincingly created for us as the normal woman" (quoted in Gezari, *Annotated*, 129). And why, despite her status as servant, Nelly "does not speak in the local dialect" but instead in the emergent orthodox language of her betters—later earning Lockwood's grandiloquent compliment that, "excepting a few provincialisms of slight consequence," she has "no marks of the manners that I am habituated to consider as peculiar to your class" (quoted in Wiltshire 20).

The halting and inexpressible collapse of the *dispositif* of the person so disgusting to Nelly is raised to the level of maxim in Catherine's conviction, noted just now, that she *is* Heathcliff. It is elaborated into plot point when, for example, Heathcliff removes the side from Catherine's coffin to become one with his love object, "dissolving with her" (255). ("[W]icked," Nelly judges, adding that Heathcliff should be "ashamed" [255].) And it functions at the level of trope in the pathetic fallacy overspreading the novel, by which the outside object world of "weather" or "environment" (as Ruskin would later scold in his essay on this technique) animistically coordinates with the "insides" of human characters, to the point that "setting" becomes inadequate to describe the permeated figure-ground, subject-object relations of this book—not dissimilar from the vortices of paint in Turner's canvases, discussed in the introduction.[48] Most dramatically, perhaps, the collapse of the subject-object relation is legible as I have indicated in the narrative structure of the book, since, to the confusion of contemporary reviewers and undergraduates, we encounter no event unmediated, no object without its interpreter, no dialogue without an interested transcriber. No one thing but with its entanglement in another.

Newman explains that *Wuthering Heights* "is structured as a monologue—in this case, a monologue containing other monologues and dialogues, captured in a diary. As a result, every perspective is presented as partial; there is no authoritative point of view, no single character with whom to identify" (12). In nested first-person accounts, Lockwood tells us what Nelly told him, this mediated testimony itself including long passages of quoted speech such as Isabella's letter. Editors since the nineteenth century have had to contend at a basic level with the formal complications of this nested construction, given that, if represented accurately, the novel's proliferating relations of address would create "the confusion of printing banks of quotation marks within quotation marks," citations inside citations inside yet other citations (Gezari, *Annotated*, 36; cf. 85)—a confusion of the subject-object division at the level of the typographic in which the book's error-filled first edition unevenly indulged.

The point is that the formal groundlessness generated by the novel's nested structure reinforces the counter-modern epistemological project of the plot, one emblematized most powerfully perhaps in the crystal of Catherine's speech. This epistemological situation is what Hillis Miller has translated into the idiom of deconstruction; what Bersani transcodes into a story about "the refusal of identity"; and what Richard Dellamora, echoing Susan Stewart's argument about love, has more convincingly described as hearkening to eighteenth-century and classical logics of friendship:

antebourgeois models of collective coupledom that defy the post-Lockean separation of subject from object and the conventional ethics following from it.[49] In fact the book's epistemological blackout denies us access to any unmediated object world or final say, and refuses to come to rest in even a negative closure. That is: it will not let readers come to the conclusion I am offering here, even as it arrays for us any number of characters who are deluded into believing such final arrest to be possible. "I believe the dead are at peace," Nelly exclaims—wrongly (300).[50]

The short-circuiting of the "verificationist style" (Parsard 94) natural to a rising bourgeois imperialism is pushed yet further by the densely historical, intricately temporal structure I've already alluded to—even if the hyper-chronological nature of the book registers mostly as perplexity with readers trained, as we all are, in the instrumentalist thought and corresponding plot sequencing the novel is interested in sabotaging. It is at last the moment to say directly that the novel is dated with fanatical specificity, the book's events insistently marked with time and specified to precise calendric accuracy but also reorganized into queerly mismatched synchronicities. Making matters worse, or better, first editions of the book were printed with page gatherings bound out of order, further scrambling its already scrambled sequence (Schuessler).

In a vividly committed article called "The Moons and Almanacs of Wuthering Heights," of 1974, A. Stuart Daley uses Brontë's allusions to time alongside the novel's precise notations of moon phases and other meteorological data—there are more than six hundred such annotations in the book—to reconstruct with a kind of fanatical empiricism a calendar for the events of *Wuthering Heights*. What Daley finds, after cross-checking the data points of these allusions against the historical record in a lost naval guide to nineteenth-century moon phases, is that Brontë "articulated [the novel's events] with calculating care into time sequences wholly consistent with the activities and the seasons they measure—consistent, that is, with themselves in their fictive calendars, but inconsistent with the historical calendar years that the novel pretends to be observing" (343).

This inconsistency derives from the fact that the calendar of *Wuthering Heights*, while internally perfectly correct, does not match the years in which the book is supposedly taking place—1784 and 1801—but instead matches other, later years—1826 and 1827—and matches them precisely, with almanac-style exactitude, down to the dates of the novel's three harvest moons (September 11, 1783; September 22, 1801; and September 11, 1802). Daley notes that "in 1784 the 20th of March fell not on a Monday [as Brontë states] but a Saturday" (341). Daley's calmly fanatical critical effort, itself a monument to the disposition I've charted so far, uncovers for us how Brontë's novel about the collapse of bourgeois thought encrypts its critique not just into dense thickets of ironic screening and interleaved subject-object relations, but also in a tightly woven set of temporal registers, elaborated with "calculating care," that it works simultaneously to sabotage. The fidelity is to the detail—but the details do not match, the paradigm of clarity invoked only to be painstakingly undone. Time thickens, then, as a recursive, traumatic, or typological time interleaves with lunar and calendric times, all of these otherwise incompatible registers cutting against the homogeneous, empty time of Lockwood's own metropolitan world. ("Time stagnates here," he famously complains, noticing exactly this.) As it perfectly transcodes 1826 into 1784 and 1827 into 1801, turning Mondays to Saturdays, the novel's queer chronologies intercut seemingly discrete—but in fact, by the tumbled-together form of the novel, united—moments in the unfolding British modernization.

The novel's extended early modernity stretches from 1757, Daley notes, when Hindley Earnshaw is born, to January 1, 1803, when "Catherine and Hareton [are] to marry" (352), this chronicle punctuated with the advent of Lockwood into the archaic zone of a residually feudal eighteenth-century Yorkshire. ("The first statement in *Wuthering Heights* sets a date," Daley observes: 1801 [Daley 337]). All this is chronicled with a hyperbolic accuracy of chronometric notation, with twenty-two of thirty-four chapters opening with a marker of time, even as this precision is also confused, muddled, or stagnated: a gibberish temporality that first readers of the novel, like I do, still, find almost perfectly inscrutable. It will not resolve into clarity.

My account has positioned Brontë as diagnostician of an emergent order predicated on use and extraction; it has suggested that her work labors via aesthetic means to unwind this cognitive system from the inside, in ways that charge material particularity with ethical significance and generate befuddlement among those encountering the book both early in the bourgeois project and at its twilight hour today. In all these efforts, *Wuthering Heights* tracks the mutually enforcing logics of capture, ownership, and identity across seemingly disparate registers, articulating the coherence of these domains as an aspirationally total system. The results defeat description in the regular grammars of sequential predication, where obvious subjects do things to clearly demarcated objects. The story of reason's internal collapse cannot be told in this normal idiom. As Cathy more succinctly explains: I cannot express it.

Dark Eyes (In Place of Conclusion)

To the extent that criticism continues to treat the Atlantic economy as one theme among others, a "background" or "context" rather than a structuring condition whose mutations and aftereffects continue to structure the present, it replicates the laundering processes and acts of intellectual partition to which Lockwoods have dedicated themselves across the ages. Against such self-insulating acts of mental hygiene, *Wuthering Heights* labors to ghost modernity's primal scenes into hieroglyphics that will not resolve into clear legibility. The crime of total commodification on the British sugar islands sets into motion a wavelike, recursive plot that is characterized by traumatic recurrence and serial repetition, not so much progressing toward happy conclusion—though Lockwood thinks it does—as swirling, recirculating, and reemerging in moments of intensity that braid together seemingly disparate phases in the long unfolding of enclosure-based accumulation and the climatic breakdown I am suggesting is its logical result. This story continues in the mudslides and firestorms of a fully commodified planet. Its reach extends to the genteel interiors and country homes of eighteenth-century merchants and twenty-first-century petroleum lobbyists alike, but also to the standardized speech staring at you from the pages of this book.

The novel's tangled and inescapable analysis is paradoxically most apprehensible, I've said, at minor scale. This long chapter's final detail is perhaps the slightest: one of the novel's mechanisms for marking the recurrence of the past in the bodies of those living in its narrative present. "Black eyes" are the proto-genetic trait shared among characters up and down the Earnshaw-Linton family tree. These gleam as a kind of shining stain in Hareton's skull—a holdover, we are meant to understand, from a previous generation and reverse image of Edgar's "great blue eyes and even forehead" (50). Catherine I and Cathy II both have black eyes, as does Heathcliff. Across time, these eyes are "precisely similar, and *they are those* of Catherine Earnshaw" (286, emphasis added). At one point in the 1847 edition Emily uses an ambiguous possessive to describe these important features, writing that "his black eyes flashed" (285). In the context and sense of the passage, "his" refers to Heathcliff, but according to rules of usage, the possessive pronoun refers to Hareton. In 1850, Charlotte corrected the ambiguity by writing "Heathcliff's black eyes flashed."

But Emily's seeming error of attribution condenses into a single agrammatical gesture the sabotage of personhood the novel is at pains to dramatize: in her original, wrong version, the pronouns refer across individuals and show the continuity of the past into the present; this relation takes shape across orthodox lines of kinship (Hareton is Hindley's son, not Heathcliff's) and defies standards of correctness modeled on metropolitan usage. From the perspective I advance here, Charlotte's solution to Emily's agrammatical staging is itself the problem, and tiny though it may be, the correction registers at world scale. If this detail seems small or the moments I've rehearsed feel tiny, it is because my claim has been that the throwaway instant and the sub-thematic detail might be seen under an aspect of care to index larger categorical claims without becoming subsumed by them.

Did she mean to do it? No one knows and, as I will suggest in coming chapters, the question itself only restages the voluntarist frameworks and desire for transparency the novel itself is working to think past. The gamble is that, protected from the desire to hold and know, the aberrant particulars of this most instrumentalized of novels might be allowed to breathe again, attention to the tiny instant now taking shape as an ethical and epistemological injunction at odds with the thematizing gaze of Lockwoods then and now.[51] The first thing to be cut from any academic book is always the close reading.

I hope it is clear by now that despite hints to the contrary, the aim of this chapter has not been to assert an allegorical connection between *Wuthering Heights*'s events and processes of wealth accumulation and the laundering of racial capital in the early fossil economy. Still less has it been to argue for the true context of Brontë's novel so as to establish via extratextual references what the novel is really about. Such habits are themselves the satiric target of the book, as its crosshairs center on the cue-ball reasoning and smooth equations that, transformed into the habits of criticism, take shapes so diverse as the faithful discovery of historical originals, thesis-based summation of argumentative takeaways, and checklists of climate action for the concerned academic.

This chapter's argument therefore follows accounts that see Brontë's work as conditioned by the historic fact of Atlantic slavery. But it pushes further to assert that the primal moment of extractive accumulation stands as origin point or crystal for an epistemic posture that extends well beyond its own moment of invention, and even into my performance here. Pushing is Lockwood's impulse, and no form of argument can avoid it. Katherine McKittrick refers to "plantation logic" as "a persistent but ugly blueprint" for the conceptual and spatial regime of racialized extraction we inhabit now (10). To invoke *plantation logic* is then to indicate a conceptual-material paradigm inaugurated in slave-based extraction: a suite of intellectual practices ranging from theories of personhood and identity to syntactical relations between subjects and objects and the idea of predication itself. This mental grammar sponsors the spreadsheet accounting and injunction-to-capture that still governs what counts as reason in scenes so seemingly disparate as international conferences on climate change and the boardrooms of corporate universities. Rough weather, they say. The truth is darker.

3

Minor Freedom and the Fragment

WITH EMILY BRONTË'S POEM-OBJECTS

> The struggle of the soul against a predestined doom is one form which the freedom motif takes in Emily Brontë's work.
>
> —C. Day Lewis, "The Poetry of Emily Brontë" (1957)

> If men wish to be free, it is precisely sovereignty that they must renounce.
>
> —Hannah Arendt, "What Is Freedom?" (1961)

Infinite Immensity

The manuscript fragment containing what is now one of Emily Brontë's best-known poems is perhaps two and a half inches tall, three inches wide. An ink blot marks the page. It seems to have been written in February 1838, but this dating is conjectural—posited based on contextual clues that are ultimately inconclusive.[1] On this scrap are scrawled two poems in black ink. One of them is canceled. The verse now titled "I'm happiest when most away" is split into two stanzas in every printed edition but compressed into a single block at the bottom of this MS page. The verse itself seems to use the conventional ingredients of lyric poetry: first-person speaker, material sensations, abstract ideas.

From its first publication in 1910 through to its canonization in the *Norton Anthology of English Literature* and its rival *Broadview*, the poem has received dashes for punctuation and a full end-stop in conclusion. In this form it stands as prototype for what one Norton reading guide calls the "extremely simple and occasionally rugged poetry" of this famous Victorian ("Reading Norton"):

I'm happiest when most away
I can bear my soul from its home of clay

On a windy night when the moon is bright
And my eye can wander through worlds of light—

When I am not and none beside—
Nor earth nor sea nor cloudless sky—
But only spirit wandering wide
Through infinite immensity.

(Black et al. 508–9; cf. E. Brontë, *Complete Poems*, ed. Gezari, 62–63; E. Brontë, *Poems*, eds. Roper and Chitham, 216)

Brontë's first-person "I" severs from physicality and wanders "through infinite immensity," becoming "not and none beside." Here the privative "not" aurally evokes "naught," zero, and flickers the poem's focus like a digital signal between *I* and *nothing*. In manuscript the verse is denuded of punctuation and all but illegible without a magnifying glass, which helps us appreciate why her only woman editor, Janet Gezari, says it is typical of Brontë to "leav[e] something open when we expect conclusion" (quoted in Helsinger 134).

The last chapter showed how *Wuthering Heights* stretched novel form while sabotaging some of that form's central features, including the Aristotelian movement toward resolution and the architecture of sympathetic identification. In related ways, poetic performances like "I'm happiest" mobilize genre signals from the romantic lyric and fragment poem in order to radicalize the split that male poets like William Wordsworth had installed at the heart of those structures. In "Tintern Abbey," for instance, the lyric speaker was defined by a wobbling division between young self and older one that paradoxically consolidated the ability of the speaker to penetrate "into the life of things" (line 49). In this dynamic of retrospective narration, aesthetic ingenuity works to disclose and aspirationally to resolve the internal difference of the speaking I from itself—a structure of chronological self-division, intimately tied to logics of development and improvement, that would come to animate *Jane Eyre*. In contrast to these parables of divided self-consolidation, the framed architecture of *Wuthering Heights* short-circuits the improvement story implicit in the romantic narrative of retrospection: intractable antagonism and looping repetition stand in place of the ready-made *bildung* stories interpolated by readers like Lockwood.

The poetry takes this internal critique even further. In "happiest," the temporal split between young and older I characteristic of the Wordsworthian lyric becomes a drama of dispersal and evacuation without clear end point or apparent effort at reconsolidation. Brontë was a sensitive student of Romantic poetry—a devoted reader of *Blackwood's*, obsessed with Byron, and "affined," in Gezari's striking phrase, to "the early Romantic period" in temperament, reading habits, and even dress (*Last* 3). Her poetry's drive toward what is often misread as transcendence activates tropes of the early nineteenth-century lyric in ways that have tricked some readers into viewing it as conventional in the extreme—a "cardboard sublime," as Muriel Spark and Derek Stanford charged in 1953 (133).[2] The accusation helps illustrate how those readers who don't force Brontë's poetry into tropes of resistant women writers and visionary seers—the two most common clichés of readerly attention today—effectively charge it with kitsch: a kind of dehistoricized signaling where the forms of a resuscitated romanticism are emptied of power and stripped down to mere convention.[3]

For historically specifiable reasons that will emerge in coming chapters, such readings miss the combined aesthetic and epistemological work of these performances. More consequentially, they defuse the threat this writing poses to the thought forms we ourselves still bring to bear on them. Rather than resistance, transcendence, or kitsch, "happiest" dramatizes at sub-grammatical scale an effort to think within the conceptual confines of the romantic lyric so as to subject that form's philosophical and political presumptions to a kind of affirmative demolition. Gayatri Spivak uses the phrase affirmative sabotage to name an approach that "doesn't just ruin." Instead, "the idea is of entering the discourse that you are criticizing fully, so that you can turn it around from inside" (Spivak and Evans n.p.). In Brontë's case, this kind of reconstructive immanent critique means that her fragment-performances inhabit the still-potent clichés of a heroic lyric romanticism so as to turn them against their own content: these agrammatical and weirdly shaped writings rework what Marjorie Levinson capitalizes as the Romantic Fragment Poem ("RFP") into a tool for investigating the limitations of the epistemological apparatus of domination that is the subgenre's raison d'être. In this sense, Brontë's scripted performances continue the work of *Wuthering Heights* described in the last chapter, which was to reconstrue the bourgeois concepts of "subjectivity" and "freedom" in light of the fact that the material corollary of those mental grammars is best described as ruin.

It must be stated right away that the deconstructive attack on something called "romantic subjectivity" is itself a kind of cliché. The open and unresolved are now habitually elevated into the crypto-heroic formulas for an aestheticized resistance, negation, or escape diagnosed, for instance, in recent calls for "affirmative instrumentality."[4] More substantively, such postures can be seen as idealist insofar as they position thought as a substitute for politics, and romantic in that they set up an alternative domain called *the imaginative* and position this as the place where salutary outcomes or perhaps transcendence might transpire, even or especially when such outcomes are foreclosed in fact—as Bloch showed in the introduction. Often the commodified idealism that would position literary and cultural work as the domain of resistance proposes the critic as the figure who might accomplish the thinking otherwise that would open "the future" as unspecified utopian space.

But instead of repeating prepackaged critiques of an allegedly hegemonic *liberal subject*—a strawman for criticism in Victorian studies since the 1980s, as I note in chapter 5—I am describing Brontë's approach in terms of a historical ontology or episteme of extraction. For Brontë, I am suggesting here, the apparently only poetic project of internally repurposing her generic forbears in fact spins out to implicate a host of conceptual-philosophical structures that follow from the lyric idea: from the aesthetic values of completion and totality to something like identity, understood in both the conventional sense as subject position or private standing, and in the philosophical sense as the "correspondence of the thing-in-itself to its concept" that is "the ideological element of pure thought, all the way down to formal logic" under capitalism (Adorno, *Negative*, 149). She does not so much "rupture" or "dissolve" these subgenres of depletionary cognition but inhabits them so as to repurpose them from within (figure 11).

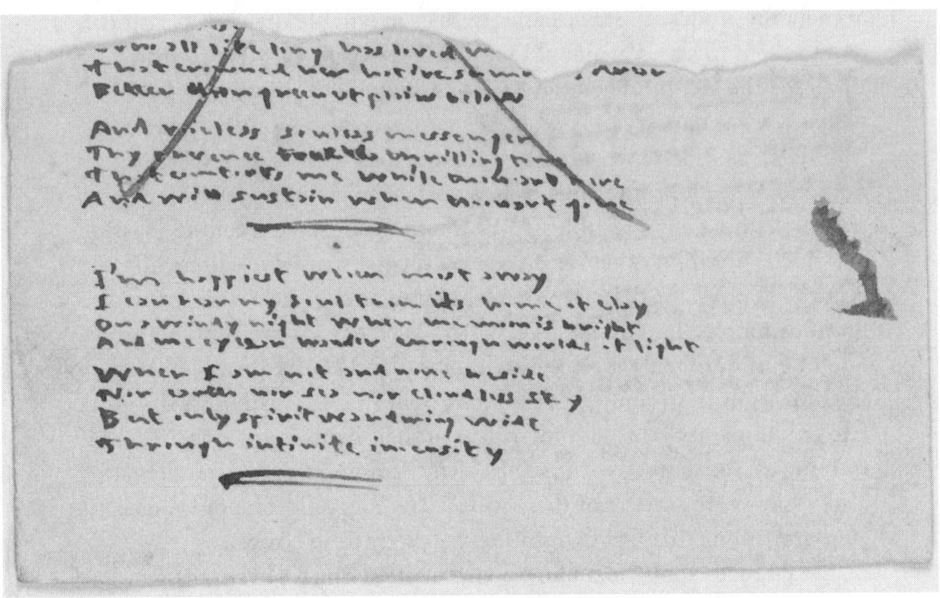

I'm happiest when most away
I can bear my soul from its home of clay
On a windy night when the moon is bright
And the eye can wander through worlds of light

When I am not and none beside
Nor earth nor sea nor cloudless sky
But only spirit wandering wide
Through infinite immensity

FIGURE 11. Emily Brontë, "I'm happiest when most away" (1838). Ink on torn paper. Henry W. and Albert A. Berg Collection of English and American Literature, New York Public Library. Photograph: New York Public Library.

It is important to note in pursuing this argument that what looks like secondhand romantic ideology comes back to ground in the inescapably physical quality of material presentation. Seeing the poems in their manuscript form discloses Brontë to be modeling as aesthetic performance a deliberately circumscribed aesthetic scene, minor in material footprint and epistemological commitment. But this very investigation of limitation joins up, in these tiny works, to the grandest dissolutions imaginable: "infinite immensity." The result is minor elaborative production, a movement-within-structure that helps forecast this book's ongoing interest in action at what I will call sub-heroic scale. Lydia Brown observes that Brontë's "poetry rests heavily on a sense of self. Yet for all their interior intensities, Brontë's poems strive not to cement the self but to dissolve it" (182–83). The comment amply summarizes one obvious reading of "happiest": here the speaking subject melts into "spirit" and becomes "not and none beside," in a move that appears to track with the typically masculine stories of escape-from-self familiar from romantic poetry and revived today in the self-aggrandizing self-renunciations of climate writers of the Dark Mountain school.

In climate circles, such Nietzschean posturing presumes catastrophe to be fait accompli and asserts the only appropriate reaction to be an auto-consolidating self-renunciation, combined with detachment: an attempt at metaphysical escape that naturalizes as inevitable the very disasters it would seem to stand against.[5] Donna Haraway glosses this posture as a thrall to "the self-indulgent and self-fulfilling myths of apocalypse" (35) whose only outcome can be a serene indifference or fatalistic remove—a "nihilism," as Bloch puts it, that is "the objectivist mask of the crisis phenomenon" (I, 4). Brontë's feeling happiest when most away would seem to track with those climate nihilists who adopt the poses of placid abnegation and docile negativity that are available only to those whose lifeworlds are secure enough that disaster can be savored as spectacle, ruin turned to gratification in the chiastic reversal characteristic of the sublime mode. Such figures are male, usually; rich, often; and ready, always, to deploy the universalizing grammar of the Anthropocene "we" to discuss the bleak fate of "humanity" through the prism of their own experience. "There is nothing we can do to save ourselves," Roy Scranton wrote in a much-cited 2013 essay symptomatic of this mode. "The biggest problem we face," is "understanding that this civilization is already dead" (n.p.).

Despite activating the sublime postures of such metaphysicians, Brontë's poetry suggests sublimity is not the entire picture. For Swinburne, Emily Brontë "love[d] the earth for earth's sake" (quoted in Gezari, *Last*, 3) and biographers note with intermittent wonder that for all her apocalyptic cast of mind, she seems to have got most pleasure from repetitive, minor acts of housework done with her hands: "brushing the carpets, kneading the bread, feeding the dogs" (Gezari, *Last*, 2). If it is metaphysical, it is a metaphysics of the mundane. She is said to have cauterized her own arm with a hot poker and said nothing about it, so as to avoid "fuss" (cf. Barker, *Wild Genius on the Moors*, 231). And so the twist, in "Happiest," is that the poem refuses to rest in its negative mode of aesthetic fugitivity or aggrandizing self-escape. Instead, the speaking subject who has been dissolved, transcended, or turned to naught finds itself rehabilitated, albeit in canceled or ghosted form in the astonishing final quatrain. The speaker returns in the form of a jarring slant rhyme that rescues the "I" even at the moment of its apparent transcendence:

> When I am not and none beside
> Nor earth nor sea nor cloudless **sky**
> But only spirit wandering wide
> Through infinite immensi**ty**.

Pronouncing "immensity" to complete its rhyme with "sky" forces a torque in voice that salvages the "I" at the moment of its undoing—or almost does.

It is just a sound, and a weird one. Substandard, in fact, from the perspective of the metropolitan speech patterns that were in this period being raised into universality under the label "RP" or received pronunciation.[6] The muted, semi-standard effect of the poem's concluding rhyme shows Brontë thinking about "self-actualization" in a self-canceling way, and more importantly, vice versa: refusing to abandon the project of affirmation even at the moment of seemingly total evacuation. It is important, I'm saying, that the effect of rhyme is voiced: physical, I mean, and inseparable from the body's performance of a written script that could otherwise seem to belong in the domain of ideas. Roper and Chitham observe that Brontë's fantastical spelling and unusual orthography reflect the habits of someone "more sensitive to the sound than to the look of words" (E. Brontë, *Poems*, eds. Roper and Chitham, 278). Here, immensity's twisted rhyme with "I" marks the commitment with which this writing instantiates in physical performance what we could call negative thought or countertheory, even while keeping faith with the positive dreams without which, Brontë suggests over and over again, the commitment she still calls "hope" would be impossible. It is a practice of thinking freedom from within the corrupted grammars of bourgeois consciousness, the regular thought of romantic liberalism shaped into nonstandard and degraded forms, then brought back again.[7]

I have focused exorbitant attention on this tiny item of writing, and have drawn introductory conclusions from a microscopic instance, rather than beginning with a thesis or stating the chapter's aim outright. Methodologically, I mean, we have begun at the level of the detail and will move, only slowly, to the "main ideas." The rest of this chapter operates inductively alongside a loose group of Brontë's most minimalist knowledge-forms, her poetic scraps. Its aim is to show how these unfinished and open-form aesthetic productions position the singular, the irresolute, and the small against the myths of grandeur and totality propagated by such men as Lockwood and Scranton, even while subjecting this minoritarian minimalism to expansion at total scale. Pursuing this double claim requires that we reconstruct how a series of male editors in the years before 1945 took the obscure and formless poetic writings of this most bristling Brontë sister and transformed them into "lyric poetry."

Such reworkings are akin to those better-documented processes to which Emily Dickinson's work has more famously been subjected. Like the editorial processes documented by Virginia Jackson and others, the edits to Brontë's poetry import a specious liberal universalism onto the idiosyncratic formal and political project of performances that, I explain, put the humanistic presumptions of their own apparent genre into question. The drama of editorial reification I chart may sound familiar from existing analysis of Dickinson, or from too-familiar critiques of the "universal subject" of liberal modernity. But my point instead is to show how Brontë's verse, in manuscript anyway, works to rescue universalism by locating its emblems in the dark and unvalued rather than the dominant; in scraps rather than finished wholes; and in glitchy, wobbling physical practices invisible as "literature" in still-conventional senses of that term. More, her writing does this work in the context of a modernizing England whose emergent fossil economy was built on what Brontë in her school essays called a principle of destruction. In this context Brontë's half-lyrics and dreamlike fragments read as broken hymns to freedom: they rethink the logics of personhood and liberty at the emergent stage (ca. 1840) of an extractive modernity her later editors inhabited in a dominant form (ca. 1945–1975) and whose aftermath gathers around us today.

Exception and Rule

Like the introductory section you just read, the chapter on *Wuthering Heights* was long and detailed and used a series of set-piece close readings of a single nineteenth-century artifact to argue for one author's insight into the self-abolishing trajectory of modern reason. The form of attention modeled there was, let us say, focused: In reading after reading, I tried to show how the novel that no contemporary reader could comprehend disrupted from within a gathering extractive rationality it associated with both chattel slavery and a then-rising bourgeois capitalism. A small thread of that argument—just a note—suggested how, in place of the standardizing logics of this rising common sense, Brontë positioned a reparative concern with the low-key, the singular, and the idiosyncratically vulnerable. Lapwing feathers and nonstandard dialects, weird religions and broken grammars: all these differently emblematized forms of being whose material specificity might escape, if just provisionally, the "monoculture of naming" that is "intended to make all things comparable" (Ghosh, *Nutmeg's Curse*, 97).

In its obsessional fidelity to such remaindered things, *Wuthering Heights*—so I implied—proves all but unique among nineteenth-century novels, in this sense replicating what Lyn Pykett has referred to as Brontë's "sense of her own freakishness and exceptionality" in comparison to the standards of her age (Pykett 47). In the context of Brontë's famous idiosyncrasy and orthogonal relation to the standard, it is worth recalling that the exception is meaningfully distinguished from the example. Where an example stands in for a wider category and is at least theoretically replaceable with other members of its set, an exception sits at remove from the category to which it nevertheless gestures by negation. Despite a defining relation to the set or rule it escapes, the exception is only itself. I treat Emily Brontë's work as exceptional in this sense because of this book's investment in identifying spaces of possibility that are antagonistic to but still within a gathering nineteenth-century normalcy whose ruins constitute our present. Brontë is neither a hero nor a "revolutionary." She did not occupy a transcendent position with respect to gathering bourgeois ideology or the material processes of despoliation it supported. Rather she was inside the storm, which means that instead of highlighting heroic resistance or romantic intransigence, I locate in Brontë's minor practice moments of non-total possibility and uncompleted predication. The gesture, the wobble, and the momentary flight—these and other low-frequency activities give shape to a practice of internal adjustment, a non-total activity that finds expression in the odd, unscripted movement rather in than the general tendency from which those movements fleetingly deviate.

This chapter takes a half-step past the reading of *Wuthering Heights* and aims to demonstrate the commitments Brontë's verse writing shows to developing models of attenuated capacity amid the gathering homogeneity of a now-total extractive system. The poem-objects redescribed here are small, fragile, and almost infinitely difficult, "not at all like the poetry women generally write," as Charlotte judged (C. Brontë, "Biographical Notice," 301). They traffic in themes of constraint and liberty while inviting and frustrating hermeneutic translation in equal measure. Above all, they redirect the interest in subjectivity traditionally associated with the lyric mode toward dissolution, evaporation, and flight, even while resisting the negative closure of escape that might seem to follow from that critical project. In so doing these bits of ephemera wrestle possibility from within the otherwise all-encompassing terms of a system from which no full escape is possible, a situation allegorized in Brontë's poetic writing, again and again, in prisons, chains, fetters, and boxes, and the flights of mind and hand only momentarily able to transcend them.[8] Against mechanisms of capture they describe as finally inescapable, the tiny acts of thought crystallized on notepaper and scrap go further even than *Wuthering Heights*, I am suggesting, to recast freedom for an age of non-transcendence.

In a 1961 essay entitled "What Is Freedom?" that will return in the next chapter, Hannah Arendt describes how, from the early modern period forward, a Western philosophical tradition transformed *freedom* from a term denoting a common life lived in public—a fundamentally social phenomenon, and a political one—into an inner state of mind. For Arendt, freedom was by this process wrestled from "the realm of politics and human affairs in general" to "an inward domain, the will" (145). In this newly privatized domain of liberty, individualized actors could engage in the acrobatic dramas of self-division and internal discipline that only confirm what Arendt calls the modern "free" subject's "estrangement from the world" (146). On this reading, the concept of *will* and its increasing isomorphism with the freedom concept over the course of early modernity confirms the narrowing and depoliticization of freedom itself. Arendt thus unpacks what she describes as the catastrophic consequences of construing "freedom" as a fundamentally individual matter of interior states "when, briefly, freedom had become free will" (163).

This transition effectively moved the freedom problem from the domain of politics to that of philosophy. In addition, Arendt suggests, it wrestled the social and political concept of common life into a notion now fundamentally aligned with the notion of sovereignty. That is because—as the projects of Rousseau and Thomas Paine indicate (163), and as Locke's appearance in the last chapter showed—freedom in the political sphere was now to be construed on the model of "sovereignty, the ideal of a free will, independent from others and eventually prevailing against them" (163). Since liberty was now to be experienced in the mind, it followed that this domain of unfettered individual activity could be imagined in terms of total self-command, or sovereignty. The final turn in Arendt's effort to rewind the clock on this depoliticizing understanding of freedom as unchecked private capacity is to note what she calls its most "pernicious and dangerous consequence[s]" (164).

These are: (1) that this model results paradoxically in "the denial of human freedom," since it cannot help but become obvious to everyone, eventually, that "whatever men may be, they are never sovereign" (164). If freedom is to name activity unaffected by other factors, people, or situations, no one is free, and all are constrained. More importantly (2), if freedom is to name sovereign will and its execution in the world, then "the freedom of one man, or group, can be purchased only at the price of the freedom, i.e., the sovereignty, of all others" (164). The point polemically redescribes negative liberty in light of ecological relation: since all action is impingement on another, no "sovereignty" can be achieved without the corresponding imposition onto someone else's sphere of autonomy—which is anyway a fiction. "Within the conceptual framework of traditional philosophy," Arendt says, "it is indeed very difficult to understand how freedom and non-sovereignty can exist together or, to put it another way, how freedom could have been given to men under the condition of non-sovereignty" (164). Arendt's description invites a consideration of "non-sovereignty" as an ante-modern but real form of freedom that is collaborative rather than private, predicated not on unscripted voluntarity but on mutual enactment in a field of necessarily plural relation. Such a recalibrated freedom could only be imagined, she suggests, outside the conceptual frameworks and approved genres of bourgeois philosophy. It would require another language.

Access Industries

Brontë fans will remember that twenty-one of Emily's poems were published by Charlotte in *Poems by Currer, Ellis, and Acton Bell* (1846), which sold a total of two copies. Another eighteen poems appeared after Emily's death, in the 1850 edition of *Wuthering Heights and Agnes Grey* edited by Charlotte. Both collections presented a heavily shaped version of Brontë's work to an all but uncomprehending public. Here as with *Wuthering Heights,* Charlotte's heavy alterations and retitling of poems flattened out rough edges, regularized syntax and sense, and aimed to fulfill the function of "interpreter" that (in Charlotte's words) "ought always to have stood between [Emily] and the world" ("Biographical Notice" 306).

She spliced in capital letters, turned dashes to periods, added end-stops, and went so far as to write and then interpolate extra lines at the end of Emily's most (to her) unsatisfactory poems, like "The Night-Wind," adding "the sort of moral lesson with which Charlotte frequently closes her own poems" (Gezari, *Last,* 134). The number of known Brontë poems expanded in 1910, when the critic, editor, and Brontë-obsessed collector Clement Shorter, working from manuscripts purchased from Charlotte Brontë's widower under dubious circumstances, added a number of previously unpublished texts even while "sometimes fall[ing] back on invention" when transcribing them (E. Brontë, *Poems,* eds. Roper and Chitham, 291). C. W. Hatfield's *Complete Poems of Emily Jane Brontë,* of 1941, offered a nearly full complement of manuscript poems to the world in print form, but regularized punctuation and fixed a kind of spelling that "exhibits peculiarities which it is not considered expedient to perpetuate in print" (E. Brontë, ed. Hatfield, 22).

It is not clear that Brontë desired publication for any poetry she wrote at all, given that even those published when she was still alive were wrestled away in what has become a famous biographical episode. "It took hours to reconcile her to the discovery I had made," Charlotte recalls, "and days to persuade her that such poems merited publication" ("Biographical Notice" 302).[9] Charlotte's recollection deploys "reconcile" as a transitive infinitive, "to reconcile her," in parallel construction with *to persuade her,* and so codes into grammar the inadequacy of the consent concept at the core of liberal concepts of action.[10] Did Emily "consent"? The question is inadequate, and the striking duration of the pressure campaign—"hours," "days"—crystallizes Arendt's point that autonomous wills and unfettered decisions are finally fictive: heuristic stand-ins or tropes, even, for papering over what Dan Stout glosses as "action's stubborn refusal to fit the forms of first-person accountability" (4).

In total there are forty-six scraps of paper or card in addition to three extant notebooks of manuscript material. The "tiny irregular slips" (E. Brontë, *Poems,* eds. Roper and Chitham, 19) that concern me here "preserve many apparently unfinished or incomplete poems, usually described as fragments," as Gezari puts it, "and we cannot know what she intended to do with them" (*Last* 5). The point is that these private or semi-private performances are assimilable into available genres of comprehension only after a kind of interpretive force-fitting: we can make sense of them only by shaping them into conceptual-aesthetic templates they nevertheless will not exactly fit.[11] "Poetry" is one of these boxes.

In "'Tis Moonlight," for instance (figure 12), Shorter presents us with a three-stanza lyric conventional in theme and structure. Brontë's own text even refers, in line 10, to "lovely form" and things happening "sweetly" and "gent[ly]." It would be easy to read such a poem and decide on its perfect isomorphism with the generic precursors it appears to emulate: just

XVIII

'Tis moonlight, summer moonlight,
All soft, and still, and fair ;
The silent time of midnight
Shines sweetly everywhere.

But most where trees are sending
Their breezy boughs on high,
Or stooping low are lending
A shelter from the sky.

And there in those wild bowers
A lovely form is laid,
Green grass and dew-steeped flowers
Wave gently round her head.

May 13, 1840.

FIGURE 12. Emily Brontë, "'Tis Moonlight." From *The Complete Works of Emily Brontë, Volume 1: Poems*, ed. Clement Shorter (New York: Hodder and Stoughton, 1908): 253. Library of Congress, Washington, DC (AIG-0355). Photograph: Library of Congress.

another Romantic poem about flowers and moonlight, "breezy boughs" and "wild bowers." But the original text (figure 13) helps us see how hard Shorter has had to work to achieve this flatly generic effect. The manuscript, about the size of a Post-It torn in half, shows no stanza breaks and includes barely legible cancelations and a semi-phallic drawing on the upper left that contemporary editor Derek Roper calls a "doodle suggesting a winged snake" (E. Brontë, *Poems*, eds. Roper and Chitham, 249n78).

Later transcriptions differ entirely from Shorter in his construal of lines three and four (E. Brontë, *Poems*, eds. Roper and Chitham, 106; E. Brontë, *Complete Poems*, ed. Gezari, 125), which are, in the manuscript, best described as a blur. The original has no punctuation at all, and the verso of the torn scrap includes a geometrical drawing of a singular point of vision being ripped apart—the perspectival regime of the Wordsworthian lyric shredded into scrap, only one of her many forays into diagrammatic representation (figure 14). "So far as is known," explains Roper, "this beginning was never continued, and bears no clear relation to other narratives

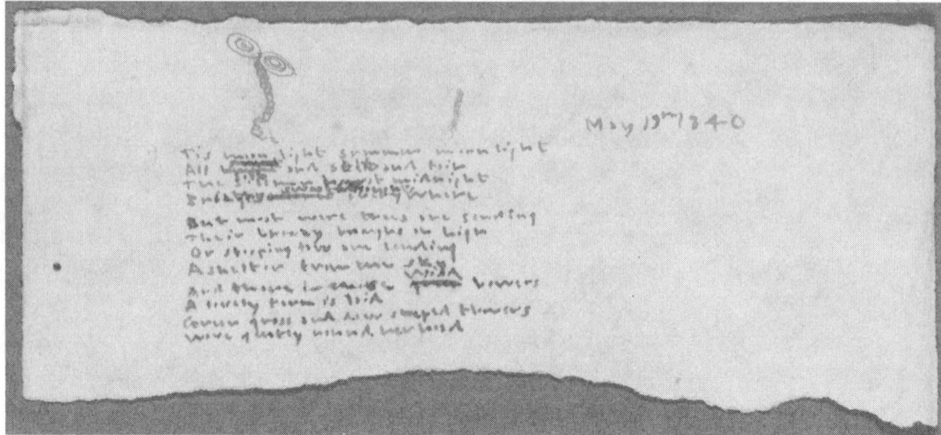

FIGURE 13. Emily Brontë, "Tis moon light summer moonlight" (1840) (recto). Ink on torn paper. Henry W. and Albert A. Berg Collection of English and American Literature, New York Public Library. Photograph: New York Public Library.

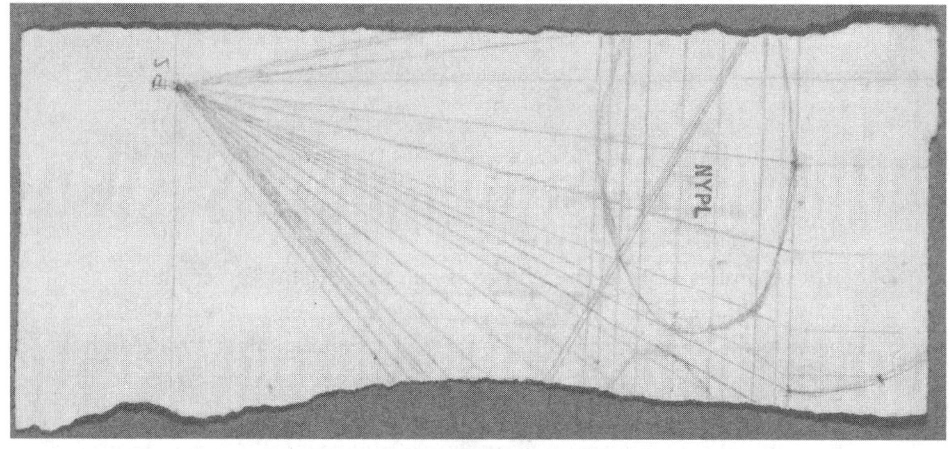

FIGURE 14. Emily Brontë, "Tis moon light summer moonlight" (1840) (verso). Pencil on torn paper. Henry W. and Albert A. Berg Collection of English and American Literature, New York Public Library. Photograph: New York Public Library.

by EB" (E. Brontë, *Poems*, eds. Roper and Chitham, 249). It is a start without a conclusion, an unfinished process. This wobbling relation to closure means that the poem that looks like an object requires us to read it instead as a moment in a longer and unfinished unfolding, a performance characterized by deviation, swerve, and unexpected elaboration without clear starting or endpoints—where the solemn hour of midnight might not "shine," as Shorter has it, but (in the manuscript version) "breath[e]s" (see E. Brontë, *Poems*, eds. Roper and Chitham, 106).

I am hinting that in even a basic material sense, a poetic performance like "'Tis Moonlight" cannot really be called a poem, except from within the lyricizing perspective shared by nearly all of Brontë's posthumous editors. Even Gezari, whose gorgeously perceptive account in *Last Things* provides inspiration for this chapter, finds it necessary to make an "argument for the integrity" of several fragmentary poetic texts, a claim backed by "a defence of their formal and semantic coherence" (97). Thus do even the work's very best readers—those sensitive, as Gezari is, to the way "avoidance of closure" might be an "achievement" in its own right (*Last* 97)—conscript these fragments into a lyric tradition that recent work has shown to be almost entirely the product of a twentieth-century criticism reading its categories backward onto earlier writing.[12] In *Dickinson's Misery*, Jackson invokes the term *scribal objects* to designate the not dissimilar manuscript fragments of Dickinson (45). (Dickinson had "No Coward Soul is Mine" read at her funeral, signaling "the powerful transferal of energy between Brontë's writing and her own" [Moon 231; see Gezari, *Last*, 128]). But even *scribal objects* stretches the truth, since in the case of Brontë's texts at least, they can come to rest as objects only after acts of arrest imposed on them by variously interested readers across the ages. Rather than achievements or objects, they may be more properly termed performances.[13]

In any case, it appears that if we continue to construe the term *poem* in the New Critical, Romantic, or simply commonsense way as a finished artifact or completed thought—a made thing, *poēma*—then these aren't really poems at all, but essays in the etymological sense of tests or attempts. They are meaningfully understood as frozen processes that, as Gezari observes above and Levinson says of romantic fragment-poems more broadly, transform "the very act of completion" into their central problematic (26). Almost all of them are scrawled on torn sheets, some on black-banded mourning stationery, ripped up and repurposed, all of which marks them as standing adjacent to a poetics of positive knowledge.[14] She hid many of them in her desk, along with a review of *Wuthering Heights* that called it "wild, confused, disjointed, and improbable" (Allott 220).

The stakes of Brontë's efforts perversely to redeem the category of the disjointed are highlighted by a recent episode in the textual history of her poetry, which I relay here despite the misfit of this anecdote with the sequential pursuit of argumentative claim. One of the three main collections of Brontë's manuscript poetry existed for decades only in the form of a photostatic copy of a notebook that was, in its original form, thought to be lost. The copy was made in 1934, and "it does not appear to have been seen since" (E. Brontë, *Poems*, eds. Roper and Chitham, 14). But in 2021, the nonexistent sheaf of holograph poems, known as the Honresfield manuscript, or "MS A," resurfaced, instantly to be monetized by means of a Sotheby's auction. A now-universal logic of value extraction meant that these resurfaced literary artifacts could be construed, in the news articles accompanying the episode, as both "priceless" and "valued at between £800,000 and £1.2m" (Flood). The apparent paradox of valuation is only one indicator of the historical victory of a conceptual and political paradigm whose ascendance is documented in *Wuthering Heights*.[15]

When I wrote to the curator of Sotheby's in June of 2021 to request access to the newly rediscovered manuscripts, he replied only briefly, his perspective so obvious as to require little explanation. "We think it most appropriate," he wrote, "for the buyer to make decisions about sharing images and other scholarly access."[16] Thus was "the Most Important Brontë Material to Come to Light in a Generation" (Sotheby's n.p.) effectively cordoned off from public use and enclosed as property, just another instance of what Carolyn Lesjak describes as the "non-evental" or centuries-long process of partition by which commons have been outfitted for the private extraction of value (22). It is usefully viewed as a minor episode in the unfinished history of enclosure, no different, really, than Heathcliff placing traps over nests on his property, open country being turned to private parcels across the eighteenth and nineteenth centuries, or the island of Bermuda, say, being "apportioned into four private estates by investors and worked by sharecropper tenants" in the "vision of corporate colonization" that remade this frontier for use after 1615 (Stern 58). As the curator's message indicated by means of matter-of-fact prose and a complete lack of further explanation, it should in no way be surprising that a salable manuscript would be cordoned off from public access: of course you can't look at it; you don't own it. But it is exactly this precognitive aspect of universal commodification that is the point here.

In the event, twenty million dollars were raised to "save" the collection from dispersal into private hands by a consortium of museums and cultural heritage sites. Half the money came from the philanthropist and investor Leonard Blavatnik, a friend of oligarchs and university patron whose spectacular wealth has its original source in Russian oil and the mining of aluminum. The Blavatnik portfolio has since diversified into petrochemicals and coal, in addition to the cultural heritage work on the part of Britain's cherished past. Among other things, the story of the Brontë manuscripts being "rescued," in the insistent parlance of the news stories, by an extraction oligarch can help us see how fully the tendrils of a catastrophic system now reach into the apparently separate domains of thought and art. It shows, too, how the extractive order whose roots lie in the Atlantic slavery, internal colonization, and coal combustion documented in *Wuthering Heights* might come full circle to embrace even those strange and haunting objects that I am suggesting labor in minor ways to interrupt that system.

Breaking the good news, the British Library reported that "Brontë treasures" had been "saved for the nation," a salvific phrasing that reappeared the same day, unchanged, in newspaper accounts from opposed ends of the political spectrum (the *Guardian*, the *Evening Standard*). The echoing of this rescued-by-billionaire template across the British press testifies to the standardization of thought under conditions of total enclosure and full media consolidation, but also to something more precise, which is the success of the public-relations campaign that invented and deployed this framing.[17]

In ghostly ways, then, the standardized rhetorics of a degraded media landscape disclose the filigrees of connection linking the ideological work of billionaire-serving PR firms to more concrete scenes of extraction and despoliation that pay the bills for such services. This circuit of culture and materialism enables us to see how *Brontë manuscript salvation* and the PR campaigns bragging about it depend upon, and are unthinkable without, say, the "ethylene, propylene, propylene oxide, ethylene oxide, tertiary butyl alcohol, methanol, acetic acid and their derivatives" that just one of Blavatnik's several petrochemical companies produces in order to "advance modern living." Far from the chemical plants and extraction zones, nearer to the grassy lawns on which Alice sat in chapter 1, the Blavatnik School of Government is "one of the University of Oxford's newest and most vibrant departments." This outlet of ideas is a "network of policymakers, government leaders, public officials and practitioners," the website tells us, a network that "reaches worldwide."[18] In April 2024, Blavatnik participated in a Zoom call with a different network, this one including hedge fund managers, a real estate investor, the CEOs of Starbucks and Dell, and other "billionaires and business titans," all of whom discussed with New York City mayor Eric Adams how they might together "pressure Columbia's president and trustees to permit the mayor to send police to the campus," in an effort to "handle" student protesters opposing the genocide in Gaza (Natanson and Felton). Blavatnik's major holding company—the umbrella under which the petrochemicals, aluminum mining, power generation, oil, media, entertainment, and biotechnology all find shelter—is called Access Industries.

The Prisoner (A Fragment)

From such all-encompassing processes of capture and unfreedom, can any escape be imagined, let alone set into motion? It could never be total: the Blavatnik Family Foundation "contributes to renowned institutions that showcase the breadth of arts and culture, including performance, exhibition and education" at some 180 museums and cultural sites worldwide, providing financial support to at least one institution, the Tate, that generously supplied this book with permissions and artwork.[19] And anyway the Blavatnik story is just an anecdote, an exemplar meant to crystallize a point about the penetration of enclosure's total system into the sphere of aesthetic and cultural practice—that is, the domain of thought.

The poems I'm talking about worry this problem at vanishingly tiny scale. It is true, I am suggesting, that the fugitive or inassimilable quality of Brontë's literary work is almost reflexively recaptured: purchased and literally commodified, yes, but also romanticized into cliché and made to fit the already established templates of heroic resistance, visionary women, or proto-modernist experiment, among others. Or it is simply read: translated into themes or takeaways we can grasp and hold, main ideas one can study in a class, put on a PowerPoint, or simply *like*. (My students, discussing these fragments in spring 2024, wondered whether they should be read at all.) This point is about aberrant knowledge and the mechanisms of seizure that the identical articles in the *Guardian* and *Evening Standard* demonstrated perhaps without realizing. The dynamics of domestication described in those formulaic news stories extend, even, to processes that see "domestication" itself as their greatest enemy. The truth is that the properties of "recalcitrance" and "idiosyncrasy" I myself argued for are ready-made for co-optation into the scripts of the outsider visionary or romantic artist; primed, too, for insertion into neoliberal clichés about the genius creator of content. All of these scripts are Brontë myths supercharged for an era in which "conceptual risk-taking" is its own academic product line (J. Wilson).[20] Among other things, the omnivorous quality of the culture industry means that the force of this poetry's non-integrative quality—and its immanent, internally disobedient relationship to its own conditions of articulation—must now be recovered rather than taken for granted, even as the countervailing risk of fetishization is suspended or held temporarily at bay. Instead, motion: "Brontë's poems," notes Gezari, "return again and again both to the prison site and to the prison break" (*Last* 6).

What momentary freedoms exist in these poems are legible at all only because the containment they strain against is so pervasive as to be almost total. Capture, as readers have long noted, is their organizing motif. The poem that appeared in the 1846 published edition as "The Prisoner (A Fragment)," for instance, is exemplary in its invocation of constraint only to imagine its opposite: the poem figures transcendence in a canceled or negative form consonant with the "darkly privative logic" organizing Brontë's poetry generally (Vine 103). The story it tells is a chronicle of de-subjectification or becoming-object by means of physical containment. It describes "lives wasting . . . away" in cells (E. Brontë, *Complete Poems*, ed. Gezari, l. 2) and inventories bodies made subject to limit, "when the pulse begins to throb, the brain to think again, / The soul to feel the flesh, and the flesh to feel the chain" (ll. 55–56). Like other of Brontë's investigations of prisons, cells, boxes, or cages, "The Prisoner" oscillates between the binary terms of freedom and restraint common to liberal-voluntarist frameworks and routes its investigations through what the poems construe as the related categories of (political) liberty and (poetic) closure.[21]

In the poem, a jailer explains to the female prisoner that no escape is possible: "sooner might the sun thaw down those granite stones" (l. 24). The imprisoned woman responds with an apparently straightforward confidence, reporting that "A messenger of Hope, comes every night to me, / And offers for short life, eternal liberty" (ll. 35–36). This reassuringly Christian article of faith seems to solve the speaker's carceral situation, responding to her terror of enclosure with "Hope." The poem appears to suggest that her jailers "had no power to work the captive woe"—that they cannot actually hurt her—since her belief in a future emancipation is so strong (ll. 62–64). She will find true freedom in a future life, and is therefore, in a way, free now. This is the "theme of Emily Brontë's 'The Prisoner'" that can be found via online searches and AI summaries of them.[22]

Yet the published version of "The Prisoner" is culled from a much longer poem of more than 150 lines, and "is marked as a fragment [in its title] because it has been excerpted from the longer poem, but it is not, therefore, incomplete" (E. Brontë, *Complete Poems*, ed. Gezari, 238). Gezari's own wavering in the double negative—"not . . . incomplete"—perhaps alerts us to a characteristic feature of the fragment form, which meditates often self-consciously on the nature of completion as such, as Gezari observes (*Last* 79–105). In keeping with this thematic concern with irresolution, while the published poem posits the prisoner's faith in a future closure of redemption, the manuscript version (E. Brontë, *Poems*, eds. Roper and Chitham, 176–81) discloses what has been chopped away and added to give this effect. The final stanza of the published version was newly composed (E. Brontë, *Poems*, eds. Roper and Chitham, 269), and seals into unity a larger dialogic conversation between "Julian M" and

"A.G. Rochelle"—two Gondal characters—who assert "never-doubting love" and "unswerving constancy" (l. 151), but not before Julian asks, "What rest could soothe—what peace could visit me / While she lay pining there for Death to set her free?" (ll. 212–22). In this way does the fuller, manuscript version of the poem dynamize and render ironic the redemptive, Christianized closure apparently offered in the published "Prisoner."

What is a fragment, anyway? Often associated with "heterogeneity, plurality, and so forth," as Rodolphe Gasché writes in his introduction to Schlegel, the fragment in its Romantic iteration works to imagine a totality that it does not, as a rule, instantiate: fragments encipher a lost whole and mark this whole as absent (vii). It helps to clarify this point to observe that the fragment is meaningfully compared to the ruin. In canonical accounts of these two key Romantic motifs, ruins are understood to presume a recognized discrepancy between a prior imagined wholeness and the partial fragment in front of us: this relation of part to whole is conceptualized under the rubric of loss and, often, in an "endeavor of retrieval" (Rajan 4). Whether construed spatially, as in a fragment, or temporally, as in the ruin, both modes arguably reassert totality as the operative register of final meaning; more consequentially, in affective terms they valorize the broken, smashed, or unfinished, non-dialectically *refusing wholeness* in ways that simply invert the aesthetic priorities of normative bourgeois aesthetics in which, as Naomi Schor has argued, sublime totalities subsume beautiful particulars (3–18). Such heroic recapturing of the anti-heroic simply transvalues the negative term into a positive one, turning the bad thing good, and will be familiar to us from Nietzsche, male modernism, and certain modalities of climate writing today. It is a species of what Schor identifies as the masculine takeover of historically feminized modes (the detailed, the fragmentary, the small), a transvaluation that "leav[es] the masculine and its prerogatives intact" (116).[23]

Examples of the fragment Brontë would have known include Coleridge's "Kubla Khan," Byron's *The Giaour* and *Don Juan*, Keats's "Hyperion: A Fragment," or Shelley's *Triumph of Life*. Brontë read Byron's *The Giaour: A Fragment of a Turkish Tale*, in July 1839 and "intensely experienced" it (Roper, "Introduction," 9). She was not alone, of course, even if belated: Francis Jeffrey observed in 1813 that "the taste for fragments . . . has become very general" (quoted in Allport 414), with nearly innumerable examples of the form appearing in the early decades of the century. Andrew Allport gives some sense of how solidly conventional this genre had become by the late Romantic period, listing out titles like "The Suicide, A Fragment" and "The Future: A Fragment" so as to note their essential interchangeability: these poems "often" feature a dying speaker while "others" reflect on the inevitability of death (Allport 415).

While indicating something factually true at a practical level, namely that the version of "The Prisoner" published in 1846 was excerpted from a larger, earlier entry in the Gondal saga (E. Brontë, *Complete Poems*, ed. Gezari, 237; E. Brontë, *Poems*, eds. Roper and Chitham, 269), the addition of "(A Fragment)" to the title of "The Prisoner" can also be seen as formalizing the poem's membership in this stable or relatively stable generic set. The parenthetical label marks the poem's exchangeability with other examples of a category, even as the poem itself emphasizes the sense of containment that follows from such acts of conceptual enclosure, where the "wings" of "inward essence" strain to be "almost free" (ll. 50–51). The detail suggests Brontë construing capture in physical and literary-aesthetic terms at once, drawing a relation between material constraint and the literary forms that would document this bondage.

I recapitulate this account of the so-called RFP microgenre because the suspension of closure on which this form meditates is among the most salient structural features of Brontë's poetry, as readers like Gezari have observed. John Maynard emphasizes Brontë's persistent rhetoric of "incompletion" and suggests how the poems "dar[e] the reader to imagine consummation" (201). The speaker of "The Philosopher," to take another example, imagines that strife will "close" with death, a crisis to be followed by "repose"—the consummation of this Christianized closure further secured by rhyme (ll. 54–56). But this completion is not guaranteed but wished for: "Oh, let me die" (l. 53). Until then, repose is suspended, resolution delayed. As in "The Prisoner" above, the intermittent quotation marks of "The Philosopher" confuse the question of who is saying what (E. Brontë, *Poems*, eds. Roper and Chitham, 265), making it impossible to tell who is the addressee and who the addressed, which positions which; the result is an oscillating motion of conceptual locations "within this little frame / . . . . warring night and day" (ll. 17–18). The poem's alternate or original title, "penciled at the head of the poem, apparently in Emily Brontë's hand," is "The philosopher's conclusion" (E. Brontë, *Complete Poems*, ed. Gezari, 233n). But in the poem, conclusion stands as both horizon and impossibility, closure itself now operating as a kind of vanishing dream: "an endless search, and always wrong!" (l. 44).

As we saw, in addition to their often inscrutable writerly marks, Brontë's manuscripts include drawings, symbols, and notations, some of them—diamonds, horseshoes—comprising "a private language, its meaning now obscure" (Lutz, *Cabinet*, 159). Some of the small sheets scrawled with pen marks could scarcely have been legible to the author herself, given that Emily's handwriting appears "to approach the asemic" (Lutz, *Cabinet*, 299). One need not be tempted into a normative evaluation of penmanship to see that the "not only very small but badly formed" script (Roper, "Introduction," 20) does not resolve immediately into legibility; there is speculation it was written this way to elude surveillance, as a secret idiom or encrypted speech. As Roper observes of one holograph fragment, "the n, r, and the u are almost interchangeable, and some letters, especially the e, are often so small as virtually to disappear. The t is not always crossed and the m often has a spiky crown, so that in several places one can only tell from the sense of the passage whether Emily wrote 'thy' or 'my'; and the sense is not always decisive" ("Introduction" 20). But if we can bear to suspend our preference for decisiveness, the inscriptions counted as bad penmanship by Roper and unscannable by OCR data-harvesting software might instead become legible as conceptually consequential refusals to specify. Brontë's asemic orthography is one mechanism by which these scripted performances decline to complete the circuit of verificationist communication they set into motion.[24]

Were they props for the Gondal characters, physically tiny to match the scale of the famous dolls gifted to the children by Patrick? Or was their physical slightness part of a practice of encipherment meant to render these productions effectively private (Lutz, "Paper Work," 295), an "open secret," in Anne-Lise François's term for modes of partial articulation that slip the trap of "the mind's own will to seize" (xvii–xviii)? Given that the diary papers she traded with Anne were also folded minutely, and fitted into a tin box two inches long, could the smallness itself be a kind of code (Lutz, "Paper Work," 300)? Are they simply . . . bad, in the sense of messy or pointless? Or unfinished in the simple sense that she meant to complete them, but didn't? The archive will not allow conclusions. What we can appreciate is how these self-consciously minor things, tiny in size and sub-heroic in physical amplitude, nevertheless treat topics of vast and seemingly universal scale: through them course images of prisons, cages, and chains while the words *liberty* and *freedom* rush like a current, even while all this content remains rigorously denuded of even the most basic context, physical or otherwise.

There is no setting, hardly any world. Whatever material action transpires in them happens in a poetic scene evacuated of concrete specificity. Yet as manuscripts the objects themselves are characterized most by precisely that: a fragile physicality that has caused generation after generation of critics to refer to them as relics. In the hand it is true their slightness is overwhelming, as their vulnerability as objects becomes palpable in the grain of torn rag paper or the smudge of graphite or ink. But my suggestion is that this vulnerability should not be viewed in the half-light of an auratic or quasi-religious mythos, since to do so would be to script these objects into yet another grid of comprehension and capture. Instead I am offering this slightness as an epistemological strategy: a form of presentation at odds with masculine maximalisms and their implicitly imperialist heroic scales, aslant too from strategies of smoothly efficient communication and the frictionless transfer of information from subject to object, even while (as I am suggesting here) the poems refuse to abandon the projects of *freedom* or *liberty* I am arguing are associated with those modes.

This dynamic of almost simultaneous proposal and withdrawal helps bring into thinkability a program of immanent critique, whereby the very terms that enable communication—generic convention, lyric assertion, lexical denotation itself—are subjected to a de-monumentalizing internal disruption, torn apart but left in broken form, still, to signify. A case in point is the untitled scrap that begins "I am the only being whose doom," numbered 85 in Gezari's Penguin edition (1992) and 49 in Roper and Chitham's *The Poems of Emily Brontë* (1995).[25] Roper and Chitham's fuller transcription also includes the date, May 17, 1839, one instance of Brontë habit of preserving a given writing's original moment of composition even after re-transcribing it multiple times over periods of years, the time-stamped "present of . . . inscription" trailing the recopied text like a ghost (Derrida, "Signature," 317).

In printed versions, "I am the only being whose doom" unfolds in regular tetrameter quatrains with an ABAB rhyme scheme, the seemingly simple cadence reinforcing Brontë's characteristically short lines and trademark monosyllabism—a tactically deceptive simplicity that will recur in chapter 5, in Christina Rossetti's similarly plainspoken verse. Here, Brontë's lilt becomes uncanny when, in the first line, "being" scans not as two beats (be-ing) but one:

> I am the only being whose doom
> No tongue would ask no eye would mourn
> I've never caused a thought of gloom
> A smile of joy since I was born.
>
> (ll. 1–4)

From this dark opening the poem continues to describe how "this changeful life has slipped away / As friendless after 18 years." The ungendered speaker is "as lone" now "as on my natal day" (ll. 6–7).

This total withdrawal from the social system, where early hope "melted off" and "Fanceys rainbow fast withdrew" (*sic*, ll. 17–18), leads to a final observation that approaches something like total negation:

> T'was greif enough to think mankind
> All [hollow] searvile insincere
> But worse to trust to my own mind
> And find the same corruption there
>
> (ll. 21–24)

This self-abolishing conclusion sets its terms of address at the widest possible scale only to fold back on the speaker and "find the same corruption there." The slant rhyme of "insincere" and "there" again confirms not just Emily's nonstandard regional dialect, in which phonetic spellings "correspond to speech around Haworth then as now" (E. Brontë, *Poems*, eds. Roper and Chitham, 278) and deviate from what is called received pronunciation; it also shows that the "mind" of the speaker is no less structured by "corruption" than anyone else's. The speaker is part of the system (s)he critiques: just as "[hollow] searvile insincere" as those (s)he might criticize. The misspelling of *searvile*, as *sear*, evokes as glitchy whisper the burning and incipiently violent quality, perfectly clear to Emily, of a fallen world in which "mankind" and "my own mind" share the same "corruption."

But the point is that even this reading becomes tendentious when set against the cryptic and inconclusive manuscript. Roper and Chitham's brackets around [hollow] tell us that the reading of this term is contested, with the Oxford editors leaving a set of brackets blank and Gezari supplying "hollow" with no editorial suggestion that it is conjectural. According to Roper and Chitham,

> EB first wrote "All hollow lying insincere." She then deleted the first two adjectives (and the "ll" of "All"), wrote "searvile" above the canceled "lying" and added "Deceitful" in the left-hand margin. "Deceitful" was later heavily deleted. (E. Brontë, *Poems*, eds. Roper and Chitham, 241n)

A glance at the handwritten text, held at Princeton University (figure 15), helps us see why there might be confusion. It is again tiny, between 22 and 63 millimeters in size, "written in a microscopic hand" (summary description for E. Brontë, "I am the only being whose doom"). The text provides evidence of a composition that is minor in physical size and gestural in execution, even as it locates these apparently private doings in relation to

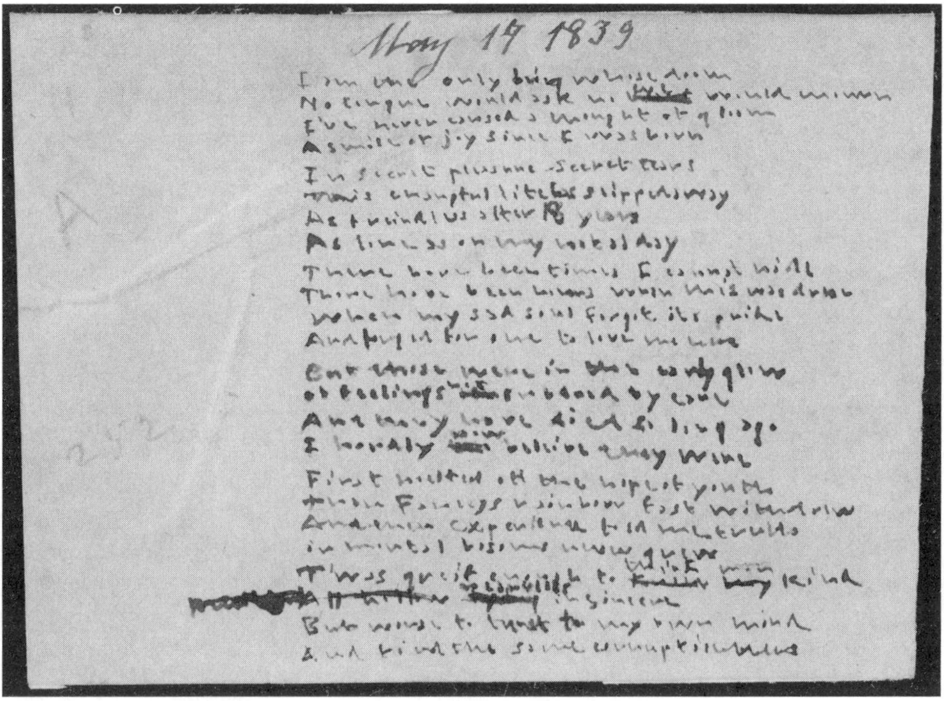

FIGURE 15. Emily Brontë, "I am the only being whose doom" (1837–1839). Ink on paper. Special Collections, Princeton University Libraries, Princeton, NJ. Photograph: Special Collections, Princeton University Libraries.

what the lines style as the corruption of an entire world. The entire performance, corrupt in spelling and insincere in its apparent conventionality, works against the very templates of poetic expression that enable it to signify in these terms. By these aesthetic means the verse meditates on the predicament of immanence by which a speaker might be both a critic of a "searvile" world and a participant in it, even while torquing from within the inherited grammar that enables this very meditation. Even these dynamics are finally unavailable to full reconstruction: [hollow] (figure 16).

In his late-career lectures, Roland Barthes refers to the "sidestepping" of "affirmation" that could "occur right at the level of language" (*Neutral* 44). He refers to "the (philosophical) critique of 'it is'" that would suspend the tendency toward affirmative imposition inherent in predication as grammatical mechanism (*Neutral* 45). *I am, I say, I argue,* are all cognate forms of this affirmative form. Barthes instantly adds, however, that any effort to do away with the fundamental linguistic copula can only fail. Predication sits at the core of all Western languages, and given that

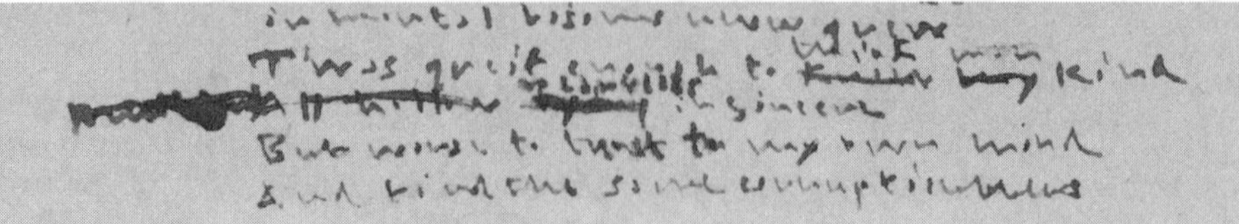

FIGURE 16. Emily Brontë, "I am the only being whose doom" (1837–1839) (detail of final stanza). Ink on paper. Special Collections, Princeton University Libraries, Princeton, NJ. Photograph: Special Collections, Princeton University Libraries.

writing is assertive in its very DNA, Barthes observes, "the best remains to accept it stoically, 'tragically': to speak, to write, and to hold still about the wound of affirmation" (*Neutral* 45, emphasis added). I am suggesting that this wound or injury of the affirmative mode is what Brontë tends to in her tangled and hard-to-parse manuscript writing. In the larger context of this book's efforts to imagine improvisation within corrupted habits of mind and broken physical systems, Brontë's practice stands as model for an improvised poetics of semi-articulation, a sabotage thought fully entangled in the structures it would work against. It speaks without hope of pure escape or final freedom, reworking languages it knows to be at best hollow and perhaps ruined too. One measure of the success of Brontë's efforts is that they have proven so vexing to later editors attempting to extract sense and profit from her literary remains.

Now is the time to note that a theme in early critical evaluations of the poetry suggested that Brontë didn't know what she was doing: that despite her theoretical mind and imperious will—an overweening sense of purpose and self-assurance, so the legends all say—she nevertheless composed without any conscious design or design at all. Charlotte's note to *Wuthering Heights* offers by way of excuse the idea that Emily "did not know what she had done" in creating characters like Heathcliff and Catherine ("Preface" 308). "She was not an artist," judged C. Day Lewis in 1957, "in the sense of a writer preoccupied with problems of form, whose material is under control and who knows more or less what he is doing with it" (85). The masculine pronoun, while conventional, helps us see the gendered priorities of the volitional understanding of consciousness Charlotte and Lewis share across nearly a century of time. From within this vocabulary, the way to rescue Brontë from the charge that she was insufficiently "preoccupied," not "under control," and didn't "know more or less what [she] is doing," would be to say that she *did* have control, *was* preoccupied, did *know what she was doing*—a tactic taken by several feminist interpreters recently.

But we need not so quickly reaffirm the voluntarist framework by which will and consciousness are construed as prerequisites for creative activity. As we will see in fuller terms in the next two chapters, consequential creative elaboration need not emerge in scenarios where isolable subjects perform voluntary deeds on identifiable objects. Instead it can emerge from gestures and interactive movements within structure: such microscaled elaborations or feedback arrangements rarely count as action in the utilitarian matrices underwriting conventional logics of the deed. In the lower-intensity model I am testing here, new beginnings can emerge not from sovereign will or directed consciousness but through the somatic work of elaboration in relation to other bodies.

Thrustful Sorts

We've seen already that the itinerary leading from the pigeonholes of Emily's portable writing desk to the most recent critical editions is a record of conjectural readings, imposed standards, enclosure, and actual fraud, with some pieces scattered in archives and private collections and many others lost or sold forever into private hands. A full engagement with the main protagonists of the story of how the poetry was "discovered" and turned to profit is beyond the scope of this writing, but a glance helps outline the system of aspirationally total capture into which Brontë's work has intervened since her death.

One key character, Thomas Wise, was a forger and a thief, who set up the Ashley Library at the British Museum and much of the Ransom Collection in Texas, where his acquisitions on behalf of one John H. Wrenn were purchased with banking and brokerage money (Oram), and eventually secured for the University of Texas by one George W. Littlefield with cash originating in cattle, dry goods, and, ultimately, plantations worked by the enslaved (Gracy). In the 1890s Wrenn began deputizing Wise to acquire culture on his behalf. Wise, who would say Wrenn "was worth £1000 a year to me" due to the volume of acquisitions he commissioned (quoted in Oram 323), counterfeited first editions of Arnold and Tennyson and cut out pages from Renaissance books to fill his own collection. In 1895, just two years after the founding of the Brontë Society, which Wise chaired, the now-infamous figure deputized his friend Clement Shorter to visit Charlotte Brontë's widower, Arthur Bell Nicholls, in Ireland, where for four hundred pounds he secured "a brown paper parcel full of manuscripts and letters by the Brontë children." In a note he lies by saying Nicholls "lent" them to him (Shorter vi). Shorter himself was, says a later account, "not a man to be easily abashed; he was of the determined, thrustful sort"

(Partington 114). Someone else called him a "pusher," "a man who was always making other men do what they did not want to do" (quoted in Partington 114).

Having got the material from Shorter, Wise would later split the manuscripts up and sell them, often fraudulently, sometimes passing off Branwell's less marketable poems as Emily's, as in one sheaf of Emily's manuscript poetry now held at the Morgan Library, whose Morocco gilt cover gives the title: "Four poems and one prose fragment by Emily J Brontë," but which, the museum now admits, is actually "by Branwell Brontë" ("Autograph Manuscripts"). A dissertation by Patricia Ayrton provides a flowchart tracing the history of these textual commodities and their circulation from one man to another in chains of industrialists and buying agents and philanthropists. In the hands of these con men and thrustful sorts, Brontë's inassimilable fragments did indeed become assimilated.

In tension with this unrelenting process of capture, I have suggested that the poem-objects we have encountered so far put into practice and in turn demand what I will call minoritarian attention: a way of observing the object world in general and artworks in particular that attends to moments of unscripted movement within rule-bound systems, local elaborations within larger-scaled orders of intelligibility. It is at these subdominant registers of intervention that, for Brontë, the grandest world-historical and metaphysical problems play out. Improvised movements of pen and hand; tiny motions of body and mind together: little things. As I will suggest in coming chapters, these glitches in the smooth running of the world open spaces through which new relations and concrete struggles might take shape. Now I am observing that these low-intensity gestures constitute material interventions into the given grammar of the world: they transform mental movement into physical act and leave the world different than it was before, if just ever so slightly. This insistence on the recessively world-tweaking capacity of tiny poems may feel aestheticizing or fetishistic, part of an involuted lyricism familiar from the Romanticist readerly modes I have reworked here. But it is key to the argument of the book that Brontë's experiments are not private at all, but instead test material circuitries by which an expansive practice of solidarity might take shape.

Wholey Lone

In 1834, Charlotte was still more than a decade away from creating one of literary fiction's most powerful first-person narrators in *Jane Eyre*. But the literary forms of bourgeois personhood had interested her from the outset, as juvenilia like "The Last Will and Testament of Florence Marian Wellesley" (1834) helps confirm. Given that the will is the generic location where personhood and property become indistinguishable, Charlotte's work in drawing up the doll-sized legal document reveals her experimenting early on with the genres proper to bourgeois individualism in its full legal and social senses. Here the legal regime of property folds together with the presumption that a will will express the will of its author in a direct or unmediated account of intention. (The next chapter explores *Middlemarch*'s own incessant punning on this word, as it undercuts the persistent fiction of *will* in bourgeois self-descriptions.) In Charlotte's early fictional will, Wellesley bequeaths diamond rings, pearl ornaments, "gold-tipt case of scented waters," and "the gold chain, three yards in length, which is braided with seed pearls and forms part of the bird of paradise headdress" ("Last Will" 318), all of these building to the main event, "the whole of that estate in Wellington's Land, value ten thousand per annum, left me by my mother" ("Last Will" 319).

I read Charlotte's childhood document as sharing a fundamental presumption about personhood with the novel that would later make her famous, *Jane Eyre*: a commitment, nascent even in these early experiments, to what Gayatri Spivak glosses as "feminist individualism in the age of imperialism" ("Three Women's Texts" 244). From within this protocol of understanding, *bildung* can be understood as the growing-into personal sovereignty that sees Jane move from object to subject, from victim of circumstance to self-assured narrator of her own story, where—in a framework of liberal-feminist understanding to be explored in this book's final chapter—she has "found her voice." As ever, this movement into subjecthood is evident at the level of syntax, entire epistemologies coded into prose. At the outset there is "*no possibility* of taking a walk that day," but the end of the novel unfolds in the famously direct predication by which Jane becomes subject and her man the object: "Reader, I [S] married [V] him [O]."

Against such clean vectors of causality, Emily's poetry coils and falls in on itself. I close this chapter with a final uncategorizable performance, "And like myself lone wholey lone," which operates at sub-grammatical scale to unwind the orthodox predication at the heart of *Jane Eyre*. Emily's performance opens up the individualist mechanisms of regular grammar to disruptive but incomplete rearticulation. At four and a half inches tall the scrap is among the larger of Emily's loose-leaf poems and is bizarrely inscribed with Anne's name, at the bottom right, though the handwriting is almost certainly Emily's. It frames a question about identity in the first line, the speaker noting that he or she is "like" myself, but not. Note the spelling of "wholey," which will become important (figure 17).

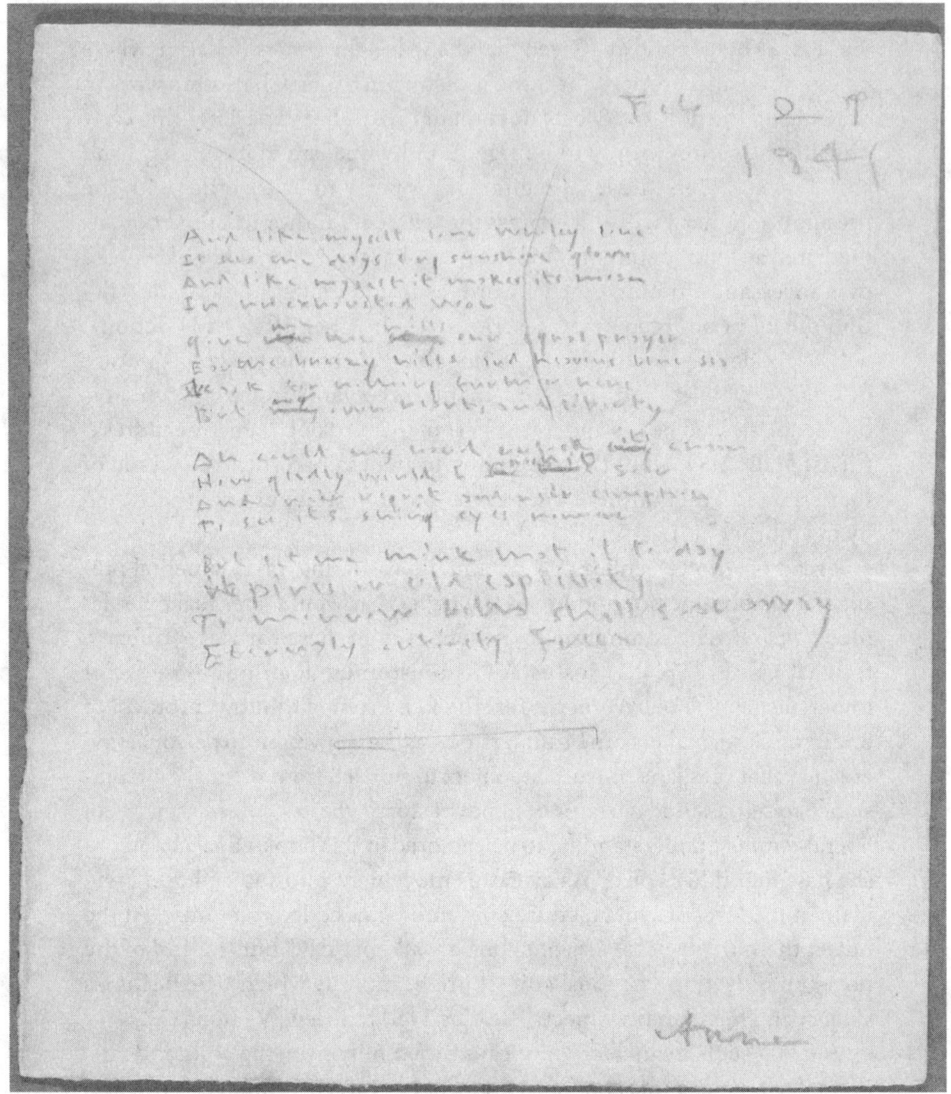

FIGURE 17. Emily Brontë, "And like myself lone wholey lone" (1841). Pencil on paper. Henry W. and Albert A. Berg Collection of English and American Literature, New York Public Library. Photograph: New York Public Library.

As Hatfield notes in his 1941 edition, the title "The Caged Bird" was added to this fragment in 1915 by one A. C. Benson in an edition that advertised its "conjectural emendations" as a selling point (quoted in Ayrton 154). But this explanatory title is nowhere in the manuscript and the poem mentions no cage, only a "chain" (l. 9). The poem describes what appears to be the speaker's imaginative experience of releasing a bird from bondage: a hawk, perhaps, like the one the family kept as a pet, but in any case a site of the speaker's "total" identification, in Juliet Barker's words (quoted in E. Brontë, *Poems*, eds. Roper and Chitham, 251). "Ah could my hand unlock its chain / How gladly would I whach it soar" (ll. 9–10, *sic*). Even many of those editions, like Gezari's, that do not introduce false punctuation into the poem persist in normalizing Brontë's spelling, transforming *whach* to *watch* and the title line from *wholey* to *wholely*, or (in both the Hatfield and Gezari editions) *wholly*. These edits resolve the latter into an adverb when it started as an ambiguous mix of adverb and adjective. Brontë's *wholey* leaves grammatical resolution unfixed while encoding as seeming spelling error the oscillation between totality and negation that the poem is also, in its content, about: it freezes into agrammatical phoneme the situation by which something can be both fully itself and absolutely nothing, whole and hole.[26]

Hatfield's edition gives a list of words Emily spelled in strange ways, "peculiarities which it was not considered expedient to perpetuate in print" and lists "wholey" among them (E. Brontë, ed. Hatfield, 22, 23). Roper and Chitham note the by-now-obvious point that "EB's spelling is neither consistent nor orthodox" (E. Brontë, *Poems*, eds. Roper and Chitham, 278) and offer "Some Unusual Spellings" as an appendix, which includes this one. The editorial transformation of *wholey* into *wholly* in nearly all available editions forces affirmative signification onto a poetic performance that works inside the epistemological presumptions of bourgeois language to stretch that idiom into other shapes. But it is not just a word game. This is the second stanza:

Give we the hills our equal prayer
Earths breezy hills and heavens blue sea
I ask for nothing further here
But my own heart, and liberty

(ll. 5–8)

Modern editions disagree on how to read the second word. For Hatfield and Gezari it is "we," while for Barker, Roper and Chitham, and earlier editions, it is "me" (figure 18). The otherwise-pointless editorial disagreement matters because it testifies to the poetry's own refusal to decide between two exclusive and, I want now to suggest, consequential pronomial forms: the first-person objective pronoun, me, and the third person subjective pronoun, we. Solitary or mutual, then? Substance or relation? Subject or object?

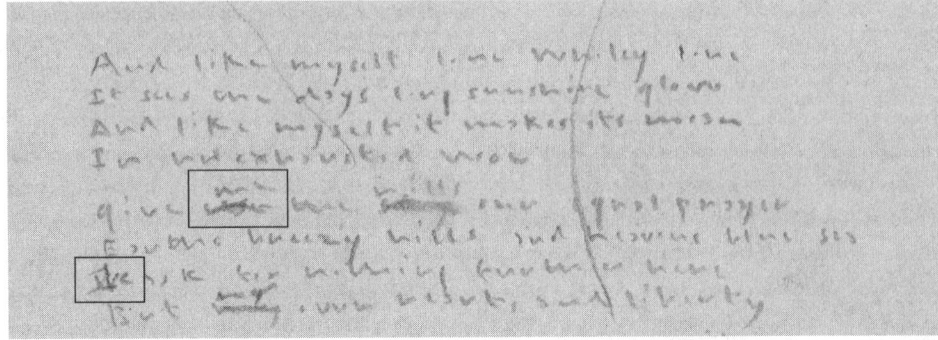

FIGURE 18. Emily Brontë, "And like myself lone wholey lone" (1841) (detail, boxes added). Pencil on paper. Note the cancelled "we/me" (line 5) and "I/we" (line 7). Henry W. and Albert A. Berg Collection of English and American Literature, New York Public Library. Photograph: New York Public Library.

In the manuscript, there's a cancelation or an overwriting, and faded handwritten gestures refuse to resolve into conclusion, leaving the question of *we* or *me* undecided. Two lines below this act of semi-specification, in the phrase, "I ask for nothing further here," the "I" is written directly on top of a "we," without apparent cancelation. The apparent error again functions as conceptual hinge, since, as Roper concedes, "the changes in pronouns" in this poem "play out the whole question of the relation of speaker to bird, one fundamental to the interpretation of the poem" (Roper, "Introduction," 21).

In the context of the claims I am tracking here, Brontë's spectacular overcoding freezes mutually exclusive pronouns, and the historical ontologies they stand in for, into unresolved asemic relation: the first-person logic of bourgeois personhood sits on top of, or underneath, or with, the plural collective: *I, we,* and *me* folding together into a single term. It is crucial that in this de-grammared performance, personhood and its appropriate lexes are not "dissolved," transcended, or done away with, as in neoromantic calls for posthuman assemblage and horizontal ontology popular among ecocritics today. Instead they remain as a problem: the *me-we, I-we* tension is here positioned as unfinished dilemma at the center of the poem's performance—"fundamental," Roper said, to this poem in which the inability to act sits at the heart of its meditation on liberty. "Ah *could* my hand unlock its chain / How gladly would I whach it soar" (ll. 9–10).

Against a tradition that continues to understand freedom as the sovereign absence of interference, Brontë conceives hands unable to work and beings locked together. This effort to redescribe freedom as a condition not outside restriction but dialectically related to it imagines these two positions, freedom and subjection, as oscillating with one another in an irresolvable analog relation. It is significant, I am suggesting, that this writing refuses to abandon the vocabulary of freedom bequeathed by the liberal tradition even as it labors by microstylistic means to unwork this vocabulary from the inside. This process of immanent recoding discloses freedom to be most possible at its moments of suspension and erasure, not in completion but as the dream of a language that might emerge from the ruins of predication itself. "Eternaly entirely Free—" she writes, erroneously (l. 16).

In an argument that remains persuasive for many on the left, Alain Badiou frames his conception of metapolitics against what he derides as "micropolitics," part of a trend among left-masculine theorists of the Jacobin set to fetishize revolutionary processes while denigrating sub-revolutionary action as at best delusional and at worst aimed at maintaining the status quo. But the Leninist fascination with the trope of revolutionary action has been recoded or twisted in the age of climate breakdown and—as I've already suggested—becomes visible now as fantasy-formation rather than strategy. Transposed into the local context of climate activism, this tendency to construe the only possible forms of action as *open* and *obvious* and *spectacular* is part of what Anahid Nersessian describes as the "mass idealization of the unrestrained and inexhaustibly available" (*Utopia* 12): a utopianism of more and all against which she positions "a vocabulary of restraint" (6), adjustment, and "low-impact aesthetics" (12). Likewise does François contest "the normative bias" toward measurable action at political scale by articulating a call for a "reticent assertion" that articulates possibility in minor notes (xvi, xix). In this way could an embrace of the constraint that enables all activity help dissolve the persistent fixation on purity that informs a politics of unfettered will and completed projects. Such a refocused attention might then locate real freedom in improvisatory movements within otherwise determining social and aesthetic contexts, languages we did not invent but must use anyway. Such a reconfigured theory of liberty might "marr[y] the generic to the improvisatory" (Nersessian, *Utopia,* 6), scaling down the ladder of action toward the pared-down forms of freedom possible inside systems designed to foreclose it.

At a moment when the mechanisms of capture, co-optation, and seizure have approached universal status, the language of overturning and structural renovation is ever more out of touch with the entrenched systemic crises we inhabit. In such a conjuncture the prospects of total erasure and epic restarting take on the status of the fever dream: they are not road maps for practice. Against Badiouian yearnings for the total event and listicles of climate action developed by well-meaning academics or petrochemical PR firms, I am suggesting with Brontë a turn toward downscaled visions of the consequential. This turn would shift us away from total renovation and unit-based action-inputs and toward what James C. Scott, in an argument I elaborate in the next chapter, calls infrapolitical activity: low-amplitude and often illegible performances invisible from within the terms of the great-men-and-revolution histories still so persuasive to even our most committed climate radicals today.[27]

In a poem called "Hope," written when she was nearly dead, Brontë in characteristic fashion struck a note halfway between the title term and its opposite, which she more often than not spelled "dispair" (E. Brontë, *Poems*, eds. Roper and Chitham, 279). Her spelling recodes the classic mood of solipsistic male Romanticism in terms of broken unions and dissolved bonds, dis-pairing; the gesture opens out by negation the idea that future-oriented practice emerges when beings are, in a strong sense, together. It is in no sense cheerful: "She would sing while I was weeping," Brontë's speaker says of a personified Hope. "If I listened, she would cease." To recover this sort of contaminated possibility, this ghosted hope is, I think, to locate in Brontë's minoritarian and I will say feminist project the seeds of a knowledge strategy adequate to a world undergoing physical breakdown. *Middlemarch* will help us consider how such vanishingly small effects might gather, join, and matter. In place of closing rhetorical summation, I offer a final scrap of someone else's writing, very small. It is written on a torn piece of mourning paper, on the back of something else, and marked with a date. The only words, smudged and without terminal punctuation, say: "my task is done" (figure 19).

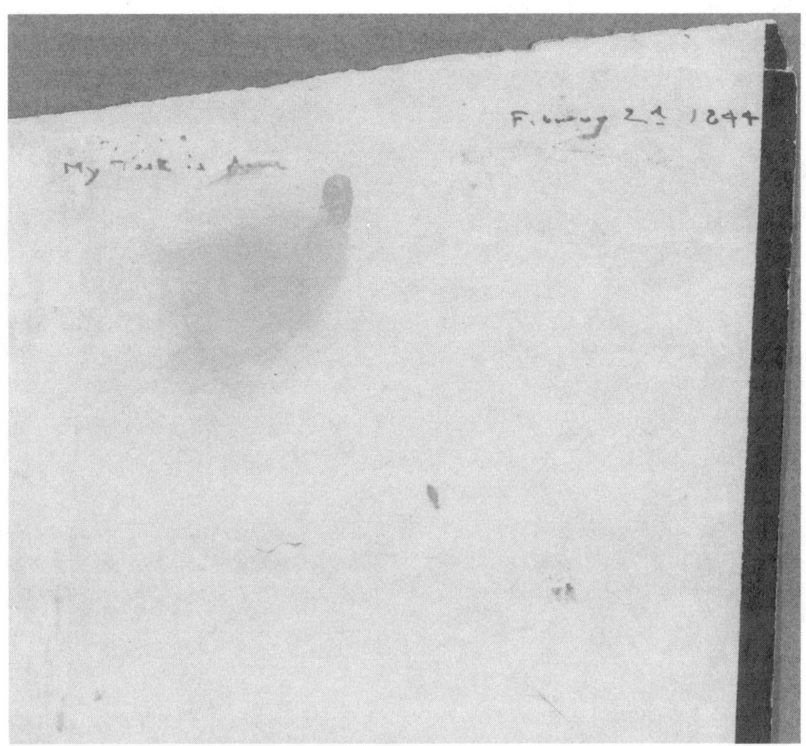

FIGURE 19. Emily Brontë, "My task is done" (1844). Smudged ink on mourning paper. Henry W. and Albert A. Berg Collection of English and American Literature, New York Public Library. Photograph: New York Public Library.

PART III

The Counterextractive Gesture

4
Feedback, Adjustment, Gesture

MIDDLEMARCH

> Now, suppose that I pick up a lead pencil. To do this, I have to move certain muscles. However, for all of us but a few expert anatomists, we do not know what these muscles are; and even among the anatomists, there are few, if any, who can perform the act by a conscious willing in succession of the contraction of each muscle concerned. On the contrary, what we will is to pick the pencil up. Once we have determined on this, our motion proceeds in such a way that we may say roughly that the amount by which the pencil is not yet picked up is decreased at each stage. This part of the action is not in full consciousness.
>
> —Norbert Wiener, *Cybernetics, or Control and Communication in the Animal and the Machine* (1948, 1961)

> 1st Gent. Our deeds are fetters that we forge ourselves.
> 2nd Gent. Ay, truly: but I think it is the world / That brings the iron.
>
> —George Eliot, epigraph to chapter IV, *Middlemarch* (1871–1872)

Prelude

In George Eliot's great novel about limitation, *Middlemarch* (1871–1872), a grandly titled "Prelude" and "Finale" bookend the dramatic action. Labeled with terms lifted from the symphony or an opera, these moments of metacommentary are set off from the plot proper and serve to underscore the novel's main purpose or what we might call—ventriloquizing the commodified language of capitalism and the new university—its takeaways. Quasi-musically, then, these bracketing sections gather into concentration this vast work's many plots or harmonic lines and distill them into the novelistic equivalent of major theme.[1] As Eliot confided to her journal in March 1871, "My present fear is that I have too much matter—too many *momenti*" (quoted in Haight, *George Eliot*, 433). Insofar as the "Prelude" and "Finale" work as discursive frames to secure the unity of these *momenti*, they help signal to readers what the point might be of a novel that otherwise, without these acts of extradiegetic totalization, might seem overly invested in detail, just so many independent particulars joined together without central purpose.[2] Like epigrams, then, preludes and finales help gather diverse instances into a conceptual structure that has, at least, the flattering illusion of concentric arrangement.[3]

To the mind outfitted for capture, such things are helpful. Headlines are useful, summaries handy. And from within a cognitive apparatus that has been shaped around the goals of clarity and utility, a concentric arrangement will always seem like order.[4] But *every limit is a beginning as well as an ending* (779), every moment of delimitation a kind of false containment. This fact means among other things that the tension between minor detail and overarching theme evident in the basic structure of *Middlemarch*—a friction between particular instances and the concept-forms that would contain and subordinate them—is not "solvable" but instead a constitutive dynamic of all knowledge-making. In addition to being built into the structure of the novel, this dynamic is also, as I suggested by citing the famous first sentence of Eliot's finale just now, among its core epistemological concerns and principles of formal organization.

Critics like Gillian Beer and Catherine Gallagher have long noted *Middlemarch*'s preoccupation with the movement between category and instance, type and example. In its obsessive tracking of "the arc of induction and deduction, deduction and induction," Gallagher notes, the novel almost always reasserts the particular, concrete instance as the site of ethical and epistemological consequence, positioning such details against the masculine knowledge projects that would gather such idiosyncratic particulars into distorting uniformity. This prioritization of specificity helps make Eliot "the nineteenth-century novelist who is most skeptical about categorical thought" (Gallagher 63) and links her project to what Naomi Schor calls the feminist task of "asserting the detail's claim to aesthetic dignity and epistemological prestige," even when the final goal must always be the dissolution of the gendered paradigm by which specificity is minoritized as feminine in the first place (xlvi). And if *Middlemarch* recognizes that the movement from instance to category is one domain in which the cognitive infrastructure of a functionally patriarchal bourgeois society finds shape, there is nevertheless—and this the novel also suggests—no escape from it, and I do not escape it here.[5]

Here is a moment of thematization. To this point I have sketched the story of the extractive episteme or ecocidal reason from its origins in monoculture sugar plantations worked by the enslaved, through the bourgeois century that is the focus of my own training and into the

PLATE 1. Kincade Fire, California (October 24, 2019). Photograph: © Associated Press.

PLATE 2. Joseph Mallord William Turner, *Rockets and Blue Lights (Close at Hand) to Warn Steamboats of Shoal Water* (1840) (detail). Oil on canvas. Clark Art Institute, Williamstown, MA (1955.37). Photograph: Clark Art Institute.

PLATE 3. "One Framed Palette, Owned by Joseph Mallord William Turner, Labelled 'Used at Chelsea'" (n.d.). Tate Gallery, London (7315.5). Photograph: © Tate Gallery.

PLATE 4. Joseph Mallord William Turner, *Keelmen Heaving In Coals by Moonlight* (1835) (detail). Oil on canvas. Widener Collection (1942.9.86), National Gallery of Art, Washington, DC. Photograph: National Gallery of Art.

PLATE 5. The structure of delusion. Edmund J. Sullivan (1900/1922) [untitled]. From Alfred, Lord Tennyson, *Maud: A Melodrama*, illustrated by Edmund J. Sullivan (London: Macmillan, [1900] 1922): 37. Booth Family Center for Special Collections, Georgetown University Library, Washington, DC. Photograph: Gabrielle Nemarich.

PLATE 6. William Berryman, Untitled/ Unfinished [*Landscape with Storm*] (between 1808 and 1815). Watercolor and pencil on paper. Library of Congress, Prints and Photographs Division, Washington, DC (96516473). Photograph: Library of Congress.

PLATE 7. William Berryman, *Sugar Estate—Negros* [*sic*] *Cutting Cane* (between 1808 and 1815). Watercolor and black ink. Library of Congress, Prints and Photographs Division, Washington, DC (96516495). Photograph: Library of Congress.

PLATE 8. William Berryman, *Piazza & Stairs at 4 Paths, 2 Negro Children at Work, Jamaica* (between 1808 and 1815). Watercolor, gray ink, pencil. Library of Congress, Prints and Photographs Division, Washington, DC (94508844). Photograph: Library of Congress.

neo-Victorian Great Acceleration that gave birth to the field of "Victorian studies" in the 1950s. This succession of historical waves, I've hinted, has broken with a crash into our present, when collapse is general but no single act seems capable of averting or even slowing what is now an accelerating intersystemic breakdown. Though this story has been about the origins of our broken contemporary, it has also been about causality in the sense that it has focused on capacity: the ability to effect change in a given order of things. As the world heats from carbon accumulated across the periods of this book's focus, the newly attenuated status of the category of action has preoccupied an influential strand of thinking about climate change as a total system.

Reflected in handbooks for reducing waste, listicles about carbon footprints, and laments that nothing can be done, the mass cultural fixation on "climate action" has been articulated conceptually in Bruno Latour's claim that earth systems collapse has defeated the long-established presumption that individual activity, understood as "agency," can create observable change in a given field of possibility. How, he asks, "can we simultaneously be part of such a long history, have such an important influence, and yet be so late in realizing what has happened and so utterly impotent in our attempts to fix it?" ("Agency" 1). While Latour's concern is to expand and complicate the story of action under climate change, his account draws on the political imaginary of the bourgeois system that is culpable in the world's ongoing immolation. That is because however fussed, reworked, and modified, liberalism's romance of personhood survives in Latour's account of actor networks, with the volitional subjectivity of Kant and Locke now reemerging as a power to be "distributed" in a fantasized scene of earth-systemic equilibration, "Gaia" ("Agency" 16; *Facing Gaia*).

As Latour acknowledges and I explore in the coming pages, the Gaia concept comes to him from the cybernetic thinkers about equilibrium and technocratic management of the Cold War period. Here we can see that the apparent incapacity under climate change that results from the network-effect of enmeshment with other beings—Latour calls it "impoten[ce]"—still presumes action to eventuate from sites of individuated activity operating in self-conscious ways. However distributed, hybridized, or assembled, agency remains a capacity enjoyed by isolable actors behaving in voluntary ways. ("To have goals is one essential part of what it is to be an agent" ["Agency" 10].) Latour's unremarked reference to sexual dysfunction in referencing man's new impotence helps underscore that in this inevitably gendered model of action, *will* matches *outcome* in a completed circuit of Kantian intentionality; these measurable, countable deeds can then be construed as inputs, theoretically scaling up to produce effects at the level of the earth system or biosphere. In reverse, this implicitly utilitarian calculus of action fails, and the actors become the acted upon, such that "human societies have resigned themselves to playing the role of the dumb object, while nature has unexpectedly taken on that of the active subject!" ("Agency" 11–12). Sealed with an exclamation mark, this two-term model imports a binary structure from the bourgeois traditions discussed in preceding chapters, reinscribing a utilitarian grammar of action—you do it or it's done to you—in the language of critique.

This chapter develops the book's larger claim about elaboration within failing systems by describing Eliot's efforts to locate sites of possibility within apparently inalterable social and historical scenarios. Redescribing decades of commentary, it locates in tiny touches and local moments of connection alternatives to the models of predication bequeathed to us by the bourgeois tradition. Locating unfree subjects within networks of constraint and mutual interactivity, Eliot's novel opens spaces for construing change beyond the concepts of will, volition, and input that continue to structure a bourgeois imaginary whose material corollary, I have argued, is a depletionary relation to the object world. As will become clear, Eliot's approach is feminist insofar as it construes the social fact of women's subordination as a precondition for elaborating its vision of possibility-within-structure. Against the cue-ball models of utilitarian reckoning in which voluntary subjects do things to passive objects, *Middlemarch* positions relational loops of intersubjective feedback among actors whose most common trait is a relatively subordinate position in a scheme of social domination. Within these circuits, barely perceptible instants of bodily contact stand as the degree zero for what I will call, following anthropologist James C. Scott, infrapolitical sociohistorical change (see *Domination* 183–201). Scott uses the term *infrapolitical* to describe forms of activity that elude orthodox mechanisms of historical reckoning. Narrative and perceptual habits trained on rebellions, riots, and other forms of overt or "properly political" counterhegemonic action—all habitually organized, in critical discourse, under the category of "agency"—simply cannot see sociopolitical effects that fall below a certain threshold of what Scott, like Eliot, understands using the metaphor of visibility.

Such fugitive activities "stop well short of outright collective defiance," Scott says, and often do not look like resistance at all (*Weapons of the Weak* xvi). That's because they transpire, "like infrared rays, beyond the visible end of the spectrum" (*Domination* 183) and are usually feminized. As Scott's accounts suggest, and as later deployments of his idea in Black studies make yet more explicit, such ultraviolet activity will arise in situations when the possibility for effective action at more obvious scales is foreclosed—when the light switch for regular action has been switched off.[6] Infrapolitical activity emerges, that is, at historical conjunctures in which direct frontal assault on the dominant order is not possible, when the "organic" basis of society, as Italian theorist Antonio Gramsci puts it, cannot immediately be altered. Gramsci's term helps distinguish methodologically between the entrenched structural features he describes as organic—"relatively permanent," he calls them"—and the "conjunctural" level at which strategic intervention may still be possible (177–79). Scott's emphasis is on vastly asymmetrical power relationships in colonial zones, but combined with the distinction from Gramsci his insight has consequences for any discussion of "climate action" in the present. As will become clear in dialogue with Eliot's account of delayed change and slow turning, the present situation is one in which effective mass dissent from fossil capitalism or the organized overhaul of the extractive paradigm have not materialized and will not soon. To the contrary, as the horrors of climatological unwinding become more evident, the infrastructural commitments sustaining these processes, and the mechanisms of capture driving them, have only accelerated—despite increasingly visible campaigns of protest and populist refusal.[7]

In an instance already noted in chapter one, Andreas Malm's *How to Blow Up a Pipeline* offers, as its exemplary instance of revolutionary climate action against the total fossil system, the deflating of Swedish SUV tires with pebbles (xx). Seen from the contemporary angle I am arguing for, *Middlemarch* is organized around similarly self-ironizing projects of total action. In the novel, a gathering fossil capitalism may be protested, ineffectually, by "six or seven men in smock-frocks with hay-forks in their hands," who physically threaten the "railroad agents" sent to build the new line soon to traverse previously common lands (*Middlemarch* 523). But the novel's relevance to a now-universal fossil capitalism consists not just in such direct references to the gathering carbon economy but in its treatment of gender and capacity. The most ambitious dreams of potency in *Middlemarch* are proposed by male agents of another sort: the projects of Casaubon, Lydgate, and Ladislaw find their comic foil in Brooke's doomed run for MP, and are figured as alternately pretentious, nobly failed, equivocally positive, or (in Brooke's case) tragicomically pointless. But given that *Middlemarch* is itself a massive "study" concerned avowedly with processes of world-historical change in what Lydgate calls "the entire structure" (139), the novel does not disavow these projects either.[8] Instead it internally repurposes them, in an ultimately reparative process of dialectical negation and restorative conceptual hybridization. By this process, the would-be revolutions of Casaubon's Key to All Mythologies or Lydgate's search for primitive tissue come to function as negative images for the subtler and more intersubjective theory of social-historical gradualism the book itself both explicitly theorizes and performs in its networked formal design.

None of these observations is new. Readers need scarcely be reminded that the novel ends with Dorothea resigned to function as helpmeet for Ladislaw's parliamentary career, "absorbed into the life of another" and "only known in a certain circle as a wife and a mother" (783). To readers conditioned by the liberal-feminist paradigms of agency and autonomy discussed more fully in the next chapter, this movement into mutuality has long stood as a prototypical instance of antifeminist female sacrifice. It is certainly not a triumph. But seen under the aspect of the novel's ironizing evacuation of individualist fantasy, this gutting moment of one life melting into another can also be understood as a model for how new solidarities might be generated among formerly atomized subjects. Such emergent solidarities and the muted forms of capacity they enable are the mechanisms by which what the novel construes as a nearly total carceral structure might be torqued and, in time, overturned. In a world unresponsive to the total gratification of hope, Eliot's novel offers adjustment, intersubjective contact, and minor possibility. To make this claim is merely to redescribe the novel in its own terms and the terms of its best readers.

This chapter revisits the terrain of the previous ones with a difference. It notes how, in *Middlemarch*, barely perceptible or properly unhistoric moments of intersubjective intimacy—too personal to be political, too small seemingly to matter, inevitably feminized—create apertures through which structural change can be elaborated. These not precisely infrared, but instead haptic and microsocial moments of possibility emerge within structures seemingly too vast and entrenched to admit of alteration by other means. Seen in light of the wavelike model of conceptual-material reappearance I described in the introduction, this account of somatic and minoritized possibility in Eliot's great novel enables new relations to emerge between Eliot's mid-Victorian project and later experiments in multifactorial causality developed during the Cold War Great Acceleration. At the far end of these fires, in our burning present, the possibility of an instantaneous transformation in the deep structure of social life has faded, and my gamble is that Eliot's explicitly counterrevolutionary model of limitation and low-intensity adjustment—redescribed, repurposed, and salvaged across its waves of historical reappearance—might be set to use again. Against fantasies of the total and complete, the circumscribed and collective. Let us start small.

The Sum of Human Things

In a throwaway comment in a little-cited scene of *Middlemarch*, the auctioneer Borthrop Trumbull advises residents not to overlook "a very recherchy lot—a collection of trifles for the drawing-room table" (569). It is just a detail. But in commenting on the dusty items, the verbose local worthy makes a quick and obscurely ironized comment on the novel's broader claims for the value of the secondhand and apparently insignificant: "trifles," he explains, "make the sum of human things—nothing more important than trifles" (569). Trumbull's line about the potential importance of the trivial comes during an auction of used or "recherchy" goods that is just one of Eliot's many structural devices for uniting the social circles of the novel's world and suturing what had started as two separate novels. His comment is itself secondhand: a quotation from Hannah More's "Sensibility" (1782), in which More's sentimental cliché is repurposed into the jovial banter of a provincial trying to hawk junk. "Come, Trumbull, this is too bad," says a Mr. Toller, "you've been putting some old maid's rubbish into the sale" (569–70).

But what is an auction, anyway, but a theater in which certain small things, even junk or waste, might acquire fresh importance; where secondhand objects, even tiny ones, could be salvaged from abandonment and redeemed into a kind of consequence? A place, too, as Eliot's careful narration demonstrates, where any number of microscaled and private acts of judgment—evanescent, internal moments of private deliberation—coagulate over the duration of the encounter into something general: a shared social force, say, which then becomes concrete in the quasi-material form of price? As Jean Baudrillard observes of all art auctions, the "dynamic of personal encounter" and "algebra of individuals" in such scenes ensure that the alchemical intersubjective relation of sociality itself is what produces material results (116). On this reading, price is merely a cipher for a whole system of downscaled relations invisible in the purchased object's form of appearance—this coding process being key to the commodity's classic status as a "social hieroglyphic" (Marx 167). It matters that, for Eliot, this social relation is simultaneously economic, social, and stylistic.

The hackneyed quality of Trumbull's repartee, I mean—its goofy clichés and trite joviality—mimics at the level of idiom the dense intersubjectivity of the auction as scene of social interchange. His speech, that is, is itself recycled, or common, or, put another way, fundamentally social. Trumbull's banter thus demonstrates something Lockwood's recycled speech did in chapter 2, while shifting emphasis: where Brontë used generic speech to highlight the tourist's commodified mental infrastructure,

Eliot helps reinforce the not unrelated fact that no speech can ever be entirely "free" of the traces of others, and any utterance is always contaminated or enabled (depending on how you look at it) by the almost endless chains of the ones that came before it. To believe otherwise—as Emily Brontë sometimes seemed to do—is to indulge in a neoromantic fantasy of autonomous creation and pure autarky. Seen this way, cliché, allusion, and citation only radicalize what is true of all language, which is that anything appearing new is but the recast or repurposed form of what others have said before. Recherchy, you could say.

The success of French structuralism in the Anglo-American academy after the 1970s means that readers of this book will likely be familiar with the idea that any idiom is never more than a channeled and reworked *parole* in a *langue* that is (in the words Ferdinand de Saussure uses to describe the delimited structure of a sign-system) "based, in principle, on collective behavior or—what amounts to the same thing—on convention" (647). Saussure's point is not exactly original either: transcribed into notes by unnamed students in the famous Course in General Linguistics of 1906–1911 for publication in 1916, later to be transmuted again, in the midcentury liberalism funded by the Rockefeller Foundation, into Roman Jakobson's more cybernetic idiom of "code" and "message" (Geoghegan 114–15). In this new form, Saussure's distinction between language and speech act would come to structure digital surveillance capitalism and the ideology of algorithmic extraction in the present. These circuits of inheritance will take clearer shape in the pages to come.

In Eliot's novel, meanwhile, a model of discursive circulation allegorized by the auction scene positions adjustment in place of pure novelty, small-scale modifications in lieu of heroic articulations of the never-heard-before. In *Middlemarch*'s densely layered auction scene, any apparently "ingenious article" (569) is but a trifle, or thing of no moment, seen through another, more sensitive angle of appreciation, and vice versa.[9] Like scratches on a polished surface, such trifles do not rise to the level of event, theme, or even really object, at least not one you can see by regular light. They elude the enumerative apparatuses of utilitarian reckoning, sliding through the screens of standard apertures for seeing and counting. Yet as Anahid Nersessian has argued in relation to Romanticism's circumscribed motifs of adjustment, activity need not be total to be real, and a "divestment from regimes of absolute, comprehensive gratification" can open space for smaller-scaled alterations in the structure of the given (*Utopia* 13). In Eliot's novel at least, anything apparently momentous is better understood as an archived repository of almost innumerable forgotten acts of adaptation and internal adjustment. As Daniel Wright observes, the *Middlemarch* narrator insists that "no movement is too minuscule to be registered . . . by the precise vision of the novel when it narrows and magnifies" (*Bad Logic* 128–29). The ethical injunction of the novel is to read with this same intensified sensitivity.

Trumbull is a decent hype-man, and Eliot specifies how bidding on the junky articles he fluffs up advances by way of social consent: the auctioneer uses his "preternatural susceptibility to all signs of bidding" (568) to read and shape the desires of the group whose aggregated judgments will determine the new value of these remaindered objects. The bidding "ran on with warming rivalry" (569), Eliot writes, as the Middlemarchers knit themselves into a collective decision-making body through private acts of valuation and speech. These are best seen not as "acts" in the traditional sense of intentions translated to outcome, nor yet as new beginnings carving a sharp turn from what came before, as Hannah Arendt's definition of action from *The Human Condition* (1958) would require (177–78). Instead, the Middlemarchers' social judgments and expressive gestures can be seen as effects coproduced in relation to other participants in the auction-encounter's mutualized scene of feedback.

Thus does the auction scene, like so many others in the novel, act as microcosm for the larger social-aesthetic experiment of the book, which tracks densely concentrated reciprocities across a vast but artificially contained social grid or system, and aggregates sometimes all-but-indiscernible instants of speech and thought to show how all these, together, might scale up to constitute history at "epic" scale (3). Gossip is one way this process works, auctions another; but the famous metaphors of microscopes and pier glasses, webs and tissues, all likewise underscore the novel's dual investments in downscaled vision and relational form. Approached with a Trumbellesque "preternatural susceptibility" to social "signs," actions that fall below the threshold of normal anthropocentric narrativity can nevertheless be seen as what they are: mutually authored and decisive, if only in the muted, slowly aggregating sense that dispersed and trembled-off events accumulate, over time, in ways that might torque the total system to which they are necessarily immanent. Trumbull's name derives from the Old English word for "strong," but it sounds just like the novel's favorite word for vulnerability (used sixteen times in the novel and cited just now): *tremble*.

This point about the quiet power of minor-scaled social decision can be emphasized by recalling that the novel is structured by compromised wills. As Jennifer Fleissner has recently suggested, *the will* is the site of liberalism's most intensely elaborative self-investigations, where the volitional presumptions of modern philosophy, and its belief in self-directed activity offered under the sign of freedom, are tested. Fleissner observes that, because of its association with rational deliberation in a world so often moved by passion, desire, and simple confusion, *will* named what was, in fact, "a problem—a sign that the individual was also a problem, if not perhaps *the* enduring problem of the modern age, as much as a sign of its triumph" (Fleissner 11). In an argument that counters just-so stories of "the individual's" triumphal "rise," Fleissner observes that the categories of bourgeois thought exploded into dilemmas almost as soon as they were posited and became sites of elaborative investigation—an epistemological program of questioning that was accomplished in its most refined terms by the novel. No surprise, then, that *will* is a key concept in Eliot's great novelistic investigation of human capacity: references to it constitute a kind of ongoing pun in *Middlemarch*, a strange wordplay that has invited critical attention since the nineteenth century and highlights the novel's engagements with the now-discrete disciplinary formations of "philosophy" and "political theory."

In Eliot's treatment, the will-concept refers to everyone's frustrated capacity to choose their preferred course of action, of course, and the entire episode of Featherstone's legal document—his will—where an "interlacement" of intentions pushes a legal system based on singular decision into crisis (315). It refers to Casaubon's dead-handed codicil, exerting agency from beyond the grave, and gives us Ladislaw's own first name. As Caleb Garth himself puts it, "For my part, I wish there was no such thing as a will" (317). While proliferating the vocabulary of will, the novel works nevertheless to think beyond it, marking it, with Fleissner, as a "problem" and replacing the simple grammar of decision and volition with a feedback system whose primary decision-making apparatus is not the *free intellect* or *executive functioning* still mythologized by bourgeois theory but instead gestures and touches, a poesis of the flesh. For Eliot, writes Felicia Bonaparte in *Will and Destiny: Morality and Tragedy in George Eliot* (1975), "there is no such static sanctuary of the self safe from continuous interaction with circumstances" (52).

I referred above to the will-aggregating auction scene as a theater of something called *feedback* and used the term again now to describe Eliot's intersubjective theory of social change. The references may have slipped by. But I now want to explain that this term bears its own history and constitutes another moment in the relay of conceptual paradigms across the extractive modernity story I've set into motion in this book. As scholars like Peter Galison, Paul Edwards, Fred Turner, and Derek Woods have shown, the feedback concept emerged from the midcentury cybernetic theory of Norbert Wiener to structure fields like ecology and climatology but also economics, human psychology, computer science, and (the pursuit that launched Wiener's career) anti-aircraft targeting (Galison).[10] Of particular interest to Woods, and relevant to this chapter's encounter with Eliot's most "ecological" text, is the importance of the feedback concept to the development of earth systems sciences in the latter half of the twentieth century.[11]

As will become clear, this itinerary of thought links Cold War defense projects funded by petrodollars to the notion of the earth system as "a single, self-regulating system comprised of physical, chemical, biological, and human components" whose behavior is defined by "interactions and feedbacks" at varying scales (quoted in D. Woods, "Genre," 1153). The Rockefeller Foundation, which funded projects by Theodor Adorno, I. A. Richards, Roman Jakobson, and Claude Lévi-Strauss in this period while financially supporting the main projects in cybernetic thought, had its roots in Standard Oil and ensured a measure of oversight over the intellectual investigations into the nature of social control it funded (Geoghegan 104).[12] Standard Oil dissolved in 1911 into subsidiary companies that have morphed today into BP, Chevron, and ExxonMobil, which via its "Exxon Education Foundation" funded the academic research in the humanities I described earlier in the book. The Rockefeller Foundation provided my own institution, Georgetown University, with two million dollars of funding in 2022 alone.[13] This writing is not separate from the processes it outlines: it, too, is part of the fossil system.

As Woods shows, the Gaia concept structuring such analyses as Latour's was devised by James Lovelock and Lynn Margulis and announced to the world in 1975. It emerged from transformations in biological and evolutionary sciences after World War II, when the cybernetic idea pushed biologists away from the analysis of individual organisms, species taxonomies, and the like, and "toward the study of populations and principles of natural selection in terms modeled on cybernetic theories of command and control" (F. Turner, *Counterculture*, 44; see Kingsland). The Gaia principle construed the earth as a functionally coherent, internally self-regulating system—"a very ticklish sort of goddess," Latour says ("Agency" 3). This vision of the world-as-system is scaled up from the related concept of bioregion but similar insofar as it construes the earth system to be equilibrated and, ultimately, self-correcting. Leah Aronowsky has tracked the funding from Royal Dutch Shell that supported Lovelock as he worked on the Gaia hypothesis, citing for instance his 1966 report for the company, "Combustion of Fossil Fuels: Large Scale Atmospheric Effects" (310), which described the greenhouse effect of atmospheric carbon but argued the world had nevertheless been getting colder after

1940. This cooling was no problem, however, since, so Lovelock reported, it "certainly would encourage the sales of products for winter heating" (quoted in Aronowsky 311).[14]

Invented to solve conceptual and political problems emerging in the context of a hypercharged postwar capitalism busy branding itself as freedom, the Gaia concept is usefully viewed as an ideological product of a Cold War liberalism, as histories of the period have demonstrated. No idea can be contained entirely by the contextual circumstances that produced it. Still it is important to underline, as scholars like Fred Turner and Woods have done, that the cybernetic moment and its conceptual products are in no way to be understood in the utopian terms of some recent criticism, eager for "transindividual" models of causality and appealingly collective ideas. The cybernetic notion of feedback is not apart from the bourgeois traditions of extraction and accumulation I have been charting but a key ideological tool in their development. Yet it must be said instantly that this relationship does not mean that the conceptual repertoire of cybernetics is "bad," either, instead that it is imbricated, as I am suggesting all ideas are, in material filaments of capture and use whose world-scale outcome is the fossil-fueled inferno of the present.[15]

The cybernetic redescription of action as the production of effects within mutualized scenes of transferential feedback was useful to an emerging democratic superpower eager to distinguish itself from a more binaristic, dominance-and-submission model it ascribed to fascism (F. Turner, *Democratic*, 161). Despite this history, it is my contention that an imperfectly matching, earlier image of that idea—the model of embodied, low-intensity adjustment Eliot develops through various sources into *Middlemarch*—can offer a vocabulary for construing action at a moment of near-total enclosure and the relentless capture of nature. To make this claim is to recover an intellectual apparatus developed in one conjuncture and redeploy it in another, vastly different one, to a separate and even opposed political purpose. But can "models," as I just called *Middlemarch*, be recovered and turned to work again, even against their own original ideological purpose? And if so, could any such movement of the mind ever make a real difference at all? Do ideas matter?

The Yellow Pie Dish, or Information Flow in a Cognitive System

To phrase the question this way is to highlight the process of mediation by which ideational procedure becomes material and vice versa. Ideas: do they found nothing? Or do they, instead, work themselves into new shapes, become concrete in small and often inscrutable ways, and, in that archival half-life—sometimes just pencil scratches or paint smears, mere letters on a page—remain available for reactivation in new struggles? Raised to formal principle, the model of discursive recirculation played out in Trumbull's auction and elsewhere in *Middlemarch* helps us see what we already know, which is that all speech is fundamentally social; and that all discourse, including what you're reading now, is but the slightly adjusted product of prior intellects, relayed further in a chain and modified, perhaps, and recontextualized, but never marking any truly new beginning in the sense Arendt uses as her definition of action in *The Human Condition* noted above. One term for this process of looping but continually amending and therefore nonidentical recirculation is *feedback*, since this term refers to the mechanism by which outputs of a given system are immediately reclaimed as inputs, only to sponsor new outputs which then become reintegrated again, in a continual process of relatively low-intensity adjustment. It is not a revolution. To make my claims about social connection in *Middlemarch*, I am drawing on Otis (2001), but she is citing Beer (1983), Shuttleworth (1987), and Stwertka (1977) (Otis 81) (figure 20).

In the decades after the 1946 Macy conferences, systems theory would build on the work of midcentury cybernetic thinkers to further develop its account of feedback into what Ervin Lázló, in his *Introduction to Systems Philosophy* (1972), called "a new paradigm of contemporary thought." It was not new, but reoutfitted the idiom of midcentury cybernetics with metaphors of *system* and *structure* developed in the years leading up to Earth Day (1970) and the EPA (founded in 1970).[16] In the sense devised collaboratively by these Cold War intellectuals—a sense that persisted, reformatted into structuralist philosophy, into what Bernard Geoghegan calls "French theory"—*structure* refers to a closed totality of individual instances that, comprehended as a whole, constitute

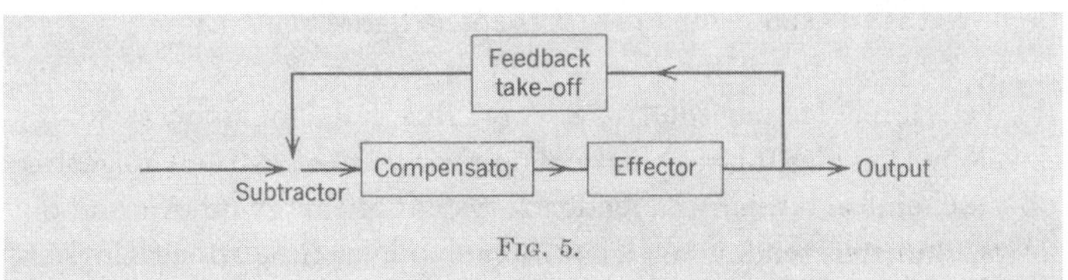

FIGURE 20. Feedback arrangement. In Norbert Wiener, *Cybernetics: Or Control and Communication in the Animal and the Machine*, 2nd ed. (Cambridge, MA: MIT Press, [1948] 1961): fig. 5, 112. © 1961 Massachusetts Institute of Technology, by permission of MIT Press. Photograph: Library of Congress.

an "underlying system of distinctions and conventions which makes . . . meaning possible" (Culler 4).

Thus construed, "structure" is an abstraction from individual particulars that takes on an autonomous analytic role of its own, in the sense that it can be understood as an entity with properties and capacities—one that, in the words of one overview, "play[s] a regulative role in social life" (Walsh 10). Imagined this way, any given structure will "constrain the behaviour of the members of society as well as enabling them to interact with one another" (Walsh 10). For Lévi-Strauss, writing in the midst of the cybernetic revolution, in 1962's *Pensée Sauvage*, "the entire process of human knowledge thus assumes the character of a closed system" (quoted in Geoghegan 97). These networks of citation help emphasize a common understanding about this definition of the structural, coalescing across seemingly separate disciplinary domains in the second half of the twentieth century.

As I suggested in the account of the Gaia concept above, the influence loop Geoghegan traces among cybernetic theory, communications theory, and French structuralism has another fold that is directly environmental. As Sharon E. Kingsland shows in *The Evolution of American Ecology, 1890–2000*, the tropes and conceptual figures of cybernetic thought in the early postwar years would sponsor developments in biological method that would lead directly to the establishment of the fields of earth systems science and thus the study of "the Anthropocene" in the years after 2000.[17] The "ecosystem" concept is a case in point: the term was coined in 1935 to denote "a natural unit including living and nonliving parts that interacted to produce a stable system" (Kingsland 189); it gained new traction in the years after World War II, and pushed ahead in the 1960s and 1970s, when influential textbooks overlaid the original concept with the now explicitly cybernetic concepts of circulation, internal regulation, and the "flow" of chemicals and energy through the "system." The emblem for this newly deployed ecosystem-idea was the model of the shallow lake I uncritically deployed as an example in the first chapter (figure 21).[18]

As Kingsland explains, the diagram appears in Eugene Odum's 1971 third edition of *Fundamentals of Ecology*. This "father of modern ecology" developed the idea that any "natural unit" could be construed "in abstract physiochemical terms," as a feedback system of energy inflows and outflows, ultimately tending toward self-regulation or circulation (Kingsland 190). The largest of these units was the "*biosphere* or *ecosphere*," Odum wrote, which is best conceived as "a steady-state system intermediate in the flow of energy between the high energy input of the sun and the thermal sink of space" (4). In this sense did the idea of a bounded system of

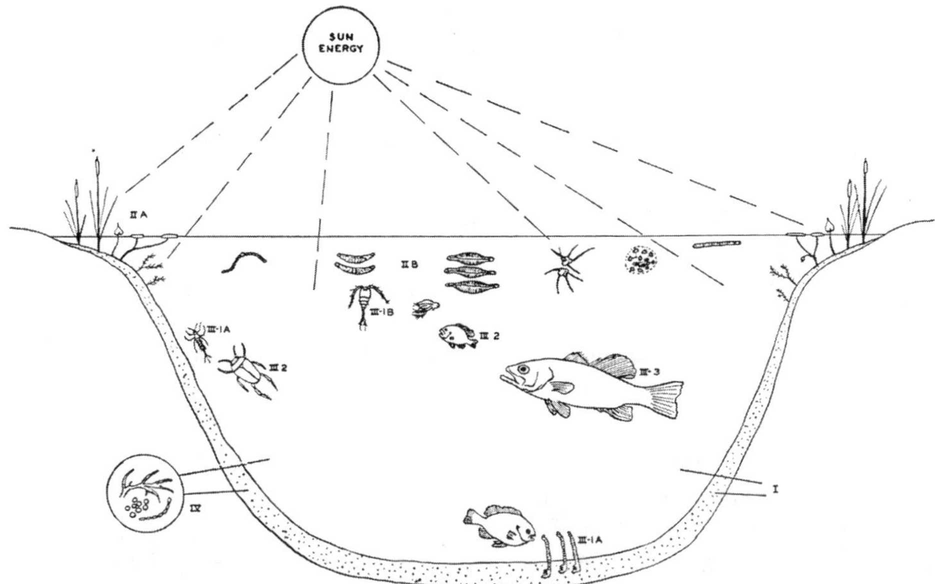

FIGURE 21. The energy chain as depicted in a pond ecosystem. In Eugene Odum, *Fundamentals of Ecology*, 3rd ed. (Philadelphia: Saunders, 1971). By permission of the Cengage Group. Photograph by the author.

causally integrated and interdependent functions come to be described in the terms of "structure" or "system." "By a *system*," Odum clarified, "we mean just what Webster's Collegiate Dictionary defines as 'regularly interacting and interdependent components forming a unified whole'" (4, emphasis original). This emphasis on the relation of organism to its "community" in the context of energy flows (5) meant that ecology itself came to function as a kind of reflecting pool for ideologies of liberty and interdependence among "free nations" in the Cold War effort to rewrite capitalist development in terms of massively determining systemic intertwinement. (The singular entity named "the economy" emerged alongside a newly minted abstraction called "the environment" in the years after 1970, as Timothy Mitchell has shown: rival tools for an emergent globalization's structuralist imaginary.) This conceptual struggle, I am suggesting, replayed with a difference the philosophical engagements with liberty, subjection, and determinism in the period of extractive fossil capitalism's emergence and maturation, when as Elizabeth Miller has observed, metaphors of sinew, nerve, and blood imagined the fossil economy as a now-globalized social body ("Industrial Ocean").

This multi-phase history helps reframe and complicate the story of *Middlemarch*'s much-vaunted "ecological" properties. John Plotz and Jayne Hildebrand have explained that the provincial novel operated as an aesthetic tool for experimenting with interactive social form in ways similar to the various structure-concepts noted above. Like Wardian cases (the sealed terraria popular in the decades after 1840) or tidepools (which Eliot visited with Lewes before writing *Middlemarch*), the provincial novel enabled a relatively artificial boundary to be set around a group of interactive organisms, creating a bounded socio-biophysical group now functionally operating as a system.[19] For Hildebrand, this experiment in biosocial limitation enabled Eliot to construe the physical environment or milieu to stand as a "common resource that mediates human connections" within its boundaries (Hildebrand 106). In this "ambient social environment," as Gage McWeeny terms it (62), novelty in any pure or total sense becomes unthinkable, given that (as Odum writes) "homeostatic mechanisms . . . , checks and balances, forces and counterforces, operate all along the line," ensuring that "a certain amount of integration occurs as smaller units function within larger units" (5). Recall that the book's exogamous characters like Lydgate, Ladislaw, and Raffles emerge into the relatively sealed or semi-detached sociocultural milieu of Middlemarch to modify only slightly the inherited equilibrium they disturb.

The system's prior steady state is enforced or *conserved* by such agents of the landed class as Mrs. Cadwallader and Sir James Chettam, whose Tory commitment to the established order inspires their efforts to thwart novelty and, should novelty emerge, to restore the system to what they understand as its former state of "self-balancing equilibrium" (Woods 123). In the terms of the cybernetic thinking I want to further develop now, their function is to introduce negative feedback: corrective equilibrating inputs in response to an initial disturbance aimed at counterbalancing that shock. "She says he is a great soul," Cadwallader observes of Dorothea, as her socially unwelcome attachment to Casaubon begins to take shape, "—A great bladder for dried peas to rattle in!" (54). This feedback is negative in a vernacular sense, of course, but it is also "negative feedback" in the sense of a counterposing adjustment to a developing disturbance in the social order; its purpose is to restore equilibrium to a relatively steadily operating structure that is—by means of a propertied young woman developing an attachment to an intellectual nearly beyond reproductive age—in the midst of being disrupted. Of two other such structurally if not politically conservative figures, Lydgate's rivals Minchin and Sprague, the narrator says: "Regarding themselves as Middlemarch institutions, they were ready to combine against all innovators" (170).

It is not original to observe that *Middlemarch* develops a systems-based, rather than unifactoral model of causation: its insistent demonstration is that action does not happen in Newtonian chains of cause and effect or sequenced operations placed on a linear array; instead causality is circular, in the sense that vectors of decision are construed to be branched, cross-linked, and (crucially) recursive. Elaborately coded episodes like the auction scene or Bulstrode's non-murder of Raffles disclose how Eliot pushes commonsense or bourgeois models of causality to their fraying limit, with consequences for the legalistic categories of guilt and innocence, or "responsibility," as Daniel Stout observes. Recall that in the novel, Raffles's death is effected by a non-act, derived from confused motivation, and effectuated by proxy. It is a servant astonishingly named Abel who, in passive voice and elaborately distended grammar, fatally fails to observe Lydgate's advice—which Bulstrode doesn't pass on—to not administer brandy (666–69). Such tangles of attenuated non-activity knit factors into "interdependence" and "interrelation" (Odum 5), and show decisive events emerging from ambiguous motives and inputs that cannot answer to the name of action. Rosamond is perhaps the savviest actor in this densely reciprocal, feedback-based environment, conscious as she is of the equilibrating internal adjustment necessary for success in her highly populated milieu, rife with organisms operating according to often inchoate private desires, or conations. (*Conation*, as Eliot knew, refers to "an inclination [as an instinct, drive, a wish, or a craving] to act purposefully."[20])

Lázló's 1972 diagram of "information flow" in what he calls a "cognitive system," visualizes the process by which internal conations engage an external world and readjust based on the feedback received from that encounter. This model could stand as image for any number of the most iconic moments of *Middlemarch*—the spots that, as Sierra Eckert and Milan Terlunen show in their data analysis of the history of criticism on the novel, readers continually come back to. But Rosamond's early interactions with Lydgate are among the most vivid examples of this almost hypercharged reciprocity. "Every nerve and muscle in Rosamond was adjusted to the consciousness that she was being looked at," Eliot writes. "She was by nature an actress of parts that entered into her physique: she even acted her own character, and so well, that she did not know it to be precisely her own" (109). After gazing at Lydgate, the sensitive actress produced a "result, which she took to be a mutual impression, called falling in love, [which] was just what Rosamond had contemplated beforehand" (109) (figure 22).

What the criticism continues to misconstrue as "egoism" in the novel—an overemphasis on self in comparison with others—takes the form

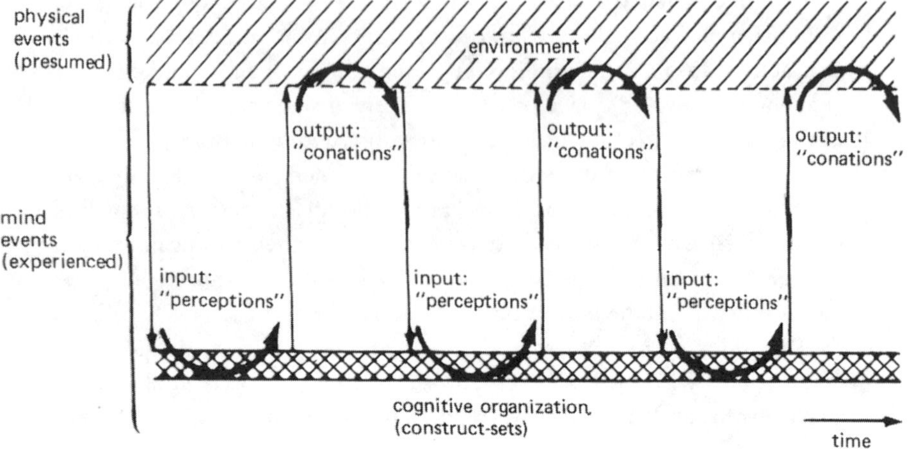

FIGURE 22. Ervin Lázló, "General Information-Flow in a Cognitive System." In *Introduction to Systems Philosophy: Toward a New Paradigm of Contemporary Thought* (New York: Harper Torchbooks, 1973). © Taylor and Francis. Photograph: Gabrielle Nemarich.

instead as the tactical weaponization of feedback loops in a situation where a subaltern or hyperbolically constrained actor (for Eliot, almost always a woman) does not control the terms of engagement. Nor do such figures have a role in designing the structures—here, the heteropatriarchal structure "called falling in love"—in which they nevertheless must operate.

Lázló's looping model helps emphasize what *Middlemarch* more elegantly discloses, which is how (1) inputs gleaned from outside the sensing body might become assimilated to that body and then help govern that body's activity going forward, and (2) how mental or ideational events can generate outputs that effect that concrete world, which then alters the shape of "mind events" in turn. Rosamond's poised utterances and pointed aperçus, for instance, perfectly pitched to the requirements of the moment, produce "compulsory admission" in their recipients (275), making concrete effects in the world. Among other things this circular process means that her most sincere-seeming statements of belief are best understood as tactical outputs into a dynamic material field she seeks to steer to advantage, the term *cybernetics* famously deriving from κυβερνήτης, "steersman" or "pilot." "'If I loved, I should love at once and without change,' said Rosamond, with a great sense of being a romantic heroine, and playing the part very prettily" (279).

One way of describing Rosamond's hyberbolic sensitivity is as social sense; another is as superficiality or falseness, the "artifice" that readers continue to judge harshly in vestigially liberal responses whose normative categories are self-reliance and autonomy. But seen in relation to the forms of structural domination I am attempting to evoke here, Rosamond's postures can be read as modes of subaltern effectivity in the face of systemic bioinformatic relations not currently organized to her advantage. These networks are horizontally reciprocal, on the one hand (instantiated in mutual relations of feedback with other bodies), and striated by relations of power, on the other (informed by social domination among parties engaged in those loops). In this context, Rosamond's actress-like apperceptive attunement enables her to carve a measure of "control" from otherwise predetermined systemic arrangements. Lázló suggests how perceptions gleaned from the external world are received by the organism via "experience," as one phase in "an ongoing multicyclic flow" (121). In this sense any given conation is effectively co-authored by the stimuli that were its mediated cause. Cited above, *conation* is the Latinate term Eliot herself knew from her translation of Spinoza's *Ethics* in the 1850s, where she translated this term for "volitional vector, impulse, or desire" (*conatur, conatus*) differently even in the same sentence: as a verb, she renders it "strives" and as a noun, "effort" (*Ethics* 171).

Completed in 1856 and never published due to a dispute between Lewes and a publisher over fees, Eliot's translation of Spinoza's 1677 text was the first ever undertaken in English. As Clare Carlisle notes in her edition of Eliot's version, Spinoza's monist materialism construed God as (in Eliot's translation) "the immanent cause of all things" such that nothing "exists in itself" or transpires of its own accord, but as a second-order expression of a single ultimate causal source (quoted in Carlisle 4). In this scheme, human beings are not self-sufficient or autarkic but instead a modal form of appearance of the only single substance there is, in the sense of something self-causing and self-sufficient: God. Among other things this paradigm means that (as Carlisle glosses it), "we are mistaken to believe ourselves or others to act from free will" (6) because, as Eliot translated Spinoza, "men believe themselves free solely because they are conscious of their actions and ignorant of the causes by which they are determined" (quoted in Carlisle 6).

To note how a vocabulary from early modern philosophy interacts with metaphors from cybernetics and systems ecology of the mid-twentieth century to structure *Middlemarch*'s procedure is to describe a historical relay of concepts across phases of extractive capitalism's long itinerary. It is also to underscore how the contained quality of the provincial novel might be redescribed in terms of Eliot's interest in structure as such, with "structure" understood now in the sense common to Lévi-Strauss, Saussure, or Foucault to mean the social set or demarcated body of instances bound into totalizing relation. The capacity for micrologic modification of such structures in light of apprehended signals has been developed in Rosamond, Eliot suggests, to the point of self-estrangement or alienation. Given the novel's much-vaunted investment in social life, one might think this sensitivity to others would be celebrated, but Eliot's moralizing irony toward this relentlessly feminized process of apprehension betrays the persistence of bourgeois voluntarism within the novel's otherwise synthetic and organicizing analysis of relational life. The novel's engagement with its conflicting paradigms is productively impure, generatively discrepant.

I have already mentioned how Eliot's studies of tidepools, recorded in "Recollections of Ilfracombe" (1856), can be understood as early exercise in her ongoing study of restricted biosocial forms and the modes of effectivity proper to them. As Hildebrand recounts, Eliot's journal entries record these marine encounters in the newly prestigious vocabulary of "environment," a term that enabled Eliot to make some of her earliest analogies between biological and social forms and generated a theory of interactive causality in which some organisms are better at effecting change than others. In her journals Eliot observed that taking polyps out of their habitats induced distress to the organisms in much the way Middlemarch characters struggle outside their native milieu. "Yellow pie-dishes were the best artificial habitat for *Actiniae*," Eliot observed (*Journals* 266), while noting that even the finest "artificial habitat" was no substitute for an organism's home water.

If the provincial novel enabled Eliot's conceptual inquiry into structure in the sense of bounded social totality, it also focalized for her the conceptual dilemma of action within unwilled context. The novel's interlocked metaphorical levels understand social bodies, microscopic organisms, political organizations, railway networks, communications systems, financial exchanges, gossip chains, webs, tissues, and scratched pier glasses as relatively cognate tropes for the mutual interdependence the novel also tests at the level of style and form. In the feedback-based causal chains elaborated in these areas, it makes little sense to ask "who or what is responsible." That is because subject and object interact continually in sequences that loop outputs back into the system as inputs, such that any "result" is only the momentary product of arrays that are effectively co-authored and ongoing: frozen into the appearance of completion only by virtue of artificial boundaries. Yet Eliot's experiment can be described in terms of what twentieth-century social scientists began to call feedback only with the proviso that both moments of conceptual-analytical investigation were conditioned by their own material situations: related but distinct moments in the unfolding of an extractive project whose late stages we inhabit now.

Inward Being, and What Lies Outside It

Historian Steven Heims observes that in the 1950s, the seemingly new conception of feedback-based causal processes

> suggested formulations of greater complexity and subtlety than traditional causal theories, but retained the scientific predictability inherent in those theories. In traditional thinking since the ancient Greeks a cause A results in an effect B. With circular causality A and B are mutually cause and effect of each other. Moreover, not only does A affect B but through B acts back on itself. The circular causality concept seemed appropriate for much in the human sciences. It meant that A cannot do things to B without itself being effected [*sic*]." (23)

Readers of *Middlemarch* unacquainted with Cold War social-scientific thought have long sought languages for describing identical models in Eliot's novel.[21] As I've suggested, the braided nature of "human lots" sponsors the novel's most direct philosophical statements in favor of an interactive or relational ontology, including the finale's famous observation that "there is no creature whose inward being is so strong that it is not greatly determined by what lies outside it" (784–85).

As the last chapter described, Arendt's "What Is Freedom?" (1968), like *The Human Condition* a decade before it, cataloged the forms of collective capacity and public life that had to be expunged in order to make space for the bourgeois era's concept of freedom as unencumbered private activity or autonomous will realized in deed. The corollary concept to this newly minted concept of freedom as sovereignty is *determinism*, which means that the pairing of "determinism and freedom" itself should be seen as a conceptual artifact of the liberal-bourgeois voluntarisms I've described to this point in the book. It is perhaps no surprise then to find that this pairing would have emerged in the inaugural years of Victorian studies as a field. George Levine's foundational essay, for instance, described "Determinism and Responsibility in the Works of George Eliot" (1962), an approach that would be fine-tuned in, say, Bonaparte's 1975 study of "Will and Destiny" in Eliot's novels and then again in Amanda Anderson's discussions of agency using Eliot, which date to early in the first decade of the 2000s. In this context, Eliot's hedging insertion of *greatly* into her claim about "inward being" being "determined by what lies outside it" can be read as a stylistic mechanism by which liberal causation can be reworked and finessed under the pressure of entangled or actual life, the "enduring problem" of the will now emerging as the occasion for stylistic and formal innovation (Fleissner 11).[22] Seen in light of the wave-based model of conceptual rearticulation I am evoking here, Eliot's gesture marks grammatically the shortcomings of the freedom-determinism binary she inherits from a bourgeois tradition she labors incompletely to transcend.

The first volume of Silvan Tomkins's *Affect Imagery Consciousness* was published in 1962, the same year as Levine's redeployment of the freedom-determinism binary in his essay on responsibility Eliot's fiction. In the book, Tomkins noted with discernible fatigue that "the debate concerning freedom of the will" involves a confusion between an insufficient binary structure and a (better) analog one. He elaborates on what he calls "the conventional concept of causality, which generated the pseudo-problem of the freedom of the will." This model "assumed that the relationship between events was essentially two-valued," Tomkins wrote, and "that man's will was therefore either slavishly determined or capriciously free." Against this digital logic and its attendant vocabularies of will, volition, responsibility, and even consent, Tomkins arranged "what may be described as the information, complexity, or degrees-of-freedom principle" ("Affects" 35). This principle imagined an analog gradient whereby something like unfreedom could be considered a general condition: because no given entity worked in conditions of complete autarkic sovereignty, any supposedly free actor was better understood as affected in more or less degree by (what Eliot termed) "what lies outside it." Like Marx in the *Eighteenth Brumaire* (1852), who noted that man makes his own history but in circumstances he does not choose, Tomkins's analog redescription of liberalism's constitutive binary offers a gloss on Eliot's "greatly": the suggestion is that the substantive work happens not when we judge something free or unfree, but when we labor to construe the inescapably qualitative entanglement of activity within the "structures" those actions in turn help to define.

In the cybernetic fold of the Great Acceleration, Tomkins finds—as Eliot did, in the 1850s and 1860s—that the best metaphors for expressing such interlocked relations are tiny organic beings. For Tomkins these beings include "amoeba[s]" and "plant[s]" ("Affects," 35). Recall that, as Otis and others note, for the cover of the first, serial version of *Middlemarch*, Eliot insisted not on the microorganisms she'd studied while devising the book but on vines. The result is a tangled organic twining, human drama folded in among the varied lots of so many other material beings (figure 23).

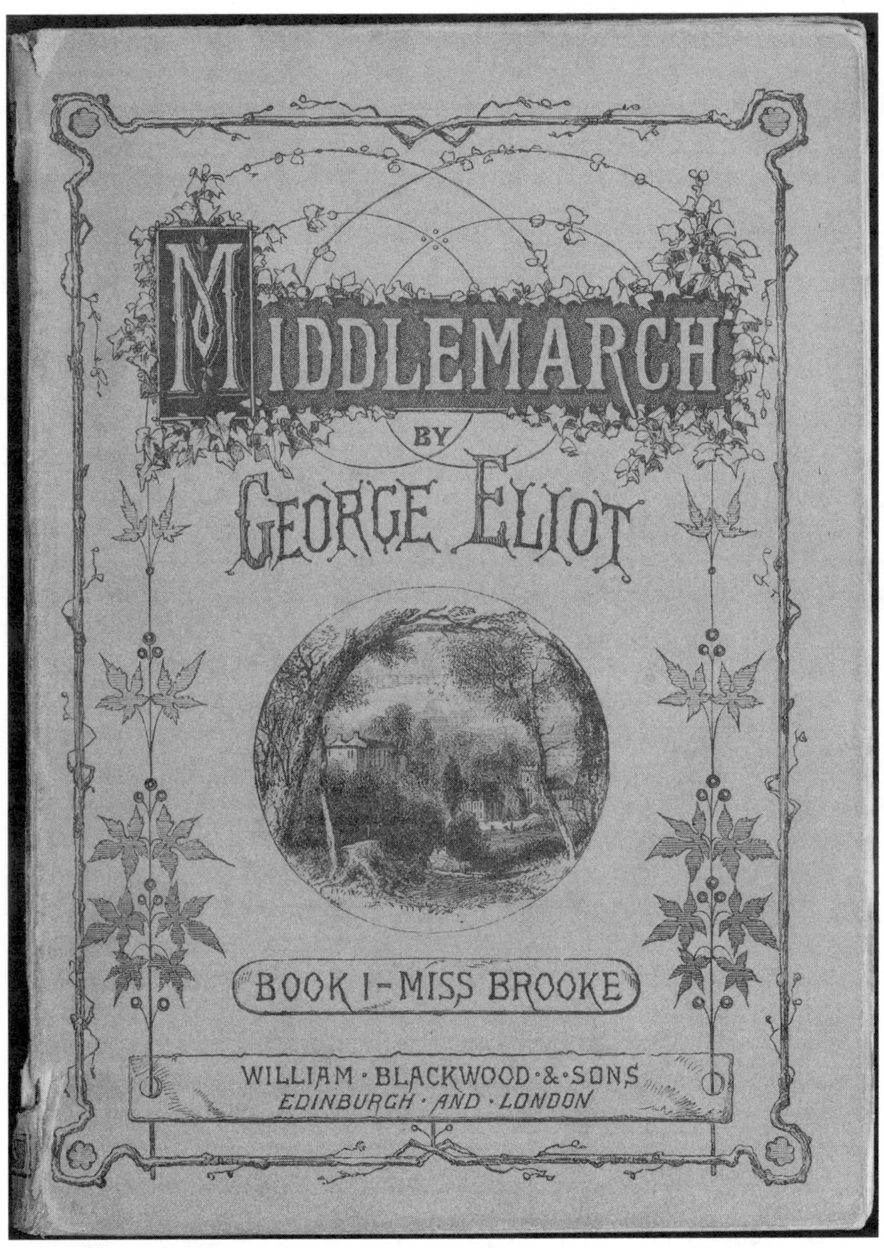

FIGURE 23. George Eliot, *Middlemarch*, book 1: "Miss Brooke" (Edinburgh and London: William Blackwood and Sons, 1871–1872). Carl H. Pforzheimer Collection of Shelley and His Circle, New York Public Library. Photograph: New York Public Library Digital Collections.

To this well-known organic vocabulary, common to Eliot's notes on tidepools and the metaphoric arsenal of *Middlemarch,* Tomkins adds "information," marking a new turn in the old story. And given that (in Tomkins's words) "a living system such as a human being" is a "feedback system" ("Affects" 36), it will always be interactively related to the other beings around it, co-comprising the system of interactivity in which it participates. "The freedom of any feedback system," Tomkins explains, "is, consequently, a conjoint function of its complexity and the complexity of its surround" ("Affects" 36).[23] In this sense does the Cold War cybernetic moment help us understand in reverse the middle decades of the nineteenth century, when a digital vocabulary of freedom confronted a consolidating extractive system whose sprawling, weblike expanse of increasingly entrenched social infrastructures was soon to render dreams of "unfettered" action self-evidently inadequate.

Writing in the early 1990s as she was developing her account of Tomkins's work in partnership with Adam Frank, Eve Sedgwick approached liberalism's digital model of freedom through the topic of addiction. In "Epidemics of the Will" (1992), she articulated a sense that a "propaganda of free will" imposes a two-term logic that enables one of two mutually confirming analytical moves. From within an analytic binary of determinism and liberty, Sedgwick observes, one might always "detect[] the compulsion behind everyday voluntarity"—showing how free choices are actually determined—or, inversely, show that any seemingly determined thing "shrivels in the equally stark light of the open secret that one might indeed at any given moment have chosen differently" ("Epidemics" 134–35). This observation continues to describe any number of apparently critical interventions today, but Sedgwick's point is historical: for her, the "mutual[ly] internal categories" of will and compulsion arise in dialogue with what she describes as the self-help crazes of the "early 1980s"—exercise addiction, shopoholicism, "sexual compulsion," and "workoholicism," among others. These vernacular theoretical interventions play out a hermetic ideological scenario by which freedom is always posited against its counterimage, compulsion, and vice versa, in "sites of subtle negotiation among reduplicated absolutes" ("Epidemics" 134).

Sedgwick's note about 1980s self-help lets us historicize some of Victorianist criticism's most enduring dilemmas. (Samuel Smiles's *Self-Help,* of course, was published in 1859, as Eliot was drafting *The Mill on the Floss.*) In particular, Sedgwick's point discloses that the long-standing debate about whether Eliot believes in free will or determinism is a symptom of how fully this conceptual model has been baked into the critical apparatus since at least the 1960s and, I am saying, long before. But Sedgwick's observation also helps us see how Eliot herself drew on and sought to rework the voluntarist languages to which she was heir in the middle decades of the nineteenth century, and better track how she supplemented those languages with conceptual idioms borrowed from biology, acoustics, or Spinozist monism, among other sources.

In the *Middlemarch* prelude, this strong theory of socio-discursive structure means that individual acts "tremble off and are dispersed among hindrances" (4), and any one speech act is condemned to fold itself into a larger interactive system of speech and counter-speech, lacing networks that form the particular webs that are the subject of the novel's documentary attentions. Construed synchronically, this dynamic means that any organism's tiny hairlets, in the famous description of Mrs. Cadwallader, will alter its scenario in a non-total but perhaps observable way. Imagined diachronically, these alterations become what Eliot calls, in "The Natural History of German Life" (1856), an "inheritance." In this temporalized feedback relation, the "internal" and "external" conditions of society—ideological and material conditions, linked together—persist intergenerationally, joining past and present into a conceptual-material paradigm that shapes (in just one of Eliot's persistent organic metaphors) "this living body in which our lives are bound up" (*Essays* 422). The operations of this body can hardly be changed. In the novel, Caleb Garth's comment to the peasant insurrectionists that the railroad "will be made whether you like it or not" (525) confirms the political stakes of this view while illustrating how an emergent extractive system provides concrete occasion for the book's social-philosophical experiments. The retrospective structure of this historical novel thus enables *Middlemarch* to suggest, among other things, that the advance of fossil capitalism and the full enclosure it relied upon is effectively inevitable.

It is worth recounting that the earlier *Felix Holt* (1866) described the same allegedly inalterable historical process explicitly as a matter of industrial advance and the enclosure of nature in an emergent fossil-capitalist system. In the famous stagecoach tour opening the novel, we glimpse a precapitalist landscape of meadows and shepherds—"silvered" by a morning light (3) and characterized by what Eliot specifies is "unmarketable beauty" (4). But this silvery scene of uncommodified life is soon demolished by the slow advance of coal-fired transformation. Unmarketable pastoralism gives way, Eliot observes, to a fully commodified world: a land "blackened with coal-pits" and noisy with "the rattle of hand-looms," marked by "coal dust" and marred by "the roaring furnace" (7). The transformation from peaceful country to roiling city took place, Eliot writes in *Felix Holt*, "five-and-thirty years ago," that is, in 1831, when *Middlemarch* is also set, the retrospective frame once more enabling present-day readers to experience the uncanny effect by which our own world of handlooms and mines was in process of emergence and formalization (3).

For political strategists like Antonio Gramsci, effective intervention in a situation requires an analysis of the relations of force that obtain at that particular moment.[24] Gramsci observes that ruling powers will want to preserve what he calls the organic basis of society—its foundational principle of organization or deep structure—even past the point when its "incurable structural contradictions" have begun to reveal themselves (178). "Since no social formation will ever admit that it has been superseded," Gramsci explains, political forces will always defend the order sustaining them, however inherently broken or crisis-prone that order may be. To do so the dominant powers will resort to "conjunctural" effects—political maneuvering, ideological manipulation, the use of police power—in order to "conserve and defend the existing structure" even past its point of organic crisis. Therefore "it is on this terrain"—the terrain of the conjunctural—"that the forces of opposition organize" (178).

In the roaring furnace of our present, scenes of sociopolitical transition such as the one we glimpse through the window of *Felix Holt*'s carriage help underscore the total nature of depletionary life today. When $140 billion oil firms, swollen on record profits and devouring smaller competitors, are still dwarfed by fossil conglomerates worth four times that much (Warner and Elliott), fantasies of frontal assault on the extractive order are legible as just that. Instead, wars of position are required: slower, more tactical, unobvious, the hairlets and vortices of microscaled procedure operating conjuncturally, in Gramsci's terms, and gathering in ways that prepare the ground for new constellations of power and a renovation at what he called, with Eliot, the organic structure of life.

Targeting Apparatus / Foundress of Nothing

I've said already that relations of feedback and adjustment structure *Middlemarch* in the active sense deployed by Rosamond in her canny manipulation of Lydgate, but they shape the novel also in their absence—as when Mr. Brooke, for instance, displays a naïve and sometimes comic blindness to the fact that any social scene will be characterized by a reciprocal interaction between subject and object. (The failed performance of his stump speech confirms his deafness to feedback in this sense.) A related deficiency is charted in Fred, likewise impervious to inputs from the world around him. This dissolute and self-interested figure "fancied he saw to the bottom of his uncle Featherstone's soul, though in reality half what he saw there was no more than the reflex of his own inclinations" (111). Eliot's prose specifies that Fred does not entirely fantasize ("half what he saw there . . ."); the problem is that he overemphasizes the subject in light of the object, runs himself over, as does Lockwood in *Wuthering Heights,* into the object with which he should be in a densely calibrated or interactive relation.

"That gossamer web!" exclaims Mr. Vincy to himself, as he contemplates the nature of young love in the case of Lydgate and Rosamond (325). The ambitious father finds himself marveling how love's "subtle interlacings are swung—are scarcely perceptible: momentary touches of fingertips, meetings of rays from blue and dark orbs, unfinished phrases, lightest changes of cheek and lip, faintest tremors" (325). Momentary, unfinished, faint: Mr. Vincy's minimalist vocabulary describes the developing courtship of his daughter as a matter of almost infinite subtlety: it is but one cluster of *Middlemarch*'s interlocked figures for imagining decision at wavelengths all but below the visible spectrum. New projects do not emerge into the world from the volitional impulses of any single actor but are coproduced in the "subtle interlacing" of encounter.

In a famous and much-revised passage of the finale, Eliot echoes the terms of Vincy's astonished spectatorship by describing how the "determining acts" of life result from an individual's "struggling amidst the conditions of an imperfect social state" (784). As Hildebrand and Otis remind us, the novel's layered metaphorics figure this social state variously as a web, a network, a tissue, or a "milieu," all of these being efforts to describe the interactive causality characteristic of complex systems.[25] Eliot revised the "determining acts of life" passage extensively, suggesting the productive challenge she saw in the question of how most precisely to describe the interplay between instance and structure, individual life and the "social state" in which that creature might find herself. In manuscript, she wrote that the "determining acts" of Dorothea's life were "the mixed result of struggling with *imperfect conditions*." In the first edition, the conditions were "prosaic" rather than imperfect, while later in the passage Eliot described the structure inhibiting Dorothea's "determining acts" variously as the "*social air* in which *morals* begin to breathe" and "the *social medium* in which *young creatures* begin to breathe" (810n784, emphasis added).

Conditions, medium, and *social air*: each term labors to name something like circumstances or setting but does so by emphasizing the material quality of these extrapersonal conditions, as Pearl Brilmyer has recently shown. It's in the context of this physicalized impingement that Lydgate, like everybody else in the book, feels what Eliot calls the "hampering threadlike pressure of small social conditions, and their frustrating complexity"

(169). In Eliot's essays it becomes clear that this importantly materialist theory of sociohistorical structure is "conservative" (as her editor puts it; see Eliot, "Natural History," 267) in the sense that it is resistant to any immediate or phenomenologically abrupt structural change; it is counterrevolutionary in arguing against the wisdom but also against the possibility of any "damaging convulsion," as Felix put it in 1868 (Eliot, "Address," 420). Instead, massively determining systems change in slow time, according to "the gradual operation of necessary laws" (Eliot, "Natural History," 287).[26] This organic gradualism means that the model's investments appear to lie in the preservation, not the overhaul, of what Gramsci called the organic basis of society, where, as Felix tells the rioters, "the nature of things in this world has been determined for us beforehand" (Eliot, "Address," 422).

Contemporary ecocide enables us to see Eliot's counterrevolutionary gradualism in new light and opens up the possibility of flipping its normative valences while learning from its analysis of how systemic change occurs. As Levine's 1962 account appreciated, the position is dangerously close to a fatalism. In *Felix Holt,* the title character rises above his fellow peasants and cautions them to wait for time itself to grant them the power to vote. In *Middlemarch* it is Caleb Garth, that moral center of the book who is modeled, biographers think, on Eliot's own father, who underlines the apparently defeatist political valences of this theory. As noted above, the kindly patriarch tells a pack of pitchfork-wielding rioters that stopping the historical process of railroad expansion is impossible: "it will be made whether you like it or not" (525). With Garth's railroad speech in mind, Michael Tondre describes the novel as an energy epic, noting further that "at times *Middlemarch* represents fossil modernity's march as a given," even while the book also "provides anticipations of industrialism's terminus" in tropes of wasted energy, expenditure, and diffusion ("Finitude" 310, 308).

Is climate collapse "inevitable"? It would be naïve to say no, given that it is already happening, and also that heating processes and systemic alterations to currents, wind patterns, and the like are already certain to accelerate based only on past inputs into the system —"inherited conditions," as Eliot said. The continued march of these processes seems, as Felix Holt put it, "determined for us beforehand." And yet. In *Middlemarch,* anyway, the incomplete nature of an apparently deterministic emphasis on structure emerges in hedging words like "greatly," in its ironic structure, and in its fussing editorial alterations between conditions and social air. But its productively incomplete investigation into the limitations of bourgeois freedom is articulated perhaps most movingly in the prelude. Here Eliot famously compares Dorothea to St. Theresa of Avila and uses analogy to scale down from the world-historical to the micrologically individual—suggesting, with Naomi Schor, that in the Western aesthetic imagination, the plight of the particular is linked fundamentally to that of woman (*Detail* 10–11).

Our narrator observes that while St. Theresa saw the realization of her dreams in the founding of a religious order, the modern Theresa, Dorothea, is "foundress of nothing" (4). Dorothea started nothing, marked no new beginning, and (as the finale says) left no great name on earth, her actions "trembling off" and "dispers[ing] among hindrances, instead of centering in some long-recognizable deed" (4). Eliot specifies that what dispersed were not her deeds at all but her "loving heart-beats" and "sobs after an unattained goodness," a difficult construction that emphasizes the somatic quality of Dorothea's engagement with the particle-field of the novel. The sentence positions desire or conation—not plans or conscious thought—as the motor of (muted) change. In Bloch's words, cited in this book's introduction, hope is in this way construed not as a disposition you choose or do not choose to have, but as a physical need or longing (figure 24).

In manuscript we see the traces of minor wobble, revisionary gesture, and momentary hesitation. In their only semi-formulaic quality, the dips

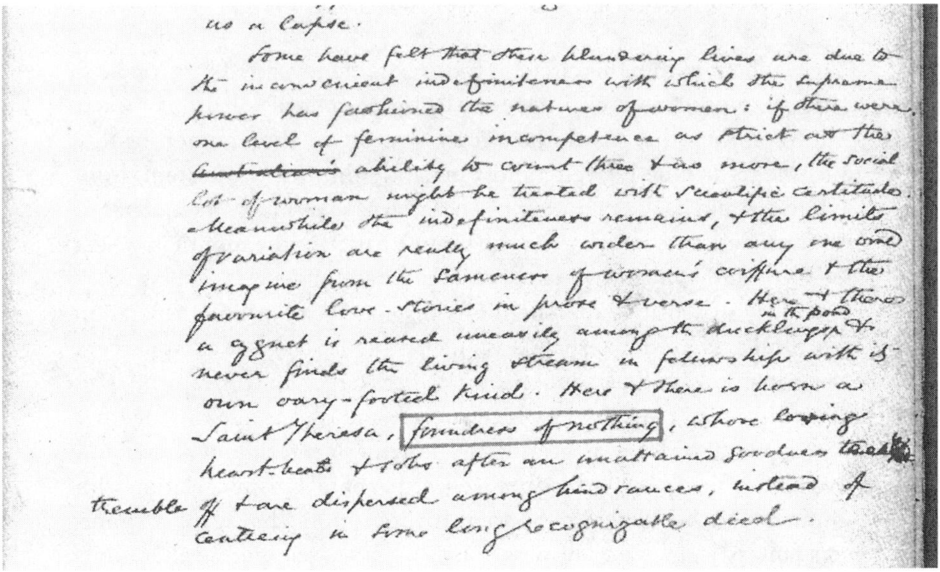
as a lapse. Some have felt that these blundering lives are due to the inconscious indefiniteness with which the Supreme power has fashioned the natures of women: if there were one level of feminine incompetence as strict as the ~~[illegible]~~ ability to count three & no more, the social lot of woman might be treated with scientific certitude. Meanwhile the indefiniteness remains, & the limits of variation are really much wider than any one would imagine from the sameness of women's coiffure & the favourite love-stories in prose & verse. Here & there a cygnet is reared uneasily among the ducklings in the pond & never finds the living stream in fellowship with its own oary-footed kind. Here & there is born a Saint Theresa, foundress of nothing, whose loving heart-beats & sobs after an unattained goodness ~~[illegible]~~ tremble off & are dispersed among hindrances, instead of centering in some long-recognizable deed.

FIGURE 24. George Eliot, "Foundress of Nothing" (1871). Manuscript page from the prelude, *Middlemarch* (Add. 34035). British Library, UK. Photograph: © British Library Board.

and swerves and tiny movements of Eliot's hand cut against what can seem like the novel's own account of total sacrifice to the already existing. In the shaking of the pen and the movement of the fingers, I am suggesting, we find the physical records of only semi-scripted activity: relayed over decades and via any number of translational recodings, these mediated signals testify, nevertheless, to a moment when something new emerged into the world—even when, as here, the new was actually a recast version of something taken down before (the manuscript in the British Library is a fair copy). It is relevant to this brief detour into handwork that for cybernetic theory from the Cold War period, the classic example of cybernetic feedback was a human hand reaching for something. For Wiener in the epigraph to this chapter, that something was an instrument for writing, but it could be almost anything. As Heims paraphrases,

> A person reaches for a glass of water to pick it up, and as she extends her arm and hand is continuously informed (negative feedback)—by visual or proprioceptive sensations—how close the hand is to the glass and then guides the action accordingly, so as to achieve the goal of smoothly grabbing the glass. The process is circular because the position of the arm and hand achieved at one moment is part of the input information for the action at the next moment. If the circuit is intact, it regulates the process. (15–16)

If the feedback within this circuit is too drastic, if movements are irregular or the communications circuit slowed by lag, the pencil will drop or water spill; if, on the other hand, the circuit is sensitive, then numerous tiny adjustments will be relayed almost instantly through the system, from hand to eye and back again, over and over, so as to produce "a sequence of 'real time' data and calculations concerning a path to the mouth in which case the mouth will always already be the future of the glass" (Pias 20).

Such highly sensitive apprehensions imagine not a Cartesian separation of "willful acts" and external consequences (Pias 20) but an apperceptive body-mind working almost holistically as targeting apparatus. It is an embodied social circuitry in which subject and object operate together in a reciprocal process of adjustment, longings centering in almost unrecognizable deeds, a hand scribbling onto paper in dynamic relation with innumerable other factors at the scene of inscription. The "agent" of bourgeois fantasy is, in effect, dispersed into a host of sub-heroic alterations and gestural interventions that together rewrite the script of the given, at inevitably minor scale.

Like handwriting or the stroke of a key, such physical motions turn ideational impulse into material performance and do so in the context of a "circular" or looping relational circuit. Cybernetics' key examples of reaching to touch a water glass or holding a pencil are surprising insofar as they use quotidian gestures to illustrate an idea that was devised to shoot down airplanes in wartime. But this emphasis on the hand and its touch helps forecast the downscaled investments of Eliot's experimental novel, where hands emerge as the key trope for social effectivity: a tiny means by which an otherwise broken conjuncture can be shifted toward what she termed "growing good."

Bodies as Knowledge-Mechanisms (Sob, Hands)

Perhaps unusually for an anthropological study based on Malay archives, James C. Scott begins *Domination and the Arts of Resistance* (1990) with a reading of George Eliot (6–10). The anthropologist of peasant uprising cites Mrs. Poyser, in *Adam Bede*, in the context of what he calls the hidden transcript, whereby official notation and traditional record keeping—the archival practices of academic readers and bureaucrats—cannot apprehend certain forms of low-intensity resistance to power. What looks from one angle like compliance is, from another, more sensitive perspective, resistance. For Scott, Mrs. Poyser's "apparently calm surface of silence and consent" in fact "carries the force of a symbolic declaration of war" (8).

For all its crucial ingenuity, Scott's account rearticulates in new form the dyadic vocabulary of "resistance" and "consent" familiar from the tradition I have tracked so far, albeit in an attempt to dynamize the relation between what Sedgwick above called the "reduplicated absolutes" of activity and passivity, "will" and "determination" ("Epidemics" 134). Spatial metaphors enable this attempt: the surface-and-depth model allows Scott to suggest that the outward appearances of peasant actors like Mrs. Poyser might *show* consent, but "war" (the site of true intention) rages underneath. The move leaves undisturbed the voluntarist presumption that true motives can be discerned if we look hard enough; the goal of his account is to provide tools to "more successfully read, interpret, and understand" the "strategic pose[s]" and "tactic[s]" of actors whose explicit representations should not be taken "at face value" (*Domination* xii).

Scott's emphasis, like Eliot's, is on the visual. His account rests on the presumption that what is required to discern secret scales of activity are more sensitive practices of reading, a more penetrative technology of sight. As Rosalind Morris has observed in an intellectual history of this period,

Scott's struggle with the vocabulary of bourgeois action from the mid-1980s formed the condition of disciplinary possibility for Gayatri Spivak's cautions, in "Can the Subaltern Speak," against the longing for authenticity and the almost reflexive desire among well-meaning academics for windowpane-clear access to the Real Motives of the Dispossessed. Writing in 2010, Morris noted that Scott's work from the mid-1980s was "the locus classicus" for the attempt to recover "resistance," restore "suppressed voices," and discern "the agency of the oppressed" in archives not obviously containing those things. Morris ties this transdisciplinary impulse to the political failures of the Reagan and Thatcher years (R. Morris 11–12).[27] I have observed already that Exxon sponsored Scott's work, but an important citational afterlife links Scott's 1980s-era arguments to sophisticated accounts of subaltern resistance and unresponsive archives in the writing of Saidiya Hartman, for instance, who cites *Domination and the Arts of Resistance* and *Weapons of the Weak* in *Scenes of Subjection* (1997).

But where Hartman's emphasis is on opacity and the final irrecoverability of archival intent, as well as the inevitably confused circuitries of desire, Scott's model understands rational intent to be discernible if we only look hard enough. I've hinted that his presumption of the importance of *visibility* helps us appreciate again the often-noted optical metaphors in *Middlemarch* and suggests by shorthand Eliot's own investment in action at the lowest ends of the discernible spectrum. Like Scott, Eliot's interest lies in finding ways to make fugitive conduct apprehensible and to show how effects invisible to the naked eye might yet scale up to consequence. But it is worth saying directly that a hydraulic Cartesian dualism structures accounts of *hidden resistance* or *secret strategy*, since in this model, the springs of action are presumed to exist an implicitly cognitive executive function, even when this site of strategic planning lies below the surface. In contrast to Scott's crypto-liberal emphasis on rational deliberation, Eliot supplements her own post-Enlightenment cognitivism with an emphasis on the work of the body.

Remember that at the Green Dragon, Fred Vincy's tingling habit and flushing blood give him the "prophetic sense" of future effect without any consciousness of choice: "It is in such indefinable movements," the narrator specifies, "that action often begins" (632). Bulstrode, too, feels his "diseased motive" as "an irritating agent in his blood" (665) as he passively acts to effect Raffles's death. Such moments find Eliot shifting the site of decision from the Cartesian dreamworld of "strategy" to a gradient responsive scenario where any effect is conditioned by material embodiment and different bodies linked together, most often, by physical touch—"indefinable movements," Eliot specifies. To make this observation is in no way to discount Eliot's obvious interest in the scopic logics of seeing and visibility: but this vocabulary, along with its cognate epistemological postures of reasoned calculation and "distance, objectivity, and dislocation" (Anderson, *Powers,* 7) is in *Middlemarch* finally displaced and countermanded by—positioned uneasily alongside—an investment in the felt and physically proximate, tingling blood and charged bodies.

Early on, we learn that Dorothea, raised "in the unfriendly mediums of Tipton and Freshitt" (36), has decided on a catastrophic course of action. It impossible, she says, that she will marry Chettam and announces instead her preference for Casaubon: "a husband . . . above me in judgment and in all knowledge" (38). Why does she do it? We have our suspicions, but it is Celia, at this early moment, whose power of interpersonal sensitivity enables her to respond effectively while Dorothea is caught in the world's iron. Celia, like Rosamond, is habitually condescended to in the criticism, but she is among the book's most sensitive operators within densely predetermined scenes of social domination, or what Hartman calls spaces of enclosure (*Wayward* 33). When Dorothea tells her sister of the disastrous choice of Casaubon, Celia's acute perceptual capacities enable her to immediately assess the feedback loops and systemic relations that have produced the outcome.

Still, not even Celia's "marvelous quickness in observing a certain order of signs" (44), an echo of Trumbull's identical skill later in the novel, can save her from being bowled over by the enormity of the choice Dorothea has just announced. It is a disturbance. Elsewhere described as insubstantial or superficial—she has just made quips about Casaubon's unseemly soup-eating and weird, Locke-like blinking (45)—Celia here shifts in the light to expose a fundamental dispensation toward care. As she cuts out paper figures in the manner of a child, her response to Dorothea's announcement registers in her flesh. "It is right to tell you, Celia," Dorothea says, "that I am engaged to marry Mr. Casaubon."

> Perhaps Celia had never turned so pale before. The paper man she was making would have had his leg injured, but for her habitual care of whatever she held in her hands. She laid the fragile figure down at once, and sat perfectly still for a few moments. When she spoke there was a tear gathering. (45)

The "habitual care" for the fragile and subordinate thing Celia exhibits here, so routine as to have become second nature, enables her to avoid translating the shock she suffers into injury for another being. Dorothea's news registers on the physical makeup of Celia's body, paling her.

But Celia has trained herself by repetition ("habitual") to receive such shocks as her social system may produce for her with negative feedback or steadying energy; she supplements this absorptive quality with a responsive care toward other "fragile figure[s]" who might be injured too. Here, Celia protects both the small and seemingly insignificant paper dolls and, by extension, her sister, as she sits stock-still and her body, generating a teardrop in the passive voice (it "was gathering") registers an investment in her relationship with Dorothea even as it prevents her from speaking out in ways that might injure. The scene taxonomizes Eliot's attention to what Sedgwick and Frank, reading Tomkins, call "bodily knowledges" (22): it is a densely physicalized encounter that happens quickly, and is gone. A trifle, really—but trifles are the sum of human things.

Such scenes of dissolved and somatized action as I just rehearsed harness the analog capacities of literary presentation to disrupt and recalibrate the bourgeois logics of action Eliot inherited from her *Westminster* colleagues and reworked with the benefit of other, stranger conceptual languages. In scenes like Trumbull's auction or Celia's protection of the dolls, Eliot's tactically deployed passive voice and perspectival shifting show action without single cause: not "unifactorial" predication (Beer 149) but multiple, multiply caused effects. In this sense, minor scenes again prefigure the novel's major storylines, these levels again repeating one another with difference in a play of scalar resonance that is itself evidence of the book's investment in complex systems and "servo-mechanical" relation. Taken as a methodological invitation, this formal experiment sets terms for what Schor describes as the political effort to "dream a universe where the categories of general and particular, mass and detail, and masculine and feminine would no longer order our thinking and our seeing" (xliii). Call it a rehabilitated universalism, a climate action model from below.

In fact, such tiny scenes as I've just reconstructed prefigure the spectacular moment of liquid "diffus[ion]" in the finale, alluded to already, when we are told that Dorothea's "full nature" has "*spent itself* in channels which had no great name on earth" (785, emphasis added). The celebrated fluid metaphor shows among other things how Dorothea's status as an actor in Arendt's sense of being endowed with the capacity to mark new beginning is canceled, spent: martyred, in fact, to an abolishing medium that renders her ardent deeds finally illegible, or nearly so. But as in any other fluid medium (a tidepool, a pond) molecule touches molecule, body influences body, such that "the effect of her being on those around her," as Eliot's narrator famously adds, "was incalculably diffusive" (785). The liquid dissipation of Dorothea's capacity has paradoxically allowed for an effectivity in social and historical terms that is both larger (it changes more things more durably) and smaller (you barely notice it).

Reading these and other passages, Pearl Brilmyer helps us see how the "dynamic materiality of the body" (55) functions as the fundamental unit of Eliot's social physics: characters are themselves composed of varying scales of physicalized materials, variously metaphorized as gluten, starch, particles, planets, and fibers, among other substances. Yet these aggregated physical entities collide with one another and interact in the Wardian case of the novel's provincial milieu, a tidepool effect by which material interactions and embodied responses co-create the effects that will come to be visible as a structure. In her translation of Spinoza, Eliot had already confronted the philosopher's resolutely materialist "geometry" of human relations, in which human social relations could be studied in physical terms, and as if (in Spinoza's words, translated by Eliot) "the subject were lines, surfaces, or solids" (quoted in Carlisle 12). As Brilmyer observes, it is in this sense of the social as a theater of interacting material bodies that we can read, for example, of "*the force* with which certain characteristics of Dorothea *impressed* those around her" (Eliot, *Middlemarch*, 447, emphasis added).

Productively out of synch with the orthodox scientific vocabularies of her moment, Eliot's approach also cuts against the cognitivist models that still construe something called *the body* as a homogeneous essence, the inversion of *mind*.[28] In the words of Sedgwick and Frank, liberal philosophies that share this rationalist presumption see the body as "a markedly homogeneous, lumpish, and recalcitrant bodily essence, one particularly unarticulated by structures or processes involving information, feedback, and representation" (19). New materialist theories of affect and embodiment follow this tendency in reverse, since these approaches reduce "the body"—now a good term, rather than a bad one—to a site of conceptual opacity and pre-ideological essence, a valorized impulsivity that stands romantically apart from "mind" now understood in its bad sense as cognitivist rationalism. Against this simplifying calculus, Eliot figures human bodies as sites of differentiated and attuned analog response, a processing mechanism of surpassing alertness. This claim can be made with the disclaimer mentioned already, which is that the metaphors I have just used, of apprehension, information, system, and processing, are themselves part of a figural arsenal common to cybernetics and its legacies in the twentieth-century Anglosphere.

Heartbeats, blushes, trembling, and tears: these and other of *Middlemarch*'s obsessively observed physiological responses give expression to sophisticated somatic processing and together advance the novel's account of embodied knowledge or what the "Natural History" essay calls incarnate history. Because it transpires only in the space of encounter, this somatized knowledge proves incompatible with fantasies of personal sovereignty and proposes instead a model of solidarity across barriers of social division. In novels like *Persuasion,* Jane Austen updated the tradition of eighteenth-century modest-heroine stories to deploy the blush as a semaphore by which women convey authentic or "natural" feeling against the artificial social idiom of manners. Being a signal of the body, it often gets its wires crossed, as the blush of embarrassment about desire can be indistinguishable from the blush of desire itself, a useful confusion for the production of plot.[29] In *Middlemarch* the blush does not so much secure the body's eventual capture by institutions of heteronormative social order (its function in Austen novels) as it enables connection across boundaries the social order presumes to be unbridgeable. It makes new relationships, enabling emergent solidarities that then enact change in a world that seemed inalterable.

It is not the blush or the tremble but the sob, however, that generates the most consequential changes in the existing social architecture of the *Middlemarch* world. Eliot's sobs transpire across moments of heightened dramatic interchange or moments of intensity. The OED tells us that to sob is to experience the affective response par excellence: "to catch the breath in a convulsive manner as the result of violent emotion."[30] "Convulsive" suggests an unwilled bodily response, and "as a result" betrays a sense that it is not any cognitive capacity but "emotion" that stands as the sob's ultimate source. Understood as saturated sites of intrapersonal feedback, sobs find social information transmitted, received, and recirculated in an intersubjective loop whose instrument of signaling and apprehension is not cognitive at all and is nonverbal too.

In total I count thirty-three such wordless instants in the book, an archive of social adjustments transpired at the level of body (see the appendix). You can consult them if you want, but trust me that these convulsions of expressive emotion function as hinge points in the novel's action and underscore the importance of this saturated affective response in what I am calling Eliot's paracognitive conception of possibility within otherwise intractable systems. To be sure, this recourse to the body at pivotal moments has habitually been taken as evidence of a conventionalized sentimentality or cheap moralizing of the kind Eliot herself critiqued in "Silly Novels by Lady Novelists" (1856).

But Eliot's understanding of the sob as a site of consequential social interchange is not reducible to a cloying, liberal-sentimental trope of fellow-feeling. It does not confirm a feminized sphere of sentiment against a male world of public reason (Arendt's procedure); nor yet does it conform to an "ideology of feeling[]" by which the social as such is dissolved into one-on-one encounters presumed to defuse political antagonism (Jaffe 14, 15–16). Instead, Eliot positions the sob as the site of alteration or adjustment in otherwise locked-in social relations, a means by which transindividual collaborative connection, effected outside verbal and conceptual structure, enables the script of the world to be altered. It is by no means innocuous. Dorothea has a "dangerous tendency to sob" (594), and the threat resides in the capacity of this paraverbal communication to create linkages between previously disaggregated characters and in so doing disturb, in some way, the prior state of social order.

Against usage, it is a transitive verb, in the prelude, to indicate a movement toward something, to "sob[] after an unattained goodness" (4); as the novel proceeds, it describes the intersubjective response of characters, nearly always Dorothea, though Rosamond sobs in their famous encounter, Mrs. Bulstrode sobs (number 25), and Will does too—the only instance of a male character experiencing this emotionally dense response. Any of these instances would repay careful reading. Number 19, for example, describes the "inward silent sob" when Dorothea speaks with a "pure voice, just trembling in the last words as if only from its liquid flexibility" (510). Here fluid metaphors combine with "trembling" to show Dorothea's embodied processing of what the novel with knowing wordplay calls the "sad necessity which divided her from *Will*." At one point (number 18), *sob* is a metaphor, describing how speech—which should arise, on the Arendtian model, from the function of public reason or *logos*—instead arises "as naturally as a sob after holding the breath" (508). The "natural" quality of this informatically dense expression shows how the sob functions as a site of effectivity without an "agent" in the Newtonian sense of isolated cause. Is it good? We can't say for sure, since the content of "change" is normatively neutral, a blank space where values should be. My point is that Eliot's attempt to dramatize how intractable social orders might be torqued from inside can offer guidance to those whose goal is the transformation of the organic order of society in an era of earth systems collapse, when full revolutionary assault has been (as James Scott wrote of Nat Turner) "foredoomed" (*Weapons* xvi).

A corollary to the sob is touch, and the last turn of this claim is to note what readers of Eliot already know, which is that *Middlemarch* positions this sense as the fundamental mechanism by which bodies interact with one another to adjust the given structure of the world.[31] In "Notes on Form in Art" (1868), written in the long period when Eliot was "brooding over her [new] 'English novel'" (quoted in Graver 201), Eliot described phenomenological interface of touch as the zero degree of apprehension, "of which the other senses are modifications" ("Notes on Form" 432).[32] Touches spark moments of plot-defining connection and structure the most consequential interactions among characters. Describing this phenomenon, Suzanne Graver observes that "regularly" for George Eliot "the meeting or joining of hands is emblematic of community, of those acts of sympathy, friendship, and love that unite one individual with another" (203–4). But the benign connectivity Graver identifies has a threatening edge and extends well beyond conventional accounts of Eliot's interest in something called sympathy. Hortense Spillers has identified "the contradictory valences" of the haptic in relation to emancipatory projects, since touch is at once the site of care and restorative intimacy and the site of coercive violence in its purest form, where one body (to use Eliot's language) "impresses" another. It is, Spillers notes, the starting point for an ethical and political program and not—as in neoromantic calls for *intimacy* and *connection*—its end point. Like "change" or "futurity," connection is normatively undefined: its ethical and political value depends on what you do with it.

Finale

In book 8, Dorothea encounters a Rosamond who is, let us say, disinclined to receive her. They are meeting because Lydgate is broke and Dorothea wants to pay his debts, but there's been a misunderstanding. Dorothea wants to put it right, but Rosamond resents her. Still, something in Dorothea's bearing breaks down Rosamond's defense. There is melodrama in this most famous scene, and the sort of sentimental connection only possible, in Victorian novels, between white women of a certain class. Like Dorothea's earlier connection with Lydgate, this one is "involuntary" (272), Eliot specifies, since Dorothea moves toward Rosamond by "impulse" and extends her hand in a gesture that produces equally involuntary response: Rosamond "could not avoid meeting her glance, could not avoid putting her small hand into Dorothea's" (745). All these impulsive movements locate the site of action in the women's bodies, not their minds or "will." In this sense, Dorothea's most important act of the novel is not an act at all:

> Dorothea, completely swayed by the feeling that she was uttering, forgot everything but that she was speaking from out of the heart of her own trial to Rosamond's. The emotion had wrought itself more and more into her utterance, till the tones might have gone to one's very

> marrow, like the cry from some suffering creature in the darkness. And she had unconsciously laid her hand again on the little hand that she had pressed before. (747)

While this scene is conventionally read as a scene of sympathy, I'd rather emphasize the crucially different idea of solidarity. As the next chapter will further emphasize, in sympathy discourse, the separation of the subject and the object are presumed and the wound is imagined to be repaired by a condescending replacement of the other with oneself: *I feel your pain.* In solidarity, repair in any final sense is neither desired nor presumed; the security of solution is exchanged for a lateral relation among differentiated and differently interested participants; and the commonality across difference that defines this relation is enabled most often by a sense of shared injury.

The book 8 passage is a climax or crescendo in an obvious sense. It has been among the most cited passages of the novel since publication, as Eckert and Terlunen observe, a fact that itself testifies to the importance of sympathy tropes to a liberal-bourgeois tradition of Victorianist scholarship I have evoked across these pages. But Dorothea's encounter with the "fragile creature who was crying close to her" (747)—no less fragile than Celia's doll—is reparative in its basic orientation. Microscopic in scale, the encounter does not in the end attempt the curative transference of liberal-democratic sympathy. Instead it is physical contact: when Dorothea "unconsciously laid her hand again on the little hand that she had pressed before," she aspires to no revolution, and leaves the organic basis of society almost entirely unmoved. Nothing happens, really. Rather than heroic action at total scale, Dorothea reacts with her body in solidarity with another who is experiencing the damage of bourgeois life alongside her, reaching "from out of the heart of her own trial" to another's.

The term *heart* here suggests a Hallmark-style sentimentalism. But importantly it is not Dorothea's *heart* that enables her speech but *the heart of her trial*: it is her subordinate position in a scheme of social domination that enables her to engage in a speech act that connects with another such subaltern, a linkage among the (relatively) disadvantaged that becomes material in the choreography of haptic contact here. Crucially, Dorothea's gesture is not a romantic outside to capitalist expropriation, nor is it—the novel makes clear—any kind of escape for these women inscribed into an effectively total patriarchal order. There is no transcendence.[33] Yet their connection instantiates a theory of action that is noncognitivist insofar as new beginnings do not spring, self-caused, from inside private wills, but emerge in physical encounters with other beings likewise subordinate in schemes of social domination—beings that need not be human, either: "creature[s]," Eliot again specifies here. The encounter, we are told, "might be a turning point in three lives" (747).[34]

A hand on another hand, an edit, a brushstroke. To this point in the book I have attempted to highlight moments of improvisation and elaboration that are fleeting, evanescent: available to us only by way of their minute archival traces if at all, and locatable as such mostly after the fact, through screens of mediation and at removes of sometimes hundreds of years. Still such elaborations make small alterations in the grammar of existence. They are in this sense poetic, from the Greek ποιέω, "to make or do." In response to Dorothea's reactive and elaborated set of gestures, Rosamond is decisively changed. She is "taken hold of by an emotion stronger than her own—hurried along in a *new* movement which gave all things some *new*, awful, undefined aspect" (749, emphasis added). The novelty of this uncertain but unscripted new life—as I noted, its normative content is undefinable—means that Rosamond finds language inadequate, grammar newly inexact: she "could find no words, but involuntarily she put her lips to Dorothea's forehead which was very near her, and then for a minute the two women clasped each other as if they had been in a shipwreck" (749).

As we survey the shipwreck of the modern project now, it strikes me that this scene of two women finding solidarity in the midst of a catastrophe they cannot meaningfully alter might be read as a scene of minor but real possibility. Given that few read nineteenth-century novels now, and fewer still care about their details, as an item of evidence it is almost comically small. But in Eliot's handling, trifling things for that very smallness are more real than the false dreams of revolution or the delusions of masculine overturning left in ruins by the end of the novel. After all, the effect of Dorothea on those around her, say the famous lines,

> was *in*calculably diffusive: for the growing good of the world is *partly* dependent on *un*historic acts; and that things are *not so ill* with you or me as they *might have been*, is *half owing* to the number who lived faithfully a *hidden* life, and rest in *un*visited tombs. (785, emphasis mine)

Whatever possibility emerges in the well-known words is fantastically muted, attenuated to an almost total degree: entangled grammatically, in fact, in negation and half-positivity and the semi-negation of negation. It is a model of possibility in the absence of hope. This socialized effectivity has abandoned the triumphalist dreamwork of solutionism and committed itself, instead, to solidarity and mutual struggle without the false consolation of transcendence.

As her biographer Rosemary Ashton recounts, Eliot's position during the *Middlemarch* years was "intermediate between optimism and pessimism": she accepted the deterministic models of social life put forward by Spencer and Comte, but remained, Ashton says, "intent on avoiding a passive fatalism . . . in the face of these inexorable laws" (305). The gamble of this chapter has been to arrange its particulars like so many scratches on a sheet of metal, and to have resuscitated or perhaps breathed through an avowedly counterrevolutionary model of sociohistorical change, reanimating it for a conjuncture when the organic basis of society is effectively inalterable but requires nothing less than a total overhaul. The infrapolitical circuitry of Eliot's experiment puts adjustment in place of revolution, solidarity in place of sympathy, and subsystemic immanent critique in lieu of the grand structural overturnings that masculine theory continues to fantasize as the domain of the properly political.

The next chapter will show how intimately scaled contact among the dispossessed can produce not transcendental change but non-total effectivity in the ruins of an extractive common sense. From an analysis of universal capture and the exposure of vulnerable life to the harms of the market, Christina Rossetti develops an account of subaltern capacity: an action without hope built from tiny details and elaborated from the grammar of a mental language that is implicated in the harms it aims to redress. This new language, like all of them, must be built from what came before. It can be generated only in the tangled aftermath of what Eliot, like the Cold War intellectuals whose work I have charted alongside her, only had words to call freedom.

5

You Companioned I Am Not Alone

ROSSETTI AND SOLIDARITY

The Surging of the Sea / And the Storms That Blow

The last chapter showed how George Eliot positioned intimate contact—solidarity among the broken and spent—as a site of possibility within functionally determined conjunctures. This chapter turns to Christina Rossetti to describe how her poetry imagines small improvisations and momentary disruptions as varieties of consequential intervention in the world. These low-intensity adjustments do not renovate or overturn the conditions that precede them but instead elaborate and rework a gathering modern condition that was, Rossetti saw, deadly in its fundamental orientation. It will help make this point, paradoxically, to begin with baby stuff. Rossetti's book of children's poems, *Sing-Song: A Nursery Rhyme Book* (1872), was published ten years after her breakout first volume (*Goblin Market and Other Poems* 1862), and roughly a decade before *Verses* (1893), which gathered together her most stringent and devotional poetry into a single book characterized, critics note, by a "wakeful anguish" fueled by a sense of the world's certain destruction (Harrison 81). *Sing-Song* thus arrived halfway between the early lyric works that continue to star in criticism and undergraduate syllabi, and those fervent exercises that have daunted secular readers since they first appeared. Yet Rossetti's children's book is not without its own metaphysics. It includes "If a Pig Wore a Wig" and "Three Plum Buns," but also "Why Did Baby Die" and "A Baby's Cradle with No Baby in It."

As the last two titles suggest, the book conjures for its juvenile readers no nursery-room consolation but a wintery world in which upward-tending resolution is deferred, canceled, or altogether thwarted. It is usefully understood as a poetics of disaster. This bleakness makes sense given Rossetti's famed sensitivity to the nonhuman world and what Emma Mason calls the "ecological love command" structuring her verse (*Rossetti*,

3), an attunement to precarious beings placed into worlds organized to exhaust or kill them. Rossetti's strict emphasis on "the inevitability of loss, betrayal, disappointment, [and] physical pain" (Harrison 81), meanwhile, was informed by her Tractarian understanding that Christ's bodily suffering was prerequisite for a future redemption that would coincide with the end of days.

But it also derived from an analysis of the modernizing process gathering around her. By the year of *Sing-Song*'s publication in 1872, the nineteenth century's emergent extractive system was coalescing into dominance, the despoliations of growth now palpable in, for example, the soot-blackened air that gave Rossetti choking fits and headaches throughout her adult years. That is to say nothing of the sacrifice zones even further from the Rossetti family home at 56 Euston Square: the open pit mines of Cornish copperworks, say, or the Afghan hillsides that, in the introduction, yielded the luminous flakes of Turner's blue. The Haunchwood Tunnel Colliery, to pick another instance, now fifteen minutes by car from George Eliot's childhood home in Nuneaton, was sunk in 1855 after its owner's prior mine ran out, and was already "on the verge of exhaustion" itself by the early 1870s.[1] In these scenes and others the disaster of what Rossetti saw as modernity's fixation on the "almighty dollar" (Rossetti, *Face*, 272) became manifest, the catastrophe of an emergent extraction-based status quo palpable in tissue of her own lungs.[2] Air pollution, extinction, and the violence of accelerating enclosure instantiated what Rossetti saw as the "materialism, consumption, greed, wealth, power, and cruelty" structuring relations in the extractive empire's capital city (Mason, *Rossetti*, 5).

Like so much other of Rossetti's austere and pared-down verse, *Sing-Song* positions cataclysm as ever-present: readers have long noted that canceled possibility is her guiding theme and "restraint" an animating principle (Harrington 4). *Sing-Song*'s "Twist me a crown of wind-flowers," for example, imagines the world as a generalized tempest or superstorm, marked by "surging" seas and "blow[ing]" wind, strange to read in a moment of serialized hurricanes and drowned coasts. It opens by imagining how a blossomed coronet might enable the speaker's flight beyond this everyday catastrophe. "Twist me a crown of wind-flowers," the speaker commands, "That I may fly away." Then the interlocutor is addressed directly, and promise evaporates:

Put on your wind-flowers:
But wither would you go?
Beyond the surging of the sea
And the storms that blow.

Alas! Your crown of wind-flowers
Can never make you fly:
I twist them in a crown today,
And tonight they die.

(ll. 5–12)

The poem holds out the promise of liberation only to reassert the priority of limit.

Here a freedom that is acknowledged to be desirable is positioned as both escape ("beyond") and, because it is an effect of wearing a "crown," a kind of quasi-sovereign power. But the supreme capacity to "fly away" from a storm-racked world is offered up in the conditional mood ("that I may").[3] The structural relationship to hope that defines the conditional, so important to Emily Brontë's poetics in chapter 3, is mobilized here only so anticipation can be thwarted, transcendence evoked only so that, in an operation imagined as dialectical ("I twist"), it can be canceled: "Alas! Your crown of wind-flowers / Can never make you fly: / I twist them in a crown today, / And tonight they die." This abnegating motion makes "Twist me a Crown" emblematic of a poetic practice that readers have long seen to be organized by restrictive truncation, a "ruthless artistry" (in Antony Harrison's words) animated by "rigorous aesthetic values" (8).

Harrison's masculine rhetoric of rigor and ruthlessness may fit uneasily with Rossetti's investment in the fragile, vulnerable, and precarious that I will describe in the pages to come. But it does help suggest how Rossetti's concern with unwilled constraint operates in these poems not only as a thematic but a formal principle. "Twist Me a Crown," for example, is like many of her poems an exercise in scalar and conceptual reduction, "simple, chaste, and severe," as Jerome McGann describes Rossetti's prevailing mode (236). In "Twist," this compression effect is achieved by metrical cropping: each of the poem's three brief stanzas ends with a five-beat line that stops us short, since the line whose rhyme it completes has six. This syllabic paring-down generates at the levels of sound and time a hobbled effect, turning the verse into a somatic performance of annulled possibility.

As I noted in the introduction, in its standard usages the concept of hope presumes that desire can achieve satisfaction, and that one's action might possibly secure a visible result: it is the "expectation of something desired," as the OED says, or "desire combined with expectation."[4] As a verb, to hope is "to entertain expectation of something desired; to look (mentally) with expectation." For the King James Bible, meanwhile, "hope deferred maketh the heart sick: but when the desire cometh, it is a tree of life" (Proverbs 13:12). In odd grammar, the verse unfolds in tension with the utilitarian presumption that results are what matter most: here desire, not necessarily its outcome, is what, "when cometh," gives life. In "Twist" and elsewhere, Rossetti refuses the presumption that desire will be fully or finally achieved on earth, but—more radically—refuses equally to abandon the commitment to the redeemed world such desires necessarily aim toward. As I noted in the introduction, in a new edition of *Hope in the Dark* focused on climate change, Rebecca Solnit writes that hope "is not the belief that everything was, is, or will be fine" and understands that failure, not achievement, will be the outcome of many movements for justice in the near term.[5]

Yet this near-certainty of inachievement need not asphyxiate the struggle for partial and real victories—often, Solnit writes, "comparatively small" or even "invisible" ones—in preparation for larger ones to come (xiv, xv). Desire need not combine with expectation to motivate work in the present. Rossetti's poetry radicalizes this constitutive tension in the concept of hope: it works at minor scales to imagine how local possibility and collaboratively engineered new beginnings might yet emerge from within scenes of almost total foreclosure. For reasons to be developed as this chapter proceeds, her condensed and dialectically twisted verse can be seen as a laboratory for understanding the conditions for struggle when the definitional requirements of hope have withdrawn.

Insofar as it imagines avenues for elaboration within conditions of near-total structural constraint, Rossetti's writing helps redirect the persistent fixation, within and outside the climate community, on the linked categories of "optimism," "hope," and affective positivity as prerequisites for commitment in a struggle. Conceived from within a fiercely devout Anglo-Catholicism, Rossetti's poetry demonstrates what life in the collapsing late carbon era confirms, which is that pleas for "hope" against "doomism" can be purchased only at the price of a fatal naïvete about the absolute nature of the present catastrophe. Rossetti at least, perfectly assured of the given world's brokenness, required little convincing that earthly life could not promise redemption, and that action at decisive scale was, in the end, impossible. Her stringent take on the *vanitas mundi* convention combined high-church fidelity and a millenarian fixation on the end of days into a negative aesthetics where the desire to achieve worldly ends culminates, over and over again, in nothing. From within the terms of bourgeois thought this philosophical and aesthetic disposition can only read as hopelessness. But Rossetti's bleak assurance paradoxically clears space for possibility at lower frequency: in the intimate spaces of observed detail and syntactic disruption emerges a future-oriented practice that positions solidarity and mutual commitment over the functionally privatized category of positive emotion.

In "Goblin Market" and elsewhere, I mean, Rossetti's calls for solidarity in catastrophe carve out a domain of connection from within a finally masculine system of extraction and violence she represents as (in our lifetime anyway) inescapable. In keeping with this project, her poetry works to anatomize the restrictions on possibility that render hope inadequate for understanding repair in an unwinding world. This chapter describes Rossetti's efforts to imagine increasingly stringent scenarios in which constraint is felt; describes the scale effect by which the minor and the small become the domain of the metaphysically vast; reconstructs her understanding of the temporal world as fundamentally inhospitable and nonprogressive; and shows how she elaborates a form of common-being I will call solidarity as bulwark against a generalized catastrophe, where no avenue of total escape remains from "the surging of the sea / And the storms that blow."

The Ruin They Have Made

Into degraded conversations about climate "doomism" and the allegedly disenabling moods of "despair" that follow from even the most basic factual analysis of our collapsing contemporary, Rossetti's verse intervenes as a bracing antidote. Is it "pessimistic"? Rather than reinstating the key presumptions of bourgeois growthism—that time will bring improvement, that individual deeds can avert the violence of a storm-ravaged and broken world, that measurable "action" will produce countable "solutions"—Rossetti transforms these presumptions into the operative friction, or even target, of the work.

A two-quatrain song like "I dug and dug," for example, also from *Sing-Song*, begins by describing futile activity in a frozen waste. In documenting this bleak negativity, the poem would seem to be setting up a redemptive turn from the first quatrain to the second. But no turn comes. This is the whole poem:

> I dug and dug amongst the snow,
> And thought the flowers would never grow;
> I dug and dug amongst the sand,
> And still no green thing came to hand.

Melt, O snow! the warm winds blow
To thaw the flowers and melt the snow;
But all the winds from every land
Will rear no blossom from the sand.

(*Complete Poems* 229)

The poem describes the mise-en-scène of Samuel Beckett's *Endgame*, described in the introduction: a barren world where forests are a memory and no seeds can grow (3, 13). Figured here in terms of repetitive, fruitless action in a dead landscape, Rossetti's understanding of a fundamentally "unteleological world" (I. Armstrong 361) means that fantasies of improvement were visible to her as precisely that: delusions made possible only by a willed incapacity to understand the consumption patterns and violence on which ideologies of improvement depend.

In "I dug and dug," the problem takes condensed shape, since in just eight lines it inverts the entire bourgeois narrative of private property, by which, as I explained in chapter 2, the enclosure of land for purposes of cultivation leads to what Locke called improvement. In Rossetti's treatment, Lockean strategies of property-making development elaborately fail. In the sand and snow of this barren world nothing can grow; improvement is no option. And in Rossetti's rewriting of modernity's paradigmatic episode of property-securing self-establishment, all the labor in the world, even two iambs' worth ("I dúg and dúg"), will produce nothing: "still no green thing came to hand."[6]

Rather than *growth* or *improvement*, then, the world Rossetti conjures in *Sing-Song* and elsewhere is defined by exhaustion, diminution, and the failure of regeneration. It describes what Elizabeth Miller calls depletionary life. In such a world the concept of hope can be only offered conditionally—as it is in another of *Sing-Song*'s short lyrics, where a stanza break again invokes the conditional mood's defining relationship with possibility only to withdraw it:

If hope grew on a bush,
And joy grew on a tree,
What a nosegay for the plucking
There would be!

But oh! in windy autumn,
When frail flowers wither,

What should we do for hope and joy,
Fading together?

(*Complete Poems* 243)

After turning on a "but," the poem's closing rhetorical question opens a space where the motions of withering and fading mean that "hope and joy" have withdrawn. But a substitute must nevertheless be imagined. "What should we do?"

This question—perhaps the central problem in the age of earth systems degradation—will return. But in the context of the specifically ecological recasting of Rossetti's poetry I am attempting here, it bears repeating that Rossetti's almost metaphysical attraction to catastrophe took special shape as a concern for the violated and broken instances of nonhuman nature. It is not a transcendentalism: nature worship is not part of it. Readers have described, instead, how Rossetti's concern for the nonhuman world and its most fragile inhabitants took shape from within the thoroughly urbanized lifeworld of the Rossetti household. She was a frequent visitor to the London Zoo, for example, where she would bring "a goodly bag of eatables" to feed the animals and once recalled seeing a fight between a porcupine and a wombat (quoted in Marsh 215). Her sketches of plants and animals display a wobbling sense of wonder at their odd angles and idiosyncrasies.

This intimacy with the world is evident, too, in her flower catalogs, her descriptions of pets, and her careful analyses of weather phenomena. All these acts of natural witness unfold in Rossetti's characteristic millennialist idiom (one of her poems is titled simply "The End of Time") but manage to be both metaphysicalizing and concretely observational at once, such that the nonhuman world is both a symbol of something else and always only itself. Mason has explained how Rossetti's interest in and amateur study of the natural sciences—"geology, biology, and astronomy, the specifics of flora and fauna, and the antivivisection movement" (Mason, *Rossetti*, 110)—accelerated in direct proportion to her sense of the universalizing obscenity of fossil-fueled progress around her. The more the natural world's vulnerable beings fell under threat, the more fervently she sought connection with them.

In the face of the organizing violence of modern life, Rossetti's commitment to the material particularity of the world was evident across her poetic and artistic production.[7] But given her related obsession with the dynamics of temporal experience and the philosophy of time, it makes sense that this commitment finds voice also in the profusion of her quasi-pastoral lyrics named after seasons: we might think of "Winter Rain," "Spring," or "A Summer Wish," among many others. ("I dug and dug" was one of these, above.) I call them quasi-pastoral because each inverts or at least troubles the customary association of spring with life, winter with death, again twisting opposed terms until they bleed into one another.

More often than not the frozen rains of winter become associated with life, and spring ciphers an incipient disaster. In "Spring Quiet," for example, the end of winter promises birdsong, "sweet scents," and "budding boughs," but also guarantees that hunting "snare[s]" will be set to silence this music (ll. 13, 10, 16) . In "Spring," "There is no time like Spring that passes by, / Now newly born, and now / Hastening to die" (ll. 36–39). In these and many other of her poems, a strategy of chiastic inversion evolves death from life and vice versa, and links Rossetti's Christian metaphysics to the related mechanism in Gerard Manley Hopkins, which may be why Hopkins admired her so much.[8]

While widening out, in scalar terms, to a wintery seasonality and even, as we will see, cosmic time and the end of the world, Rossetti's catastrophic poetics describe disaster most often in familiar terms, and they redeem this domain of feminized particularity as the most consequential register at which God's vulnerable creation is threatened. As with Brontë and Eliot in chapters 3 and 4, this insistence on the seemingly insignificant as the domain of ethical consequence—trifles, raised to the sum of human things—finds shape in a formal practice dedicated to the condensed and apparently colloquial. Plain speech resonates at grand scale.

In another eight-line micro-poem, "Hear What the Mournful Linnets Say," for example, the melancholy birds of the poem's title lament the destruction of their nest by "cruel boys" (l. 3):

Hear what the mournful linnets say:
"We built our nest compact and warm,
But cruel boys came round our way
And took our summerhouse by storm.

"They crushed our eggs so neatly laid;
So now we sit with drooping wing,
And watch the ruin they have made,
Too late to build, too sad to sing."

(*Complete Poems* 230)

Here, an injury to the physical world is unmotivated and literally anthropogenic: it has its source only in the "cruel boys" who "t[ake] our summerhouse by storm" (ll. 3–4). This scene of masculine invasion describes an unprovoked, gender-inflected "ruin," while the audience, identified with the mature linnets as "we," can only "sit with drooping wing" / "And watch the ruin they have made." *Ruin*, it bears noting, is a term that recurs across Rossetti's natural and devotional writings, freighting her well-known "pre-occupation with death" (Harrison 59) with metaphysical resonance. The normal operation of modern life was, for Rossetti, brutally harsh and antithetical to flourishing. More specifically, it was predicated on an original violence, coded as male, that subjects the vulnerable world to an almost endless assault.

In the "Linnets" poem, this assault takes the form of crushed eggs and a broken nest and is, we are told, "too late" to be healed by "build[ing]." The line references the moment in bioseasonal reproductive cycles at which linnets (*Linaria cannabina*) can no longer successfully restart their process of regeneration. But it also evokes the futility of attempts to repair worldly damage: it is too late to build. In addition to being irreparable, the loss is "too sad to sing." But in the poem itself at least, it has been sung. That the linnet is *linaria*, linen-weaver, named for its diet of the flax seeds from which linen is made, reemphasizes this minor-key association between birds and poetic production, as the poem in a gorgeous performative contradiction weaves a fabric of lines and sings a doomed song about an injury that cannot be ameliorated in the present, nor even be "sung" at all. A sense of the world's precarity and availability to injury, then, organizes the "Linnets" poem and structures much of Rossetti's dark nature poetry. Her evident care for nonhuman life—wild animals, plants, pets, flowers, seasons, and weather—and her emphasis on the various modalities by which such things can vanish might serve by itself to recommend Rossetti as a poet for the era of climate collapse. My own acts of sustained attention—long readings, elaborate redescriptions—transpire in response to the ethical and political invitation of these performances.

But in the same way that a negation of a negation is not quite a positive, the "Linnets" poem finds a kind of muted possibility in the performative contradiction by which a song might be sung even when its occasion makes it "too sad to sing." This space of minor positivity or imperfectly canceled hope will recur for us later in the images of solidarity organizing her most famous poem, "Goblin Market." But in contrast to even the most fractured hint of possibility in "Linnets," a poem like "A Baby's Cradle with No Baby in It" is just what it sounds like. Another poem about child death, "Why Did Baby Die," also from *Sing-Song*, meets a child's imagined questions about mortality with mute indifference. The picture it paints cannot be consoling, since as with "Linnets," it depicts a historical ontology or episteme defined by loss:

Why did baby die,
Making father sigh,
Mother cry?
Flowers that bloom to die,
Make no reply
Of "why"?
But bow and die.

(ll. 1–7)

For the chaste and nonreproductive Rossetti, this and other of the startlingly bleak poems of *Sing-Song* build out a theory of nonregenerative or futureless earthly life. It is a version of Lee Edelman's "queer negativity" (6), albeit one inflected by a rigorously Anglo-Catholic vision of a future state beyond embodied existence.

For Rossetti, however, eschatological promises of future redemption do not cancel or even dull the pain of disaster now. Her original illustrations for *Sing-Song*, stark and awkward, give visual shape to the nonteleological account of temporal life her poetry codes into verbal form. (They are "merely my own scratches," she said, "and I cannot draw" [quoted in Marsh 384].) "Naïve" they may seem (Marsh 384), but as the gasping thrush of figure 25 suggests, the sketches also underscore the thematic centrality of vulnerability to Rossetti's worldview, even as this general availability to injury is construed entirely outside any verbal or visual rhetoric of the sentimental.

As we saw in relation to Dorothea Brooke's haptic encounter with Rosamond in the last chapter, Victorian sympathy discourses deploy an individuating logic of equivalence and marshal this emotional calculus in scenes of damage or injustice. In the sympathetic encounter, that is, the wounded other is placed onto a matrix of exchange by which it might be evaluated in terms of potential equivalence with the self, even when the purpose of this assessment is to emphasize the difference between compared terms (Greiner 4): you are suffering and I am not. This comparability between instances becomes the starting point for a process of aspirationally recuperative cognitive and emotional engagement by which a lost or fallen wholeness is imagined to be restored: something that was injured might now, by the emotional attention of the observer, be healed (cf. Rada 11). According to this logic of affective fungibility, we might see a dead thrush and shed a tear for it, then take our outpouring of feeling as the conclusion of a process of emotional exchange by which we have softened the harsh edges of a brutal world.

Audrey Jaffe has explained how the sympathy paradigm mandates that an empowered onlooker pick out from the crowd representative individuals deemed to be deserving of repair—virtuous beggars, innocent babies, tiny birds. These pitiful exemplars then come to embody "ideals of universality" that "invit[e] the harmonious resolution of social conflict" by the ministration of sympathetic affect (Jaffe 21). This individuating motion has the function of hiding the factors that have produced the suffering, transforming politics into ethics in much the way Solnit means when, writing about liberal disinformation regarding allegedly lethal wind turbines, she notes that "stories about individual birds can distract us from the slow-motion calamity that will eventually threaten every bird" ("Big Picture").

In the model Jaffe and others chart through Adam Smith, and that Solnit critiques as the infrastructure of liberal-journalistic storytelling about climate collapse today, this individuating equivalence recodes structural factors as individual plights and understands the emotional process of sympathetic interchange as an adequate mechanism of repair for the damage on view. (Its logic is inevitably scopic.) In this sense the central albeit disavowed function of sympathy is as an apparatus of mental hygiene for the empowered onlooker. The result is that the conditions generating the suffering remain unchanged. As Solnit instructs: "You need to look past the sparrow and see the whole system that allows—or allowed—the birds to flourish" ("Big Picture").

Sympathy's fantasy, then, is that emotional interchanges with individual wounded beings such as those that populate *Sing-Song* might heal, resolve, or redress the structural injury under view. But for Rossetti the conflict cannot be resolved, since it is endemic to a fallen modernity whose violence has only accelerated under industrialization. Against the privatizing and sentimental moralism of liberalisms then and now, Rossetti arrays what Mason has styled as a commitment to stand in solidarity with the precarious. By this anti-sentimental and, I am suggesting, politically consequential social and aesthetic universalism, the weak are in fact the greatest and "even the smallest details" can be seen as "part of a participatory creation that was made not for humans to subjugate, but as an expression of God's love for all" (Mason, *Rossetti,* 12).

Rossetti's goal is collective, then, and predicated not on restoring an alleged harmony but on bearing witness to "the ruin they have made," and to the specific bodies on which that organizing violence has fallen. Often, as in "Linnets," Rossetti's speculations on catastrophe at local scale draw forth meditations on the nature of poetic production, since the poems again inscribe at the level of their construction the conceptual content of their invocations of the minor and the tiny and the dying. The thrush poem described above, also in *Sing-Song*, is brief and crisp, memorializing a dead songbird while writing an obituary for the poet herself (figure 25):

> Dead in the cold, a song-singing thrush,
> Dead at the foot of a snowberry bush,—
> Weave him a coffin of rush,
> Dig him a grave where the soft mosses grow,
> Raise him a tombstone of snow.
>
> (ll. 1–5)

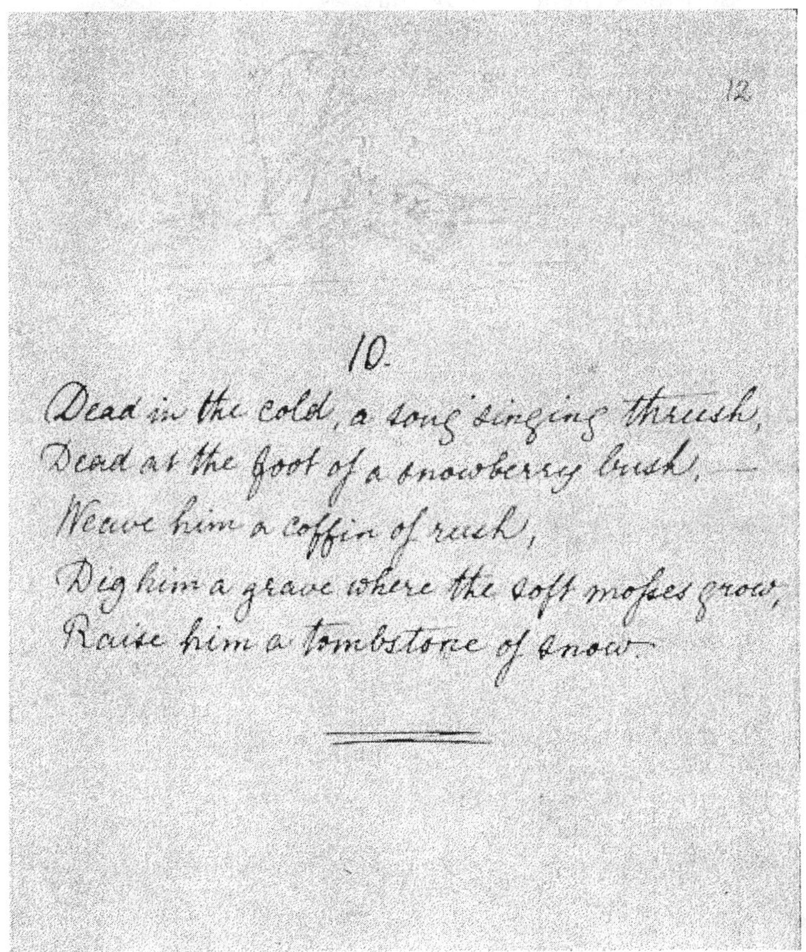

12

10.

Dead in the cold, a song singing thrush,
Dead at the foot of a snowberry bush, —
Weave him a coffin of rush,
Dig him a grave where the soft mosses grow,
Raise him a tombstone of snow.

FIGURE 25. Christina Rossetti, "Dead in the Cold" (1869–1870). Manuscript page from *Sing-Song: A Nursery Rhyme Book* (Add. 011652, g.16). British Library, UK. Photograph: © British Library Board.

The poem begins with a two-line prepositional duplication of "dead"—dead in, dead at—and proceeds to offer three actions as commands to the reader who has survived this violence: we are to *weave, dig,* and *raise.* But as Rossetti's original illustration helps emphasize, this is in no way a resurrection story, and no actions promise "solution." The speaker addresses those who have outlived the death event, directing auditors to build a physical monument that will not so much ameliorate the loss, nor yet restore it: instead we are left to gaze, in the repetitive structure of the lines, at three successive substitutes for what is gone: "coffin," "grave," "tombstone."

"Dead in the Cold" in this way figures its addressees as survivors who inhabit the same frozen world that proved fatal to the being over whose awkward corpse we now stand vigil. The fact that Rossetti directed in her will to have her own coffin be "perishable"—that is, that she be buried in a biodegradable wicker casket (quoted in Mason, *Rossetti,* 1), a coffin of rush—only enhances the autoreferential closure of the poem. In Rossetti's hands, the lyric poet or "song-singing thrush" imagines not his transhistorical persistence via song (Keats's and other Romantics' solution to this always bird-associated predicament) but rather her physical fragility and the fidelity of survivors who outlive her. Nightingales and thrushes are closely related passerine birds known as old-world flycatchers. But *thrush* also names a throat infection that carried a significant threat of death for infants in the mid-Victorian period. The echo adds a further turn to Rossetti's condensed inversion of the Keatsean problematic: here the poet does not live forever in masculine-heroic song but dies like any other biotic part of the world, singing itself now rendered impossible. "Our" predicament is to figure out how labor in the present (weave, dig, raise) might be organized in solidarity with this loss.

Rossetti's work articulates an autoreferential sense that scarce consolation will come with the fact that death is inescapable, disaster inherent to life, and transcendence a dream for a different world—"*nell'altro mundo,*" in her phrase from the Italian (quoted in Marsh 375). It is relevant that Rossetti's own health during the *Sing-Song* period was precarious in the extreme, her body a constant reminder of mortality and human finitude. She was spitting up blood as early as 1864, suffering acutely from the toxic London air, and by 1871 was "wretchedly ill," in her brother William's words (quoted in Battiscombe 140), with a version of Graves' disease. After a March 1871 doctor's visit—one of many—she was unable to climb stairs and couldn't hold a pen, experiencing "acute weakness and tremor in all limbs, together with high fever" (Marsh 396). Between 1871 and 1873, we are told, she

> suffered from a bewildering variety of ills, a swelling on her throat, heart-attacks, choking, frequent vomiting, sensations of intolerable heat, cough, neuralgia, fainting fits, and, not surprisingly, total exhaustion. (Battiscombe 141)

These wracking failures of her biotic system produced physical deformity, skin discoloration, and loss of hair. In Battiscombe's misogynist account these details are adduced to suggest that Rossetti's "worst trial" was "the ruin of her delicate beauty" (141). Her brother William claimed that his sister's "life and character" could not be grasped "without recognizing the fact that she was almost constantly invalid and often very ill" (Marsh 168), her symptoms extending even beyond the above to include "heart palpitations, stifling sensations, [and] breathing difficulties." Her throat and neck were ravaged by swelling, the voice of this song-singer transformed now to a "rasping croak" (Marsh 397). Like the nauseous and whirling figures of chapter 1, Rossetti found the seat of experience itself, the body, to be as broken as the world burning into soot around her.

During the whole of her mature period, I mean, Rossetti's physical self was proof that any life could only ever unfold in tactile and embodied anticipation of death. (Her descriptions of ailments included references to symptoms she refused to name, too intimate to be shared even with her closest friends.) But it was not just her own experience that proved that the upward plot of life was always aimed toward undoing. Her brother Dante would spin into an anomie of addiction and illness that culminated in his 1882 death from a kidney disease at age fifty-three. Her sister Maria, the person closest to her aside from their mother, died after a torturing bout of ovarian cancer in 1876, triggering in Christina fervent consideration (she said in a letter) "of the responsibilities of time & the all-importance of eternity" (*Letters* II, 121). Her mother died in 1886. It was during the intense illnesses of the *Sing-Song* period that she wrote "Mirrors of Life and Death," which begins this way:

> The mystery of Life, the mystery
> Of Death, I see
> Darkly as in a glass;
> Their shadows pass
> And talk with me.
>
> (ll. 1–5)

The syntactic structure of the sentence means that life and death fold ambiguously into a single phenomenon or mystery that can be "see[n]." But this figure is only visible, as Rossetti's reworking of 1 Corinthians 13:12 specifies, "darkly as in a glass." The shadows of this mystery themselves take shape as a kind of character, with whom Rossetti's speaker is strangely, colloquially intimate. They talk together.

Equally haunted but more famous artifacts like "Introspective," "Echo," "['When I Am Dead']," "After Death," and "At Home" pivot their inquiries into the inescapable quality of earthly disaster on a scene of death. In all of these so-called death lyrics, each one narrated by a disembodied voice from beyond the grave, de-subjectified speakers address living humans in a key of ambiguous indifference: "So lost from chime to everlasting chime / So cold and lost for evermore" ("Dead before Death," ll. 13–14). But it is in keeping with Rossetti's full-spectrum and (I am suggesting) counter-bourgeois investigations into death as inescapable finitude that she in no way restricted this condition to human speakers. Her lyrics often grant voice to nonhuman entities like water spirits, stars, trees, seasons, and the sea, each of which assumes the role of *I* in various poems (Mason, *Rossetti*, 35). These entities, too, experience the ruin that is the sole guarantee, she suggests, of temporal life.

Rossetti's animal poems, apocalyptic writings, and death lyrics stretch conventional presumptions about lyric personhood and provide evidence of a philosophical concern with finality and ending. They also help us see how this formally inventive woman poet, long cast as a religious scold and anti-secular mystic, drew on the capacities of her medium to probe the paradoxes of temporal representation occasioned by a world tending to crisis. In the frozen milieu of Rossetti's verse, bromides about happy endings and upward resolution dissolve into thin cold air. Consistently her poems articulate instead how vulnerable beings are conscripted into gendered relations of ownership and destruction. Rather than spurring improvement or growth, the Lockean paradigm is disaster itself, as the "plough in its flawless track pursuing / Involved them in one common ruin" ("A Handy Mole," ll. 15–16).

Writing here about moles and earthworms "of low degree" (l. 8), Rossetti describes how the metal implement of agricultural cultivation, the plow, works as a weapon for a relentless instrumentality toward the object world. This feminized and devalued sphere—"blind," Rossetti adds (l. 9)—stands on the receiving end of a motiveless rapine, in the full sense discussed in chapter 1, by which *rapio* means both capture by possession and a sexualized violation. "The impartial ploughshare of extinction," Rossetti concludes in the mole poem, "Annulled them all without distinction" (ll. 19–20). Against this almost metaphysicalized sense of gendered destruction, Rossetti arrays the minor and the fragile, vulnerable particulars "of low degree."

Minor Cry: Against Maximalism

As we've seen, the bleakest laments in *Sing-Song* are tiny and meditate on tiny losses: a nest, a bird, a baby. But Rossetti's scalar procedure finds over and over that the most cosmic scales of consequence are to be found in the lowest detail, the largest topics contained in the trifle—and vice versa. This process of scalar inversion insists on the downscaled and counter-heroic as the sphere in which a reparative materialist thought must transpire. The poetics of disaster and limitation is, in this sense, a poetics of the small—albeit (as I will suggest now) a poetics aimed toward the redemption of those details at a universal register. Among other things, Rossetti's dialectical emphasis on the slight and the exposed counters the widespread tendency, in techno-scientific narratives of climate change solutionism, toward grand narratives and planet-scaled analytic frameworks. "Climate" is itself part of this maximalist vocabulary, since it recasts multisystemic and always localized phenomena into a planet-sized object of analysis, this newly upsized object now available for potential manipulation by geoengineering and other techno-capitalist interventions.

It is now familiar to note that the world-scaled discourses of the Anthropocene increasingly voguish in the years after 2000 presume scientistic reason and market capitalism as the default languages in which "solutions" can be construed, and view "us"—an unthinking pronomial form coincident with Euro-American affluent whites, "Man"—as looking on at events from "a strategic external position from which the Earth system may be managed and piloted" (Bonneuil and Fressoz 62). As Christophe Bonneuil and Jean-Baptiste Fressoz among others have shown, this techno-managerial scalar maximalism essentially positions the poison (scientific managerial reason) as cure, a pharmakon-effect by which Anthropocene-speak becomes "a legitimizing philosophy" for ever more intensified capitalist domination (288). The historical fibers linking the neo-utilitarian ecological thought of Anthropocene ideology with the Cold War reoutfitting of freedom by cybernetic theorists was one topic of the last chapter.

It is less remarked upon that, in reverse fashion, leftist and anticapitalist analyses that have been concerned polemically to reanimate the era of "grand theory" (Fraser and Jaeggi 9) recapitulate the same tendency. Reinvigorated calls for abstraction and systemic analysis are salutary insofar as they counteract a narrow-minded particularism that has tended to abdicate responsibility to think in structural terms. Yet the new abstractionists also recapitulate Anthropocene-talk's maximalist overrunning of sensuous detail, recoding as critique the mandarin indifference to the lived scale of experience characteristic of neoliberal technics. System-level analyses aim to leave particularity behind so as to better consider "large historical processes, systemic conflicts, and deep-seated contradictions and crisis tendencies" in the system as such (Fraser and Jaeggi 9–10). Such upsizing brings important relations into view but adopts a view-from-nowhere scientism while overrunning the domain of material specificity that should be ground zero for materialist method. Chapter 2 explored this deductive epistemological approach in terms of its smothering and homogenizing approach to the object world it overcodes. One irony of the chapters you've read so far is that their unruly length arises paradoxically from a formal and ethical investment in details, a commitment to the particular waged against the deductive maximalisms of method.

In its literary-critical instantiations, anyway, the upwardly tending analytical bias toward the "general horizon" of method (Kornbluh, "Abstraction," 57) is a move away from the plane of immanent specificity and historical experience. Such motions are symptomatically expressed by an almost universal focus on plot form and a tendency toward argumentative paraphrase in place of direct citation or sustained reading. And from one angle it makes sense that calls for analytical abstraction would rely most on abstract or architectonic models of incident, character, and the total structure of a work; it makes sense, too, that such approaches would exhibit a corresponding apathy toward or inability to see the interference effects produced at what we might call lower frequencies: in substructural details such as metrical pattern and wobbled rhymes, for example, or productive ambiguity at the level of syntax, syllable, and phoneme. And it makes sense as well that the most vociferous interventions into the new abstractionism therefore tend to avoid poetry so as to focus on narrative forms like novels, films, and television series—stories. That is because from the abstracting perspective of summary and paraphrase these forms can more readily be made to yield the thesis-based results that themselves become amenable to polemical deployment.[9]

But for critical thought at least, the point is that the tiny detail and total system are linked in an ensemble that can only be construed in its momentary forms of appearance, never as totality, and never in ways reducible to thesis statement or polemic. Naomi Schor describes the feminized category of the detail as emerging as the undervalued other in masculine aesthetics of abstraction and totality. But her point is that this gendered dynamic is itself an artifact of patriarchal domination as a lived structure, and therefore to be inhabited and unworked from within (xliii). The process-based and unreifiable quality of dialectical analysis means that any materialist procedure will inevitably respond to the impossible requirement for a multitiered or split approach, one able to honor the fact that even the most abstract system is experienced always in particular form and, inevitably, in the body. Writing of Marxist historian and geographer Mike Davis, Gabriel Winant describes Davis's "insistence," unusual among his peers, "that, while the social world could be—and ultimately had to be—grasped as a unified totality, this totality could at the same time only be understood as a complex system of differentiated parts, each of which in turn had to be comprehended in its own specificity" (n.p.).[10]

Thinking with Rossetti along these lines helps us appreciate her efforts to develop an aesthetic procedure that arrays a concern for the fragile and small against world-scaled frameworks and totalizing analyses, albeit in an effort to make these local details resonate at total scale. (For Harrison, Rossetti was "preoccup[ied] with the details of quotidian experience," and convinced of "the potentially transcendental value of even the most ordinary images and events" [58, 59].) Compressed, colloquial, and most seemingly modest when reaching toward the "ruin" of general life, this prosaic metaphysics is easily misread by critics conditioned to presume, in line with the bourgeois principle of logical identity, that small things are small and big ones big.

A brief, seemingly simple late-career poem called "Time Seems Not Short" compresses all this work into just three stanzas, which together reorient the distinction between minor and the major, small and large, presumed in contemporary polemics about method. Again, flat language belies dramatic conceptual work and monosyllables cipher the world. The poem moves from spans of time perceptible to human speakers and "humankind" upward, outward—toward "eternity" and the interlocked movements of heavenly "sphere[s]," whose vastness makes motion feel like stillness:

Time seems not short:
If I so call to mind
Its vast prerogative to loose or bind,
And bear and strike amort
All humankind.

Time seems not long:
If I peer out and see
Sphere within sphere, time in eternity,
And hear the alternate song
Cry endlessly.

(ll. 1–10)

Characteristically these first two stanzas advance by negation, and in their play of canceled appearances—"Time seems not short," "Time seems not long"—readers are made to stumble over whether the abstract noun at the center of the poem is to be experienced as long or short, big or small. The point is that it is both, or rather that it can seem like either, depending on the aperture of evaluative vision we bring to the problem.

The first two stanzas underline this antinomy of temporal experience by highlighting death: the extinction of the human species, on the one hand, and the "endless" "cry" of eternity, on the other. The poem's final stanza radicalizes this rendering of temporal finitude, as it collapses the first two stanzas' opposed perspectives into disjunctive adverbial phrases that seem to unite them:

> Time *greatly short,*
> O time so *briefly long,*
> Yea, time sole battle ground of right and wrong;
> Art thou a time for sport
> And for a song?
>
> (ll. 11–15, emphasis added)

The poem ends by turning toward a personified time, now both infinite and human, to ask it a question the poem itself has already performatively answered, which is whether the problem of human-scaled and cosmically scaled temporalities, compressed into a single narrative, can become a fit subject for poetry at all.

Two points are important to this argument about the interface between maximal and minimal scales in Rossetti's poetry. The first (obvious) is that the poem itself is tiny: three five-line stanzas, composed almost entirely of plainspoken monosyllables. The second (less obvious) is that its central thematic content plays out at micrological scale as poetic effect, in an aesthetic version of the typological thinking Rossetti developed in dialogue with John Keble's Tractarianism, by which minuscule details instantiate "higher Truth" in analogical mode (Harrison 76). Here, each stanza of this poem about discrepant scales is organized according to a perfectly symmetrical scalar pattern, a bell curve by which lines of two, three, five, three, and then two iambic feet move us up and then down a graded scale of regular increment.

Yet the poem's rhyme scheme injects into this perfectly symmetrical rising and falling action a slight wobble, three b rhymes to two a's, such that the lines' evenness of scalar distension—scaling up, then scaling down—is overlaid with a kind of imbalance or irresolution: abbab. Coded into structure, this hesitation becomes thematic again when expressed in the poem's final question, which asks how human verse might measure against the vaster music of divine perfection. What can human language, segmented into measured feet and clipped stanzas, signify against its "alternate song," the "endless cry" of "eternity"? Such seemingly fussy metrical notation helps recover how Rossetti positions the sub-thematic singular effect—the wobbling feature or errant detail, barely perceptible at all—as the domain of final consequence, even as these sub-historical devices turn out to encode problems of maximal philosophical and material significance. Poetry becomes the necessary instrument for this impossible conceptual exercise.

The stakes of Rossetti's crucially poetic movement between opposed levels of address become clearer when considering that she is speaking of the actual universe. "Time Seems Not Short" appeared in Rossetti's 1893 collection, *Verses*, which gathered poems previously interspersed through her hybrid-format religious works, in a section called "Divers Worlds. Time and Eternity." This period of Rossetti's career was focused on what would come to be called her devotional works, expressions of fervent piety that would find shape in poems like "All Flesh Is Grass" and "Before the Beginning Thou Has Foreknown the End." It would also be expressed in her extended, line-by-line commentary on the book of Revelation published the previous year by the Society for Promoting Christian Knowledge (SPCK). Entitled *The Face of the Deep: A Devotional Commentary on the Apocalypse* (1892), that work is monumental and strange, a kind of *S/Z* of biblical hermeneutics. As in Barthes's fanatically close reading of Balzac's *Sarrasine, The Face of the Deep* finds Rossetti proceeding sentence by sentence through St. John's prophecy of the end of the world, offering a close reading of each verse conjoined to her own commentary and, occasionally, original poems.

Like much of Rossetti's work in this period and earlier, *The Face of the Deep* gravitates toward the Christian chiasmus by which death and redemption are dialectically linked. But its orientation toward the time of ends means that its emphasis falls most pressingly on death. The volume took Rossetti seven years to complete and was the only book she wrote after her mother died. In this sense it is a record of calamity's aftermath. Here as in her more seemingly secular poetry, the apocalyptic arrival of God's kingdom occasions meditations not just on glory and redemption but the character of diminishing worlds.

Filtered through Rossetti's "temperamental austerity" (Curran 292), apocalyptic cast of mind, and attraction to "neutralized and evened emotion" (Hassett, "Reticence," 501)—the frozen affect of detachment she shares with the cold women of her death poems—even the Good News of God's eventual reclamation of the world registers as disaster:

> I lift mine eyes to see: earth vanisheth.
> I lift up wistful eyes and bend my knee:
> Trembling, bowed down, and face to face with Death,
> I lift mine eyes to see.
>
> ("I lift mine eyes to see," ll. 1–4)

The tendency of these poems to refuse consolation in favor of impartial engagements with the bleakest outcomes of temporal life sits uneasily with what Battiscombe incomprehensibly refers to as the "general impression" of "deep happiness" given by *The Face of the Deep* (203). Seen together, the collection's apparently contradictory impulses toward tragedy and rejuvenation—the mystery of life, the mystery of death—mean that the arrival of Judgment registers not just as happy advent but as fulfillment of the "trembling" that has preceded it. Eschatology is salvation, but disaster too. As Rossetti explains in her preface to *The Face of the Deep*, the book will offer not just descriptions of how the apocalypse will reveal God's permanent glory, "but terrors likewise, doom, the Judgment, the opened Books, the lake of fire" (15). In the poem cited above, "earth vanisheth."

Critics have noted Rossetti's "developing apocalyptic vision" during this later period (Hu 186n) and cited her "fascination with the apocalypse" (Heady 150; cf. Humphries). Rossetti's always sharpening Tractarian fidelities meant that her interest was in apocalypse, not catastrophe, apocalypse being derived from *apokálupsis*, "revelation," and naming a process of disclosure or uncovering rather than world ending. (Catastrophe, too, is by etymology neutral, meaning "sudden turn or overturning"; its negative associations arrived only in modernity.) Though her own beliefs were most directly shaped by Keble's Tractarian high Anglicanism and the Oxford movement—as well as by its ideological successor, Ritualism—Rossetti refused the Oxford movement's drift toward Catholicism and maintained close ties to the lower-church traditions of premillenarianism and evangelical enthusiasm (McGann 240–41).

Here too, details matter. Though Rossetti's early religious education was relatively conventional, and her brothers wound up essentially atheists, by 1843 the family had begun attending the Christ Church Albany Street, where the incumbent was William Dodsworth, a Catholic-leaning supporter of Keble, Pusey, and Newman. Rossetti, her sister Maria, and their mother embraced this stringent and doctrinal version of Tractarian Anglo-Catholicism "with all the fervour of converts" (Battiscombe 30);

in her brother William Michael's words, Rossetti was "an Anglo-Catholic, and, among Anglo-Catholics, a puritan" (lxvi). For the Tractarians with whom Rossetti developed kinship, the natural world appeared as a system of revelations of God codified into material form: like Hopkins she viewed every particular instance in the world as charged with God's presence, in the sense that it was interfused with and coterminous with the divine. This univocal way of construing grace understood "all things to synchronously participate in the reality of God and the created world" (Mason, *Rossetti*, 44).

McGann and Harrington both note how, yet more idiosyncratically, Rossetti also subscribed to the notion of "Soul Sleep," whereby (in contrast to both Catholic and High Church doctrine, where the soul is judged individually at the moment of death and then at the final Judgment), a dead soul waits, unredeemed but frozen into inertia or suspension, until the Second Coming. The haunting force of an anthology piece like "Song ['When I Am Dead, My Dearest']" comes from this uncanny stasis, a disembodied sentience that maintains a semi-consciousness that can perceive but is also severed from embodied sense experience.

The poem that begins by urging "When I am dead, my dearest, / sing no sad songs for me," continues: "I shall not see the shadows, / I shall not feel the rain; / I shall not hear the nightingale / Sing on, as if in pain" (ll. 9–12). Again advancing by negation, Rossetti's nonliving speaker here explains all that she will not see, not feel, and not hear, a canceled apprehension Kathy Psomiades glosses as a "state of dreamlike suspension between life and death . . . described from within" (*Beauty's Body* 62). Rossetti composed "Song ['When I Am Dead']" during the Advent season of 1848, when she would have heard sermons delivered by Dodsworth at Christ Church that focused "on the end of the world and the Second Coming" (cited in D'Amico 34). Diane D'Amico speculates that "such sermons might easily have encouraged Rossetti to wonder about the time between death and resurrection" (34), but the detail confirms the traffic between personal and eschatological scales of disaster in Rossetti's project.

As I've suggested, this typological scalar doubling relied crucially on effects of poetic form. Here that point helps us appreciate Rossetti's ongoing effort to link dilemmas of lifelessness and disembodiment to what Barbara Herrnstein-Smith calls poetry's "closural effect[s]" (212): the specific capacity of poetic forms to model closure and its refusal on multiple, interlocking registers simultaneously. Stuart Curran observes that Rossetti "has only one real subject, mortality" (291), but we could more properly call her subject limitation or, as Emily Harrington terms it, "restriction," since mortality and the temporal processes appropriate to it provide typological images for the singsong measurements and allegedly simple structures of her clipped form. Hassett observes that Rossetti's "preference for short measures and full stops" and instinct toward the "confinement" of regular stanza forms (509) recast at ultraviolet scale her thematic obsession with boundaries and enclosure. Meanwhile, the time of verse itself—its status as temporally unfolding speech marked into intervals—is implicated in the content of these poems about duration and chronological experience. I recount these prior readings because I am merely adjusting them. The wobbling meter of "['When I Am Dead']," for instance, introduces irregular seven- and even eight-beat lines into the tick-tock trimeter of its regular form, generating a model at micro scale of temporal extension and compression. Again poetry emerges as the medium best able to perform these conceptual feats, albeit at a level undetectable from the top-down views of paraphrastic summary or instrumentalizing synopsis.

Performed likewise at the subverbal level of meter and the overt scale of theme and message, the poetry's minoritarian concerns with extension and limit are legible in yet another idiom in, for example, the interlocking calendric regimes that organize the "reading diary" of *Time Flies* (1885), published by SPCK seven years before *The Face of the Deep*. Dedicated to Rossetti's mother during a period when her health was collapsing (Frances Polidori would die in April of the next year), *Time Flies* is a kind of compendium for yearlong prayer and private study; it features an entry in prose or verse (or both) for each day of the calendar year, these followed by an appendix with entries for each holy day in the Anglican church calendar. Entries shift between modes and jump unexpectedly between topics, all of them religious. The volume's concerns with time and scale are not limited to its formal decision to follow in lockstep the Gregorian calendar. It also meditates on time in extended prose passages about death and eternity whose formal effects again experimentally enact the modulations they describe. *Time Flies* thus demonstrates in multiple registers Rossetti's materialist concern for biological and embodied life and its ends. But it suggests too that these resolutely particularized damages are legible best, or only, when viewed against vaster, spiritual, and even cosmic scales. Material harm and spiritual redemption must be thought in the same frame, and again it is the office of poetic presentation—here, a hybrid mixture of annotation, exegesis, and verse—to fold these diverse worlds into an almost impossible single configuration.

Performances like this show, among other things, how fiercely Rossetti (following Augustine, to whose writing she alludes) remained committed to thinking of time as a conceptual and therefore linguistic or poetic problem. Her late verses show her working out tentative solutions to it.

In the manner I've traced out already with "Time Seems Not Short," it would be possible to unpack yet further the fractal procedure by which Rossetti's death poems, for instance, coordinate macro- and microscaled time signatures and in so doing imagine interlocked scales of disaster: love lost, death in nature, and ends of worlds all folded together. In this typological mode, "world" is both the physical domain of biotic life and a metonym for a more general scene of plunder and avarice, a fallen totality metaphorized—as "Goblin Market" will demonstrate shortly—perhaps most vividly in the lapsarian vocabulary of sensual excess and sexualized domination. Perhaps surprisingly, however, Rossetti's counter-solutionist analysis did not generate despair, or at least not only despair. Rather, Rossetti finds in her diagnosis of a world built on capture the seeds for possibilities that do not answer to the name of hope. The poised or self-canceling quality of Rossetti's presentations mean that no positivity can unfold except from within elaborate negations and privative structures—the ultimate purity of redemption deferred, finally, to another world. In this one, only limitation.

Light Switch On, Light Switch Off

In a scholarly world still operating inside the bourgeois mental vocabulary charted in previous chapters, Rossetti's insistence on systemic foreclosure and inescapable limitation in the present can only seem perverse or even—in the habitual language of the criticism—"masochistic." That is because with important exceptions, readings of Victorian women's poetry continue to be organized by the dyadic conceptual schema I've suggested in other chapters is the hard-wiring or base code—the everyday common sense—of our burning world. This cognitive template holds out as positive values those categories of self-assertion, "voice," and authentic desire truly realized that are the moral idiom proper to "the self-possessed persons and discrete actions that liberalism presumes" (Stout 8).

In the more particular domain of feminist literary criticism, this impressively durable bourgeois schema means that women poets' *resistance* to male *dominance* must be figured in quasi-heroic and almost unfailingly individualist terms as a drama in which female *agents* struggle against the *structure* of a patriarchal literary and political culture that would restrict or thwart them. This version of the repressive hypothesis construes a domain of freedom against another zone, exactly antagonistic to it, that would hydraulically stifle freedom in the name of constraint, crushing agency in the name of structure.[11] In environmental quarters, cognate formations are legible in the solutionist rhetoric of "defeating" climate change or "beating" mass extinction, since these pet formations of the owning class cannot help but imagine a transcendent realm of freedom or Edenic domain of escape as the goal toward which "your individual actions" must necessarily be aimed.

This common sense has responded to Rossetti since the earliest days with a revealing form of befuddlement. William Michael Rossetti wrote in his 1904 introduction to his sister's poems that "one finds in her verse a noticeable combination of the outspoken with the self-repressing" (x), a confused formula that crisply introduces the binary model that has organized reactions to Rossetti for more than a century. William Michael Rossetti was no feminist, but the dynamic he describes can be recognized as the prototype for a liberal-feminist analytic committed to understanding an "outspoken" movement beyond constraint as opposed to "repressi[on]" by self and others. From the liberal-bourgeois perspective this dynamic can ever only satisfactorily be resolved in favor of "agency" or its related terms: action, resistance, transcendence, and the finding of voice or outspokenness. In place of these and other tropes of transcendence alluring to well-meaning readers even today, Rossetti presents tableaux of limitation and an insistence on the determining power of systemic processes beyond the individual's capacity to alter. It is in this context that we can best appreciate the observation that Rossetti is a poet "whose ideology . . . is largely uncongenial to the ideologies of the academic scholars who are most likely to study her today" (Harrison ix).

Into the complacent presumptions of bourgeois thought then and now, Rossetti's poems intercede like a short circuit. *Speaking Likenesses* was judged "peculiarly revolting" for its violence and oddity in 1874, and Jan Marsh in 1994 agreed that it was "not . . . charming" (418): critics in the late twentieth century especially observed the jarring movements of what Sandra Gilbert and Susan Gubar described in 1979 as Rossetti's "aesthetics of renunciation" (539), a refusal of transcendence and countervailing embrace of "captivity" (Harrison 80) that can be assimilated only with great difficulty into the liberal-bourgeois presumptions that freedom will be measured at the level of the individual unit; that liberty be defined as the absence of constraint; and that action can be assessed by visible outcome.[12]

Tacking away from this suite of post-Lockean presumptions, the poems also (so I will suggest) open a supra-individual beyond to the very tropes of suffocating circumstance and inevitable injury that obsess the liberal mind in the form of negative fantasy, as the dark flipside of "agency's" coin.[13] For these reasons Rossetti's (for us) confusing tendency to join containment, truncation, and reduction with a drive toward mutual being and solidarity has proven challenging to a liberal-feminist common sense still organizing much study of Victorian poetry, among many other domains of the cultural field, today, as Devin Garofalo has noted in relation to Elizabeth Barrett Browning.[14] But in the terms I have developed across this book, our confusion measures Rossetti's success, as she labors to develop a concept of possibility adequate to life in a broken world.

It bears repeating, therefore, that the agency-structure problematic has supplied a framework for the habits of mind that inform not just critical activity in Victorian studies and beyond since the 1980s but thinking about climate doom and "agency" today. As prior chapters suggested, this enduring bourgeois dilemma operates digitally insofar as it positions a domain of freedom against one of determination. Like the ones and zeros of binary code, the model works on a logic of purity to name a domain in which no external determination exercises force on the organism. For Hannah Arendt at least, the prophylactic separation between one category called "agency" from another called "determination" has the perverse effect of denying that human freedom is possible at all. That is because, if freedom is to mean "sovereignty" in the sense of the perfect autarkic capacity for self-directed activity that John Stuart Mill means, for example, when in *On Liberty* he writes that "over himself, over his own mind and body, the individual is sovereign" (13), then it's plain enough that it doesn't exist at all. In Arendt's words already cited in chapter 3, "whatever men may be, they are never sovereign" ("What Is Freedom?" 164). The problem then becomes displaced, as the freedom-determinism binary now takes shape as an almost endlessly reworked, constantly reconfigured oscillation between good freedom and bad determination, ever-new twists on what Jennifer Fleissner powerfully describes as the "enduring dialectic" at the core of the autonomy concept itself (29).

I have noted that Fleissner's intervention locates in the will and its cognate concepts of agency, autonomy, and voluntary decision not an answer but a problem: it is the "scene of an irreducible conflict" by which a "gap" inevitably opens up between what Arendt calls the "I-will" and the "I-can" (Fleissner 23). Whether framed in the affirmative terms of bourgeois mythmaking or in the critical terms of modern self-analysis charted by Fleissner, the alleged tension between agency and structure can only be ideologically explained away or "solved" with varying degrees of increasingly self-ironizing ingenuity. For Eve Sedgwick and Adam Frank, this ineluctable antinomy of bourgeois thought produces what they describe as an "impoverishing" "bipolar analytic framework." Elaborated and made complex though it often is, the light-switch-style flipping between freedom and determinism, agency and structure, results in analytical outputs that can (they say in a famous phrase) "adequately be summarized as 'kinda subversive, kinda hegemonic'" (5).[15]

One of this book's efforts has been to locate criticism's entanglement within the historical and conceptual dynamics it offers to analyze, as the traceries of bourgeois thought ramify not only in allegedly "external" sites like neoliberal climate policy but in "internal" ones like the very critical mechanisms we might use to understand or even critique that formation. This immanent model means that attention to otherwise tedious details of disciplinary genealogy can be instructive. In this case, the resurgence of *agency* as a fetish term in Victorianist criticism from the 1990s and early in the first decade of the 2000s is usefully symptomatic, since it can be taken as evidence of the surprising durability of the extractive order's logical categories across historical moments, and of their relative success in infiltrating even the most highly mediated domains of avowedly critical analysis.

Given the efficiency with which the woman question tends to detonate liberalism's operative binary, it makes sense that the most sophisticated treatments of the agency-structure dialectic in the domain of Victorianist criticism have come from feminist readers concerned to move past the myths of transcendence anchoring accounts from the 1970s and early 1980s. Describing the predicament of Victorian women's poetry, for example, Sandra Gilbert and Susan Gubar's treatment of 1979 described "the maze of societal constraints by which women poets have been surrounded." In their account, the result of this hegemonic surround is "a passionate renunciation of the self-assertion lyric poetry traditionally demands" (564). Here the renunciation can be *passionate* (that is, "subversive"), but what is renounced is "self-assertion" itself, meaning that hegemonic structure is ultimately reinstated. Kinda subversive, kinda hegemonic.

Writing a generation later in *Uneven Developments* (1988), meanwhile, Mary Poovey reworked Louis Althusser's notion of the ideological apparatus to explore the shaping functions of extant social orders on women's capacity in the mid-Victorian period. A year earlier, Nancy Armstrong's analysis in *Desire and Domestic Fiction* (1987) had focused on the *dispositif*, Michel Foucault's term for the flexible ensembles of force that generate and maintain a given order of knowledge. Foucault's term for this grid of enabling constraints has been translated variously as "device," "machinery," "apparatus," "construction," and "deployment," any one of which, as Armstrong showed, enabled the analysis of power to focus on not only its constraining qualities but its productive ones too.[16]

This vocabulary for a productive form of control enabled Armstrong's reworking of the structure-agency problem away from the hydraulic models of the repressive hypothesis into a kind of dialectical ensemble, where (in her Foucauldian inversion of the Gilbert and Gubar formulation above) bourgeois women could be construed as the positive producers or agents of the very social structures ensuring their own and others' subjection. However newly finessed, though, such accounts as Poovey's and Armstrong's reasserted the determining power of structure against a prior generation of liberal models, effectively flipping the light switch back again—as countervailing projects of the following generation, flipping the switch one more time, worked to show.[17] My point is that all these projects participate in a structure-agency oscillation that should itself become the object of historical analysis.

Drafted in the late 1990s and published in 2000, Amanda Anderson's "The Temptations of Aggrandized Agency" imagined itself as an exposé of Marxist and Foucauldian accounts of the prior decade, aiming to show that these "structure"-focused accounts secretly depended on the category of agency against their own argumentative thrust. In the sinews of their argumentation and grammar of their claims-making, Anderson suggested, those projects evinced a contradiction insofar as the critic's own interventions remained somehow exempt from the totalizing recapture of Althusserian ideology or Foucauldian discourse being described at the level of content—something Poovey acknowledged herself in some exceptionally perceptive paragraphs of *Uneven Developments* (20–23). Expanding on these in a withering late-career self-assessment, Poovey deepened this autocritique, dismissing her own early work as "a product of its time" ("Twenty Years" 10).

Anderson's attempt was to expose an allegedly symptomatic reliance, among the previous generation of feminist critics, on the categories of "critical lucidity and political potency"—agency—even in claims for the total force of "networks of power" ("Temptations" 44), or structure. Seen from the angle I am taking here, this micro-genealogy can be recognized not as the trail of disagreements it appeared to be but as a decades-long effort to toggle the switch of the constitutive antinomy of bourgeois thought. Among other things, this claim means that what such polemics as Anderson's highlighted best were the limitations of the conceptual language in which the entire discussion had taken place, and how successfully (I am suggesting) an extractive bourgeois liberalism's core analytic categories had come to structure even such admirably self-critical knowledge projects as the ones I've just rehearsed. This tiny reconstruction of a single cycle of academic argumentation thus stands to show how the intellectual architecture of a definitionally imperial ecocide remained intact throughout the period of my subdiscipline's unfolding. Poovey in particular had articulated her project in elaborative dialogue with her forbears, even (in the late work) with herself. And if Anderson's intervention claimed to supersede and cancel her mistaken predecessors, I offer this genealogy in a different key: as evidence that any speech act or conceptual intervention, including this one, unfolds only in dialogic relation to the prior utterances that have made it possible. Everything I just explained, I learned in a seminar taught by Kathy Psomiades decades ago.[18]

It scarcely needs repeating—though I will repeat it anyway—that the fantasy of unscripted voluntarism and its attendant logic of "agency" continues to prove persuasive in domains far more consequential than literary-historical micro-polemics. It drives orthodox rhetorics of environmental policy, for example, and sponsors the persistent fascination with rational-choice modeling even among progressive environmental groups. Funded by oil conglomerates, dark-money think tanks, and tech giants, this common sense is laundered by corporatized universities into spreadsheet to-do lists and carbon footprint worksheets, the PowerPoint decks of official climate thought now exhaling the pure serene of liberal metaphysics in ways that—whatever their stated concerns to mitigate fossil capitalism and its subsidiary processes—function most of all to ensure the smooth operation of the very extractionist paradigm whose consequences they purport to relieve.[19] Solutionism is one rhetoric in which this paradigm finds voice.

Then as now, from within an official perspective that joins meliorist progressivism with the implicitly binary metaphysics of agency I've been elaborating, any prolonged investigation into collapsed possibility and thwarted liberation can only be "pessimistic." The counter-discourses from within the humanities most often arrayed to combat this technocratic common sense are themselves implicated in the dilemma. An institutionalized environmental humanities, I am saying, awash in funding from provostial initiatives, has risen up to critique the techno-scientific liberalism just described by offering no shortage of hybrid agencies and flattened ontologies.

Yet as we've seen already, efforts to discover the implicitly salutary category of "agency" in ever more unlikely places recapitulates the bourgeois problematic at new scale, while freighting it with an aura of heroic, even neoromantic resistance. It is evidence of this unwilled compact between the technocrats and the new materialists that an entire sub-discourse has arisen from within the culture industry to critique the supposed "doomism" of pessimistic or overly negative appraisals of the current conjuncture. A search for books on the topic of hope and climate change yields an impressive list, by authors ranging from Elizabeth Kolbert to Michael Bloomberg. While their answers to the problem differ, all sides agree that more optimistic stories must be told: more hopeful paradigms are required, more agency must be discovered, so that we do not "fall into despair" and "lose the power for action." The point is that the oscillation between a tacitly privatized "agency" and totalized "structure" is common to technocratic managerialism and the neoromanticisms that would critique it. From within this shared grammar, as old as Locke and Kant, any suggestion that individual deeds will not effect structural change can only signify hopelessness or despair. Light switch on, light switch off.[20]

Sonnet Form and the Necessary Constraint

On the spectrum of all possible discourses, poetic speech surely rates as among the most highly constrained. That is because even its "freest" instantiations mobilize pre-given forms and play out already set patterns that will always at least partially predict (that is, determine) what can be said next. Rhyme is a particularly condensed instance of the algorithmic effect of all linguistic structures, given that the first term will set parameters that the second must fulfill, even if the fulfillment of this programmed expectation is partial or slanted.[21] Yet any given instance of human-generated poetic speech, however apparently wooden, mechanistic, or bound by formula, will always at least minimally torque the constraints of the sayable: it will reconfigure received languages, adjust the material that came before, such that the question of whether poetry is "autonomous," or emerges "freely," is a kind of elaborate joke.

This structurally ineradicable wobble sits at the heart of all speech and is radicalized, I am suggesting, in strongly formalized speech like poetry. This recombinatory creativity is captured in the term *idiom*, which describes the untranslatable specificity of a given linguistic pattern or verbal repertoire, while highlighting also that any given idiomatic system can always be internally repurposed or transformed. Indeed it is in the nature of an idiom that it is always undergoing such internal modifications. The point for this account of Rossetti's practice is that the metaphysical dilemma of idiom—the tension between pre-given template and the necessary elaboration that is then folded back into the system from which it deviated—is, in poetry, turned into a kind of organizing principle or animating problem: what it is about. Poetry is in this sense a technology of adjustment, since it names the necessary alterations, at local scale, of a preexisting algorithmic pattern or protocol without which that alteration could not have existed in the first place.

If poetry radicalizes the tension between code and message characterizing all speech, the sonnet pushes these dynamics even further. For

Andrew Galloway, a protocol, like an algorithm, is a "*proscription for structure* whose form of appearance can be any number of diagrams or shapes" (30, emphasis added). Galloway's description of coded digital procedure is useful in drawing out the specific features of the Petrarchan sonnet Rossetti sets to work in her career-long engagement with that form. The Italian sonnet, like any poetic structure but more so, is protocol-based or algorithmic object insofar as it obeys a set of laws or rules that restrict but also enable the output-form of certain likewise restricted thematic inputs: it will be about love, or love lost, or desire, etc., and it will have fourteen lines, an octave and a sestet, a volta, and a recognizable rhyme scheme familiar from undergraduate classrooms.

It is from within these rule-bound procedures that artificial intelligence engines for processing natural language might theoretically generate a sonnet with relative superficial believability—more so, perhaps, than it might be able to replicate more "open" forms like a free verse epic, an ode, or indeed a novel.[22] Still, from this narrowly formal perspective a perfect sonnet, if such a thing could be imagined, would display all the features of code-based or algorithmic art, in which (in artist Sol LeWitt's words) "all of the planning and decisions are made beforehand and the execution is a perfunctory affair" (quoted in Galloway 164). It was William Carlos Williams, deep into the twentieth century, who said that a poem is a machine made out of words (256), but earlier than that Coventry Patmore, in "An Essay on English Metrical Law" (1857) and George Saintsbury in *A History of English Prosody* (1910) had construed poetic form as its own kind of shaping apparatus or machine in this sense. As Yopie Prins notes in a reading of Swinburne, poetry's measure was "disciplinary" insofar as it was understood as participating in the regulative logic by which, as Kant says in the *Critique of Judgment*, an otherwise shapelessly "free" art would find its "constraint." Citing Patmore, not Kant, as her key example, Prins further explains how in the Victorian period meter itself was understood to constrain the unruly motion of spoken utterance: meter was "a formal grid or pattern of spacing, created by the alternation of quantifiable units" that would provide structure to otherwise free matter (90).

What Prins recovers is how Victorian metrical theory imagined rhythmic segments of individual "voice" to be smoothed out, disciplined into a grid of networked or "coordinated" constraint.[23] When Patmore refers to this effect as "the bonds of verse," he only makes explicit the extent to which the freedom-bondage dynamic central to early modern sovereignty theory, Enlightenment philosophy, and later liberalisms had transcoded itself into presumptions about the putatively *regulative* capacities of poetic meter (8).[24] This transmutation of prosodic theory into the light-switch problem of bourgeois thought and vice versa has led Meredith Martin and others to observe the political valences of seemingly arcane nineteenth-century debates about prosody. For Paul Fussell writing in the Cold War, anyway,

> meter is the most fundamental technique of order available to the poet. The other poetic techniques of order—rhyme, line division, stanzaic form, and over-all structure—are all projections and magnifications of the kind of formalizing repetition which meter embodies. They are meter writ large. (5)

Insofar as it radicalizes the various interlocked "techniques of order" central to metrical arrangement, it may be that the sonnet is the most rule-bound of rule-bound forms. That at least seems to be what attracted Rossetti to it, driving what critics have acknowledged as her "intense and lifelong" interest in the form (Hassett, *Patience*, 156). She is most famous for her crystalline and depersonalized sonnets like "After Death," but she deploys the form in many contexts, most often religious. *Verses* (1893) begins with a section called "Out of the Deep I have Called unto Thee, O Lord," and while the rest of the collection includes a diversity of stanza structures and metrical forms, this opening section contains seventeen sonnets and nothing else.

The editors of the *Cambridge Companion to the Sonnet* channel Foucault when they call this the form that best shows "how a formal pattern shapes and suggests desires" (Cousins and Howarth 4). In contrast to the binary or digital accounts that continue to construe "desire" as somehow unscripted and "pattern" as the structural constraint that would impinge on it, Rossetti develops by means of poetic structure an analog theory of attenuated effectivity. As I've tried to indicate, Rossetti's work is obsessed with showing how seemingly external or inherited constraints do not "restrict" or oppose otherwise free motion or original content; instead it suggests that all speech must transpire inside idioms inherited from the past and the pre-given forms in which those idioms unfold. Each new utterance thus develops not "freely"—whatever that might mean—but immanently through the structures that make them possible.

For Saintsbury, the sonnet is the most compressed and artificial and thus "lawful" of all poetic structures (349, 391). For this reason it is the machine whose orderly processes most call out for disruption from those interested in the dilemma of aesthetic or linguistic novelty. It is the structure Rossetti's correspondent Hopkins turns to, for example, when he decides to inhabit so as to rework convention in his so-called curtal sonnets, which reconfigure the fixity of this very old form by condensing its mathematical ratios; reworking the volta between octave and sestet; and adding half-lines at the end. Hopkins's famous diacritical annotations and wordy elaborations on the technical dimensions of sprung rhythm help suggest how his stretched or distended sonnets aspire to mathematicity or pretend to, even as they alter those very regulative formulas—not just by adding "tail-pieces" but by (for example) demolishing the pivot between octave and sestet by not *turning*, as the volta would normally require, but *adding* ("I say more," as he writes in "Kingfishers" [129, l. 9]). That is to say nothing of the constant transmutation of verbs into nouns, objects into subjects, a grammatical innovation that rewires the circuitry of conventional love poetry and devotional work by turning the objects that typically receive action into subjects that do it.

But also vice versa, since Hopkins's internal adjustment of the sonnet form also discloses how the apparent agents of action in fact receive inputs from beyond themselves. The windhover or airborne kestrel is just one instance of this relational quality, since here wind and bird fuse into mutuality, such that the subject-object distinction of normal grammar dissolves into incoherence (132, ll. 9–10). My point is that Hopkins goes to the sonnet to think through this insoluble paradox of individuation. He also deploys the form as a means to imagine how seemingly inert features of the world instantiate consequential activity on earth: birds, trees, and pieces of shaken foil all enact verbal processes and, in the only language we have to describe this not-inert quality, *become subjects*. Going further, however, and in the opposite direction from this Latourian commonplace (see "Agency" 5), Hopkins shows how such newly consequential particulars live out their membership in a universal set, folding their "agency" into larger processes of which they and their acts are only expressions. Against the durable bourgeois philosophies of contemporary ecocriticism, then, Hopkins's final turn discloses that the grammar of subjects and objects is finally inadequate to the mutualized univocity of being that is, he believes, the ontological condition of the created world. But it is also the only structure we have to describe that very problem.[25]

I have said already that Rossetti's verse, so marked by its fervent deferral to authority, has for decades generated confusion for a liberal feminism dedicated to post-Enlightenment principles of self-actualization and autonomy, what our students call finding their voice. Since Dante, the Petrarchan sonnet has been the form most closely associated with heteronormative love and, therefore, with the sexualized domination and patriarchal rule couched in that idea. No doubt because of this association, Rossetti focused on the Petrarchan sonnet to the point of near-obsession across her career, drawing on this template repeatedly in a sustained effort to trade the clichés of liberal feminism for focused studies of restriction and minor-scaled adjustment within scenes of seemingly total domination—places where "agency" is difficult to find. Canonical eviscerations of supposed love relations like "In An Artist's Studio" or "After Death" are examples of the Petrarchan sonnet's suitability for this purpose. *Later Life*, the hyper-religious "Double Sonnet of Sonnets" (1881), sharpens this dynamic of form and content to a zealous extreme. Its twenty-eight linked sonnets, divided into two fourteen-poem arcs, are best understood as a fractal, insofar as the poem cycle, like crystals or certain kinds of broccoli, repeats its form and ratios across multiple scales internal to itself. *Later Life* works fractally in this sense to intensify the restrictive qualities of the sonnet form, repeating its features at double scale so as to radicalize the dynamic of closure and elaboration that Herrnstein-Smith and others describe as constitutive of all poetic form, and that Gayatri Spivak has seen as the insoluble dilemma of speech within systems of domination. If "your voice" is supposed to be authentic, emanating from some pure or unscripted domain within you—do you even have one?

In Spivak's account as in Rossetti's, the repertoire of expression by which subaltern speech might be conveyed is itself part of the power structure rendering the speaker subaltern or under-other in the first place. The grammar of thought is part of the power relation, which means that relations of domination cannot be transcended or escaped but must be reworked from within. Seen from this perspective, the sonnet can be recognized as a formal technology by which the problem of a post-light-switch, inevitably immanent relationship to domination can be first focalized and then brought into dynamic play. That is because the sonnet form ensures that "speech," whether conceived in the voluntarist sense of direct self-expression or in the representational sense as the windowpane-clear communication of "ideas," is, in the context of this supersaturated formal and thematic inheritance, impossible. Any pure ideas or individual idea that a given speaker could bring to the poetic occasion will always be effectively overcoded by the inherited or pre-given structural grid—the algorithm—inside of which her verbal and epistemic performance will transpire.

It is worth pointing out in the context of this so-far-only philosophical argument about sonnet form that *Later Life* in some ways fits comfortably with its age: it participates in the revival of sonnet sequences especially among religious poets in the middle decades of the nineteenth century. The Victorian revival of the sonnet sequence or cycle included not just Browning's *Sonnets from the Portuguese* (1850), Meredith's *Modern Love* (1862), or Dante Rossetti's own *The House of Life* (1881).[26] Isaac Williams's

The Altar (1847) was a series of more than two hundred sonnets that engaged at length with what its subtitle calls "all aspects of 'the Great Christian Sacrifice'" (quoted in Harrison 70).

In Williams's liturgical exercise, the device of thematically linked sonnets ensured a wooden metronomic quality of near-stultifying (because pious) repetition. In the hands of Rossetti, the same device enables a delicately poised formal experiment on the nature of unwilled structure. *Later Life* starts by describing a total and explicitly masochistic fidelity to God: "For though He slays us we will trust in Him" (*Complete Poems* 346, sonnet 1, l. 9). It then pulls us on a journey of renunciation, constrained hope, and "promise unfulfilled" (357, sonnet no. 26, l. 3), only to alight, at last, on death, which at least—because it is a limit—holds to the chance of some future redemption (358, sonnet no. 28, ll. 1–4). What Rossetti models across these twenty-eight linked sonnets is how total liberation, naïve freedom, or authentic desire is unthinkable within the poetic and indeed conceptual constraints of what she calls "This Life" (357, sonnet no. 26, ll. 1, 9)—real life, she means, and also "this life," the poem we are reading about it.

Later Life is astonishing, but Rossetti's subtlest engagement with the problems of constraint and adjustment via the sonnet form is *Monna Innominata,* the "Sonnet of Sonnets." Published like *Later Life* in the 1881 collection *A Pageant and Other Poems, Monna Innominata* is another fractal experiment, since it tracks a sonnet-like movement of octave-to-sestet across its fourteen fourteen-line poems. It announces itself as a recovery of lost female voices. A prose preface to the poems, the only one Rossetti ever wrote (Hassett, *Patience,* 161), explains that the sequence to follow will be literally about a silenced or anonymous subject finding the power to speak. In this way does the poem cycle confront the liberal-feminist paradigm head on and in its own terms. As Rossetti explains, the work will unfold as the speech of an unnamed woman, a *Monna* or "madonna" who is *Innominata,* unnamed, and will help readers gain insight into what love poems might be like "had such a lady [as Petrarch's Laura] spoken for herself" (*Complete Poems* 294).

As criticism continues to observe, this preface suggests that the project is concerned fundamentally with the poetess tradition, and Rossetti's prefatory nod to Elizabeth Barrett Browning as "the Great Poetess of our own day" (*Complete Poems* 294) helps in this reading of *Monna Innominata* as a paradoxically low-key ratification of the *outspokenness* of female voices against their *silencing* by masculine structures. In fact it was this thematic binary that likely supplied her brother William Michael with the comment about Rossetti I cited above, in which she's alleged to be both outspoken and repressed at the same time. In this sense the sequence promises, so the preface seems to indicate, to "address and repair the aesthetic legacy of Petrarchanism" (Hassett, *Patience*, 162).

It is inconvenient, then, that the sonnets following this preface describe not agency achieved or desire consummated—someone finding her voice—but thwarted desire and a broken mutuality in which individual want can never be satisfied. Rather than the full personhood or liberal autonomy desired in bourgeois accounts, Rossetti depicts how a woman speaker is swallowed up, canceled, and introjected. With sharp economy, the sequence accomplishes the abolition of female personhood that is usefully viewed as the paradigmatic logic of coupledom under patriarchy. In "The Ontology of the Couple," Pearl Brilmyer, Filippo Trentin, and Zairong Xiang explain feminist theory's understanding of the logic of domination secreted within heteropatriarchal love, which can be expressed mathematically as a kind of zero-sum game. That is because the male term (1) is added to another term (1) to make a couple (2) in an equation that might be represented as 1 + 1 = 2. The problem under patriarchy is that the second, female term, cannot stand for itself, and does not "count" on its own. It is "a *zero* whose sublation into the male one" in the love relation means that it finally stands not as any autonomous integer, but as a "lack and absence": a no one. The woman is a null term, a one that, in political terms, "does not exist" (Brilmyer, Trentin, and Xiang, "Ontology," 227).

This dark mathematics is what Rossetti charts in *Monna Innominata*. The speaker of these sonnets declares her complete fidelity to her lover and confirms in the process her total subordination to him, her introjection into his number. In a twist on Rossetti's typical move of typological expansion, this male lover now becomes the speaker's entire world, a kind of total universe: "For one man is my world of all the men / This wide world holds; O love, my world is you" (*Complete Poems* 294, sonnet 1, ll. 7–8). This total collapse of world into man overleaps any notion of the female speaker's autonomy and represents, instead, the complete forfeiture of worldliness or feminine agency. The sonnet performs what Ronjaunee Chatterjee in an important reading calls Rossetti's "relentless interest in oneness that arise[s] from the failing 'two' of heterosexual difference" (94).

Monna Innominata's bleak sequence includes the infamous line that "woman is the helpmeet made for man" (*Complete Poems* 297, sonnet 5, l. 14) and sets up the general feminist predicament by which, under a smothering and fundamentally inescapable patriarchy, the choice becomes whether one will be subsumed under another or be discarded. In one gloss on *Monna Innominata*, the "alternatives" become (1) a "fusion in which individual identity and, by implication, female identity, are canceled," or (2) a "hierarchical subordination in which the female identity can be defined only in relation to male identity" (D. Rosenblum, *Christina Rossetti*, 206). The collapse of freedom's promise into a choice between two forms of self-annulment means that *Monna Innominata* radicalizes even the stringent and apparently critical analysis of objectification in a more famous sonnet like "In an Artist's Studio," mentioned above. In that most archetypal of Rossetti's sonnets, the gendered dynamic of subject-object separation is properly vampiric, as the male artist "feeds upon her face by day and night," and (in the famous lines) sees his female muse "Not as she is, but was when hope shone bright; / Not as she is, but as she fills his dream" (ll. 9, 13–14).

Monna Innominata pushes the other-abolishing masculine logic of "In an Artist's Studio" even further. It documents that the final result of heteropatriarchal love's introjective accounting is, Rossetti writes, "one":

> I loved and guessed at you; you construed me
> And loved me for what might or might not be—
> Nay, weights and measures do us both a wrong.
> For verily love knows not 'mine' or 'thine;'
> With separate 'I' and 'thou' free love has done,
> For one is both and both are one in love:
> Rich love knows nought of 'thine that is not mine;'
> Both have the strength and both the length thereof,
> Both of us, of the love which makes us one.
>
> (ll. 6–14)

In the scenario Rossetti imagines here, the conventional I-thou relation is abolished and the misogynist magic act seems perfectly in place. But for Rossetti—as she repeats the terms *I* and *thou*, *you* and *me*, *one* and *both* and *nought* across the grid of the sonnet like a koan—the resulting unity is not imagined in terms of the null-set accounting of the love relation as described by feminist critique. To be sure, she puns on exactly this reading, noting that "love knows *nought* of 'thine that is not mine.'"

But this nought does not describe the subtractive procedure by which a self (1) is lost. Instead, the argument takes shape as a scandal to erotic reckoning, as Rossetti's new math aims to short-circuit the spreadsheet logic of human relations it nevertheless alludes to constantly. The new relation will defeat the "weights and measures" that "do us wrong." It suspends transactional ordering, refuses the fungibility of compared terms. Love is "rich," we read, but the very concept that something could be "thine that is not mine" no longer makes sense. In lieu of privatized ownership and possessive individualism, something else: in the final lines, a thrice-repeated "both" enmeshes sonically with a twice-repeated "love" to resolve into—but not add up to—the final term, "one": *Both of us, of the love that makes us one.* Poetic presentation makes this nonstandard thought possible.

Lodged at the center of *Monna Innominata*'s problem-setting octave (it's number 4 in the sequence), "I loved you first" thus plays out a counter-accounting by which the linked mechanisms of bourgeois individuation and property ownership dissolve into something like mutual life. In this new solidarity, the problem's initial integers do not so much add up but disband and coalesce into a new term, "one," that stands orthogonal to the zero-sum erotic domination that sits, Rossetti suggests, at the core of post-utilitarian or normal thought. The next sonnet in the sequence picks all this up and turns it again, pronomial forms and possessives now bearing the burden of this syntactic and philosophical experiment in non-bourgeois relation. The speaker's male lover is now "my heart's heart, and you who are to me / More than myself myself" (*Complete Poems* 296, sonnet 5, ll. 1–2): two fold now into one, the hiccuping repetition of *myself myself* doubling the reflexive pronoun and disclosing how this union of two into one cannot be fit into standard syntax. It will always sound weird.

In the context of a heteropatriarchal erotics that Rossetti elsewhere figures as explicitly vampiric, it is possible that from within our presumptions about autonomy and self-directed autarky, this dynamic can only feel cringey. It runs afoul, I mean, of ethical programs built on liberal ideas of differentiation and autonomy, as we saw in relation to the similar experiments of *Wuthering Heights* in chapter 2. In refusing "erotic complementarity produced through gender binaries," as Chatterjee observes of *Goblin Market* (113), *Monna Innominata* opens a different space: its emphasis on what appears to be total female submission counteracts our residual bourgeois values to such a degree that its experiment is all but impossible not to greet with almost somatized political revulsion.

Can "liberty" be thought, outside the masculine vocabulary of fraternity, equality, and sovereignty bequeathed to us from the bourgeois tradition? For readers deep inside the ethical and historical-political programs Rossetti aims here to disrupt, Rossetti's experiment with transpersonal solidarity seems regressive, like its own form of domination—and that is how it has been read, with a mixture of embarrassment and incomprehension, since at least the mid-twentieth century. Yet here again the shame of critical practice measures our cognitive immersion in the paradigms Rossetti herself associates with a depletionary and cancerous ideology of freedom, capturing the world and taming it for use. Her work is poetically to reoutfit the logic of bourgeois relation under the aspect of union and solidarity. It is our task, at the tail end of the social and environmental crises she diagnosed in their emergent phase, to make ourselves adequate to this effort.

The speaker reports that "we stand / As happy equals in the flowering land / Of love" (*Complete Poems* 297, sonnet 7, ll. 2–3). The seemingly trite phrase in fact redeems a relation of misogynist hierarchy into a revised conception of equality. Here a subtractive equationalism of bourgeois erotics (1+1/0=1) now appears as restoring surplus, "love's liberty" transpiring "in the flowering land" (297, sonnet no. 7, ll. 8, 3). Rossetti's test of this flowering mutuality, in the sororal scenario of *Goblin Market*, will help lay bare the stakes of this restorative experiment shortly. Here the double bind of subaltern positioning means that *Monna Innominata* enacts the problems of coverture, subsumption, and solidarity formally too, in the poetic structure radicalized in the sonnet-of-sonnets device. Poem 12 in the sequence tells of another masochistic renunciation, tough to read in our age of self-help, in which the speaker defers her whole being to the male lover who rejects her for somebody else. Here's the sestet:

> For if I did not love you, it might be
> That I should grudge you some one dear delight;
> But since the heart is yours that was mine own,
> Your pleasure is my pleasure, right my right,
> Your honourable freedom makes me free,
> And you companioned I am not alone.
>
> (*Complete Poems* 300, sonnet 12, ll. 9–14)

When Rossetti's speaker writes that "the heart is yours that was mine own," and when she says that "your pleasure is my pleasure, [your] right my right," she evacuates "herself" and gives over precisely the dream of agency (as "right") that an implicitly extractionist liberal theory continues to offer as the only rubric under which action might transpire. This effect of canceled will and smothered legal personhood is doubled insofar as it comes at a formal level too, as the female poet's individual discourse, whatever that may be, is subordinated to, made possible only within, the shaping grid of one of the oldest and most masculine forms in literature, the Petrarchan sonnet.

Rather than unfettered freedom or transcendent individualism we get something like Hopkins's notion that you speak yourself most fully when you participate in something else; or T. S. Eliot's sense that the poet's work is "a continual surrender of himself" to tradition (55). In a less heroic idiom we might think of Elizabeth Grosz, drawing lessons from Darwin, who sees all new forms as but the reanimation of older ones, with mutations. Adding a turn to this point about path dependency and elaboration, what Rossetti's vision of liberty-in-renunciation helps us imagine is that freedom and constraint are but a depletionary modernity's own vocabulary for understanding how action transpires. Rossetti's poetic undoing of the jargon of agency exposes the ones and zeros of this binarist code as a target of epistemological sabotage and installs in its place an analog solidarity that cannot easily be assimilated into the scripts of sovereign freedom we still bring to bear on it. And as Rossetti continually reminds us, the very speech that makes up these poems is borrowed and recirculated, "dead for all its breath" (*Complete Poems* 357, sonnet 26, l. 9). But it is also the shadow or typological image of some purer language, God's, whose domain of purer liberation calls out as the object of struggle in the unredeemed world we actually inhabit. "Total victory," Solnit writes, "has always seemed like a secular equivalent of paradise" (*Hope* xxiv): on earth, victory will always be partial, if you get it at all.

It matters to the argument of this book that Rossetti's immanent critique of the ideology of emancipation was launched at the moment when the early extractive empire was developing its most enduring self-reports. Out of the ruins of bourgeois predication she engineered new models for imagining the constraints that shape all thought. In so doing she hints at how a fallen conceptual and political language might be salvaged, its broken grammars twisted into new shapes adequate to the idea that you, companioned, might leave me not alone.

Locked Together in One Nest

Rossetti's most famous poem does not come from *Sing-Song, The Face of the Deep,* or any of the other devotional works that gave polygeneric shape to her developing fidelities as her body failed over the last decades of her life. *Goblin Market and Other Poems* (1862) was her first publication and was organized around a title poem that continues to feature as its author's signature production, a star of undergraduate syllabi and courses on nineteenth-century feminisms to this day. Following sisters Lizzie and Laura as they attempt to resist the delicious but appalling ministrations of goblin men bearing "evil gifts" (l. 66), the poem is an ambiguous investigation of the market economy and its vampiric relationship to women's bodies and the earth itself. For "who knows," Laura says, "upon what soil they fed / Their hungry thirsty roots?" (ll. 44–45)

Rossetti represents the market for these voracious goods as a dark but alluring place, a zone of domination that nevertheless exerts an almost gravitational attraction on those who would attempt to avoid or escape it. The delicious temptations of the goblin economy are addictive, then, but also nonregenerative: like the products of the actual economy, the goblin world's fruits are the result of a system predicated on what Rossetti, in a short story, called the "woe and ruin" inherent to a rising industrial capitalism (Marsh 367). The plot of her 1867 story "A Safe Investment," published in *Churchman's Shilling* magazine, describes modernity as a "gross darkness" that "covered the land" (241) and, in just a few pages, takes the failure of a bank as microcosm for a series of yet more sensational disasters, including storms, shipwreck, and a gasworks explosion, the fossil-capitalist system now turning into an emblem of a Carlylean fantasia of modernity's self-destruction. (The story references *Signs of the Times* on the first page, 241, and its scenario bears a nontrivial relationship to that of *Maud*, discussed in chapter 1). Rossetti's story describes a nighttime cityscape, draped in its now metaphorically freighted "darkness."

> Then a cry went up, then there came the crash and crush of a tremendous explosion, and then darkness settled once more over its own dominion; whilst through the darkness those who could not see each other's faces heard each other's groans, cries for help, shrieks of terror or of agonizing pain. All the gas-lamps of the city had gone out as though at a single whiff, for it was an explosion of the great central gasworks which had taken place. And the darkness deepened. ("Safe" 243)

"A Safe Investment" works straightforwardly to condemn this self-immolating fossil economy. It moralizes against a contemporary society that had been riven by actual bank failures no less than by the apparent disorder of the riots and other spasms of social instability in the leadup to the Second Reform Bill. Yet within its rearguard condemnation of modern darkness, the story locates a key truth, since it construes a blinded social atomization as intimately linked to, and even deriving from, the fossil system. This social reality is defined by garish "flare[s] of red light" (242) and explosions, which are linked in turn to a financial apparatus that is fundamentally unstable—since even the "old-established county bank," when beset by shipwreck, explosion, and fraud, will topple (244). "Every man beheld an enemy in his neighbor," Rossetti writes, "an enemy who would forestall others and save himself at all costs" (245).

The nightmare of capitalist life takes shape in "A Safe Investment" as a clunky morality story in which a "solitary traveller" on a white horse offers the only hope for resolution (242). In this approach it replicates the techno-managerial logics of climate liberalism, which can only construe heroic instances of magic—carbon capture, atmospheric seeding, travelers on white horses—as capable of ameliorating a fully entrenched status quo. "Goblin Market" is subtler. It recodes the extractive system into fairy terms while trafficking in the very sensuality and enjoyment it otherwise warns against (Mendoza 914). In keeping with this internally contradictory relation, Rossetti shows how the market economy of the goblin world offers an intense form of pleasure that shifts instantly, Lizzie finds, into its opposite: "She sucked and sucked and sucked the more / Fruits which that unknown orchard bore; / She sucked until her lips were sore; Then flung the emptied rinds away" (ll. 134–37). Lizzie's painful experience of pleasure produces a form of somatic gratification that, routinized across thumping iambs ("She sucked and sucked and sucked the more"), transforms into a disaffected aphasia that is, Rossetti adds, extractive in its central logic: she "flung the emptied rinds away."

Consumption, disorientation, waste: Rossetti's cryptic analysis of market capitalism finds that practices of consumer behavior mimic at smaller scale the extractive processes yielding the goods in the first place, as "fruits" are stripped from "an unknown orchard" and sold. It is important that, contrary to readings that insist on the Edenic valences of Laura and Lizzie's scenario, these fruits are not depicted as natural at all: they are not, contra the Goblins' advertisements, "wild [and] free-born" (l. 11), nor yet are they the spontaneous issue of pastoral processes. Their origins are, rather, elaborately obscured (Menke, Mendoza), revealed as "unknown," even as the "hungry thirsty roots" of these delicious commodities are presumed to deplete the soil. Relentlessly sexualized and issuing from supply chains that are darkly exploitative and of undetermined shape, these wares—like any other fruit of an extractive economy—arrive to their consumers bearing no trace of the despoliation that produced them: they are "full and fine," "plump," and "bloom-down-cheeked": "sweet to tongue and sound to eye" (ll. 21, 7, 9, 30).

These and the many other moments of connection between sexualized fruit and women's bodies mean that the process of consumption is imagined in *Goblin Market* as another form of violent introjection: one more mechanism by which the other is subsumed into a feeding self. The original violence of the subject-object relation under extractive consumption extends now to the mode of payment in the poem. Laura clips a lock and drops a tear in exchange for her fruits, confirming that the price of participation in the market economy is the attrition and sacrifice of one's own body, "precious" and "rare" (ll. 126–27). Here an extractive system of supposedly free exchange—driven by desire for sensual gratification, supplied by raw materials of unknown source, defined by relations of "feeding," "eating," and "crushing"—is also self-harming in a literal sense or, in Miller's term, depletionary. It converts rare and precious singularities into values on a balance sheet of exchange.

The poem's original title was to be "A Peep at the Goblins": a riff on Anna Eliza Bray's 1854 *A Peep at the Pixies*. But on encouragement from her brother Dante, Rossetti settled on a title that emphasized the social form—capitalism—the poem allegorizes. "Come buy," the small men command. By figuring the predatory relation of "goblin *men*" toward their woman customers, the poem anatomizes the gendered violence at the core of the extractive economy, giving fairy form to the nonreciprocal relationship of exploitation, organized by *rapio*, seizure, that secretly structures any scene of supposedly free exchange. If bourgeois thought cannot understand social relations except in the voluntarist terms of consent and compulsion, free choice or its negation, Rossetti gives shape to the structures of coercion that persist in scenes of apparent choice, disclosing the mechanisms of capture that threaten structurally dominated bodies "with gibe or curse / Or something worse" (ll. 457–58).

Laura enters this theater of unfreedom freely, in a way—but is driven by something inside her, too, a "sweet-tooth" (l. 115) and something in her essence: she is "curious Laura" (l. 69), the Homeric epithet signaling an essential or unwilled quality predating the modern subject's putatively voluntary relation to its desires. Did she choose? Once sampled, the products are powerful enough in their appeal to erode any capacity to decide by means of something called will. It is a scene of compulsion re-narrated as choice, bourgeois liberalism's central value category dissolved under the pressure of a somatized desire in ways Eve Sedgwick noted of addiction narratives of the 1980s, in the essay I discussed in chapter 4, "Epidemics of the Will." Like Jeanie, who died from her addiction to the fruits, Laura didn't just *want* them or *choose* them but "pined and pined away; / Sought them by night and day" (ll. 154–55).

Such phrases show the breakdown of liberal voluntarism at the site of desire and whisper with what Chatterjee calls "the murmurs of a different architecture of selfhood" (93). After setting out to acquire an antidote for her sister, Lizzie too enters into the commodity relation, this time "freely" paying a penny in a decision she immediately wants to reverse. But the masculine machine of accumulation will not restore her payment.

Lashing their tails
They trod and hustled her,

Elbowed and jostled her,
Clawed with their nails,
Barking, mewing, hissing, mocking,
Tore her gown and soiled her stocking,
Twitched her hair out by the roots,
Stamped upon her tender feet,
Held her hands and squeezed their fruits
Against her mouth to make her eat.

(ll. 398–407).

The extravagant violation of her body produces in Lizzie a kind of broken trauma, and, dazed, she doesn't know what day it is. She endures, however, and the disruptive force of her refusal carves out some small space of possibility for her: "At last the evil people, / Worn out by her resistance, / Flung back her penny" (ll. 437–39). When Lizzie returns to her sister after this refusal, she asserts a lateral sororal connection (Chatterjee 101, cf. Harrington) and says to her sister, "never mind my bruises" (l. 467). The request confirms that their connection, and the feminine solidarity it figures, is born in shared injury. They have both been bruised. It is not freedom.

As Isobel Armstrong points out, whatever liberty Laura may enjoy consists in her "assent to being overwhelmed" (quoted in Hassett, *Patience,* 24), while Lizzie's autonomy, such as it is, appears to subsist in her total abnegation of her self for the benefit of her sister: "Eat me, drink me, love me," she says, "Laura, make much of me: / For your sake I have braved the glen / And had to do with goblin merchant men" (ll. 471–74). Psomiades notices how whatever power Lizzie has emerges from refusal: she keeps her silver coin, refuses to grant access to her body, and "emerges victorious, even though the goblins take their frustrations out on that very body" (*Beauty's* 50). Lizzie is then a bearer of injury inflicted in the masculine sphere of extractive accumulation: an endurer of its violence who uses the trace of this harm (the fruit, now spangling her skin) to nourish her ailing sister. Observed the flummoxed male editor of *English Poetesses* in 1883: "I do not think this is a pleasant story" (quoted in Hassett, *Patience,* 24).

By thus recoding injury as the site of a rejuvenation based on female solidarity, Rossetti places the degree zero of a renovated concept of possibility not in myths of transcendence but in the inevitable injuries sustained in a heteropatriarchal extractive economy where brutality is built into the normal order of things. Lizzie cannot dictate terms, redirect the goblins, or meaningfully alter the course of their efforts to generate value for themselves in the marketplace. But her commitment becomes a kind of weapon, confirming Chatterjee's observation that the poem "sidestep[s] entrenched notions of individualism and completeness" by emphasizing a sororal solidarity that emerges, against patriarchy and masculine rapine, as a "generative structure in its own right" (112, 115). Lizzie is not allowed truly to refuse, of course; her resistance is, at one level, futile. But the residue of that refusal—the juice of the fruits that she does not eat, smashed across her own skin—registers on the surface of her body, becoming food for her sister.

Whether read as Christianized sacrifice or erotic indulgence, *Goblin Market* thus describes a fundamentally self-sacrificing logic that is less like the vampirism it is still mistaken for and more like mutual aid, in the sense Peter Kropotkin understands as "the kinds of care animals, birds, and humans tend to show other members of their species when surviving in the face of common environmental struggles" (Gammage n.p.). Against nightmare visions of a goblin world defined by self-interested violence and extraction-based accumulation, mutual aid posits care work and solidarity as the means by which survival can be secured and struggles continued in the future. In the poem, Lizzie says Laura should consume her "never mind my bruises" and asks Laura to "make much of me": to use her to produce something curative to herself. Self and other dissolve as Laura wonders whether her sister will be "Undone in mine undoing / And ruined in my ruin" (ll. 482–83). The line underscores what *Sing-Song* called a "common ruin" while suggesting that out of this shared disaster some new capacity might yet emerge—in the same Christianized dialectical motion, perhaps, by which "life" emerges "out of death" (l. 524).

The total system of goblin economy is an extractionist nightmare and delicious catastrophe, no less addicting than fossil fuels or cheap red meat. Yet from within this depletionary conjuncture a muted form of possibility takes shape: it does not follow from myths of escape or fairy tales of purity, but from acts of material connection in a shared struggle, and at moments of anti-individual self-abolition stolen from the ruins of a world that has been designed to annul us all without distinction. This refusal of naïve or first-order ideas of freedom in favor of the mixed—or, I will say, dialectical—qualities of mutual being exposes terms like *will, autonomy,* and even *freedom* as fairy stuff: in place of these dreams stands a form of intimacy and struggle characterized by the effort to sustain one another in a wasted world. Here the residues of collective trauma are redeemed, outside the logic of monetary exchange, into a nourishment by which one's sisters might be kept alive until tomorrow (figure 26).

I hope it is clear enough how this form of solidarity might stand against privatized dreams of "action" and oppose, too, PowerPoint lessons about

FIGURE 26. Dante Gabriel Rossetti's frontispiece for Christina Rossetti's *Goblin Market and Other Poems* (London: Macmillan, [1862] 1865). Booth Family Center for Special Collections, Georgetown University Library, Washington, DC. Photograph: Jay Silvestre, Booth Family Center for Special Collections.

your carbon footprint still offered as the only conceivable genre of climate action while the world drowns. In the poem, this interinvolved mutuality is modeled physically, I've suggested, in scenes of eroticized feeding and self-abnegating mutual aid; it takes shape too when the sisters merge grammatically into a single body, "'two' who are the same" (Hassett, *Patience*, 25–26). In the scene, the prime integer of bourgeois thought, one, now rolls out to contain two, and this double form returns again to become a single, entangled thing, a new one whose proper value is no longer counted on the ledger but in the natural world, where counting means nothing at all:

> Golden head by golden head,
> Like two pigeons in one nest
> Folded in each other's wings,
> Like two blossoms with one stem,
> Like two flakes of new-fall'n snow,
> Like two wands of ivory

Tipped with gold for awful kings.
[. . .]
Cheek to cheek and breast to breast
Locked together in one nest.

(ll. 184–98)

Pastoral it may seem, but the nest in which the sisters are locked is lacerated by the violence of the world to which it would seem to stand as remedy and counter-term. It is not only "snow" that is "new-fall'n" but Laura too; and the sovereign violence of "awful kings" and their phallic "wands" disturb the feminized image of touching bodies in a shared bower. Like the linnets' nest broken by "cruel boys" in *Sing-Song*, this nest offers no escape.

Chatterjee observes how, sealed poetically with the repetition of the basic simile structure "like" "like" "like," Lizzie and Laura's folding-together cuts against bourgeois fantasies of autonomy, but also (we can add) the whole suite of ethical categories following from it—will, voluntariness, agency—and, I am suggesting, the institutional forms that materialize these fictions in practice: from tort law and carbon budgets to environmental literary criticism focused on "agency" and its supposed distribution. The dissolution of these fairy tales is acted out here in a choreography of sisterly closeness, suggesting that the ultimate form of self is involvement with another, "new logics of gendered difference" now emerging into view that "may be partial and laterally organized" (Chatterjee 101). Having endured the burning world's marketplace, the sisters no longer appear as the unchained free subjects of bourgeois myth. Instead they are, Rossetti specifies, "locked together."

As Michelle Rada observes, solidarity is usefully understood as the apparently paradoxical construction and maintenance of identity across difference: it is "a link of care and commitment . . . between divided subjects and between their overdetermined desires" (Rada 11, citing Zeavin). This process of bond building across the gulf of subjective difference is crucially distinct from liberal technologies like sympathetic identification or empathy, which not only individuate and depoliticize but strive "toward a feeling of cohesion between the self and other (and self and self)." Against this drive toward homogenized sameness, solidarity places value in the formation of "a collective of bodies bonded in care and desire" (Rada 11): a sum of human belonging greater than its parts, such that one plus one does not make two, but one, or zero, or the entire world:

She clung about her sister,
Kissed and kissed and kissed her:
Tears once again

Refreshed her shrunken eyes,
Dropping like rain
After long sultry drouth;
Shaking with aguish fear, and pain,
She kissed and kissed her with a hungry mouth.

(ll. 485–92)

For Rossetti, the boundary between two beings becomes scarcely discernible in the additive syntax and repeat rhyme of "kissed her." It's true that the simple grammar of this transitive verbal phrase seems to insist on a distinction between acting subject and receiving object. Yet these positions fold together, as predication implodes under the pressure of union. After the kiss, "her lips began to scorch," and the sense of the passage appears to indicate that the *her* of line 493 is Laura. But grammatically it's ambiguous, syntax again playing out the collapse of distinction physicalized in the repetitive touching and introjecting consumption described in the prior lines.

Performed here as the breakdown of normal predication (the lips both receiving the scorching and, perhaps, performing it), this transferential scene means that the two sisters now "cling together" as they later suggest their own children should (l. 561). And in the singsong conclusion many have found cloying, we find instead a repetition of the personal pronoun "one" emphasizing how the mathemes of bourgeois accounting dissolve into something outside financial reckoning. There's no friend like a sister, writes Rossetti,

In calm or stormy weather;
To cheer one on the tedious way,
To fetch one if one goes astray,
To lift one if one totters down,
To strengthen whilst one stands.

(ll. 563–67).

Against algorithmic action models and cue-ball sequences of cause and effect, Rossetti offers a vision of sororal entanglement and common struggle. *One stands*: this picture of mutual aid without guarantee emerges, Rossetti specifies, from the ruins of a scorched marketplace that is figured as finally inescapable. In our veering new atmosphere, freedom is unavailable. Escape from stormy weather is not on offer. But if tears can "refresh[ ]" and injury give food for struggle, it may yet transpire that the ones and zeros of a world outfitted for capture can add up to something that, if small, might also exceed calculation.

CONCLUSION
The Women on the Stairs

Fires burn, winds blow. Whipsaws of temperature have de-linked biorhythms coevolved over millennia, shredding the domain of vernacular experience and leaving the Holocene as a memory for those old enough to remember it. None of this is news. Across a looping, traumatic timeline, this book has tracked the intensification of an extractive epistemology or mental grammar whose material instantiations take terminal shape, I have suggested, in mudslides, mass extinction, and superstorms. But I have evoked fossil capitalism's lifespan recursively: not as a linear progression or lockstep sequence but in a series of moments of intensity or nonsequential instants, a constellation. This story has connected the primal violence of chattel slavery and monoculture enclosure to the consolidating fossil capitalism of the Victorian period; it has shown, too, how an emergent carbon inferno, naturalizing itself across the nineteenth century, reached another inflection point in the post–World War II Great Acceleration, when the ecocidal logic of bourgeois acquisition kicked into hyper-speed.

The period after 1945 was defined by modernization theory and bilateral rivalry, when the Victorian idea that time would bring development and growth found shape in a scenario where two superpowers vied to master an earth now construed as resource. In this way did the postwar era bring the domination of nature latent in the Enlightenment project to dark fruition, often bewilderingly indistinguishable from progress. Petrochemicals, synthetic fertilizers, the mass consumption of domesticated animals, and the trawling of the ocean floor to total emptiness: these and other material facts indicated how extraction had been raised to the world's unofficial religion or common language. The universalist dreams of the Enlightenment culminated in an Esperanto of total capture, where "the history of global fisheries," to pick just one theater of its operation, "is one of full . . . exploitation" (Victorero et al.). And so the long-durational story of extractive thought now reaches into the more familiar timescales of decades and lifespans: my parents' lifetimes (b. 1948), my lifetime (b. 1976), yours. Here, in the ruins of the liberal project, 75 percent of all insects measured by weight have vanished since I was eighteen years old (Hallmann et al.). But the era of unwinding is unlivable for humans too: David Wallace-Wells explains that in a world warmed by just two degrees, 150 million human beings will die from air pollution alone. "Numbers that large may be hard to grasp," Wallace-Wells says, "but 150 million is the equivalent of 25 Holocausts" (28).

Thus has the problematic identified by Theodor Adorno and Max Horkheimer in the shattered aftermath of the Shoah—the question of how knowledge could proceed, after the emancipatory dreams of the Enlightenment had become identical with death—returned to us in sharpened and seemingly terminal form.[1] Yet we are entangled in our collapsing world, enmeshed in its logics and material practices, invested in its pleasures. We speak its language and taste its fruit. As I have noted more than once across these chapters, an episteme can be understood as the preconceptual background for thought, the condition of possibility or basis for any given instance of knowledge, theory, or practice (cf. Gutting 9; Canguilhem, "Death," 76–77). In these terms, the episteme of any person who might conceivably read these words can be described as being defined by fossil capitalism and its logics of extraction, enclosure, and domination. It is this preconceptual grammar that organizes even the style of my own critical account, organized as it is by tropes transmitted from my predecessors and along vectors of predication by which subjects do things to objects.

Given this unavoidable entanglement, it has been my contention that the work of any environmental humanities now must be to inventory the extractive episteme whose logics and presuppositions breathe and speak through our very acts of analysis. To do so would be to develop a historical account or critique, in the Kantian sense, of ecocidal reason. Any such necessarily unfinished effort of epistemic accounting would need to go further still, I have tried to suggest, to track how conceptual procedures ramify in material contexts: in paint sourcing and manuscript production, but also in oil-funded institutions, co-opted critical projects, and inevitably implicated scenes of elaboration and transmission that concretely mediate intellectual performances often mistaken for mere ideas. But even that diagnostic effort would only set the stage for the most pressing labor, which would be to inventory counter-knowledges, so as to begin building repertoires of disruptive possibility from within the inescapable confines of our own cognitive language. It is crucial to add once more that these new grammars cannot remain in the idealist domain of mental experiment or "thinking otherwise." They are not just an aesthetics. Instead, nonstandard knowledges and corrupted common sense must be traced out along the route that all thought travels, as it wends from intuition, concept, and mental image to the concrete realm of embodied behavior and intervention in the world.

As we've seen, sometimes the physical traces of thought appear to us merely as gestures: a brushstroke or cancelation, a movement on the page. Usually they are small. They often take shape as mistakes. "To common eyes," in Eliot's words in *Middlemarch*, the gestures that make thought real will seem like "mere inconsistency and formlessness" (3). Still such materialized instances of unscripted activity modify, at some scale, the smooth reproduction of the given. In so doing, these internal aberrations from the order of things shift, if just slightly, the relationship of bodies to other bodies on earth. It was in this sense that I tried to suggest how the broken syntaxes and undone grammars of Brontë, Eliot, and Rossetti in particular modeled internal disturbance as a domain of tiny but consequential adjustment within the shipwreck of the modern project. That such gestures were nearly insignificant was part of the point.

What those sub-historical movements enacted and brought into the world at tiny scale was a political epistemology of steadfastness, improvised collaboration, and intimacy: gesture redeemed into the domain of practice. These minor notes did not achieve the status of completion or totality, nor did they seek that status. For that reason they remain all but illegible from within dominant frameworks of comprehension—"common eyes," as Eliot put it. To such eyes the fleeting instants in which possibility reside can only appear as marginal or abject—valueless, feminized, or pointless, if they can even be noticed at all. "S[u]nk unwept," Eliot says, "into oblivion" (*Middlemarch* 3). Plot summary will not find them. Tracking them takes time. A "thesis" based on them would seem extravagant. But as Rossetti and Eliot both helped show, tiny moments of hesitating creation and nonstandard expression, however vanishing, also sketch out how material connection between remaindered lives might be made real, the sobs of one unprotected body connecting its trial to another's. You, companioned, leaving me not alone. Solidarity with others in struggle, therefore, was one possible concrete outcome of these infrared adjustments to the given. It is in this all-but-indiscernible sense that the otherwise aesthetic performances I have tracked here can be understood as political (plate 6).

This is not, however, a happy ending. In fact it is no ending at all. To conclude this book's nonlinear account I turn back to the beginning, or near to it: to painting, again, and to the catastrophic scenes of early extraction on the British sugar islands, those experiments in Lockean improvement worked by stolen people and the nonpersons hovering at the edges of the Carolina Constitution, and that the *Second Treatise* could only euphemize as "servants." Here, among the crushing machines and mosquitoes, mortality rates were legendary and monoculture production the order of the day. As David Brion Davis observes in *The Problem of Slavery in the Age of Revolution*, the British sugar islands, like contemporary factory farms, ran on an "extreme model of speculative profits, absentee proprietorship, monoculture, [and] soil exhaustion," as well, of course, as the mass death of laborers, who died at such rates, perhaps 8 percent a year, that their populations, unlike in the United States, could not be sustained without a steady supply of new imports (52).

Then as now, human catastrophe went hand in hand with the war on nature. In a ten-year span, the entire island of Barbados, once "soe full of wood and trees," was successfully denuded of the "relatively dense forests" that had covered it—little surprise, given that an average sugar mill burned "the equivalent of one huge tree per hour" (quoted in McNeill 27; Dunn 11). Stripped to the roots to make way for cash crops, the woodlands of Jamaica, meanwhile, wound up burned for fuel or in England, mahogany fixtures now connoting status for newly enriched slave profiteers in the areas outside London and Liverpool (Nelson 243). At Gateshead, Jane notices these signs twice in a paragraph, the Atlantic sacrifice zones now appearing as "darkly polished" mahogany in the "largest and stateliest chamber in the mansion," the red room (C. Brontë, *Jane Eyre*, 17; cf. Freedgood). The total burning was, in a sense, successful. Already by the 1660s, Dunn writes, the white colonists had "cleared the entire island [of Barbados] and were cultivating all of the arable land," their victory over nature now total. This victory didn't stop them from "complaining of a timber shortage" (Dunn 27–28).[2]

The confusions of these early improvers suggest how, in the experimental zone of Britain's slave colonies, always testing-grounds for new practices of extraction, total capture and full exploitation had reached their self-abolishing zenith. Yet the suicidal qualities of their emergent form of depletionary life could not be admitted to the minds of those overseeing its expansion. Instead it looked like beauty. "A most delightful place," it was said of Barbados: "the beautyfulls't spott of ground I ever saw" (quoted in Dunn 28). Such obscene dialectics mean that the visual archive of the unfree Caribbean is, in general, hard to look at. Richard Ligon's illustrated 1657 map of Barbados, for instance, shows some of the island's very few remaining trees, likely fantasized, with a more believable depiction of a white planter or his agent riding down two enslaved people and shooting them (Ligon).

Later fantasias of Jamaica include such titles as *West Indian Scenery: Illustrations of Jamaica* (1837–40) and *Sketches of Character, in Illustration of the Habits, Occupation, and Costume of the Negro Population on the Island of Jamaica* (1840). Such Victorian-era works betray a "nostalgia for the most opulent days of the sugar industry under slavery" (Modest and Barringer 15), exuding by means of aesthetic form a melancholic longing for the days of slave accumulation. Like these and other mythologizing retrospectives, James Hakewill's *Picturesque Tour of the Island of Jamaica* (1825) was made in an aftermath: it lacquers the plantocratic regime in the gauzy effects of its title genre, converting routinized murder into the picturesque.

Hakewill's lavishly illustrated volume offers up the geography of the Jamaican deathworld like a female body to the gaze of an implicitly male viewer. Bays extend, hills roll, trees puff and flower, grottos beckon. It is a master's view. Only oblique notation tells us that these charming landscapes have been produced through disaster, that their supposed charm is itself disastrous. Deforestation, extraction, and the systematic exhaustion of soil: the vistas in Hakewill's volume make little note of such processes. They show less interest in the human beings entangled in the disastrous agro-industrial system he tries to romanticize—lives conscripted into a labor scheme organized around death and perfectly at odds with any concept of liberty then being developed in the pages of Romantic-era poetry or elsewhere. Instead, in plate after plate, Hakewill gives us a planter figure dressed in coattails, proxy for the viewer. This character gestures to a field, points at water, shows a monument to a Black man and a dog. He enjoys a "commanding view," as Hakewill's commentary specifies, the earth falling always "beneath his eye" (56).

Such scenes of opulent mastery are interspersed, in Hakewill's text, with spreadsheets of export sugar tonnage (for example, 30). The volume's naïve formal hybridity in this way confirms an internal bond between the aesthetic technology of the picturesque and the statistical rationality of the export table. Brontë's Lockwood, recall, sees the earth like a tourist but has "business" in town. Eighteenth-century innovations in the "seasoning" of enslaved people in Caribbean slave ports directed those commodities to be prepared for market in closed pens, overseen by piazzas (Nelson 31–32). This process of human resource management was known to increase efficiency, since it reduced financial loss from death while adding pre-sale value to each unit via a process of minimal acculturation involving food and exercise. It was improvement.

Surveying the ruined byways of extractive globalization in the contemporary Philippines, Neferti X. M. Tadiar has described the experiential horizon or lifeworld of dwellers in the slums and lean-to shantytowns of a hyper-urbanized Manila. These people are, Tadiar explains, futureless: orbiting the edges of economies of digital servitude, they are exposed to toxic effluents and aerosolized poisons, functionally abandoned, and remaindered by an extractive order to which they count as almost nothing. In this sense, these disposable human beings might be seen as modern replays of Hakewill's mute onlookers or Brontë's Heathcliff, the other half of Lockwood's suitable pair, who is claimed as "starving, and houseless, and as good as dumb" from the Liverpool streets and does not receive a personal pronoun until weeks after his supposed salvage (E. Brontë, *Wuthering Heights,* 31). He spoke no language his owners could decipher. In Manila, the experience of one subset of the extractive order's human refuse is of a life without a future, the living-through of catastrophe.

Tadiar notes how this withdrawal of possibility forces the production of new idioms, fresh vernaculars to describe this lifeworld's qualitative effects, as the victims of macroeconomic common sense develop figural repertoires to inventory their position. These torqued grammars emerge to give shape to wasted experience, expressing the textures of improvised life eked out in the crush of an extractive project long in the making. "*Buryong,*" for example, is

> the stifling experience of the worthless, useless, meaningless time of disposable life, [and] is the other side of *diskarte,* a slang word (from the Spanish, *descartar,* to discard) for 'the ability to make something out of the tiniest possibility,' a kind of creative resourcefulness in places of scarce and diminishing resources. *Diskarte* is an art form and a form of getting by and surviving, the profane art of making life out of scraps, fissures, and shifts of space and time[.] (313)

The erosion of hope demands new grammars and invites makeshift forms. The scene Tadiar describes is one of an almost infinite supply: a single snapshot taken among the ruins of a still-unfinished nineteenth century. What the image discloses is a total carceral situation defined by foreclosed possibility and fully entrenched social processes, where hope is a foreign term. Responses to this futureless condition are necessarily improvisatory and become real in acts of risk-taking and connection, mostly small, all vernacular, by which the given world is adapted and adjusted into new shapes. There is no revolution.

To witnesses and outsiders—you, me—this condition of life can be known only after mediation, through the translating idioms of scholarship and via almost infinitely recoded relays of adaptation, reframing, and citational deployment. Specifically: Tadiar's source is Steffen Jensen, a Danish anthropologist writing in English, based in Denmark, working in South Africa and the Philippines. The passage above is cited from a book, having appeared in slightly altered from, first, as an essay. But through these screens, across global circuits of inevitable mistranslation, we intuit that on the underside of the extractive lifeworld's pleasures, in the ruined spaces of progress, minor gestures perform counter-movements against the reasonable and sensible efforts that have been designed, far from Manila slums or the Liverpool sidewalks, to capture the entire globe.

In contrast to Hakewill's sweeping views of Jamaica plantations, the tiny and unfinished watercolor by William Berryman reproduced in plate 6 is roughly the size of a greeting card: never circulated and, a later title tells us, "Unfinished." It shows a weather event gathering darkly, sometime between 1808 and 1815. Pencil notations at the bottom of the sketch are ciphers for qualities of sky: "1. blue de[ep?], 2. indigo, 7. 'darkest blue green with some appearance of [ ] color at bottom'" (Berryman, *Landscape with Storm*). The subjects of Berryman's Jamaican studies range from generic-seeming landscapes such as the one just mentioned to much more intimate tableaux, scenes of labor and daily life: cotton spinning and cane threshing, water carrying and hole digging, heaving plantains on a pole.

These tableaux are interleaved with depictions of family life among the enslaved and, more surprisingly, stolen moments of rest (plate 7; figures 27–31). I reproduce some here, along with details whose successive reframings disclose Berryman's acts of translational notation at increasingly proximate resolution. *Detail,* recall, is a conventional term for captioning images selected from larger works: it is also "an item, a particular (of an account, a process, etc.); a minute or subordinate portion of any (*esp.* a large or complex) whole."[3] To read in detail, Naomi Schor observes, "is, however tacitly, to invest the detail with a truth-bearing function," even if "the truth value of the detail is anything but assured" (xlvii).

What survives of Berryman is minimal. The notes that accompany his paintings at the Library of Congress, among the only known records of his work, say that he is "a British artist of whom little is known."[4] The same notes state that he made a "group of 292 pen, pencil, and watercolor sketches of Jamaica as it appeared during his tour from 1808 to 1815." An unpublished dissertation by Rachel Grace Newman draws on research by B. W. Higman to suggest Berryman may have been a sign painter or bookkeeper, and that he may have sought the favor of a key figure on the

FIGURE 27. William Berryman, *Planting Corn. Old Driver. Planting Corn. House Negro Digging Corn Holes* (between 1808 and 1815). Gray and brown ink. Library of Congress, Prints and Photographs Division, Washington, DC (2007675692). Photograph: Library of Congress.

FIGURE 28. William Berryman, [*Negro Portraits, 16 Small Drawings with Notations*] (between 1808 and 1815). Brown and gray ink, pencil, watercolor. Library of Congress, Prints and Photographs Division, Washington, DC (96522174). Photograph: Library of Congress.

FIGURE 29. William Berryman, *Sugar Estate—Negros [sic] Cutting Cane* (between 1808 and 1815). Watercolor and black ink. Library of Congress, Prints and Photographs Division, Washington, DC (96516495). Photograph: Library of Congress.

FIGURE 30. William Berryman, *Sugar Estate—Negros [sic] Cutting Cane* (between 1808 and 1815) (detail). Watercolor and black ink. Library of Congress, Prints and Photographs Division, Washington, DC (96516495). Photograph: Library of Congress.

FIGURE 31. William Berryman, *Sugar Estate—Negros* [*sic*] *Cutting Cane* (between 1808 and 1815) (closer detail). Watercolor and black ink. Library of Congress, Prints and Photographs Division, Washington, DC (96516495). Photograph: Library of Congress.

island, Edward Long, whom Catherine Hall, citing Peter Fryer, calls the "father of English racism" (quoted in Hall, "Return," n.p.). Proper names index particularity.

The Longs owned property on Jamaica from the outset of British colonization and, by the early nineteenth century, oversaw the perversely named Lucky Valley Estate, in Clarendon, "probably the most graphic example" of plantation efficiency in the period, since its layout of concentric circles and arcs shortened the distance between field and works to mathematical minimums: straight lines from point to point (Higman 84). For Hall, Lucky Valley crystallizes historical processes reaching into the present, an aftermath defined by haunting, recurrence, and disavowal (xxviii, 31–33).[5] "*That's slavery breathing on you*," recalled Orlando Patterson in 2013, on revisiting his place of birth near Long's plantation. "You're just walking through cane. It's like walking through history, walking through a strange time zone to the past" (quoted in Hall, *Lucky Valley*, xxiii, emphasis original). Patterson's *Slavery and Social Death* was published in 1982, reissued in 2018 with a new preface. A committed improver, Long authored the three-volume *History of Jamaica* (1774), the canonical source for knowledge about the island for at least a century. The figure from whom Berryman seems to have sought patronage was therefore an icon of an extractionist white intelligentsia, infamous to this day as a metonym for racial capitalism as total process. Despite hustling for patronage from such worthies, the itinerant watercolorist seems to have failed, come home, then died suddenly from a skin infection, "leaving a widow and two children" (quoted in Higman 87). Transfer grids enable the artist to divide a scene into smaller parts so as to move from sketch to total picture while retaining accuracy of scale. But the gridwork of partition and capture cannot offer guarantees, only more chances for slippage and, in the end, escape (figures 32–34).

The final unfinished work in this book's incomplete account is called *Piazza & Stairs at 4 Paths, 2 Negro Children at Work*. It is done in pencil, uncolored but for two bright shocks of green—shutters on a house (plate 8). Piazzas were an architectural form borrowed from Spanish Cuba and designed to provide shade for commercial activities and, at certain seasoning houses, oversight of the enslaved for purchase. On these stairs, two young women bend over handwork. We see only one face; the other turns away. As Newman explains, Berryman consistently trained attention on spaces of Black life that were usually of little interest from within the genre confines of the white picturesque.

The "alternative space[s] of production" that most interested Berryman, Newman says, "had no part in the export economy that dominated the colonial sphere" or its official visual genres. In this, "Berryman presents us with a view and concept of the plantation that we do not see in the work of any of his contemporaries" (R. G. Newman 104). The subjects of *Piazza & Stairs* are engaged, from one perspective, in *buryong*, the passing of the evacuated, unvectored time spent in disposable living. But from another view, they also express *diskarte*, a making of novelty from vanishingly small possibility. The truth is that we do not know what they are doing. On the young women's faces, no expression is discernible; the interior life of these enslaved individuals is at once noted as existing—it is the subject of the work—and locked away from our gaze. It is marked for the bourgeois viewer as unreachable: held as opacity.

Berryman's Jamaica had already been "liberated" but was not yet free and would never be. The transportation of human beings for purposes of forced labor had ended March 1, 1808, just before Berryman seems to have arrived; enslaved Africans were emancipated by decree in 1834, long after he had gone. Like *Piazza & Stairs*, the other watercolors Berryman made during this interregnum teeter on a razor's edge of undecidability, refusing to coalesce for latter-day moralists. Instead the images bear witness, from within the vocabulary of white supremacist visual representation, to shards of life that will not be contained by that language. They testify to

FIGURE 32. William Berryman, *A Most Charming Picture—Admirable Figures* (between 1808 and 1815). Gray ink and pencil. Library of Congress, Prints and Photographs Division, Washington, DC (96522186). Photograph: Library of Congress.

FIGURE 33. William Berryman, *A Most Charming Picture—Admirable Figures* (between 1808 and 1815) (detail). Gray ink and pencil. Library of Congress, Prints and Photographs Division, Washington, DC (96522186). Photograph: Library of Congress.

FIGURE 34. William Berryman, *A Most Charming Picture—Admirable Figures* (between 1808 and 1815) (closer detail). Gray ink and pencil. Library of Congress, Prints and Photographs Division, Washington, DC (96522186). Photograph: Library of Congress.

forms of experience elaborated in the ruins of a fully modern industrial system, local gestures and particular lives that evade notation by our most canonical genres and are even, when glimpsed or painted or written about, finally unavailable for full reconstruction.

The Library of Congress typescript explains that "the sketches, which are 24 × 33 cm or smaller, were received in an album with a modern 20th century binding of unknown origin. The Library dismantled the album and left the drawings numbered as they were arranged in the album." Thus has the life's work of one witness to subaltern life in the long unfolding of the climate disaster been collated into just a few boxes. That is where I saw them for the first time in 2020, just before the world was locked down and public life sealed into the memory of semi-available childcare and a half-functional state apparatus. Three years before, I had tested the first steps toward this book in Houston, after Hurricane Harvey, as described in chapter 1. When I held them in my hands, Berryman's paintings were small, more delicate than the generously scanned digital copies had suggested to me. Minor, you could say.

One point of these concluding notes is to insist that treating "climate change" in its full amplitude requires that we track the genealogy of dispossession and human misery that developed alongside the "ecological crises" of a nineteenth century that we have not and will not escape. In the archives of this extractive modernity, within this unfinished project, some of our most pressing work will be to scan for moments of hesitation, blank spaces and instances of impenetrability. Such eddies in the flow of representation offer chances to attend to the human capacities almost completely overcoded by established idioms, aesthetic and academic both. Such movements are only barely registered in archives, artworks, and official records. Monographs by midcareer academics cannot grasp them. Still, such tiny adjustments in the field of possibility are scratches on the glass, infinitely minute, of a world calling out for total renovation. Reading them by the dim lights of the present will require that we do more than *offer new theses* or *propose fresh theories* in the way that factories produce widgets, brands establish identities, or mines dig up treasures. Instead it asks that we take up the unfinished itself as concept and practice, and frame inheritance and collaboration as strategies of knowledge-making, solidarity as a domain of practice. But none of that will be possible without turning our eyes to the young women on the stairs (plate 8), who nevertheless refuse to meet the critic's gaze.

Acknowledgments

Authorship makes the social work of creative elaboration look like the product of a single actor's isolated mind. This book was not really written by me: it has taken shape over many years, in many scenes of exchange, input, and rearticulation; and it could never have become real without far more instances of support than even an overlong acknowledgments section could list.

The financial help I received over the long course of this book's development is one example of its argument, which is that no sustained thinking can now transpire except in the context of profoundly unequal structural conditions that call out for total renovation. For material backing at Georgetown University, I thank the Virginia Graham Healey Fund for Excellence in English; the Lafferty Family Endowed Fund for English; the College of Arts and Sciences, for Summer Faculty Fellowship Awards and a Senior Faculty Fellowship; and, for a course release intended to offset the research freeze of the pandemic, the Provost's Office. During the entirety of this book's career I had secure terms of employment, access to libraries, and health insurance. Today such arrangements are obscenely rare privileges: they must be extended beyond the province of elite universities if conceptual activity is to have a future in our time.

Archivists and librarians provided help far in excess of what was ever required. I thank Ethan Henderson, Melissa Jones, and Jay Sylvestre at the Georgetown University Library and the Booth Family Center for Special Collections; Liz Fawcett and Katie Waring at Lancaster University Library Special Collections; the British Library; the Henry W. and Albert A. Berg Collection of English and American Literature at the New York Public Library, and Mary Catherine Kinniburgh at the Berg in particular; the Prints and Drawings Rooms, Tate Britain, and Laura Murphy there specifically; the Library of Congress Prints and Photographs Department; Peter Armenti at the Library of Congress; and Aaron T. Pratt at the Harry

Ransom Center. Thomas Frantz, Jennifer Swift, and Joyce Townsend generously shared their expertise.

I have been lucky to test these ideas in variously unfinished forms with audiences at (in chronological order): Marymount University; Duke University; the e-flux lecture series; Binghamton University; Carleton University; Columbia University; the University of Pennsylvania; the University of Maryland, College Park; American University; Brown University; the University of California, Davis; the Graduate Center, City University of New York; Colby College; the University of Wisconsin, Madison; the University of Delaware; Lehigh University; the University of British Columbia; Vanderbilt University; the University of North Carolina at Chapel Hill; the BMW Center for European Studies, Georgetown University; the University of Toronto; the Future of the Humanities Project, Georgetown University; the University of North Texas; the Georgetown University Department of History's "Archives" class; King's College, London; Cambridge University; and Sewanee, the University of the South. I thank those audiences for pushing on the claims and evidence here.

The people who arranged those visits and helped handle material logistics put in hard work to help create this book, even though, of course, nothing bad in it is their fault. Specifically, I am grateful to Megan Cook, Thom Dancer, Jane Danielewicz, Sierra Eckert, Dustin Friedman, Zach Fruit, Devin Garofalo, Will Glovinsky, Matt Irvin, Maha Jafri, Erica Kanesaka, Barbara Leckie, John McGowan, Elizabeth Carolyn Miller, Vin Nardizzi, Rick Ness, Clare Pettitt, Michelle Rada, Rithika Ramamurthy, Jessie Reeder, Aaron Rosenberg, Adam Rothman, Jason Rudy, Talia Schaffer, Lorenzo Servitje, Katrin Sieg, Stephen Squibb, Kathryn Temple, Rachel Teukolsky, Aaron Vieth, Chris Walker, Sarah Wasserman, and Danny Wright. Specific input from Pearl Brilmyer, Jennifer Fay, Scott J. Juengel, and John McGowan helped me a lot. I learned immensely from a 2016–2018 Mellon-Sawyer Seminar, and thank Megan Dean, Meredith Denning, Mabel Denzin Gergan, Dana Luciano, and John McNeill.

For reading parts of the book and buoying me when I was drowning or offering sharp help when floating too high, I am grateful to Nan Da, Sarah Dowling, Jed Esty, Devin Garofalo, Corbin Hiday, Meredith Martin, Patrick O'Malley, Stephanie O'Rourke, Sarah Osment, Karen Pinkus, Zach Samalin, Dan Shore, Andrea Kaston Tange, and the VCologies Working Group, especially Sukanya Banerjee, Kate Flint, Devin Griffiths, Barbara Leckie, John MacNeill Miller, Kyle McAuley, Elizabeth Carolyn Miller, Benjamin Morgan, Daniel Williams, Tobias Wilson-Bates, and Lynn Voskuil. Deanna Kreisel helped me more than she's aware with a stray comment about hope. Friends and collaborators are also co-authors, though again not responsible for my mistakes: Tanya Agathocleous, Emma Davenport, Anna Gibson, Owen King, Anna Kornbluh, Kristin Mahoney, Mary Mullen, Nasser Mufti, Gautham Rao, Zach Samalin, and Philip Steer.

At the Georgetown English department I am lucky for colleagues I've drawn upon and learned from, particularly Caetlin Benson-Allott, Manu Samriti Chander, Jennifer Fink, Brian Hochman, M. Lindsay Kaplan, Lakshmi Krishnan, Peggy Lee, Amani Morrison, Sarah McNamer, Lindsey O'Neil, Patrick O'Malley, Ricardo Ortiz, Cóilín Parsons, Seth Perlow, John Pfordresher, Libbie Rifkin, Dan Shore, and Duncan Wu.

I thank Amy Ding, John Patrick James, Gabrielle Nemarich, and Bridget Sellers for inventive and reliable research assistance in the long preparation of this book. Karen Lautman offered administrative expertise over its entire career and before, and worked hard to help me and many others. The anonymous readers received the manuscript with care and an acute generosity and made it better. I am grateful to Alan Thomas, Randy Petilos, and the staff at the University of Chicago Press for helping these ideas become a physical artifact. In different shapes, parts of the conclusion and chapter 5 appeared in the *Victorian Review* 47, no. 1 (Spring 2021), © 2021 Victorian Studies Association of Western Canada; and *Nineteenth-Century Contexts* 38, no. 5 (2016): 399–415, https://www.tandfonline.com, respectively. I thank the editors, Vanessa Warne and Jill Ehnenn.

It is hard writing something, and there are no guarantees. Over the development of this project I worked closely with Max Brzezinski, Thomas S. Davis, and Nicole Rizzuto, whom I trust with my life and for whose encouragement and brilliance I am indebted. Kathy Alexis Psomiades read a chapter at the end and reminded me why all my writing aims to be adequate to her example. Students have co-created and elaborated these ideas with me over many years, and nothing in these pages could have been done without them. Not one of the people mentioned here is responsible for any errors of fact or interpretation in the book. There are some, I'm sure, and they are on me.

My family has been with me from the beginning. I send love to Jeffrey Hensley, Lynne Ashbeck, and Dr. Paula Solomon, as well as to William Hensley and Jennifer Hensley and their amazing families. Anne O'Neil-Henry turns every scenario toward something new and bright that could never have been predicted: I am so thankful to know her. June and Irene Hensley bring beauty and humor and fun into the world. I love you: you and your friends are in charge now.

Silver Spring, MD, May 2024

APPENDIX

Sobs in Middlemarch

Sobs in *Middlemarch* (1871–1872). All page numbers refer to the Oxford World's Classics edition (ed. Carroll).

1. Here and there is born a Saint Theresa, foundress of nothing, whose loving heart-beats and **sobs** after an unattained goodness tremble off and are dispersed among hindrances, instead of centering in some long-recognizable deed. (4)
2. Celia colored, and looked very grave. "I think, dear, we are wanting in respect to mamma's memory, to put them by and take no notice of them. And," she added, after hesitating a little, with a rising **sob** of mortification, "necklaces are quite usual now; and Madame Poinçon, who was stricter in some things even than you are, used to wear ornaments. . . ." (11)
3. Dorothea trembled while she read this letter; then she fell on her knees, buried her face, and **sobbed**. (40)
4. "I beg your pardon, if I have said anything to hurt you, Dodo," said Celia, with a slight **sob**. She never could have thought that she should feel as she did. (45)
5. "No; but music of that sort I should enjoy," said Dorothea. "When we were coming home from Lausanne, my uncle took us to hear the great organ at Freiberg, and it made me **sob**." (61)
6. I am sorry to add that she was **sobbing** bitterly, with such abandonment to this relief of an oppressed heart as a woman habitually controlled by pride on her own account and thoughtfulness for others will sometimes allow herself when she feels securely alone. (180)
7. I will write to your dictation, or I will copy and extract what you tell me: I can be of no other use." Dorothea, in a most unaccountable, darkly feminine manner, ended with a slight **sob** and eyes full of tears. (187)

8. It was in that way Dorothea came to be **sobbing** as soon as she was securely alone. But she was presently roused by a knock at the door, which made her hastily dry her eyes before saying, "Come in." (191)
9. "But you do forgive me?" said Dorothea, with a quick **sob**. In her need for some manifestation of feeling she was ready to exaggerate her own fault. (197)
10. Dorothea was silent, but a tear which had come up with the **sob** would insist on falling. (197)
11. "Oh, poor mother, poor father!" said Mary, her eyes filling with tears, and a little **sob** rising which she tried to repress. (238)
12. At Fred's last words she felt an instantaneous pang, something like what a mother feels at the imagined **sobs** or cries of her naughty truant child, which may lose itself and get harm. (239)
13. When Sir James entered the library, however, Mr. Casaubon could make some signs of his usual politeness, and Dorothea, who in the reaction from her first terror had been kneeling and **sobbing** by his side now rose and herself proposed that some one should ride off for a medical man. (267)
14. Lydgate rose, and Dorothea mechanically rose at the same time, unclasping her cloak and throwing it off as if it stifled her. He was bowing and quitting her, when an impulse which if she had been alone would have turned into a prayer, made her say with a **sob** in her voice— (272)
15. For four hours Dorothea lay in this conflict, till she felt ill and bewildered, unable to resolve, praying mutely. Helpless as a child which has **sobbed** and sought too long, she fell into a late morning sleep, and when she waked Mr. Casaubon was already up. (451)
16. This was too much for Dorothea's highly-strung feeling, and she burst into tears, **sobbing** against Tantripp's arm. But soon she checked herself, dried her eyes, and went out at the glass door into the shrubbery. (452)
17. But Dorothea's effort was too much for her; she broke off and burst into **sobs**. (462)
18. Still "I do wish it" came at the end of those wise reflections as naturally as a **sob** after holding the breath. (508)
19. Something which may be called an inward silent **sob** had gone on in Dorothea before she said with a pure voice, just trembling in the last words as if only from its liquid flexibility— (510)
20. She did not know then that it was Love who had come to her briefly, as in a dream before awaking, with the hues of morning on his wings—that it was Love to whom she was **sobbing** her farewell as his image was banished by the blameless rigor of irresistible day. (515)

21. [B]ut Rosamond did not go on **sobbing**: she tried to conquer her agitation and wiped away her tears, continuing to look before her at the mantelpiece. (558–59)
22. "Oh, what sad words!" said Dorothea, with a dangerous tendency to **sob**. (594)
23. "I have never done you injustice. Please remember me," said Dorothea, repressing a rising **sob**. (596)
24. She looked at him silently, still with the blank despair on her face; but then the tears began to fill her blue eyes, and her lip trembled. The strong man had had too much to bear that day. He let his head fall beside hers and **sobbed**. (659)
25. But she needed time to gather up her strength; she needed to **sob** out her farewell to all the gladness and pride of her life. (707)
26. "My poor Rosamond! has something agitated you?" Clinging to him she fell into hysterical **sobbings** and cries, and for the next hour he did nothing but soothe and tend her. (734)
27. She could only cry in loud whispers, between her **sobs**, after her lost belief which she had planted and kept alive from a very little seed since the days in Rome (739)
28. [Dorothea] lay on the bare floor and let the night grow cold around her; while her grand woman's frame was shaken by **sobs** as if she had been a despairing child. (739)
29. But she lost energy at last even for her loud-whispered cries and moans: she subsided into helpless **sobs**, and on the cold floor she **sobbed** herself to sleep. (740)
30. . . . and in looking at Rosamond, she suddenly found her heart swelling, and was unable to speak—all her effort was required to keep back tears. She succeeded in that, and the emotion only passed over her face like the spirit of a **sob** . . . (745)
31. . . . and while her hand was still resting on Rosamond's lap, though the hand underneath it was withdrawn, she was struggling against her own rising **sobs**. (747)
32. He took her hand and raised it to his lips with something like a **sob**. (760)
33. In an instant Will was close to her and had his arms round her, but she drew her head back and held his away gently that she might go on speaking, her large tear-filled eyes looking at his very simply, while she said in a **sobbing** childlike way, "We could live quite well on my own fortune—it is too much—seven hundred a-year—I want so little—no new clothes—and I will learn what everything costs." (762)

Notes

Introduction

1. See also a July 27, 2016, Reddit comment from user Meggs2011, who wrote, "Mr Turner is a beautiful movie. Vastly underrated" (https://www.reddit.com/r/movies/comments/4uuond/mr_turner_deserves_to_be_recognised_as_one_of_the/).

2. Late in life, Turner sold land to make way for the South Western Railway Company, rival to the Great Western Railway of the *Steam* painting: "a few square yards of a copyhold meadow land . . . detached from the three pieces of freehold land mentioned in the indenture of 1844" (Finberg 423). The terms for successive stages of land enclosure describe an emergent fossil capitalist system that is also the railway plot of *Middlemarch* (chapter 4). On the emergence of the "ecocide" concept in the Vietnam era, see Zierler.

3. *The Fighting Temeraire* (1838) depicts the emblem of patriotic feeling being "tugged to her last berth to be broken up," as Turner's full title has it. Through a gauze of yellows and ochres we see a steam-powered tugboat dragging the reluctant sailing ship to its unmaking, a tidy allegory for what is depicted as an inevitable transition between a residual energy regime, freighted with nostalgia, and its smoky successor. Since 2020, *Temeraire* has featured on England's £20 note, Turner's motto—"Light is therefore colour"—transformed into cliché and the image's equivocal meditation conscripted into the project of post-Brexit nationalism.

4. In *"Probable Exhaustion": Progress Fictions in the Era of Fossil Capitalism* (unpublished book manuscript, 2024), Corbin Hiday describes the intertwinement of progress and decay across an extended nineteenth century. Jason Moore's notion of cheap nature highlights the depletionary tendency of extraction-based economies while theorists of degrowth observe that capitalist accumulation presupposes expansion (Saito; Hickel).

5. *Oxford English Dictionary*, s.v. "exploit (v.), sense 6," September 2023, https://doi.org/10.1093/OED/1208309960.

6. "Allons, camarades, le jeu européen est définitivement terminé, il faut trouver autre chose. Nous pouvons tout faire aujourd'hui à condition de ne pas singer l'Europe, à condition de ne pas être obsédés par le désir de rattraper l'Europe. L'Europe a acquis une telle vitesse, folle et désordonnée, qu'elle échappe aujourd'hui à tout conducteur, à toute raison et qu'elle va dans un vertige effroyable vers des abîmes dont il vaut mieux le plus rapidement s'éloigner" (Fanon, *Les Damnés*, 302).

7. On Fanon's project and the figure of "the earth," see Wenzel, "Turning Over a New Leaf," which I draw on gratefully here.

8. Fanon's text was published in French by Éditions Maspero in 1961, translated into English in 1963; *Silent Spring* appeared in September 1962 with Houghton Mifflin but was significantly complete by fall 1960. Beckett's text is slightly earlier: first performed April 1957 and published in English in 1958. I thank Jed Esty for the *Endgame* connection.

9. *Oxford English Dictionary*, s.v. "hope (n.1)," last modified December 2023, https://doi.org/10.1093/OED/4820602771.

10. Nan Da observes this demotivated or evacuated model of action-as-input in internet discourse, where speech acts are functionally de-linked from any context that might have produced them; thus liberated, they become algorithmic objects that circulate or don't based on other input-actions to the system (likes, retweets, views).

11. See Hacking, *Historical Ontology*, 8–9.

12. E. Miller notes that while *Extraction Ecologies* treats the connection between the nineteenth century and the present, "a limitation" is that it "does not address the important developments in exhaustion, depletion, finitude, and extraction that occurred between the 1930s and today, e.g. the Great Acceleration, the revolution in plastics, or even, really, the rise of oil and petroculture, which began before the 1930s and which this book only touches on" (207n22). No history can be complete: mine alludes to the story Miller describes but also cannot offer a full account of the "interconnected 'long exhaustion' extending from the industrial era to today" (*Extraction Ecologies*, 207n22).

13. Blue Carbon home page, accessed December 12, 2023, archived at https://web.archive.org/web/20231225030519/https://bluecarbon.ae/. According to the Internet Archive, Blue Carbon's website was being reworked regularly as news stories about its purchases in Africa and elsewhere emerged, following the announcement of COP28's Africa Carbon Markets Initiative (ACMI). The text I saw on December 12 was fully deleted by February 2024. In late December 2023, it existed only in a glitched transition on the home page.

14. The migration of these tropes into the domain of academic production is evident in Caroline Levine's *The Activist Humanist: Form and Method in the Climate Crisis* (2023), published as I was finalizing this book. There, a lament about the "political withdrawal and inaction all around me" culminates in a to-do list that presumes *action* to name self-directed activity transpiring within recognizable liberal-democratic institutions, undertaken by middle-class or even wealthy subjects in the anglophone Global North, the *you* of its unremarked second-person address (see 150). As I explain, this structure of address is common to well-intentioned climate journalism aimed at middle-class American readers (see McKibben, *Falter*, 1–17).

15. The "Climate Aware Therapist Pledge" notes that "new forms of distress are arising as a result of global crises" and offers therapies to "meet multiple, mounting mental health crises, which reflect the overall increasing instability of our planetary system" (the pledge's text can be read as pop-up under the registration link at "Become a Climate-Aware Therapist," Climate Psychology Alliance of North America, accessed May 15, 2024, https://www.climatepsychology.us/become-climate-aware-therapist.

16. Turner's apocalypticism is a running theme: in 1846, a Miss Rigby saw *Hannibal and His Army Crossing the Alps* (1812) and asked Turner whether it was a picture of the end of the world (Finberg 414). And Turner's early bid for history-painting grandeur, *The Fifth Plague*, actually depicts the Seventh Plague, but this discrepancy makes sense since "Turner had no interest in any part of the Bible but the Apocalypse" (Gowing 9).

17. He was known to wander the seaside "looking out for storms and shipwrecks," and by the 1840s, sea paintings were three-fourths of his output (Concannon 194, 192), with wrecks a heavy portion of these.

18. For many critics Turner's method was "indeterminate and wild" (quoted in Finberg 78) and displayed a shocking "laxity of form" (quoted in Finberg 401). Ruskin purchased *Slave Ship* and had it at the foot of his bed, then became repulsed by it and gave it away—evidence, I am saying, of the work's unsettled tone and resulting resistance to moralizing thematization.

19. For critics, *Snow Storm* was a "frantic puzzle. . . . Where the steam-boat is—where the harbour begins, or where it ends—which are the signals, and which the author . . . are matters past our finding out" (quoted in Finberg 390). The words could describe nearly all of Turner's late-career experiments, so often marketed as predecessors to impressionism and the nonrepresentational tradition to follow.

20. Rosalind Grooms, email to author, January 26, 2023. The book on voluntarism is Noel Malcolm, *Hobbes and Voluntarism* (Cambridge: Cambridge University Press, 2000). See chapter 1, note 10 below.

21. On immanent critique, see, e.g., Buck-Morss 66–69 and Jay 5. Buck-Morss describes Adorno's "use of the philosophical past against itself, his immanent criticism of traditional concepts to foster the liquidation of tradition" (94).

22. On interruption as a formal strategy for committed writing on climate, see Leckie.

23. Farrington "found as she read and translated this book, a sense of the familiar about it—the resemblance between Algerian freedom struggle and the Irish" (Callinen n.p.).

24. "To act," writes Arendt in *The Human Condition*, "in its most general sense, means to take an initiative, to begin (as the Greek word *archein*, 'to begin,' 'to lead,' and eventually 'to rule,' indicates), to set something into motion (which is the original meaning of the Latin *agree*)" (177). I discuss Arendt's account of action as beginning in chapter 4.

25. "The greatest evidence for the use of new materials is in the yellows, which themselves constitute at all periods the largest proportion of colours in his pigment range . . . Among the colours preserved from Turner's studio . . . are a dozen varieties of yellow, four of which were developed during Turner's lifetime; and many others are among the recipes in the sketchbooks" (Gage 19).

26. "City of Fresno," EWG Tap Water Database, January–March 2021, https://www.ewg.org/tapwater/system.php?pws=CA1010007.

27. Cobalt blue is "a mixture of cobalt oxide and aluminum hydrate to form, in part, cobalt aluminate"; discovered in France in 1802, it was the result of a massive national effort to generate a synthetic blue and Turner used it immediately—though its use was not observed in Holland until 1840 (Gettens and Stout 108). Of the Parys copper mine, in Anglesea, Wales (now the setting for *Doctor Who* and *Hard Sun*, a "pre-apocalyptic" BBC drama), Warner continues: "Its appearance is waste, wild, and barren in the extreme; not a vestige of green is seen on its parched and scarified surface, all vegetation being prevented by the sulfurous fumes which arise from the roasting heaps and smelting-houses, and extend their destructive effects for miles around" (quoted in Leifchild 220).

28. Turner was unusually sensitive to the material aspects of his practice. With his father, he stretched and primed his own canvases; made frames from salvaged wood; and starting in early works like *An Artists' Colourman's Workshop* (c.1807), reflected on the grinding work of human, animal, and mineral undergirding his practice (in the painting, vermillion scars the center of a room yellowed by aging linseed varnish). As this book went to press, I learned of Michael Lobel's *Van Gogh and the End of Nature*, which shows how Van Gogh's work is "inseparable from the modern industrial era in which the artist lived . . . and how his art drew upon waste and pollution for its subjects and even for the very materials out of which it was made" (see the book description at "Van Gogh and the End of Nature," Yale University Press,

accessed June 1, 2024, https://yalebooks.yale.edu/book/9780300274363/van-gogh-and-the-end-of-nature/). I thank Michelle Wang for this reference.

29. "Turner continued to use ultramarine for finishing skies throughout his career, having often done the original lay-in with smalt [a far cheaper cobalt-based glass powder]" (Townsend, "Techniques," 176).

30. "Thomson's Aeolian Harp," Manchester Art Gallery catalog entry, accessed April 1, 2024, https://artuk.org/discover/artworks/thomsons-aeolian-harp-206224.

Chapter 1

1. For the definition of experience as *what it is like to be,* I thank Adrienne Ghaly, who channels Thomas Nagel's famous argument about bats. This paragraph draws on Dan Shore's "The Limits of the Worst in Milton's Late Poems" and our conversations about it.

2. In an unpublished manuscript entitled *Worlds Unmanned,* Garofalo engages the work of Sylvia Wynter to show how "world" develops as an implicitly white-supremacist universalism, an imperialist humanism that extends even to the astronomical account of stars and planets (MS shared with author via email on December 13, 2021).

3. On Wells and scale see, e.g., Cole 160 and Rosenberg 36–56, who both note Wells's canonicity in treating this issue. I am grateful to Tobias Wilson-Bates for sharing his expertise on *The Time Machine* with me.

4. On second-person address in bourgeois climate writing, see note 14 of the introduction.

5. Gramsci's now-famous quotation is: "The old world is dying and the new world struggles to be born. Now is the time of monsters." Popularized by Slavoj Žižek (Achcar and Muehlebach), the maxim is now best seen as evidence of the portability of concepts reduced to fungible units or cliché. On the cliché as form, see chapters 2 and 4.

6. But even this event had duration: scientists have determined that about ten minutes after the asteroid's impact, debris would have stopped falling from the sky and the mile-high waves would have begun to form (Cappucci, "Asteroid").

7. Emmett and Nye refer to "the emergence of the environmental humanities as an academic discipline early in the twenty-first century" (see "Description: *The Environmental Humanities: An Introduction* by Robert S. Emmett and David E. Nye," MIT Press, accessed January 17, 2023, https://mitpress.mit.edu/9780262534208/the-environmental-humanities/). *Environmental Humanities* was founded in 2012 and *Resilience: A Journal of the Environmental Humanities* two years later, "indicating the development of the field and the consolidation around this terminology" in the years after 2010 (see Wikipedia, s,v, "Environmental Humanities," last modified January 3, 2024. https://en.wikipedia.org/wiki/Environmental_humanities).

8. As I was preparing this chapter in August 2022, an entirely separate flood event, in Dallas, was "'another 1-in-1000 interval flood'" (quoted in Van Brugen). Two days later, the sequence of reporting I'd noticed in 2017 repeated almost exactly: "Five 1,000-Year Rain Events Have Struck the U.S. in Five Weeks. Why?" (Cappucci, "Five"). The traumatic recurrence of this journalistic arc, separated by five years and discussing entirely separate storm cycles, paradoxically confirms the erosion of stability that concerns me here.

9. A report filed a year after the hurricane noted "a staggering 79 percent of all homes in the Kashmere Gardens Super Neighborhood flooded during Hurricane Harvey. . . . Of those households 'lucky' enough to get FEMA aid, four in ten still had thousands of dollars of unmet needs in that zip code" (Purser).

10. Quoted in Rosalind Grooms, email to author, January 26, 2023. According to current series editor David Armitage, "the last of the [Exxon] money ran out in 2013" (email to author, December 21, 2023). I thank Armitage and Liz Friend-Smith for facilitating my inquiries and Rosalind Grooms for generously investigating on my behalf. I am grateful to Max Brzezinski for the initial observation about Hacking's text.

11. "Our Houston Campus," ExxonMobile Corporate, September 27, 2018, https://corporate.exxonmobil.com/locations/united-states/houston-campus.

12. I use "extractive order" to name the total system in which bourgeois values like instrumental reason and self-proprietorship link up to the material structures, expansionist processes, and social infrastructures they support and enable. For more on the relation between material and ideal registers see the introduction, above.

13. Community water system monitoring results from 2012 through February 2022 are made available by the California State Water Resources Control Board at https://www.waterboards.ca.gov/drinking_water/certlic/drinkingwater/docs/hexchrome_cws_10-yr-avg.xlsx (see the link at note 1 on "Hexavalent Chromium (Chromium-6)," California State Water Resources Control Board, accessed June 21, 2024, https://www.waterboards.ca.gov/drinking_water/certlic/drinkingwater/Chromium6.html). I thank Tom Frantz for sharing his expertise on Fresno-area environmental issues.

14. For Husserl, *world* is the "totality of everything intramundane" and *perception* names "the original object-giving experience," where objects are first encountered as separate from background and apprehended as such (quoted in Landgrebe 6).

15. In nonstationary climates the referent for *usual* or *normal* is what is at stake, this baseline being effectively redefined, one study found, every five years, as phenomena formerly experienced as exceptional rapidly come to form new standards. The familiar metaphor for shifting-baseline syndrome is the "boiling frog effect," whereby even lethal extremity can be naturalized in short order. Leaving the feasibility of the study's "sentiment analysis tools" aside we can note that intuiting causal probability from a dynamic dataset produces something we might for short call confusion, since (as the study puts it) there is an "inherent ambiguity in choosing a stable reference period in a nonstationary series" (Moore et al.).

16. For the imperial valences of instinct, see Frederickson as well as Samalin, *Masses*. I describe the cultural conditioning of apparently somatic response in chapter 4.

17. Using a reading of *The Time Machine* to make exactly this point, MacDuffie opposes soft denial to the "hard denial" of open refusals to believe in the truth of climate change; by contrast, soft denial is "a divided state of mind in which one lives as if something one knows to be true is not" ("Victorian Pre-History" 544). Of the novel's conclusion, MacDuffie comments that Wells's narrator "doesn't bother trying to refute the future vision or the science informing it," but aims to "reinvest in the ordinary world by strategically pretending things are other than they are" (*Climate of Denial* 108).

18. See Harskamp. Crawford tracks the interfaces among dwindling green sea turtles, local Caymanian harvesters, and the twentieth-century regime of international law that enabled both endless extraction and the conservation regimes that exploited Caribbean populations.

19. For Carroll's reading on probability and statistics, see Lovett 321–38. For an account of mathematics and *Alice* adjacent to mine here, see Kornbluh, *Order of Forms*, 104–21.

20. *Oxford English Dictionary*, s.v. "queer," last modified March 2024, https://www.oed.com/dictionary/queer_adj1?tab=meaning_and_use.

21. In the closing lines of "The Lived Experience of the Black Man," Fanon describes the feeling of being caught between lifeworlds as an "eviscerated silence," a paralyzed revulsion

that comes "at the crossroads between Nothingness and Infinity." The last words of the chapter: "I began to weep" (*Black Skin, White Masks* 119).

22. According to de Rozario, "the original form of the asterisk (※) included four dots placed in the north, south, east and west positions with a diagonal cross intersecting from top left to bottom right and top right to bottom left. The cross and four dots version of the asterisk gradually rotated 90° over time[;] slowly these dots and lines merged into a star shape with eight points." This history means that the mark was always associated with the question of orientation and its turning; I discuss cardinal directions and experience below.

23. Beer says of growth that it "is a primary sense experience just beyond the reach of consciousness" and thus curiously unavailable to representation: and "if it lies beyond the reach of consciousness it must lie beyond the reach of language" (99). Puckett refers to as Alice's "ongoing series of attempts to be the Alice between big Alice and little Alice" (17).

24. "People imagine that I have described myself in *Maud*, that it is the flower of my own life, and they ask, 'Is this all he has to give us?' Nothing could be more absurd. It is the vice of the age that a man cannot say anything without its being supposed to be personal" (quoted in H. Tennyson 815). All citations to *Maud* are to the 1989 *Tennyson: Selected Edition* (Christopher Ricks, ed.).

25. O'Gorman argues for the "parodic and ironic energies after and against *In Memoriam*" (293), in this extending Lowell's contemporary account of the two poems' dialectical relation (quoted in H. Tennyson 331).

26. *In Memoriam* was a sensation, going through three editions in its first year of publication (1850), a fourth coming out in 1851. Compared to its later, weirder cousin, *In Memoriam* enjoys much more enduring popularity: a search turns up 330 instances on the MLA bibliography for Tennyson / *In Memoriam*, and for Tennyson / *Maud* just 131. I am suggesting that its relation to psychic closure makes it recognizable to bourgeois thought, then as now. On *In Memoriam* and mass extinction, see Oak Taylor.

27. Devin Garofalo discusses orbs, spheres, and circles in the poem in *Worlds Unmanned*; on the same subject, see also Taaffe. Mershon observes how the *In Memoriam* speaker "escapes his non-progressive melancholia via [Robert] Chambers's narrative of evolutionary progress" (1).

28. Isobel Armstrong notes that "it is tempting to associate *In Memoriam* with 'normal' mourning and *Maud* with the 'pathological' mourning of melancholia . . . : this can lead to some insights but can also obscure the nature of *In Memoriam* as exceptional text in the Tennyson canon by virtue of its very struggle to normalise itself" (255). But "healthy" mourning does not preclude the struggle for normalization and is defined against melancholia primarily by the fact that after such a period of struggle it does, in the end, come to conclusion, as Armstrong notes. The *In Memoriam* stanza's ABBA scheme models a form of closure as the return of the A rhyme after a suitable and varied dilation or delay ("struggle") in the middle lines.

29. See especially Dransfield and Markovits.

30. On the pastoral and violence, I am drawing here on R. Williams *Country and the City*, and on recent work by Zach Fruit and Carolyn Lesjak.

31. I discuss extractivism more directly in the introduction. Relations of mediation can be complicated, but are not in the case of Adam Trexler, who wrote a concerned and entirely orthodox monograph in the environmental humanities, *Anthropocene Fictions: The Novel in the Time of Climate Change* (2015), before going on to found Valaurum, Inc., a "minting technology" company that "offers the smallest, most affordable and secure form of physical precious

metal in the world" (see Trexler's LinkedIn profile, accessed April 4, 2024, at https://www.linkedin.com/in/adam-trexler-802b1564). I thank Anna Kornbluh for this point.

32. "We really know little of what the other characters are like, only how they impress the mind of a man who is constitutionally unable to perceive them except as projections of his own psyche" (R. Martin 386). I discuss Adorno's account in the introduction and chapter 2.

33. As Derrida summarizes and *Maud* plays out here, processes of introjection can be understood as a function of extraction-imperialism at the level of psychic relations, since "by including the object . . . the process [of introjection] expands the self. It does not retreat; it advances, propagates itself, assimilates, takes over" (Derrida, "Foreword," xvi).

34. I borrow this phrase from Nasser Mufti, who draws on Edward Said to describe the extractive economy and consequently nonlinear plot forms of Conrad's *Nostromo*.

35. The speaker's genre-coded delusions shift among singsong fantasies, hyperromanticized fugues, and mock-serious Carlylean rants. The formal templates couched inside these generic microclimates comprise (in one reader's tally) "ballad and sonnet, epithalamion and elegy, iambic pentameter, alexandrine, heroic couplet, and doggerel" (Berglund 45)—to say nothing of the "anapaestic movements" that Tennyson thought among the best of "the many metres he invented" in his lifetime (H. Tennyson 285).

36. Surveying Tennyson's manuscripts, Tucker notes that *Maud* and *In Memoriam* are both poems "open in structure while strictly observant of such local formations as metre and rhyme" (Tucker, "Better Yet," 62). *Maud*, explains Buckley, so full of "ironic reversals," is both chaotic and perfectly poised: "Despite the frenzy of its content, *Maud* is the most carefully constructed of Tennyson's longer poems; and the verse throughout, for all its onrush of sentiment, is calculated and controlled with great discretion" (144). Thus do the frenzied trochees and anapests of the first four sections give way to "colloquial recitiatives" conducted "on the dead level of iambic prose" (Buckley 144).

37. "The ending [where the speaker goes off to war] cost Tennyson much anxiety and effort; he did not make the division into three parts until 1865 (in 1859 he had divided it into two parts), and he retained—with a suggestive anomaly—the numbering of sections, so that Part III does not begin again, as Part II does, with a section I, but begins with section IV" (Ricks, *Tennyson*, 262).

38. The book sold well despite critical mockery and widespread confusion about what it meant: some eight thousand copies in three months (Shaw 81). Hallam Tennyson reports that the book sold out its ten-thousand-copy first edition quickly but that—after the bad reviews came out—a second run of three hundred never completely sold.

39. For his part, Swinburne, perhaps more alive to the nuances of the monologue form, thought *Maud* "the poem of the deepest charm and fullest delight, pathos and melody ever written, even by Mr. Tennyson" (quoted in H. Tennyson 358n1).

40. As I discuss in the next chapter, "the not merely theoretical but practical tendency toward self-destruction has been inherent in rationality from the first" (Adorno and Horkheimer xix). "Red cedar" picks up a cedar-tree image from earlier in the poem and shuttles it to the enervated edges of the extractive world system (the eastern red cedar, *juniperus virginiana*, is native to the US).

41. "Global Mean CO2 Mixing Ratios," NASA, accessed September 27, 2021. https://data.giss.nasa.gov/modelforce/ghgases/Fig1A.ext.txt.

Chapter 2

1. See in particular Elizabeth Miller, *Extraction Ecologies*; Pinkus; Tondre, "Finitude"; and Morgan.

2. In the 1850 "Biographical Notice" and "Editor's Preface," Charlotte herself set these warring strategies into motion, arguing on the one hand for the novel as a documentary account of the "ways" and "language" of the countryside—"detail[ed], minute, graphic, and accurate" ("Biographical Notice" 308); on the other, that it emerged from a "creative gift" from another sphere that "strangely wills and works for itself" ("Preface" 310). Eagleton observes that the novel's "dialectical vision" (*Myths* 120) places metaphysical and historical alternatives into relation. As critics of the New Historicism pointed out, a fetishized "context" functions to scale down total systems into units of some size (a day, a week, a specific city, etc.), then construes this historical mini-structure as causal with respect to a text. On the domesticating aspiration to containment of "context" in this sense, see Jay 33. I evoke the transfer-grid effect of this procedure and its inevitable failure in the conclusion.

3. Nersessian critiques the tendency in allegedly committed literary criticism to "subpoena[] literature to testify to the existence and the experience of this cause or that effect," a process of domestication that merely "applies one cultural form to another" while pretending to real-world effectivity (*Calamity* 7). I describe this impulse to "read[] texts as if to solve them" (*Calamity* 7) as a solution-impulse native to the rising bourgeois thought embodied in Lockwood.

4. House and Heritage, "Halsteads, Thornton in Lonsdale, Yorkshire," Facebook post, December 29, 2016, https://www.facebook.com/houseandheritage/photos/halsteads-thornton-in-lonsdale-yorkshire/1326651404073020/.

5. I thank Dan Shore for his help in translating this variation on the golden rule.

6. In one powerful moment of decipherment, Heywood explains that a ledge that is "twice referenced" in *Wuthering Heights* evokes the word *sill*, which is a "cypher" for the Sill family, known slavers residing at Dent ("Yorkshire Slavery" 192).

7. On the "architectural imaginary" of *Wuthering Heights*, see Kornbluh, *Order*, e.g., 65.

8. Historical maps and real estate records disclose that fully two dozen country homes were built or rebuilt by slave traders within a six-mile radius of the center of the Atlantic extractive economy from which Heathcliff originates, Liverpool, more of them around Lancaster. These mansions could have been rural retreats or primary residences, and at least ten of them around Liverpool were purchased from wealth primarily derived from the slave trade, a number that does not count ancillary but related sectors of the economy like shipbuilding or insurance (Longmore 43–45).

9. Nelson refers to a 1957 study, but newer work has placed the Royal Africa Company in the larger context of joint-stock companies and early corporate entities that gave British imperialism its shape across the modern period; this work confirms that the political project of imperialism was always inextricable from the processes of enclosure and the progressive value-generation of uncapitalized nature construed on the model of efficiency; see Stern. On efficiency and the "spirit of experiment" and "continual improvement" in the early slave colonies (in planter Edward Long's 1774 words) see Nelson, especially 102–16.

10. "George Welch," WikiTree, accessed July 1, 2020, https://www.wikitree.com/wiki/Welch-2222.

11. See also "Leck Hall: A Grade II Listed Building in Leck, Lancashire," British Listed Buildings, accessed April 5, 2024, https://britishlistedbuildings.co.uk/101164984-leck-hall-leck#.YbpYzX3MJz8.

12. A further fact: The Brontës attended Clergy Daughters' with Eliza Rawlins Walwyn, daughter of one Reverend John Walwyn, of St. Kitts, whose descendants owned sugar mills in St. Kitts through 1975. On transformations in the Atlantic economy and *Jane Eyre*, see C. Taylor.

13. Poovey notes that "the epistemological unit of the fact" emerges across the course of bourgeois modernity to "register[] the tension between the richness and variety embodied in concrete phenomena and the uniform, rule-governed order of humanly contrived systems" (*Fact* 1).

14. Titles and land "followed the wealth accrued over decades or centuries of different forms of involvement in the slave economy" (Draper 168).

15. "About," Harewood.org, accessed July 12, 2020, https://www.harewood.org/about/.

16. "About the Project," *Lascelles Slavery Archive*, accessed May 20, 2024, https://www.york.ac.uk/projects/harewoodslavery/about.html.

17. No evidence survives to suggest that enslaved people lived at Harewood, but more than forty Black people lived in the Lancaster area in the eighteenth and nineteenth centuries, Heywood informs us, a population that "owed its presence in rural Lunesdale to Lancaster and Liverpool trading contacts with Africa" ("Yorkshire Slavery" 194).

18. Richard Dellamora says that the Brontës visited Harewood House itself in 1833 (547) but I find no reference to this visit in the existing biographical evidence. Dellamora may be thinking of this visit to Lascelles Hall (not the same as Harewood).

19. See Spivak, "Three Women's Texts." Taylor shows how Spivak's account refers to an undifferentiated "imperialism" that flattens the history of post-slavery domination in the "east" and "west" Indies into a single phenomenon.

20. Compare Hiday, who notes that the novel stages "the coproduction of 'decay' and 'progress'" ("Heathcliff Walks" 250) and cites this passage of Emily's schoolwork to show how the novel refuses progressive temporalities (253). I am indebted to his comprehensive account of extraction in the novel. See also H. Scott.

21. Said observes of *Mansfield Park* that "the right to colonial possessions helps directly to establish social order and moral priorities at home" (62), meaning that every scene of pastoral refinement or country civility was always a boneyard in disguise. Said's point is thickened by recent work refining Eric Williams's original thesis that slave-based Atlantic accumulation was integral to the development of "free" industrial modernity in England. It is relevant to the historical argument of this book that Williams's *Capitalism and Slavery* (1944) was published the same year as the first edition of *Dialectic of Enlightenment*.

22. For Marx, landed property "presupposes that certain persons enjoy the monopoly of disposing of particular portions of the globe as exclusive spheres of their private will to the exclusion of all others" (752). Thus, the "the monopoly of landed property is a historical precondition for the capitalist mode of production and *remains its permanent foundation*" (754, emphasis added).

23. Sanger notes that "after Lockwood has been ill three weeks Heathcliff sends him some grouse, the last of the season. Since the Game Act, 1831, grouse may not be shot after 10th December, so we may take this as about the date for the last grouse" (13). From such clues Sanger builds out the chronological sequence of the novel detailed later in this chapter.

24. Beaver felt is made by "pummeling" and boiling the soft underhair of beavers killed by metal trap; demand for hats had extirpated the animal from Europe by the sixteenth century and drove expansion of the fur extraction industry into upper North America via the Hudson Bay Company, the resource frontier always pushing further "to tap new areas

of the more valuable furs" (Innis 6). Trapping reduced a beaver population of some sixty million to as few as one hundred thousand ("Escaping into the Wild").

25. For Sedgwick, the "single, overarching narrative" of the New Historicism aims to disclose "hidden violences in the genealogy of the modern liberal subject" (*Touching Feeling* 139), a faith in exposure that is motivated by a desire for the satisfaction presumed to follow from such discovery. *Wuthering Heights* tempts but does not satisfy this desire to grasp and hold.

26. One slaver's house featured "numerous and splendid apartments," as a contemporary observed, with walls covered in "crimson velvets and blue damask and lined with gilded furniture" (quoted in Nelson 257). The crimsoned room Catherine and Heathcliff observe at Thrushcross Grange is not dissimilar to *Jane Eyre*'s red room, which like Harewood House is paneled with the colonial mahogany, emblem of West Indian deforestation (see Freedgood 30–54 and the conclusion, below).

27. As H. Scott and Hiday note, in 1801, when the novel's main action begins, the fires at Wuthering Heights blaze with a heat "compounded of coal, peat, and wood" (Hiday, "Heathcliff Walks," 7). Because of ongoing deforestation and the increased tendency in northern areas especially to use coal for domestic applications, these fires would be, by Brontë's own moment, entirely fueled by fossil carbon—the energy history of northern England coded into the details and temporal sequence of the novel.

28. In formulating the question I'm indebted to Garofalo's treatment, in her unpublished manuscript *Worlds Unmanned*, of E. B. Browning's ties to the Atlantic slave economy (MS shared with author via email on December 13, 2021).

29. Over the course of the eighteenth century, new tactics for planting enabled year-round production, while, as I note in the conclusion, plantation layouts featuring concentric circles connected by radial paths more efficiently conveyed cane to the presses; meanwhile "clock-based modes of plantation management emerged on the Caribbean sugar plantation well before [they] appeared in other agricultural or industrial contexts" in Europe (Nelson 105–6).

30. For Dorothy van Ghent, Lockwood is an "effete" and "well-mannered urbanite" (190, 189); for Edgar F. Shannon, he is "gregarious and affable" ("Lockwood's Dreams" 98), with a mind that, in Gezari's words, "can make only limited sense of the inhabitants of Wuthering Heights" ("Introduction" 3). Eagleton describes him as "farcically incapable of deciphering the characters' relationships" (Eagleton, *Great Hunger*, 114).

31. "Works of art are ascetic and shameless," but "the culture industry is pornographic and prudish" (Adorno and Horkheimer 111).

32. Wiltshire summarizes Lockwood's speech as an idiom that "stands out as received English, based on the speech of southern England, and characterized by the predominance of Latinate abstract words" (19).

33. Rousseau's *Second Discourse on the Origins and Founding of Inequality Between Men* (1755) sketches the origin of civil society through enclosure too: "The first men, who, having enclosed a piece of land, bethought himself to say '*this is mine*,' and found people simple enough to believe him, was the true founder of civil society" (quoted in François 36n55.).

34. Nelson identifies improvement as the key driver of material change on the slave islands of the early British system. New designs for boiling houses, aqueducts, waterwheels, and "trash houses" all spoke to the plantation system's commitment to efficiency and "continual improvemen[t]," as slave owner Edward Long put it (quoted in Nelson 103). Long's "mentor in these matters," as C. Hall puts it, was John Locke, whom the slaver called "judicious Locke" (Hall, *Lucky Valley*, 19). "Trash" refers to the leaves, stalks, and waste cane

left after pressing that was increasingly used to fuel boiling-house furnaces as forests were cleared for new monoculture plots.

35. *Oxford English Dictionary*, s.v. "comprehend (v.)," last modified December 2023, https://doi.org/10.1093/OED/6832997497.

36. In *The Nutmeg's Curse*, Ghosh glosses this thought form as fundamental to a logic of global enclosure, where "it was by planting, and creating 'plantations,' that the settlers claimed the land. . . . [T]heir claim of ownership was founded on the notion that they were 'improving' the land by making it productive in ways that were recognizable as such by Europeans. As the historian William Cronon notes, 'European perceptions of what constituted a proper use of the environment . . . thus became a European ideology of conquest'" (63).

37. *Oxford English Dictionary*, s.v. "homely (adj.)," last modified December 2023, https://doi.org/10.1093/OED/9937319759.

38. This mechanism of imperial hygiene is ongoing, since it is a feature of bourgeois humanism and not a bug. "We are fighting against animals," said Israeli defense minister Yoav Gallant in October 2023, "not people" (TOI Staff; see Wynter; see also Garofalo *Worlds Unmanned*).

39. Esposito's inattention to chattel slavery in the Americas is symptomatic of a "philosophical" approach to these problems that separates epistemic mechanisms ("philosophy") from the material arrangements of a developing Atlantic capitalism ("history"). Further symptoms are the fetishization, shared with Agamben, of Roman law as mythic origin point for "law" as such, and a positioning of the Holocaust as an un-analogizable paradigm, outside of time or history. This odd blindness to New World genocides is transposed from Arendt's Cold War account and can thus be seen as ironically symptomatic of the specific form of liberal humanism Esposito and Agamben purport to critique.

40. Like George Eliot, the three surviving Brontë sisters invested what capital they had in railway shares and, ever punctilious about detail, Emily managed the investment. According to Charlotte, Emily "made herself mistress of the necessary degree of knowledge for conducting the matter, by dint of carefully reading every paragraph and every advertisement in the news-papers that related to rail-roads" (quoted in Gezari, *Annotated*, 86).

41. Wiltshire, in a side-by side reading of the altered passages, points out that most of Charlotte's changes had to do with orthography and pronunciation, and are thus "phonological"; her "amendments rarely extended to the lexis of the dialect speech" (25–26), even when the avowed intention was to push toward standardization.

42. My claims here track with Victoria Baena's argument that *Wuthering Heights* "fashions a vision of the 'provincial' as linguistic difference, involving asymmetrical access to economic resources as well as social and cultural capital," and that formal structure and political antagonisms of the novel are "built out of mistranslation rather than communication" (107–8).

43. I thank Nicole Rizzuto for her advice on this point and everything else in this chapter.

44. Daniel DeWispelare uses "metalinguistic writing" to refer to the usually nonfictional "writing that takes language itself as a topic" (2); Charlotte's edits help us see *Wuthering Heights* as metalinguistic in a related sense. Daniel died just as this book was going to press, an awful loss. I am sorry I did not get to talk about this idea with him.

45. Like Kant, Brontë positions the subject-object relation at the center of bourgeois consciousness; like Kant's critics Adorno and Fred Moten, she marks it as the zero point of administrative reason, where the modern project of subjectification and capture manifests as conceptual grammar (see, e.g., Moten, *In the Break*, 1; and for alternatives to this grammar, Moten, *Black and Blur*).

46. Wright observes of this passage that its "stuttering punctuation" was "radically altered" by Charlotte in the second edition, this passage being revised "much more thoroughly than any other" in the novel (*Bad Logic* 33). "Perhaps," Wright speculates, "she sensed something dangerous in that statement ["I *am* Heathcliff"] and desired to cordon it off from what surrounds it" (33).

47. "What we call the face," Levinas writes in *Totality and Infinity*, "is precisely this exceptional presentation of self by self" (202).

48. Recall that in the novel's first pages, the "atmospheric tumult" (2) of the exterior weather environment extends as by osmosis to the interior domain of the house, which is a "tempest" and a "storm" just pages later; the tumult extends further to Zillah, who "heav[es] like a sea after a high wind" (4–5), all of these entities now exhibiting characteristics of the same mood or setting. Writing in the aftermath of WWII and at the outset of the Great Acceleration, Kenneth Burke observes that the assigning of human emotions to nonhuman entities in literature "seems to have come into prominence precisely at the time when the breach between man and nature was being intensified" (234).

49. In a special issue of *GLQ* devoted to "the ontology of the couple," Brilmyer, Trentin, and Xiang "attempt to comprehend what it means to be *in two*—that is, to have one's identity or experience bound up for some duration with another" ("Introduction" 217–18). By collapsing the bourgeois mathematics that keeps ones separate, *Wuthering Heights* makes a similar attempt, even as it historicizes the emergence of that thought form with Lockwood's arrival at the gate. See chapter 5 for further discussion of Brilmyer et al. on this topic.

50. Parsard observes that attention to the empire's self-reports necessarily discloses other configurations of relation beyond the good and the useful, and that "uncertainty is an epistemological and a temporal problem for empire" (94). I revisit spaces of such uncertainty in the conclusion.

51. Schor reconstructs the ambivalent place of the detail in modern aesthetic theory, observing that the relentlessly feminized individuum has inspired derision in favor of theme and order from theorists of the masculine sublime like Edmund Burke. It has also inspired fetishization in anti-thematizing projects whose reflexive rejection of the abstract brings them closer to nominalism. My aim is to see the two in a dialectical relation that is (now) to be tactically rebalanced away from abstracting homogenization. I thank Kathy Psomiades for bringing Schor's argument to my attention.

Chapter 3

1. Roper and Chitham list it as an "undated fragment" (E. Brontë, *Poems*, eds. Roper and Chitham, xiv) but Gezari places it in February 1838, "conjecturally placed in the compositional sequence on the basis of no. 36, which appears on the reverse side of the same ms. leaf" (Brontë, *Complete Poems*, ed. Gezari, 254n).

2. Anne Carson cites this line alongside other uncomprehending responses in "The Glass Essay" (1995); see note 26, below.

3. The *Broadview*, e.g., notes that her "perspectives . . . connect Brontë to her Romantic predecessors much more than to her Victorian counterparts" (Black et al., eds., 502). I take this asynchronous quality as a sign of the work's own investments in destabilized models of periodization and historicity; see chapter 2.

4. Caroline Levine argues that "scholars across the humanities return, again and again, to three key moves: the pause, the rupture, and the dissolve" and describes these as "aesthetic"

and therefore insufficiently concerned with "action" (*Activist* 1). One understands the fatigue with what has become an approved repertoire of pre-set moves, but absent any attempt to account for the relations between conceptual structures (the domain of ideology) and material conjuncture (the domain of politics), the call for action offered in place of these allegedly empty moves can be described as anti-intellectual. It is the space of mediation—the processes by which concepts become actual—that I seek to address here. For more on mediation, see introduction, above.

5. For Bloch, such gestures reaffirm the order they congratulate themselves on critiquing, "loaning the idea of transcendence . . . from the bank" in a cheap substitute for struggle (I, 5). Wenzel describes "*world-imagining from below*" as the process by which subaltern figures "situate their precarious local condition within a transnational context" (*Disposition* 9, emphasis original). How such acts of imaginative situating become concrete is the question of politics, or (as I will say) infrapolitics: a problem of mediation I address in the conclusion via Tadiar's account of remaindered life.

6. Sky / Immensity would thus be considered a "Cockney rhyme," in the parlance of metropolitan opponents of figures like the early John Keats and Leigh Hunt. The flamboyant, dialect-based rhymes of the so-called Cockney School were "presented as non-standard and indeed sub-standard, and as a distinguishing mark of the incorrect as opposed to the correct speaker" (Mugglestone 59). I thank Greg Kucich for teaching me about Cockney rhymes years ago.

7. "It lies in the definition of negative dialectics that it will not come to rest in itself, as if it were total. This is its form of hope" (Adorno, *Negative*, 406).

8. Roper counts "the dungeon theme" as providing the "subject or setting" for fourteen of the poems and "references" for twelve others ("Introduction" 11).

9. It is well-established in accounts of Brontë juvenilia that the concept of a "public" or "audience" is far from stable for these private or semi-private textual performances, most of which, Lutz writes, "are the right size to fit in a closed hand—and the larger ones show signs of being folded to palm size" ("Paper Work" 294).

10. Pateman describes the "'standard embarrassment'" around consent in feminist analysis (150) and analyzes the failures of the consent concept to secure women's status as fully human even in societies built around the fetish of self-sovereignty. The collapse of consent as an analytic category thus marks "the success of three centuries of mutual accommodation between liberalism and patriarchalism" (162). I am indebted here and throughout to Psomiades, *Primitive Marriage*; see especially 81–132.

11. "Why ask to know the date, the clime?" of 1846, is a 264-line fragment to which Hatfield appends the following note, one of many such notes that underscore the editorial difficulty of transforming these writings into what he presumes to be "poems": "The poem was left in an incomplete state by its author. Lines 1 to 148 contain comparatively few alterations, and were probably copied from an earlier draft, but from line 149 onwards the alterations and cancellations are very numerous and much of the script is almost unreadable. Some of the printed words are partly conjectural. Lines 149 to 156 and 172 to 189 are cancelled by lines drawn across them in manuscript. A few almost illegible trial lines and parts of lines have been disregarded . . ." (Brontë, ed. Hatfield, 252). None of these difficulties deters him from converting the text into a finished poem.

12. Romantic lyric poetry was well known to Brontë but the "lyric tradition" into which her work was conscripted is largely an artifact of twentieth-century New Criticism, entirely unknown to her of course. Gezari hinges interpretation on the idea of "Emily Brontë as a

lyric poet" (*Last* 19–20). On lyricization, see Jackson; for a historical account of the ideology of poetic form see Meredith Martin.

13. Jackson borrows "scribal objects" from the Dickinson Electronic Archives (45–46). Lutz observes of Brontë's writings that "their fragmentary, roughshod nature should be understood as a deliberate choice, part of the works' creative whole" ("Paper Work" 296), installing a preference for completed forms and actualized intention in ways that confirm the penetration of voluntarist thought into even our best criticism.

14. The processes of recycling by which all the Brontës salvaged paper from other domains of life and transformed them into poetic formats is a key fact of their remediating procedure (Lutz, "Paper Work," 303n16). The practice responded to the general scarcity and cost of paper at the time, but also suggests an eye to repurposing and redeployment—a salvage aesthetics—that I am drawing out here.

15. Ayrton tracks the textual history of Brontë's "EJB" notebook from "1844 to the Present" and so describes the gauntlet of capture and monetization through which these tiny fragments have traveled since their composition. I thank Peter Armenti for this reference and for sharing his expertise.

16. Gabriel Heaton, email to author, June 1, 2021.

17. "Brontë Treasures Saved for the Nation," said the press release ("Honresfield Library"): "Lost Library of Literary Treasures Saved for UK after Charity Raises £15m," wrote the *Guardian* (Flood); while, with admirable directness, the *Evening Standard* proclaimed "Brontës' Manuscripts Saved for the Nation Thanks to £7.5m from UK's Richest Man Leonard Blavatnik" (Dex).

18. Blavatnik School of Government at the University of Oxford, accessed April 10, 2024, https://www.bsg.ox.ac.uk/.

19. "Art and Cultural Institutions," Blavatnik Family Foundation, accessed April 10, 2024, https://blavatnikfoundation.org/beneficiary/art-cultural-institutions/.

20. Frank's *A Chainless Soul: A Life of Emily Brontë* (1990) mocks the "purple heather school of Brontë biography," but posits in its place a "far more troubled, solitary and austere" Emily who "made her own choices boldly and stuck by them. She cared nothing for the opinions and values of others" (1). Davies's *Emily Brontë: Heretic* (1994), inflects this lean-in framing even further, showing "that *Wuthering Heights* and the poetry are transgressive testaments to the active experience of female sexuality" (S. Davies, "Emily Brontë: Heretic," n.p.). I address the imbrication of liberal feminism and the extractive paradigm in chapter 5.

21. I am indebted to Gezari's readings of Brontë's work throughout this chapter. As Isobel Armstrong writes in a gloss of "Enough of Thought," "the powerful energies of Emily Brontë's poetry . . . tend to reaffirm terrible alternatives despite the move to the third term—heaven or hell, spirit or man, male or female, a gendered or an ungendered world: the negations sound with the force of affirmation, and the affirmations with the force of negations" (336).

22. Google search results, "theme of Emily Brontë, The Prisoner," accessed May 29, 2024.

23. In a 2007 foreword to Schor's *Reading in Detail*, Rooney clarifies that Schor's positioning of "masculine" and "feminine" aesthetic modes is not an endorsement of these associations as in any way natural but a nod to the misogynist cognitive architecture that secured and continues to enforce this binary; within "the conceptual system of phallocentric culture" the work, for its critics, is double: "to press the claims of the detail," even "as we dismantle [the] enabling conditions" of a distinction between allegedly feminine and masculine aesthetic modes (xxxii).

24. As is well known, so-called Captcha technology works to differentiate machine reading processes from human ones, using a "distorted image" to "obscur[e] its message from

computer interpretation by twisting the letters and adding a slight background color to the gradient" (*Wikipedia*, s.v. "CAPTCHA," last updated June 17, 2024, https://en.wikipedia.org/wiki/CAPTCHA). An acronym for "Completely Automated Public Turing test to tell Computers and Humans Apart," the technology protects from one form of capture (by spam, bots, and machine-driven reading processes), by enabling another (the retrieval of securely "human" signals for transactional operations in the future). Brontë's writing, I'm suggesting, slips through the grid of both.

25. Gezari's edition appears in the "Penguin English Poets" series, whose house style requires that spelling be "modernized" and "made correct and consistent." This text has also "silently added apostrophes for possessives, for contractions, and for elisions" (E. Brontë, *Complete Poems*, ed. Gezari, xxiv, xxv, xxviii).

26. *Whach*, meanwhile, enables Anne Carson, in "The Glass Essay," to ruminate on how "Emily's habitual spelling of this word, / has caused confusion." But "whacher is what she wrote":

> Whacher is what she was.
> She whached God and humans and moor wind and open night.
> She whached eyes, stars, inside, outside, actual weather.
>
> She whached the bars of time, which broke.
> She whached the poor core of the world,
> wide open.
>
> (ll. 94–105; cf. Gezari, *Last*, 2–3)

27. Malm's "ecological Leninism" was greeted with a breathless forum of responses by male writers in the *London Review of Books* in November 2021 (see, e.g., Tooze), while Jenny Turner's follow-up piece, reporting on the ground from the outer lobbies of the COP26 conference, emphasized the almost hopeless-seeming efforts of women and the dispossessed in that scene of inertia, and construed these vernacular efforts as the secret center of the climate movement: "not much, but it'll have to be a start."

Chapter 4

1. Eliot mailed the "Finale" to John Blackwood a full two weeks after her final shipment of regular manuscript pages: it was written with the benefit of hindsight (Beaty 132). Eliot wrote "Armgart," about an opera singer who loses her voice, while working on *Middlemarch*, confirming that in this period musical composition was on her mind.

2. Famously, *Middlemarch* began as two projects, joined by means of the painstaking process reconstructed by Beaty, who notes that the serial publication of the book, decided upon only after the writing had begun, helped force Eliot to discipline her particulars into unification: "The unity of *Middlemarch* may be an outgrowth of the increasing interrelationship of the characters and interdependence of the plots. But the need to jump back and forth from one story to the other within the half-volume undoubtedly made George Eliot consider more carefully the relation of one story to the others and one group of characters to the others. . . . The requirements of parts publication thus virtually forced George Eliot to unify *Middlemarch* in a way that she had not originally intended" (Beaty 55).

3. On Eliot's epigraphs as "shrunken, subsidiary structures subsumed within a vast novel" see Hall 820.

4. In a digital analysis of the most-quoted bits of *Middlemarch* since its publication, Sierra Eckert and Milan Terlunen have shown that many of the novel's most excerpted moments come from these theme-setting passages of auto-explication (Eckert; Eckert and Terlunen). Alongside early efforts at mining Eliot's work for valuable bits like Alexander Main's *Wise, Witty, and Tender Sayings in Prose and Verse Selected from the Works of George Eliot* (1893), this study confirms the appeal of moments of overt summation, discursive condensation, and thematic reification to help make sense of the novel's mass of particularized information. Main's comment that the "wealth" in "George Eliot's treasury" is of a "supply that would seem to be actually without a limit" betrays awareness of the danger of depletion inherent in the strip-mining of "extracts" (xii, xi).

5. "With musical compositions it is obviously the whole that matters; but the whole is not something which simply reduces the individual single moments to insignificance. The whole . . . is itself the relation between the whole and its individual moments, within which these latter obtain throughout their independent value. Analysis exists only as the uncovering of the relationship between these moments, and not merely by virtue of the obtuse and aconceptual priority of the whole over its parts" (Adorno, "Problem," 174).

6. In a chapter called "Revolution in a Minor Key," Hartman describes the activities of Harriet Powell as she "engag[es] in the very ordinary everyday practice of defiance" that falls "beneath the scrutiny" of orthodox political figures of the day (*Wayward* 218). Hartman cites James Scott on the "infrapolitics of the dominated" in *Scenes of Subjection* (62).

7. It is symptomatic of a broader phenomenon that oil companies have not been subjected to sanction, mass boycott, or general strike—let alone organized armed insurgency—but instead posted record profits: "In 2022, the six largest western oil companies made more money than in any year in the history of the industry: over $200bn" (Wilson and Brower n.p.). Crary calls for "an active prefiguration of new communities and formations" against the gathering catastrophes of the present (*Scorched* 123–24). The allusion is to Raymond Williams's understanding of pre-emergent social forces and the call is for collaborative action that might not overturn the regnant order but prepare ground for social struggles that could themselves, in future, alter the organic basis of life.

8. As Duncan summarizes, "With *Middlemarch,* George Eliot realizes in full the project of the novel as a medium of scientific inquiry" (167), but the point could be reversed. In making this claim he extends Beer, who notes how Eliot "opens *Middlemarch* by presenting it as a series of experiments" (148).

9. *Oxford English Dictionary,* s.v. "trifle," accessed April 12, 2024, https://www.oed.com/search/dictionary/?scope=Entries&q=trifle.

10. As Galison explains, the idea of anti-aircraft targeting, "along with its associated engineering notions of feedback systems and black boxes, became, for Wiener, the model for a cybernetic understanding of the universe" (229).

11. Hildebrand and J. M. Miller both describe *Middlemarch* in ecological terms; accounts of links between the novel and the ecological rarely historicize this concept with the care of their treatments.

12. Geoghegan notes that in the years after World War II the Rockefeller Foundation shifted away from "textual, historical, and critical inquiries" into communication and society (Adorno, Krakauer), and toward "functionalist and ahistorical approaches that more closely resembled the structuralist approach developed by Jakobson and his colleagues" (108). This description of a shift in institutional funding away from the historical and textual to the functionalist empiricism of applied technics reverberates into the present, when immediate engagement with politics and social life is increasingly construed as compulsory for all

scholarship; a related reorientation of funding is one explanation for the rise of "environmental humanities" as a discrete field since the early 2000s.

13. "Our Grants, Georgetown University," Rockefeller Foundation, accessed April 12, 2024, https://www.rockefellerfoundation.org/grant/georgetown-university-2022/.

14. For an evaluation of Aronowsky's argument, see Howles. Jay addresses the tension between "contextualist" and "transcendental" approaches to historical ideas in *Genesis and Validity*; see especially 28–33.

15. The cybernetic complex also offers a host of tools for critical procedure, too, of course, as a cluster of recent essays in *New Literary History* demonstrate (see Love and Pao 1195). It is a core principle of this book that conceptual procedures do not have inherent relationships to political outcomes but are tools in material struggles, available for deployment in different conjunctures and to different ends. The identification of those ends is a matter of principled conviction; the matching of tools to ends is the domain of strategy; the study of how ideas become concrete is the study of mediation.

16. For accounts of this history, see Mitchell, *Carbon Democracy*, 189–93; and F. Turner, *Counterculture*.

17. Paul Steffen and Eugene Stoermer deployed the term in 2000, and the Anthropocene working group was established in 2009. In the literary humanities, the Anthropocene concept achieved status as conceptual commodity during and after this period, with books and essays trafficking in and debating the merits and demerits of the term. I am arguing that this conceptual-ideological formation must be understood historically as a symptom as much as a strategy. See chapter 1, note 7.

18. A book given to me by a family friend, *Basic Ecology* (1957), explains that "the word ecology is beginning to appear regularly in newspapers and magazines," but that "twenty years ago the senior author of this book could find no reading materials suitable for supplementing the lectures and discussions of the general ecology section of a course" in biology (Buchsbaum and Buchsbaum vii, viii).

19. Nathaniel Blagshaw Ward's *On the Growth of Plants in Closely Glazed Cases* (1842) is often credited with setting off the craze for these sealed glass cases, which protected "foreign" plants from indigenous English weather and aided in the movement of plant species across the Victorian ecological imperium.

20. *Merriam-Webster Dictionary*, s.v. "conation," accessed June 17, 2024, https://www.merriam-webster.com/dictionary/conation.

21. Otis catalogs these metaphorical registers while hierarchizing them through the figure of the network. This preference for one over the other of Eliot's figural registers may disclose less about the novel than about the critics' historical position (in 2001), when networks emerged as a preferred trope for thinking connectivity, as the early dot-com moment replayed with a difference the cybernetics group's computer-age preference for this metaphor. On network ideology in the dot-com period, see F. Turner, *Counterculture*, 175–206; in the Cold War see Woods 124–25.

22. Stout summarizes that "causality is never merely a one-to-one relationship (where one X is the cause of one Y) but a complex structure of relations in which the explanation for any event can be traced back to a potentially unlimited number of contributory causes and in which the 'event' in question is simply one link in a proliferate chain that stretches off into an endless future" (178).

23. On this key term see F. Turner, *Democratic*, esp. 151–80.

24. See, e.g., Gramsci, "Analysis of Situations. Relations of Force" (*Selections* 175–85).

25. Canguilhem noted that by the 1830s, when Comte used the term *milieu*, he believed he was touching up to "the verge of creating a dialectical conception of the relationship

between organism and milieu" ("Living" 10) but was in fact redescribing ideas from Lamarckian biology and Hippolyte Taine. I am grateful to Hildebrand, *Novel Environments*, for this reference.

26. "Here again," Felix reminds his auditors in the "Address to Working Men," "we have to submit ourselves to the great law of inheritance" (Eliot, "Address," 429).

27. Morris notes that the drive to recover suppressed agency in the social sciences during the 1980s and early 1990s was conditioned by "an intuition of the collapse of Soviet socialism" and a growing "exhaustion with or turning away from more overtly organized oppositional politics" during the Reagan and Thatcher regimes (R. Morris 12). It is germane to this book's argument that Scott reports being "an Exxon Fellow" at MIT in 1984, as *Domination and the Arts of Resistance* (1990) took shape (xvi); the note repeats his gratitude, in the earlier *Weapons of the Weak* (1985), that his "most recent" financial support has come from "a postdoctoral Exxon Fellowship awarded by the Science, Technology, and Society Program of the Massachusetts Institute of Technology," which "made it possible to complete the final draft and most of the revisions" (*Weapons* xxi). The year Exxon funded Scott's Boston fellowship, it was sued by New York State for dumping toxic ballast water into the Hudson River, a "flagrant example of environmental crime" ("Exxon is Sued"). On the imbrication of knowledge practices and extraction, see the introduction.

28. Cohn describes Eliot's refusal of the metaphorical drift among her scientific peers—Spencer especially—who saw in the "cell" a useful positive metaphor for the emergent regime of liberal citizens, Eliot imagined not cells but fibers, using fiber and related images (thread, web, "gossamer" linkages) to suggest how bodies might share material relation without full individuation. Cohn adds that the fiber was an outdated metaphor by the time Eliot was using it—a curious detail given that *Middlemarch* can also "be seen to prefigure advancements in materialist science" (Brilmyer 49). Her approach was simultaneously "ahead of" and "behind" its time.

29. I thank Max Brzezinski for helping me see this distinction.

30. *Oxford English Dictionary*, s.v. "sob," accessed April 16, 2024, https://www.oed.com/search/dictionary/?scope=Entries&q=sob.

31. "Even more immediately than other perceptual systems, it seems," Sedgwick observes, "the sense of touch makes nonsense out of any dualistic understanding of agency and passivity" (*Touching* 14).

32. In manuscript, the phrase appears in a footnote to the MS page, apparently added later (cf. *Essays* 432 n4), again suggesting how the supplement (here, touch) turns out always to be central to Eliot's conceptual-aesthetic program.

33. Fraser notes that a "romantic view is widely held today by a fair number of left-wing thinkers and activists," who "treat 'care,' 'nature,' 'direct action,' or 'commoning' as intrinsically anti-capitalist. As a result, they overlook the fact that their favorite practices are not only sources of critique but also integral parts of the capitalist order" (Fraser and Jaeggi, *Capitalism*, 57).

34. Manning shows that changes in the structure of the world can result from activity that is "decisional" rather than volitional: such moments might be narrated as decisive shifts after the fact, but in the event they are improvised and collaboratively engineered through any number of conscious and nonconscious factors. If "the more typical view of freedom has us standing outside the event," in her words, *Middlemarch* locates a non-volitional freedom actuated from within a field of which any one actor comprises only a part (22).

Chapter 5

1. "Haunchwood Colliery." *Our Warwickshire*, accessed June 1, 2024, https://www.ourwarwickshire.org.uk/content/article/haunchwood-colliery.

2. An 1843 issue of the Rossettis' collaboratively written family magazine, *Hodge-Podge*, described capitalist accumulation in environmental terms, rereferring to the "money hunting city" with its "hot smithy smoke," "where the air has lost its freshness and its purity, where all that once was white puts on a dingy hue, where no harmonious sound salutes your ear, but all is crash and dash, squeak and creak" (F. M. L. Rossetti, ed., *Hodge-Podge*, n.p.). Rossetti was removed on doctor's orders from the air pollution of London to spend time by the sea, and throughout the mid-1860s "suffer[ed] from wracking headaches and an alarming cough that brought up blood" (Arseneau and Terrell 3).

3. Hassett observes that the "cropped form" of Rossetti's verse "allows opposing feelings to remain in suspension" ("Reticence" 504).

4. *Oxford English Dictionary*, s.v. "hope (n.1)," last modified December 2023, https://doi.org/10.1093/OED/4820602771.

5. In *A Dream of John Ball* (1888), William Morris has his title character meditate on peasant revolt and consider "how men fight and lose the battle, and the thing that they fought for comes about in spite of their defeat, and when it comes turns out not to be what they meant, and other men have to fight for what they meant under another name" (n.p.). I thank Kathy Psomiades for the reference.

6. In *Endgame* (1958), Samuel Beckett's Hamm asks Clov, "Did your seeds come up?"

> *Clov*: No.
> *Hamm*: Did you scratch round them to see if they had sprouted?
> *Clov*: They haven't sprouted.
> *Hamm*: Perhaps it's too early.
> *Clov*: If they were going to sprout they would have sprouted.
> (*Violently.*)
> They'll never sprout! (13)

Rossetti and Beckett's related insights into to the failure of the Lockean improvement paradigm recur across the waves of time or moments of intensity described in the introduction, above.

7. For William Michael Rossetti, the love of animals is "but a minor matter." But "it was, however, a very persistent lifelong predilection with Christina, and is not unworthy of figuring among her 'key-notes of feeling.' She was not at all addicted to accumulating 'pets' or cockering them up with spinsterish effusion: no neighbor had to get her summoned for keeping seven cats and nine dogs. Broadly speaking, she liked any and every animal—they were all the objects of her fellow-feeling: a frog paired with a dog, and an owl with a fowl. She had even a certain preference for an odd or awkward animal over a showy or elegant one" (x).

8. A copy of *The Prince's Progress: and Other Poems* (1866) was given to Hopkins by his sister Millicent on the day he entered the Society of Jesus—a token, now held at Georgetown's Booth Family Center for Special Collections, of a shared cast of mind.

9. Caroline Levine's *Forms* focuses on novels and teleplays; *The Activist Humanist* skips the readings entirely to emphasize "affirmative instrumentality" (1), while noting that "the questions I posed in this book kept returning me not only to the repetitive patterns of popular culture generally but specifically to realism" (20). Kornbluh's *The Order of Forms* seeks

polemically to reanimate abstraction against what it styles as the nihilistic particularisms of Agambenian anarcho-vitalism and Latourian actor-network theory. Here again the focus is on novels, and specifically realism. Kornbluh's "In Defense of Feminist Abstraction" argues that "an abiding eschewal of abstractions has not capacitated feminist emancipation" and that developing "a feminist abstraction" is required "in these appalling times" (53). I follow Schor and Rooney in seeing the dialectic of general and particular as definitionally irresolvable and therefore requiring tactical adjustment based on circumstance and desired outcome. My shifting toward the particular is conditioned by a sense that thematizing mental habits and a concomitant blindness to detail are encouraged by a world-devouring paradigm of utility and capture.

10. As I observe in the introduction, this oscillation between levels is fundamental to any dialectical analysis, which is why Mezzadra and Neilson observe that "the global scope of the operations of extraction, logistics, and finance *cannot be thought* without attention to the uneven and heterogeneous patterns they create *in specific material circumstances*" (8, emphasis mine).

11. "Part of the excitement of reading Victorian women's poetry," writes Shires in a 1999 omnibus review of the field, "lies in its manifold *refusals* to adopt wholesale the codes and conventions of the male poetic tradition" (601, emphasis added). The idea of "refusal" suggests a voluntarist model of subversion on straightforward bourgeois terms. But "refusal to adopt *wholesale*" describes instead a partial resistance or entangled relationship to those constraints. The delicacy of Shires's formula thus discloses how criticism of Victorian women's poetry reanimates and attempts by various means to resolve the structure-agency dynamic I am suggesting is, at least in the case of Rossetti, the poetry's own guiding problematic.

12. For Gilbert and Gubar, the tragedy of Rossetti's career, like Dickinson's, is that she did not believe in herself. As they write of Dickinson: "Considering how brilliantly she wrote under extraordinarily constraining circumstances, we might . . . properly wonder what she would have done if she had had Whitman's freedom and 'masculine' self-assurance, just as we might reasonably wonder what kind of verse Rossetti would have written if she had not defined her own artistic pride as wicked 'vanity'" (557–58). Rossetti's "willing acceptance of passionate or demure destitution" unfortunately inhibited this fantasized self-expression (564).

13. Of Rossetti, Mermin observes that "her poetry has been valued . . . for its affirmations of female piety, passivity, and submission, while her strength and independence of thought and art have hardly been recognized at all" (xi). Isobel Armstrong's *Victorian Poetry* (1993) includes only a single chapter with any women poets and there finds that Rossetti's poetry produces a similar oscillation between freedom and restraint: Rossetti, Armstrong says, "claimed . . . expressive rights for the unmarried woman in poetry" (344), while *Monna Innominata* is the story of a woman who "has something important . . . to say about sexual feeling, but is blocked by convention from saying it" (345). To point out the vestigially bourgeois vocabulary structuring these important accounts is to appreciate the incredible persistence of liberalism's core categories into the work of Rossetti's greatest readers.

14. Devin Garofalo, *Worlds Unmanned*, unpublished manuscript, shared with author via email on December 13, 2021.

15. From within this paradigm, the injunction for the critic becomes to assess the formula by which any given cultural instance is either "resistant" or "dominant," and in what particular configurations that hydraulic digital relation resolves, reverses, or reconfigures

itself, according to what Sedgwick and Frank perhaps uncharitably describe as "the good dog/bad dog rhetoric of puppy disobedience school" (5).

16. For Foucault, the apparatus (or *dispositif*) is the system of regularities subtending all thought, or, later, a flexible set of intensifications or force-lines, a "process" or mutually supporting "chain or system" of "strategies" (*Introduction* 92). It is "an art," Foucault writes in *Discipline and Punish* (1977), "of composing forces in order to obtain an efficient machine" (164). This figure of an "efficient machine" generated by "composed forces" is importantly different from Latour, who disaggregates the force-concept into "the *composition* of all these *agents* that are connected in some way" ("Agency" 48, emphasis original).

17. On Amanda Anderson's gloss, "within historicist-theoretical feminism of the late 1980s, the lure of a constructionist victimology was repudiated and to a large extent replaced by a conception of women as instrumental agents of those forms of power that were potentially seen to determine them" ("Temptations" 46).

18. Which means that, for a better version of some of these ideas, see Kathy Psomiades's *Primitive Marriage*.

19. As recently as December 2022, a *New York Times* infographic offered to assess "the climate impact of your neighborhood," with a tool "based on research from the University of California, Berkeley." The research was in fact supplied by a think tank operating with major funding from American Express, Apple, and Facebook parent company Meta (Popovich, Rojanasakul, and Plumer).

20. Wendy Brown critiques the "liberal presumption that freedom transpires where power leaves off," noting instead that freedom "requires for its sustenance that we take the full measure of power's range and appearances—the powers that situate, constrain, and produce subjects as well as the will to power entailed in practicing freedom" (25).

21. In *Cyberformalism*, Dan Shore analyzes the imperfectly predictive quality of linguistic forms, which "narrow and partially specify the infinite range of things it is possible to say so that we can say something finite" (9).

22. In practice this task may be more complicated: When asked "What is a sonnet?" ChatGPT was able to explain that sonnets are fourteen-line poems and that "the Italian sonnet is divided into two parts, an octave and a sestet, with the rhyme scheme of abbaabba cdecde or cdcdcd." But when asked to produce "a Petrarchan sonnet in the style of Christina Rossetti" it offered a four stanza, eighteen-line poem that offered two similes for the heart ("like a rose, so bright and fair," "like a bird that takes flight") before tying things up in a repetitive bow: "But like a bird, my heart is wild and free, / And so my love, like rose, is wild and free" (prompts submitted by author to Chat GPT, January 25, 2023, https://chat.openai.com/chat).

23. Sedgwick in "A Poem Is Being Written" compares metrical form to "the rhythmic hand whether hard or subtle of authority itself" (115).

24. Harrington's *Second Person Singular: Late Victorian Women's Poetry and the Bonds of Verse* draws out the crucial doubleness of this phrase using gorgeous readings of Rossetti I draw on gratefully in this chapter.

25. More prosaically, Hopkins in the journals worries over the "circumstance of free choice" in the context of "God's power to determine the creature to choose, and freely choose, according to his will; but not without a change or access of circumstance, over and above the bare act of determination on his part . . ." (283–84).

26. For more on this context, see Phelan and Billone.

Conclusion

1. As a proper noun, *Holocaust* refers to the Jewish genocide that provided concrete occasion for Adorno and Horkheimer's analysis; in lower case it is a common noun, from the Greek *holo kaustos,* or whole burning. On burning as a metaphor for environmental collapse, see Pyne.

2. Unlike Barbados, Jamaica retained wooded areas because these were on mountains and uncultivable for sugar, beyond the reach of (that type of) extractive development. A history of mining in Jamaica explains that the "well established mineral industry of Jamaica" "only dates back to 1952," and arose in this Cold War as a result of "a successful exploration and development programme" based on mineral surveys completed in 1867 by one J. C. Sawkins. This Victorian project was paused until 1942, when "attention was [first] given to the possible economic significance of red earth, bauxite, as aluminum ore" on the island ("Geography and History of Jamaica"). Charles Leslie's 1741 *A New History of Jamaica* referred to the island as "a Constant Mine, whence *Britain* draws prodigious Riches" (quoted in Hall, *Lucky Valley*, 95, emphasis original).

3. *Oxford English Dictionary*, s.v. "detail," accessed April 19, 2024, https://www.oed.com/search/dictionary/?scope=Entries&q=detail.

4. Higman cites a British Library record (Add. Ms. 43379 F) and refers to "five sketches," noting that "unfortunately, only the last of Berryman's sketches survives" (89).

5. "We live in the aftermath," Hall writes in *Lucky Valley: Edward Long and the History of Racial Capitalism*, which was published as this book was in press, and "must recognize responsibilities and focus on the possibilities of repair" (xviii).

Works Cited

Achcar, Gilbert. 2017. "Morbid Symptoms: What Did Gramsci Mean and How Does It Apply to Our Time?" *International Socialist Review* 108 (Winter): https://isreview.org/issue/108/morbid-symptoms/index.html.

Adebayo, Bukola, and Nita Bhalla. 2023. "With Africa's Carbon Sinks Up for Grabs, Offset Debate Heats Up." *Context News*, December 11. https://www.context.news/nature/with-africas-carbon-sinks-up-for-grabs-offset-debate-heats-up.

Adorno, Theodor W. 1992. "Parataxis: On Hölderlin's Late Poetry." In *Notes to Literature*, vol. 2, edited by Rolf Tiedemann and translated by Shierry Weber Nicholsen, 109–49. New York: Columbia University Press.

Adorno, Theodor W. 1993. "Skoteinos, or How to Read Hegel." In *Hegel: Three Studies*, translated by Shierry Weber Nicholsen, 89–148. Cambridge, MA: MIT Press.

Adorno, Theodor W. 2002. "On the Problem of Musical Analysis." In *Essays on Music*, edited by Richard Leppert, translated by Susan H. Gillespie, 162–80. Berkeley: University of California Press.

Adorno, Theodor W. 2007. *Negative Dialectics*. Translated by E. B. Ashton. New York: Continuum.

Adorno, Theodor W., and Max Horkheimer. 2002. *Dialectic of Enlightenment: Philosophical Fragments*. Translated by Edmund Jephcott. Stanford, CA: Stanford University Press.

Ahmed, Sara. 2006. "Orientations: Toward a Queer Phenomenology." *GLQ: A Journal of Lesbian and Gay Studies* 12, no. 4 (September): 54374. https://muse.jhu.edu/article/202832.

Ahmed, Sara. 2016. *Queer Phenomenology: Orientations, Objects, Others*. Durham, NC: Duke University Press.

Akpan, Nsikan. 2017. "Hurricane Harvey Damages Petrochemical Refineries, Releasing Thousands of Pounds of Airborne Pollutants." PBS, August 29. https://www.pbs.org/newshour/science/exxonmobil-texas-refineries-damaged-hurricane-harvey-release-thousands-pounds-pollutants-air.

Ali, Shirin. 2022. "How Gluing Oneself to Something (and Ungluing) Actually Works." *Slate*, October 28. https://slate.com/news-and-politics/2022/10/how-to-glue-yourself-to-something-climate-protests.html.

Allott, Miriam, ed. 1974. *The Brontës: The Critical Heritage*. London: Routledge.

Allport, Andrew. 2012. "The Romantic Fragment Poem and the Performance of Form." *Studies in Romanticism* 51, no. 3 (Fall): 399–417. https://www.jstor.org/stable/24247307.

Anderson, Amanda. 2000. "The Temptations of Aggrandized Agency: Feminist Histories and the Horizon of Modernity." *Victorian Studies* 43, no. 1 (Fall): 43–65. https://www.jstor.org/stable/3829601.

Anderson, Amanda. 2001. *The Powers of Distance: Cosmopolitanism and the Cultivation of Detachment*. Princeton, NJ: Princeton University Press.

Arendt, Hannah. 1958. *The Human Condition*. Chicago: University of Chicago Press.

Arendt, Hannah. 1961. "What Is Freedom?" In *Between Past and Future: Eight Exercises in Political Thought*, 143–72. New York: Viking.

Arendt, Hannah. 1963. *On Revolution*. New York: Viking Penguin.

Armitage, David. 2004. "John Locke, Carolina, and the *Two Treatises of Government*." *Political Theory* 32, no. 5 (October): 602–27. https://doi.org/10.1177/0090591704267122.

Armstrong, Isobel. 1993. *Victorian Poetry: Poetry, Politics, Poetics*. London: Routledge.

Armstrong, Nancy. 1987. *Desire and Domestic Fiction: A Political History of the Novel*. New York: Oxford University Press.

Armstrong, Nancy. 1999. *Fiction in the Age of Photography: The Legacy of British Realism*. Cambridge, MA: Harvard University Press.

Arnold, Matthew. 1867. "Stanzas from the Grande Chartreuse." In Matthew Arnold, *New Poems*, 208–19. London: Macmillan.

Aronowsky, Leah. 2021. "Gas Guzzling Gaia, or: A Prehistory of Climate Change Denialism." *Critical Inquiry* 47 (Winter), 306–27. https://doi.org/10.1086/712129.

Arseneau, Mary, and Emery Terrell. 2019. "'Our Self-Undoing': Christina Rossetti's Literary and Somatic Expressions of Graves Disease." *Humanities* 8, no.1 (March): 1–15. https://doi.org/10.3390/h8010057.

Ashton, Rosemary. 1997. *George Eliot: A Life*. New York: Viking.

Austen, Jane. 2003. *Persuasion*. London: Penguin.

"Autograph Manuscripts of Three Poems and Two Prose Fragments: [Haworth], 1836 July." Catalog record, Morgan Library, New York. https://www.themorgan.org/literary-historical/81558.

Ayrton, Patricia A. 2018. "A Study of the 'Post-Genetic': Emily Bronte's 'EJB' Notebook, 1844 to the Present." PhD diss., University of Edinburgh. https://era.ed.ac.uk/bitstream/handle/1842/33031/Ayrton2018.pdf.

Badiou, Alain. 2005. *Metapolitics*. London: Verso.

Baena, Victoria. 2023. "History's Borrowed Languages: Emily Brontë, Karl Marx, and the Novel Of 1848." *ELH* 90, no. 1: 107–35. https://doi.org/10.1353/elh.2023.0004.

Bailyn, Bernard. 1982. "The Challenge of Modern Historiography." *American Historical Review* 87, no. 1 (February): 1–24. https://www.historians.org/about-aha-and-membership/aha-history-and-archives/presidential-addresses/bernard-bailyn.

Barker, Juliet, ed. 1998. *The Brontës: A Life in Letters*. London: Abrams Press.

Barker, Juliet. 2010. *The Brontës: Wild Genius on the Moors: The Story of a Literary Family*. New York: Pegasus.

Barthes, Roland. 1989. "The Reality Effect." In *The Rustle of Language*, translated by Richard Howard, 141–48. Berkeley: University of California Press.

Barthes, Roland. 2005. *The Neutral: Lecture Course at the College de France*. Translated by Rosalind E. Krauss and Denis Hollier. New York: Columbia University Press.

Battiscombe, Giorgina. 1981. *Christina Rossetti: A Divided Life*. New York: Holt, Rinehart, and Winston.

Baudrillard, Jean. 1981. *For a Critique of the Political Economy of the Sign*. Translated by Charles Levin. Candor, NY: Telos Press.

Beaty, Jerome. 1960. *Middlemarch, from Notebook to Novel: A Study of George Eliot's Creative Method*. Urbana: University of Illinois Press.

Beckett, Samuel. 1958. *Endgame: A Play in One Act*. New York: Grove.

Beer, Gillian. (1983) 2009. *Darwin's Plots: Evolutionary Narrative in Darwin, George Eliot, and Nineteenth-Century Fiction*. 3rd ed. New York: Cambridge University Press.

Belkin, Gary. 2021. "Psychiatry's Climate Reckoning: Time Is Now." *Psychiatric News* 10 (February). https://doi.org/10.1176/appi.pn.2021.2.33.

Benjamin, Walter. 1969. "On Some Motifs in Baudelaire." In *Illuminations: Essays and Reflections*, translated by Harry Zohn and edited by Hannah Arendt, 155–200. New York: Schocken Books.

Benjamin, Walter. 1969. "Theses on the Philosophy of History." In *Illuminations: Essays and Reflections*, translated by Harry Zohn and edited by Hannah Arendt, 253–64. New York: Schocken Books.

Benjamin, Walter. 1999. *Arcades Project*. Translated by Howard Eiland and Kevin McLaughlin. Cambridge, MA: Harvard University Press.

Berglund, Lisa. 1989. "'Faultily Faultless': The Structure of Tennyson's 'Maud.'" *Victorian Poetry* 27, no. 1 (Spring): 45–59. http://www.jstor.org/stable/40002314.

Berlant, Lauren. 2011. *Cruel Optimism*. Durham, NC: Duke University Press.

Berryman, William. n.d. *Landscape with Storm (Unfinished)*. [Between 1808 and 1815]. Watercolor. Prints and Photographs Division, Library of Congress, Washington, DC.

Berryman, William. n.d. *Piazza & Stairs at 4 Paths, 2 Negro Children at Work, Jamaica*. [Between 1808 and 1815]. Watercolor, Prints and Photographs Division, Library of Congress, Washington, DC.

Bersani, Leo. 1976. *A Future for Astyanax: Character and Desire in Literature*. New York: Little, Brown.

Betts, Kris. 2018. "Grandmother Recalls Emotional, Physical Toll of Hurricane Harvey One Year Later." KHOU, August 22. https://www.khou.com/article/news/grandmother-recalls-emotional-physical-toll-of-hurricane-harvey-one-year-later/285-586749466.

Billone, Amy Christine. 2007. *Little Songs: Women, Silence, and the Nineteenth-Century Sonnet*. Columbus: Ohio State University Press.

Black, Joseph, Leonard Conolly, Kate Flint, Isobel Grundy, Wendy Lee, Don LePan, Roy Liuzza, Jerome J. McGann, Anne Lake Prescott, Barry V. Qualls, Jason Rudy, and Claire Waters, eds. 2021. *The Victorian Era*. Vol. 5 of *The Broadview Anthology of British Literature*. 3rd ed. Peterborough, ON: Broadview Press.

Blackburn, Robin. 1997. *The Making of New World Slavery: From the Baroque to the Modern, 1492–1800*. London: Verso.

Bloch, Ernst. 1986. *The Principle of Hope*. 3 volumes. Translated by Neville Plaice, Stephen Plaice, and Paul Knight. Oxford: Basil Blackwell.

Bonaparte, Felicia. 1975. *Will and Destiny: Morality and Tragedy in George Eliot's Novels*. New York: New York University Press.

Bond, David. 2022. *Negative Ecologies: Fossil Fuels and the Discovery of the Environment*. Berkeley: University of California Press.

Bonneuil, Christophe, and Jean-Baptiste Fressoz. 2017. *The Shock of the Anthropocene*. Translated by David Fernbach. London: Verso.

Bosworth, Kai, Jesse Goldstein, Andy Hines, and Eli Meyerhoff. 2025. "Sustainability." In *University Keywords*, edited by Andy Hines. Baltimore: Johns Hopkins University Press, forthcoming. MS shared with author by email December 19, 2023.

Bourdieu, Pierre. 2003. *Outline of a Theory of Practice*. Cambridge: Cambridge University Press.

Brathwaite, Edward Kamau. (1984) 1995. "Nation Language." In *The Post-Colonial Studies Reader*, 1st ed., edited by Bill Ashcroft, Gareth Griffiths, and Helen Tiffin, 309–13. London: Routledge.

Braverman, Irus. 2018. *The Coral Whisperers: Scientists on the Brink*. Berkeley: University of California Press.

Brilmyer, Pearl. 2022. *The Science of Character: Human Objecthood and the Ends of Victorian Realism*. Chicago: University of Chicago Press.

Brilmyer, S. Pearl, Filippo Trentin, and Zairong Xiang. 2019. "Introduction: The Ontology of the Couple." *GLQ: A Journal of Lesbian and Gay Studies* 25, no. 2 (April): 217–21. https://doi.org/10.1215/10642684-7367703.

Brilmyer, S. Pearl, Filippo Trentin, and Zairong Xiang. 2019. "The Ontology of the Couple; or What Queer Theory Knows about Numbers." *GLQ: A Journal of Lesbian and Gay Studies* 25, no. 2 (April): 223–55. https://doi.org/10.1215/10642684-7367717.

Briscoe, Amy. 2020. "A 'Mars' Walk on Anglesey: Exploring Parys Mountain's Rugged Landscape." *Independent*, September 14. https://www.independent.co.uk/travel/uk/anglesey-wales-walk-parys-mountain-mars-b421571.html.

Brontë, Charlotte. 1834. "Last Will and Testament of Florence Marian Wellesley, Marchioness of Douro, Duchess of Zamorna and Princess of the Blood of the Twelves." Morgan Library, New York. https://www.themorgan.org/literary-historical/81757.

Brontë, Charlotte. 1991. "Duro, Duchess of Zamorna, and Princess of the Blood of the Twelves." In *The Rise of Angria 1833–1834*, edited by Christine Alexander, 317-20. Vol. 2 of *The Early Writings of Charlotte Brontë*. Oxford: Basil Blackwell.

Brontë, Charlotte. 2006. *Jane Eyre*. New York: Penguin Classics.

Brontë, Charlotte. (1850) 2009. "Biographical Notice of Ellis and Acton Bell." In *Wuthering Heights*, edited by Ian Jack and Helen Small, 301–6. Oxford: Oxford's World's Classics.

Brontë, Charlotte. (1850) 2009. "Editor's Preface to the New Edition of Wuthering Heights." In *Wuthering Heights*, edited by Ian Jack and Helen Small, 307–10. Oxford: Oxford World's Classics.

Brontë, Emily. 1839. "I am the only being whose doom: Six Quatrains: Manuscript, 1837–1839." Poetic manuscript. Princeton University Special Collections, Princeton, NJ. https://catalog.princeton.edu/catalog/9934150443506421.

Brontë, Emily. 1986. *The Poems of Emily Brontë*. Edited by Derek Roper with Edward Chitham. Oxford: Oxford University Press.

Brontë, Emily. 1992. *The Complete Poems*. Edited by Janet Gezari. New York: Penguin.

Brontë, Emily. (1941) 1995. *The Complete Poems of Emily Jane Brontë*. Edited by C. W. Hatfield. New York: Columbia University Press.

Brontë, Emily. 1996. "The Butterfly." In Charlotte Brontë and Emily Brontë, *The Belgian Essays*, edited by Sue Lonoff, 176–79. New Haven, CT: Yale University Press.

Brontë, Emily. 2009. *Wuthering Heights*. Edited by Ian Jack and Helen Small. New York: Oxford World's Classics.

Brown, David Blayney. 2014. "'Born Again': Old and New in Turner's Later Work." In *Late Turner: Painting Set Free*, edited by David Blayney Brown, Amy Concannon, and Sam Smiles, 33–38. London: Tate.

Brown, Lydia. 2018. "Absent Emily: Ecstasy, Transgression, and Negative Space in Three Emily Brontë Poems." *Victorians: A Journal of Culture and Literature* 134 (Winter): 181–92.

Brown, Wendy. 1995. *States of Injury: Power and Freedom in Late Modernity*. Princeton, NJ: Princeton University Press.

Browne, Randy. 2017. *Surviving Slavery in the British Caribbean*. Philadelphia: University of Pennsylvania Press.

Buchsbaum, Ralph, and Mildred Buchsbaum. (1957) 1980. *General Ecology*. Pacific Grove, CA: Boxwood Press.

Buck-Morss, Susan. 1977. *The Origin of Negative Dialectics: Theodor Adorno, Walter Benjamin, and the Frankfurt Institute*. New York: Free Press.

Buckley, Jerome Hamilton. (1960) 1974. *Tennyson: The Growth of a Poet*. Cambridge, MA: Harvard University Press.

Bullard, Robert D. 1994. "Unequal Environmental Protection: Incorporating Environmental Justice in Decision Making." In *Worst Things First? The Debate over Risk-Based National Environmental Priorities*, edited by Adam M. Finkel and Dominic Golding, 237–66. Washington, DC: Resources for the Future. https://levszentkiralyi.com/wp-content/uploads/2017/05/bullard_unequal-environmental-protection-1994.pdf.

Burke, Kenneth. 1969. *A Grammar of Motives*. Berkeley: University of California Press.

Callinen, Luke. 2022. "The Struggle to Decolonize the Mind: Frantz Fanon and His Irish Translator." *CultureMatters*, January 15. https://www.culturematters.org.uk/index.php/culture/theory/item/3875-the-struggle-to-decolonise-the-mind-frantz-fanon-and-his-irish-translator.

Canguilhem, Georges. 1994. "The Death of Man, or Exhaustion of the Cogito?" In *The Cambridge Companion to Foucault*, edited by Gary Gutting, 71–91. Cambridge: Cambridge University Press.

Canguilhem, Georges. 2001. "The Living and Its Milieu." Translated by John Savage. *Grey Room* 3 (Spring): 7–16. http://www.jstor.org/stable/1262564.

Cappucci, Matthew. 2022. "Asteroid That Wiped Out Dinosaurs Triggered 'Megatsunami,' with Mile-High Waves." *Washington Post*, October 19. https://www.washingtonpost.com/climate-environment/2022/10/19/tsunami-dinosaur-meteor-extinction-waves/.

Cappucci, Matthew. 2022. "Five 1,000-Year Rain Events Have Struck the U.S. in Five Weeks. Why?" *Washington Post*, August 23. https://www.washingtonpost.com/climate-environment/2022/08/23/flood-united-states-climate-explainer/.

Carlisle, Clare. 2020. "George Eliot's Spinoza: An Introduction." In Baruch Spinoza, *Spinoza's Ethics*, edited by Clare Carlisle, translated by George Eliot, 1–60. Princeton, NJ: Princeton University Press.

Carroll, Lewis. 1899. *The Lewis Carroll Picture Book*. Edited by S. D. Collingwood. London: Collins' Clear-Type Press. https://ia600807.us.archive.org/15/items/lewiscarrollpictoocarr/lewiscarrollpictoocarr.pdf.

Carroll, Lewis. 1998. *Alice's Adventures in Wonderland and Through the Looking Glass*. Edited by Hugh Haughton. New York: Penguin Classics.

Carson, Anne. 1995. "The Glass Essay." In *Glass, Irony, and God*, 1–38. New York: New Directions.

Chatterjee, Ronjaunee. 2022. *Feminine Singularity: The Politics of Subjectivity in Nineteenth-Century Literature*. Stanford, CA: Stanford University Press.

Chuh, Kandice. 2019. *The Difference Aesthetics Makes: On the Humanities "After Man."* Durham, NC: Duke University Press.

Cohn, Elisha. 2022. "Materializing Feeling and the Limits of Metaphor." *Victorian Studies* 64, no. 4: 586–91. https://doi.org/10.2979/victorianstudies.64.4.07.

Cole, Sarah. 2019. *Inventing Tomorrow: H. G. Wells and the Twentieth Century*. New York: Columbia University Press.

Concannon, Amy. 2014. "Horizons: Sea and Sky." In *Late Turner: Painting Set Free*, edited by David Blayney Brown, Amy Concannon, and Sam Smiles, 192–213. London: Tate.

Cousins, A. D., and Peter Howarth. 2011. Introduction to *The Cambridge Companion to the Sonnet*, edited by A. D. Cousins and Peter Howarth, 1–5. New York: Cambridge University Press.

Crary, Jonathan. 2014. *24/7: Late Capitalism and the Ends of Sleep*. London: Verso.

Crary, Jonathan. 2022. *Scorched Earth: Beyond the Digital Age to a Post-Capitalist World*. London: Verso.

Crawford, Sharika D. 2020. *The Last Turtlemen of the Caribbean: Waterscapes of Labor, Conservation, and Boundarymaking*. Chapel Hill: University of North Carolina Press.

Culler, Jonathan. 1975. *Structuralist Poetics: Structuralism, Linguistics, and the Study of Literature*. London: Routledge.

Curran, Stuart. 1971. "The Lyric Voice of Christina Rossetti." *Victorian Poetry* 9, no. 3: 287–99.

Da, Nan Z. 2023. "On Twitter." Zoom lecture. Kulturwissenschaftliches Institut Essen. January 23. https://idw-online.de/en/event73314?ipc_year=&ipc_month=.

Daley, A. Stuart. 1974. "The Moons and Almanacs of Wuthering Heights." *Huntington Library Quarterly* 37 no. 4 (August): 337–53. https://www.jstor.org/stable/3816819.

D'Amico, Diane. 1999. *Christina Rossetti: Faith, Gender and Time*. Baton Rouge: Louisiana State University Press.

Daston, Lorraine. 1988. *Classical Probability in the Enlightenment*. Princeton, NJ: Princeton University Press.

Davies, Jeremy. 2016. *The Birth of the Anthropocene*. Berkeley: University of California Press.

Davies, Stevie. 1994. *Emily Brontë: Heretic*. London: Women's Press.

Davies, Stevie. 2019. "Emily Brontë: Heretic." StevieDavies.com. Last modified May 17. https://www.steviedavies.com/sd_nf_eb_heretic.html.

Davis, David Brion. 1975. *The Problem of Slavery in the Age of Revolution*. Ithaca, NY: Cornell University Press.

Davis, Mike. 2010. "Who Will Build the Ark?" *New Left Review* 61 (February): 29–46.

Deleuze, Gilles, and Felix Guattari. 2012. *Kafka: Toward a Minor Literature*. Translated by Dana Polan. Minneapolis: University of Minnesota Press.

Dellamora, Richard. 2007. "Earnshaw's Neighbor / Catherine's Friend: Ethical Contingencies in *Wuthering Heights*." *ELH* 74, no. 3 (Fall): 535–55. https://www.jstor.org/stable/30029571.

De Rozario, Stuart. 2017. "Punctuation Series: The Asterisk." *Fontsmith* (blog), March 29. https://web.archive.org/web/20210724072841/https://www.fontsmith.com/blog/2017/03/29/punctuation-series-the-asterisk.

Derrida, Jacques. 1982. "Signature Event Context." In *The Margins of Philosophy*, translated by Alan Bass, 307–30. Chicago: University of Chicago Press.

Derrida, Jacques. 1986. "Foreword: *Fors*: The Anglish Words of Nicolas Abraham and Maria Torok." In *The Wolf Man's Magic Word: A Cryptonomy*, translated by Nicholas Rand. Minneapolis: University of Minnesota Press.

Derrida, Jacques. 1998. *Monolingualism of the Other; Or the Prothesis of Origin*. Translated by Patrick Mensah. Stanford, CA: Stanford University Press.

Derrida, Jacques. (1967) 2011. *Voice and Phenomenon: Introduction to the Problem of the Sign in Husserl's Phenomenology*. Translated by Leonard Lawlor. Evanston, IL: Northwestern University Press.

DeWispelare, Daniel. 2017. *Multilingual Subjects: On Standard English, Its Speakers, and Others in the Long Eighteenth Century*. Philadelphia: University of Pennsylvania Press.

Dex, Robert. 2021. "Brontë Sisters' Manuscripts Saved for Nation Thanks to £7.5m from UK's Richest Man Leonard Blavatnik." *Standard*, December 16. https://www.standard.co.uk/news/uk/Brontë-sisters-manuscripts-saved-leonard-blavatnik-b972375.html.

Dodgson, Henry (Lewis Carroll). 1885. "Euclid and His Modern Rivals." London: Macmillan. Internet Archive, June 8, 2009. https://archive.org/details/euclidhismodernroocarr/page/n11/mode/2up.

Dransfield, Scott. 2008. "The Morbid Meters of Maud." *Victorian Poetry* 46, no. 3: 279–97.

Draper, Nicholas. 2013. *The Price of Emancipation: Slave Ownership, Compensation, and British Society at the End of Slavery*. New York: Cambridge University Press.

Dresser, Madge, and Andrew Hann, eds. 2013. *Slavery and the British Country House*. Swindon, UK: English Heritage.

Dresser, Madge, and Mary Wills. 2020. *The Translatlantic Slave Economy and England's Built Environment: A Research Audit*. Eastney, Portsmouth: Historic England. https://historicengland.org.uk/research/results/reports/8203/TheTransatlanticSlaveEconomyandEngland%E2%80%99sBuiltEnvironment_AResearchAudit.

Drew, Philip. 1973. "Tennyson and the Dramatic Monologue: A Study of 'Maud.'" In *Tennyson: A Reader's Guide*, edited by D. J. Palmer, 114–46. Columbus: Ohio University Press.

Duncan, Ian. 2019. *Human Forms: The Novel in the Age of Evolution*. Princeton, NJ: Princeton University Press.

Dunn, Richard S. (1972) 2000. *Sugar and Slaves: The Rise of the Planter Class in the English West Indies, 1624–1713*. Chapel Hill: University of North Carolina Press.

Eagleton, Terry. 1996. *Heathcliff and the Great Hunger: Studies in Irish Culture*. London: Verso.

Eagleton, Terry. 2005. *Myths of Power: A Marxist Study of the Brontes*. New York: Palgrave Macmillan.

Eckert, Sierra. 2019. "The Way We Quote Now: Reading *Middlemarch*, 1960–2015." Presented at the NAVSA Conference, Columbus, OH, October 17.

Eckert, Sierra, and Milan Terlunen. 2025. "What We Quote: Disciplinary History and the Textual Atmospheres of *Middlemarch*." *Victorian Studies* 66 no. 4, forthcoming.

Edelman, Lee. 2004. *No Future: Queer Theory and the Death Drive*. Durham, NC: Duke University Press.

Edwards, Paul. 1996. *The Closed World: Computers and the Politics of Discourse in Cold War America*. Cambridge, MA: MIT Press.

Elder, Melinda. 2007. "The Liverpool Slave Trade, Lancaster and Its Environs." In *Liverpool and Transatlantic Slavery*, edited by David Richardson, Suzanne Schwarz, and Anthony Tibbles, 118–37. Liverpool: Liverpool University Press.

Eliot, George. 1954. *The George Eliot Letters: 1862–1868*. Vol. 4 of *The George Eliot Letters*. Edited by Gordon S. Haight. New Haven, CT: Yale University Press, 1954–1978.

Eliot, George. 1963. "Address to Working Men, by Felix Holt." In *Essays of George Eliot*, edited by Thomas Pinney, 415–30. New York: Columbia University Press.

Eliot, George. (1856) 1963. "The Natural History of German Life." In *Essays of George Eliot*, edited by Thomas Pinney, 266–99. New York: Columbia University Press.

Eliot, George. 1963. "Notes on Form in Art." In *Essays of George Eliot*, edited by Thomas Pinney, 431–36. New York: Columbia University Press.

Eliot, George. 1963. "Silly Novels by Lady Novelists." In *Essays of George Eliot*, edited by Thomas Pinney, 300–24. New York: Columbia University Press.

Eliot, George. 1979. *George Eliot's Middlemarch Notebooks: A Transcription*. Edited by John Clark Pratt and Victor A. Neufeldt. Berkeley: University of California Press.

Eliot, George. 1995. *Felix Holt, The Radical*. London: Penguin.

Eliot, George. 2000. *The Journals of George Eliot*. Edited by Margaret Harris and Judith Johnson. New York: Cambridge University Press.

Eliot, George. 2008. *Middlemarch*. Edited by David Carroll. New York: Oxford World's Classics.

Eliot, George. 2020. *Spinoza's Ethics*. Edited by Clare Carlisle. Translated by George Eliot. Princeton, NJ: Princeton University Press.

Eliot, T. S. 1919. "Tradition and the Individual Talent." *Egoist* 6, nos. 4–5 (September and December): 54–55, 72–73. https://www.sas.upenn.edu/~cavitch/pdf-library/Eliot_Tradition_1919.pdf.

Escalante-De Mattei, Shanit. 2022. "Just Stop Oil Protestors Found Guilty of Property Destruction in England." *ARTnews*, November 23. https://www.artnews.com/art-news/news/just-stop-oil-protestors-found-guilty-property-destruction-england-1234647715/.

"Escaping into the Wild: A History of Canada's Fur Trade." 2014. *Animal Justice* (blog), June 24. https://animaljustice.ca/blog/escaping-wild-history-canadas-fur-trade.

Esposito, Roberto. 2012. "The *Dispositif* of the Person." *Law, Culture, and the Humanities* 8, no. 1. https://doi.org/10.1177/1743872111403104.

Esposito, Roberto. 2012. *Third Person: Politics of Life and the Philosophy of the Impersonal*. Translated by Zakiya Hanifi. Cambridge, UK: Polity Press.

Esposito, Roberto. 2015. *Persons and Things: From the Body's Point of View*. Translated by Zakiya Hanafi. Cambridge, UK: Polity Press.

Eve, Kimberley. 2014. "Mr. Turner Movie Reviewed!" *Victorian Musings*, December 30. https://kimberlyevemusings.blogspot.com/2014/12/mr-turner-movie-reviewed.html.

"Exxon Is Sued by New York over Use of Hudson Water." 1984. *New York Times*, April 26, 1984. https://www.nytimes.com/1984/04/26/nyregion/exxon-is-sued-by-new-york-over-use-of-hudson-water.html.

Fanon, Frantz. 1961. *Les Damnés de la Terre*. Paris: François Maspero.

Fanon, Frantz. (1961) 1963. *The Wretched of the Earth*. Translated by Constance Farrington. New York: Grove.

Fanon, Frantz. (1952) 2008. *Black Skin, White Masks*. Translated by Richard Philcox. New York: Grove.

Ferguson, Frances. 2004. *Pornography, the Theory: What Utilitarianism Did to Action*. Chicago: University of Chicago Press.

Feuerstein, Jacob. 2022. "How Two 1-in-1,000-Year Rain Events Hit the U.S. in Two Days." *Washington Post*, July 29. https://www.washingtonpost.com/climate-environment/2022/07/29/kentucky-stlouis-flood-climate-explainer/.

Finberg, A. J. 1961. *The Life of J. M. W. Turner*. Oxford: Oxford University Press.

Finlay, Victoria. 2003. *Color: A Natural History of the Palette*. New York: Ballantine Books.

Fleissner, Jennifer. 2022. *Maladies of the Will: The American Novel and the Modernity Problem*. Chicago: University of Chicago Press.

Flood, Alison. 2021. "Lost Library of Literary Treasures Saved for UK after Charity Raises £15m." *Guardian*, December 16. https://www.theguardian.com/books/2021/dec/16/lost-library-of-literary-treasures-saved-for-uk-after-charity-raises-15m.

Fodor, J. A. 2001. "Language, Thought, and Compositionality." *Mind and Language* 16, no.1: 1–15.

Forrester, Gillian. 2007. "Joseph Mallord William Turner, 1775–1851, British, Leeds, 1816." Catalog entry. In John Baskett, Jules David Prown, Duncan Robinson, William S. Reese, and Brian Allen, *Paul Mellon's Legacy: A Passion for British Art*, 283–84. New Haven, CT: Yale Center for British Art. https://collections.britishart.yale.edu/catalog/tms:5508.

Foucault, Michel. 1972. *The Archaeology of Knowledge and The Discourse on Language*. Translated by A. M. Sheridan Smith. New York: Pantheon.

Foucault, Michel. (1976) 1990. *The History of Sexuality*. Vol. 1: *An Introduction*. New York: Vintage.

Foucault, Michel. 1994. *The Order of Things: An Archaeology of the Human Sciences*. New York: Vintage.

Foucault, Michel. 1995. *Discipline and Punish: The Birth of the Prison*. New York: Vintage.

Foxcroft, George. 1745. "Continuation of Will of Geo. Foxcroft Dated 20 Jan 1745." Lancaster University Special Collections, SLA/8/1. Lancaster, UK.

Foxcroft, George. 1795. "Will of George Foxcroft dated Singore 16 July 1795." Lancaster University Special Collections, SLA/8/3, Foxcroft MSS Hinton. Lancaster, UK.

François, Anne-Lise. 2008. *Open Secrets: The Literature of Uncounted Experience*. Stanford, CA: Stanford University Press.

Frank, Katherine. 1992. *A Chainless Soul: A Life of Emily Brontë*. New York: Ballantine Books.

Franta, Benjamin. 2022. "Weaponizing Economics: Big Oil, Economic Consultants, and Climate Policy Delay." *Environmental Politics* 31, no. 4 (August): 555–75. https://doi.org/10.1080/09644016.2021.1947636.

Fraser, Nancy, and Rahel Jaeggi. 2018. *Capitalism: A Conversation*. Cambridge, UK: Polity Press.

Frederickson, Kathleen. 2014. *The Ploy of Instinct: Victorian Sciences of Nature and Sexuality in Liberal Governance*. New York: Fordham University Press.

Freedgood, Elaine. 2006. *The Ideas in Things: Fugitive Meaning in the Victorian Novel*. Chicago: University of Chicago Press.

French, Adria. 2021. "Report Finds Extreme Heatwaves Would Have Been 'Virtually Impossible' without Global Warming." *World Socialist Web Site*, July 10. https://www.wsws.org/en/articles/2021/07/10/heat-j10.html.

Frow, John. 2006. *Genre*. London: Routledge.

Fruit, Zach. 2018. "Enclosure." *Victorian Literature and Culture* 46, no. 3–4 (August): 672–75. https://doi.org/10.1017/S1060150318000530.

Fussell, Paul. 1979. *Poetic Meter and Poetic Form, Revised Edition*. New York: McGraw Hill.

Gage, John. 1969. *Color in Turner*. New York: Praeger.

Galison, Peter. 1994. "The Ontology of the Enemy: Norbert Wiener and the Cybernetic Vision." *Critical Inquiry* 21, no. 1: 228–66. http://www.jstor.org/stable/1343893.

Gallagher, Catherine. 2005. "George Eliot: Immanent Victorian." *Representations* 90, no. 1 (Spring): 61–74. https://www.jstor.org/stable/10.1525/rep.2005.90.1.61.

Galloway, Alexander. 2004. *Protocol: How Control Exists after Decentralization*. Cambridge, MA: MIT Press.

Gammage, Jennifer. 2021. "Solidarity, Not Charity: Mutual Aid's An-Archic History." *Blog of the APA* (blog), January 25. https://blog.apaonline.org/2021/01/25/solidarity-not-charity-mutual-aids-an-archic-history/.

Gasché, Rodolphe. 1991. "Foreword: Ideality in Fragmentation." In Friedrich Schlegel, *Philosophical Fragments*, translated by Peter Firchow, vii–xxxii. Minneapolis: University of Minnesota Press.

Gaskell, Elizabeth. (1857) 2009. *Life of Charlotte Brontë*. Edited by Angus Easson. Oxford: Oxford University Press.

Gawthrop, Humphrey. 2013. "Slavery: *Idée Fixe* of the Brontës." *Brontë Studies: The Journal of the Brontë Society* 28, no. 4 (December): 281–89. https://doi.org/10.1179/1474893213Z.00000000082.

Gayle, Damien. 2022. “Just Stop Oil Activists Glue Themselves to Turner Painting in Manchester.” *Guardian*, July 1. https://www.theguardian.com/environment/2022/jul/01/just-stop-oil-activists-glue-themselves-to-turner-painting-in-manchester.

Geduld, Harry M., ed. 1987. *The Definitive Time Machine: A Critical Edition of H. G. Wells' Scientific Romance, with Introduction and Notes by Harry M. Geduld*. Bloomington: Indiana University Press.

Geoghegan, Bernard Dionysius. 2011. “From Information Theory to French Theory: Jakobson, Lévi Strauss, and the Cybernetic Apparatus.” *Critical Inquiry* 38 (Autumn): 96–126. https://doi.org/10.1086/661645.

“Geography and History of Jamaica, Published by *The Gleaner*.” *Discover Jamaica*. Accessed April 18, 2024. http://www.discoverjamaica.com/gleaner/discover/geography/mining.htm.

Gerard, Ralph W. 2016. “Some of the Problems Concerning Digital Notions in the Central Nervous System.” In *Cybernetics: The Macy Conferences 1946–1953. The Complete Transactions*, edited by Claus Pias, 171–202. Zurich: Diaphanes.

Gettens, R. John, and George L. Stout. (1942) 1966. *Painting Materials: A Short Encyclopedia*. New York: Dover.

Gezari, Janet. 2007. *Last Things: Emily Brontë's Poems*. New York: Oxford University Press.

Gezari, Janet, ed. 2014. *The Annotated Wuthering Heights*. Cambridge, MA: Harvard University Press.

Gezari, Janet. 2014. “Introduction.” In Emily Brontë, *The Annotated Wuthering Heights*, 1–32. Cambridge, MA: Harvard University Press.

Ghaly, Adrienne. 2022. “What Does Biodiversity Loss Feel Like? Realism in the Age of Extinction.” *New Literary History* 53, no. 1: 33–57. https://doi.org/10.1353/nlh.2022.0001.

Ghosh, Amitav. 2015. *The Great Derangement: Climate Change and the Unthinkable*. Chicago: University of Chicago Press.

Ghosh, Amitav. 2021. *The Nutmeg's Curse: Parables for a Planet in Crisis*. Chicago: University of Chicago Press.

Gilbert, Sandra M., and Susan Gubar. (1979) 2020. *The Madwoman in the Attic*. New Haven, CT: Yale University Press.

Glissant, Édouard. 1990. *Poetics of Relation*. Translated by Betsy Wing. Ann Arbor: University of Michigan Press.

Gowing, Lawrence. 1966. *Turner: Imagination and Reality*. Garden City, NY: Doubleday.

Gracy, David B. 1995. “Littlefield, George Washington (1842–1920).” Texas State Historical Association. https://www.tshaonline.org/handbook/entries/littlefield-george-washington.

Gramsci, Antonio. (1971) 2012. *Selections from the Prison Notebooks*. Edited and translated by Quintin Hoare and Geoffrey Nowell Smith. New York: International.

Graver, Suzanne. 1984. *George Eliot and Community: A Study in Social Theory and Fictional Form*. Berkeley: University of California Press.

Greiner, Rae. 2012. *Sympathetic Realism in Nineteenth-Century British Fiction*. Baltimore: Johns Hopkins University Press.

Grosz, Elizabeth. 2004. *The Nick of Time: Politics, Evolution, and the Untimely*. Durham, NC: Duke University Press.

Guha, Ranajit. 1997. *Dominance without Hegemony: History and Power in Colonial India*. Cambridge, MA: Harvard University Press.

Gutting, Gary. 1994. "Introduction: Michel Foucault: A User's Manual." In *The Cambridge Companion to Michel Foucault*, edited by Gary Gutting, 1–27. New York: Cambridge University Press.

Hacking, Ian. 1990. *The Taming of Chance*. Cambridge: Cambridge University Press.

Hacking, Ian. 2004. *Historical Ontology*. Cambridge, MA: Harvard University Press.

Haight, Gordon. (1968) 1992. *George Eliot: A Biography*. London: Penguin.

Hakewill, James. 1825. *Picturesque Tour of the Island of Jamaica, from Drawings Made in the Years 1820 and 1821*. London: Hurst and Robinson. Internet Archive, December 23, 2009. https://archive.org/details/picturesquetourooohake.

Hall, Amelia. 2020. "Epic-Graphic Proportions in George Eliot's *Middlemarch*." *Studies in English Literature 1500–1900* 60, no. 4 (Fall): 805–24. https://doi.org/10.1353/sel.2020.0033.

Hall, Catherine. 2023. "Return to Jamaica: Diary." *London Review of Books* 45, no. 14 (July 13). https://www.lrb.co.uk/the-paper/v45/n14/catherine-hall/diary.

Hall, Catherine. 2024. *Lucky Valley: Edward Long and the History of Racial Capitalism*. Cambridge: Cambridge University Press.

Hall, Catherine, Nicholas Draper, and Keith McClelland. 2014. Introduction to *Legacies of British Slave-Ownership: Colonial Slavery and the Formation of Victorian Britain*, by Catherine Hall, Nicholas Draper, Keith McClelland, Katie Donington, and Rachel Lang, 1–33. New York: Cambridge University Press.

Hallmann, Caspar A., Martin Sorg, Eelke Jongejans, Henk Siepel, Nick Hofland, Heinz Schwan, Werner Stenmans, Andreas Müller, Hubert Sumser, Thomas Hörren, Dave Goulson, and Hans de Kroon. 2017. "More than 75 Percent Decline over 27 Years in Total Flying Insect Biomass in Protected Areas." *PLoS One* 12, no. 10 (October). https://doi.org/10.1371/journal.pone.0185809.

Halsey, Katie. 2006. "The Blush of Modesty or the Blush of Shame: Reading Jane Austen's Blushes." *Forum for Modern Language Studies* 42, no. 3 (July): 226–38. https://doi.org/10.1093/fmls/cql015.

Handler, Jerome S. 1978. *Plantation Slavery in Barbados: An Archaeological and Historical Investigation*. Cambridge, MA: Harvard University Press.

Haraway, Donna. 2016. *Staying with the Trouble: Making Kin in the Chthulucene*. Durham, NC: Duke University Press.

Harrington, Emily. 2014. *Second Person Singular: Late Victorian Women Poets and the Bonds of Verse*. Charlottesville: University of Virginia Press.

Harrison, Antony. 1988. *Christina Rossetti in Context*. Chapel Hill: University of North Carolina Press.

Harskamp, Jaap. 2020. "When Eating Turtle Was All the Rage." *New York Almanack*, June 14. https://www.newyorkalmanack.com/2020/06/when-eating-turtle-was-all-the-rage/.

Hartman, Saidiya V. 1997. *Scenes of Subjection: Terror, Slavery, and Self-Making in Nineteenth-Century America*. New York: Oxford University Press.

Hartman, Saidiya V. 2019. *Wayward Lives, Beautiful Experiments: Intimate Histories of Social Upheaval*. New York: Norton.

Harvey, Fiona. 2021. "World's Climate Scientists to Issue Stark Warning over Global Heating Threat." *Guardian*, August 8. https://www.theguardian.com/environment/2021/aug/08/worlds-climate-scientists-to-issue-stark-warning-over-global-heating-threat.

Hassett, Constance. 1986. "Christina Rossetti and the Poetry of Reticence." *Philological Quarterly* 65, no. 4: 495–514.

Hassett, Constance. 2005. *Christina Rossetti and the Patience of Style*. Charlottesville: University of Virginia Press.

Heady, Chene. 2011. "'Earth Has Clear Call of Daily Bells': Nature's Apocalyptic Liturgy in Christina Rossetti's Verses." *Religion and the Arts* 15: 148–71.

Heims, Steve Joshua. 1991. *The Cybernetics Group*. Cambridge, MA: MIT Press.

Heise, Ursula K. 2019. "Science Fiction and the Time Scales of the Anthropocene." *ELH* 86, no. 2 (Summer): 275–304. https://doi.org/10.1353/elh.2019.0015.

Helsinger, Elizabeth K. 2015. *Poetry and the Thought of Song in Nineteenth-Century Britain*. Charlottesville: University of Virginia Press.

Hensley, Nathan K. 2015. "Network: Andrew Lang and the Distributed Agencies of Literary Production." *Victorian Periodicals Review* 48, no. 3 (Fall): 359–82. http://www.jstor.org/stable/43663388.

Herrnstein-Smith, Barbara. 1968. *Poetic Closure: A Study of How Poems End*. Chicago: University of Chicago Press.

Herschel, John. 1850. "On Quetelet and Probability." *Edinburgh Review* 92 (July): 1–57.

Heywood, Christopher. 1987. "Yorkshire Slavery in Wuthering Heights." *Review of English Studies* 38, no. 150 (May): 184–98. http://www.jstor.org/stable/515422.

Heywood, Christopher. 1993. "A Yorkshire Background for 'Wuthering Heights.'" *Modern Language Review* 88, no. 4 (October): 817–30. https://doi.org/10.2307/3734416.

Heywood, Christopher. 1998. "Yorkshire Landscapes in *Wuthering Heights*." *Essays in Criticism* 48, no. 1 (January), 13–34.

Heywood, Christopher. 2002. "Introduction." In *Wuthering Heights*, edited by Christopher Heywood, 18–90. Peterborough, ON: Broadview.

Heywood, Christopher. 2013. "Pennine Landscapes in *Jane Eyre* and *Wuthering Heights*." *Brontë Society Transactions* 26, no. 2 (July): 187–98. https://doi.org/10.1179/030977601794164295.

Hickel, Jared. 2020. *Less Is More: How Degrowth Will Save the World*. New York: Random House.

Hickman, Caroline, Elizabeth Marks, Panu Pihkala, Susan Clayton, R. Eric Lewandowski, Elouise E. Mayall, Britt Wray, Catriona Mellor, and Lise van Susteren. 2021. "Climate Anxiety in Children and Young People and Their Beliefs about Government Responses to Climate Change: A Survey." *Lancet Planet Health* no. 5: e863–73. https://www.thelancet.com/action/showPdf?pii=S2542-5196%2821%2900278-3.

Hiday, Corbin. 2021. "Heathcliff Walks." *Novel: A Forum on Fiction* 54, no. 2 (August): 248–69. https://doi.org/10.1215/00295132-9004513.

Higman, B. W. 2001. *Jamaica Surveyed: Plantation Maps and Plans of the Eighteenth and Nineteenth Centuries*. Kingston: University of the West Indies Press.

Hildebrand, Jayne. 2023. *Novel Environments: Science, Description, and Victorian Fiction*. Oxford: Oxford University Press.

"Honresfield Library Saved for the Nation!" 2016. Annebronte.org. https://www.annebronte.org/2021/12/16/honresfield-library-saved-for-the-nation/.

Hopkins, Gerard Manley. 2002. *The Major Works*. Edited by Catherine Phillips. New York: Oxford University Press.

Howles, Timothy. 2022. "'Gas Guzzling Gaia': Some New Camera Angles on a Pivotal Scene." *Critical Inquiry* 49, no. 1 (Autumn): 117–25.

Hu, Esther T. 2008. "Christina Rossetti, John Keble, and the Divine Gaze." *Victorian Poetry* 46, no. 2: 175–89.

Humphries, Simon. 2008. "Christina Rossetti's 'My Dream' and Apocalypse." *Notes and Queries* 55, no. 1: 54–57.

Husserl, Edmund. 1970. *The Crisis of European Sciences and Transcendental Phenomenology: An Introduction to Phenomenological Philosophy*. Translated by David Carr. Evanston, IL: Northwestern University Press.

Husserl, Edmund. 1973. *Cartesian Meditations*. Translated by Dorian Cairns. The Hague: Martinus Nijhoff.

Ingraham, Christopher. 2017. "Houston Is Experiencing Its Third '500-Year' Flood in 3 Years. How Is That Possible?" *Washington Post*, August 29. https://www.washingtonpost.com/news/wonk/wp/2017/08/29/houston-is-experiencing-its-third-500-year-flood-in-3-years-how-is-that-possible/.

Innis, Harold. 1970. *The Fur Trade in Canada: An Introduction to Canadian Economic History*. Toronto: University of Toronto Press.

Jackson, Virginia. 2005. *Dickinson's Misery: A Theory of Lyric Reading*. Princeton, NJ: Princeton University Press.

Jaffe, Audrey. 2000. *Scenes of Sympathy: Identity and Representation in Victorian Fiction*. Ithaca, NY: Cornell University Press.

James, Simon. 2012. *Maps of Utopia: H.G. Wells, Modernity, and the End of Culture*. Oxford: Oxford University Press.

Jameson, Fredric. 1982. "Progress vs. Utopia, or Can We Imagine the Future?" *Science Fiction Studies* 9, no. 2: 147–58.

Jameson, Fredric. 2019. *Allegory and Ideology*. London: Verso.

Jameson, Fredric. 2022. "Criticism and Categories." *PMLA/Publications of the Modern Language Association of America* 137, no. 3 (May): 563–67. https://doi.org/10.1632/S003081292200044X.

Jay, Martin. 2022. *Genesis and Validity: The Theory and Practice of Intellectual History*. Philadelphia: University of Pennsylvania Press.

Jessop, Bob. 2006. "Spatial Fixes, Temporal Fixes, and Spatio-Temporal Fixes." In *David Harvey: A Critical Reader*, edited by Noel Castree and Derek Gregory, 142–66. Oxford: Blackwell.

Jevons, William Stanley. [1906]. *The Coal Question*. Edited by Alfred William Flux. London: Macmillan. https://www.google.com/books/edition/The_Coal_Question/TFcpAAAAYAAJ.

Johnson, Barbara. 2014. "Euphemism, Understatement, and the Passive Voice: A Genealogy of African-American Poetry." In *The Barbara Johnson Reader: The Surprise of Otherness*, edited by Melissa Feuerstein, Bill Johnson Gonzalez, Lili Porten, and Keja Valens, 101–7. Durham, NC: Duke University Press.

Johnson, Scott. 2017. "Hurricane Harvey Studies: Yesterday's 100-Year Storm Is Today's 30-Year Storm." *Ars Technica*, December 17. https://arstechnica.com/science/2017/12/more-studies-examine-role-of-climate-change-in-hurricane-harvey/.

Johnson, Weldon. 2017. "Is Harvey a 500-Year Storm or a 1,000-Year Storm? What Does That Even Mean?" *Arizona Republic*, August 29. https://www.azcentral.com/story/weather/2017/08/29/harvey-500-year-storm-1000-year-storm-definition/613832001/.

Kant, Immanuel. 1998. "What Does It Mean to Orient Oneself in Thinking?" In *Religion within the Boundaries of Mere Reason and Other Writings*, translated and edited by Allen Wood and George Di Giovanni, 1–14. Cambridge: Cambridge University Press.

Kaufman, Mark. n.d. "The Carbon Footprint Sham." *Mashable*. Accessed April 1, 2024. https://mashable.com/feature/carbon-footprint-pr-campaign-sham.

Kidd, Colin. 2024. "Antidote to Marx." *London Review of Books* 46, no. 1 (January): 13–14.

Kingsland, Sharon E. 2005. *The Evolution of American Ecology, 1890–2000*. Baltimore: Johns Hopkins University Press.

Kornbluh, Anna. 2019. *The Order of Forms: Realism, Formalism, and Social Space*. Chicago: University of Chicago Press.

Kornbluh, Anna. 2021. "In Defense of Feminist Abstraction." *Diacritics* 49, no. 2 (2021): 53–59. https://doi.org/10.1353/dia.2021.0021.

Landgrebe, Ludwig. 1973. "The Phenomenological Concept of Experience." *Philosophy and Phenomenological Research* 34, no. 1 (September): 1–13.

Latour, Bruno. 2014. "Agency at the Time of the Anthropocene." *New Literary History* 45, no. 1: 1–18. https://doi.org/10.1353/nlh.2014.0003.

Latour, Bruno. 2017. *Facing Gaia: Eight Lectures on the New Climatic Regime*. Cambridge, UK: Polity Press.

Lázló, Ervin. 1972. *Introduction to Systems Philosophy: Toward a New Paradigm of Contemporary Thought*. New York: Harper Torchbooks.

Leckie, Barbara. 2022. *Climate Change, Interrupted: Representation and the Making of Time*. Stanford, CA: Stanford University Press.

Lee, Stephanie M. 2023. "Big Oil Helped Shape Stanford's Latest Climate-Research Focus." *Chronicle of Higher Education*, May 4.

Leifchild, J. R. 1857. *Cornwall: Its Mines and Miners, with Sketches of Scenery*. London: Longman, Brown, Green, Longmans, and Roberts.

Leigh, Mike, dir. 2014. *Mr. Turner*. Film 4, Focus Features: New York.

Lesjak, Carolyn. 2021. *The Afterlife of Enclosure: British Realism, Character, and the Commons*. Stanford, CA: Stanford University Press.

Lévi-Strauss, Claude. (1962) 1968. *The Savage Mind*. Translated by George Weidenfeld and Nicolson Ltd. Chicago: University of Chicago Press.

Levinas, Emmanuel. 1969. *Totality and Infinity: An Essay on Exteriority*. Translated by Alphonso Lingis. Pittsburgh, PA: Duquesne University Press.

Levine, Caroline. 2015. *Forms: Whole, Rhythm, Hierarchy*. Princeton, NJ: Princeton University Press.

Levine, Caroline. 2023. *The Activist Humanist: Form and Method in the Climate Crisis*. Princeton, NJ: Princeton University Press.

Levine, George. 1962. "Determinism and Responsibility in the Work of George Eliot." *PMLA* 77, no. 3 (June): 268–79. https://www.jstor.org/stable/460486.

Levinson, Marjorie. 2011. *The Romantic Fragment Poem: A Critique of a Form.* Chapel Hill: University of North Carolina Press.

Lewis, C. Day. 2013. "The Poetry of Emily Brontë." *Brontë Society Transactions* 13, no. 2 (November): 83–99. https://doi.org/10.1179/030977657796548944.

Ligon, Richard. 1657. "A Topographicall Description and Admeasurement of the Yland of Barbados in the West Indyaes, with the Names of the Severall Plantaceons." Wikimedia Commons. https://commons.wikimedia.org/wiki/File:The_earliest_printed_map_of_Barbados_by_Richard_Ligon,_1657,_KITLV_1407468.tiff.

Locke, John. 1988. *Two Treatises of Government.* Edited by Peter Laslett. New York: Cambridge University Press.

Longmore, Jane. 2013. "Rural Retreats: Liverpool Slave Traders and Their Country Houses." In *Slavery and the British Country House,* edited by Madge Dresser and Andrew Hann, 43–53. Swindon, UK: English Heritage.

Love, Heather A., and Lea Pao. 2023. "Introduction, Literary Cybernetics: History, Theory, Post-Disciplinarity." *New Literary History* 54, no. 2 (Spring): 1193–205. https://doi.org/10.1353/nlh.2023.a907164.

Lovett, Charlie. 2005. *Lewis Carroll among His Books: A Descriptive Catalogue of the Private Library of Charles L. Dodgson.* Jefferson, NC: McFarland and Company.

Lukács, Georg. (1968) 1972. "The Antinomies of Bourgeois Thought." In *History and Class Consciousness: Studies in Marxist Dialectics,* translated by Rodney Livingstone, 110–48. Cambridge, MA: MIT Press.

Lutz, Deborah. 2016. *The Brontë Cabinet: Three Lives in Nine Objects.* New York: Norton.

Lutz, Deborah. 2016. "Emily Brontë's Paper Work." *Victorian Review* 42, no. 2 (Fall): 291–305. https://doi.org/10.1353/vcr.2016.0065.

MacDuffie, Allen. 2018. "Charles Darwin and the Victorian Pre-History of Climate Denial." *Victorian Studies* 60, no. 4: 543–64.

MacDuffie, Allen. 2024. *Climate of Denial: Darwin, Climate Change, and the Literature of the Long Nineteenth Century.* Stanford, CA: Stanford University Press.

Macey, David. 2000. *Frantz Fanon: A Biography.* New York: Picador.

Main, Alexander. 1893. *Wise, Witty, and Tender Sayings in Prose and Verse Selected from the Works of George Eliot.* London: William Blackwood and Sons.

Malm, Andreas. 2020. *The Progress of This Storm: Nature and Society in a Warming World.* London: Verso.

Malm, Andreas. 2021. *How to Blow Up a Pipeline: Learning to Fight in a World on Fire.* London: Verso.

Mangla, Ravi. 2015. "True Blue: A Brief History of Ultramarine." *Paris Review,* June 8. https://www.theparisreview.org/blog/2015/06/08/true-blue/.

Manning, Erin. 2016. *The Minor Gesture.* Durham, NC: Duke University Press.

Markovits, Stefanie. 2009. "Giving Voice to the Crimean War: Tennyson's 'Charge' and Maud's Battle-Song." *Victorian Poetry* 47, no. 3: 481–503.

Marsh, Jan. 1994. *Christina Rossetti: A Writer's Life.* New York: Viking.

Martin, Meredith. 2012. *The Rise and Fall of Meter: Poetry and English National Culture 1860–1930.* Princeton, NJ: Princeton University Press.

Martin, Robert Bernard. 1980. *Tennyson: The Unquiet Heart*. New York: Oxford University Press.

Marx, Karl. 1991. *Capital: A Critique of Political Economy*. Vol. 3. Translated by David Fernhach. New York: Penguin Classics.

Marx, Karl, and Friedrich Engels. (1848) 2000. "Manifesto of the Communist Party." Marx/Engels Internet Archive. https://www.marxists.org/archive/marx/works/1848/communist-manifesto/index.htm.

Mason, Emma. 2002. "Emily Brontë and the Enthusiastic Tradition." *Romanticism on the Net* 25 (February). https://id.erudit.org/iderudit/006008ar.

Mason, Emma. 2018. *Christina Rossetti: Poetry, Ecology, Faith*. New York: Oxford University Press.

Maynard, John. 2018. "Emily Brontë and Will." *Victorians: A Journal of Culture and Literature* 134 (Winter):193–203. https://doi.org/10.1353/vct.2018.0018.

McGann, Jerome. 1985. *The Beauty of Inflections: Literary Investigations into Historical Method and Theory*. Oxford: Oxford University Press.

McKibben, Bill. 2019. *Falter: Has the Human Game Begun to Play Itself Out?* New York: Henry Holt and Co.

McKittrick, Katherine. 2013. "Plantation Futures." *Small Axe* 17, no. 3 (November): 1–15. https://muse.jhu.edu/article/532740.

McNeill, John. 2010. *Mosquito Empires: Ecology and War in the Greater Caribbean, 1620–1914*. Cambridge: Cambridge University Press.

McWeeny, Gage. 2016. *The Comfort of Strangers: Social Life and Literary Form*. New York: Oxford University Press.

Mendoza, Victor Roman. 2006. "'Come Buy': The Crossing of Sexual and Consumer Desire in Christina Rossetti's 'Goblin Market.'" *ELH* 73, no. 4 (Winter): 913–47. https://www.jstor.org/stable/30030043.

Menke, Richard. 1999. "The Political Economy of Fruit: Goblin Market." In *The Culture of Christina Rossetti: Female Poetics and Victorian Contexts*, edited by Mary Arseneau, Antony H. Harrison, and Lorraine Janzen Kooistra, 105–36. Columbus: Ohio University Press.

Mentz, Steve. 2015. *Shipwreck Modernity: Ecologies of Globalization, 1550–1719*. Minneapolis: University of Minnesota Press.

Merleau-Ponty, Maurice. (1945) 2014. *Phenomenology of Perception*. Translated by Donald A. Landes. London: Routledge.

Mermin, Dorothy. 1986. "Foreword." In Dolores Rosenblum, *Christina Rossetti: The Poetry of Endurance*, ix–xiv. Carbondale: Southern Illinois Press.

Mershon, Ella. 2023. "Tennysonian Retrogressions: Maud's Reworking of *In Memoriam*'s Geologic Imaginary." Presented at the NAVSA Conference, Bloomington, IN, November 11.

Mezzadra, Sandro, and Brett Neilson. 2015. "Operations of Capital." *South Atlantic Quarterly* 114, no. 1: 1–9.

Mill, John Stuart. (1848, 1870) 1909. *Principles of Political Economy, with Some of Their Applications to Social Philosophy*. London: Longman's, Green, and Co. https://oll-resources.s3.us-east-2.amazonaws.com/oll3/store/titles/101/0199_Bk.pdf.

Mill, John Stuart. 1989. *On Liberty and Other Writings*. Edited by Stefan Collini. New York: Cambridge University Press.

Miller, Elizabeth. 2021. *Extraction Ecologies and the Literature of the Long Exhaustion*. Princeton, NJ: Princeton University Press.

Miller, Elizabeth. 2023. "Extraction." *Victorian Literature and Culture Keywords Redux* 51, no. 3 (Fall): 403–6.

Miller, Elizabeth Carolyn. 2024. "The Industrial Ocean." Paper presented at the "Vcologies" panel, North American Victorian Studies Association conference, January 19, online. https://www.event2024.org/digital-events/vcologies-panel/.

Miller, J. Hillis. 1963. *The Disappearance of God: Five Nineteenth-Century Writers*. Urbana: University of Illinois Press.

Miller, J. Hillis. 1980. "*Wuthering Heights* and the Ellipses of Interpretation." *Notre Dame English Journal* 12, no. 2 (April): 85–100. https://www.jstor.org/stable/40062402.

Miller, J. Hillis. 1992."Optic and Semiotic in *Middlemarch*." In *Middlemarch (New Casebooks)*, edited by John Peck. New York: St. Martin's Press.

Miller, John MacNeill. 2020. "Ecological Plot: A Brief History of Multispecies Storytelling, from Malthus to Middlemarch." *Victorian Literature and Culture* 48, no. 1: 155–85.

Miller, Lucasta. 2001. *The Brontë Myth*. New York: Knopf.

Mitchell, Timothy. 2011. *Carbon Democracy: Political Power in the Age of Oil*. London: Verso.

Modest, Wayne, and Tim Barringer. 2018. Introduction to *Victorian Jamaica*, edited by Tim Barringer and Wayne Modest, 1–48. Durham, NC: Duke University Press.

Moon, Michael. 2008. "No Coward Souls: Poetic Engagements between Emily Brontë and Emily Dickinson." In *The Traffic in Poems: Nineteenth-Century Poetry and Transatlantic Exchange*, edited by Meredith L. McGill, 231–49. New Brunswick, NJ: Rutgers University Press.

Moore, Frances C., Nick Obradovich, Flavio Lehner, and Patrick Baylis. 2019. "Rapidly Declining Remarkability of Temperature Anomalies May Obscure Public Perception of Climate Change." *Proceedings of the National Academy of Sciences* 116, no. 11 (March): 4905–10. https://doi.org/10.1073/pnas.1816541116.

Moore, Jason W. 2015. *Capitalism in the Web of Life: Ecology and the Accumulation of Capital*. London: Verso.

More, Hannah. (1782) 1868. "Sensibility: An Epistle." In *The Works of Hannah More, Complete, in Seven Volumes*, 373–82. New York: Harper and Brothers.

Moretti, Franco. 2013. *The Bourgeois: Between History and Literature*. London: Verso.

Morgan, Benjamin. 2016. "*Fin Du Globe*: On Decadent Planets." *Victorian Studies* 58, no. 4 (Summer): 609–35. https://doi.org/10.2979/victorianstudies.58.4.01.

Morris, Rosalind C. "Introduction." In *Can the Subaltern Speak? Reflections on the History of an Idea*, edited by Rosalind C. Morris, 1–20. New York: Columbia University Press.

Morris, William. 1887. "The Voice of John Ball." In *A Dream of John Ball*. London: Reeves and Turner. Reprinted at the William Morris Internet Archive. https://www.marxists.org/archive/morris/works/1886/johnball/chapters/chapter4.htm.

Moser, Susanne C. 2013. "Navigating the Political and Emotional Terrain of Adaptation: Community Engagement When Climate Change Comes Home." In *Successful Adaptation to Climate Change: Linking Science and Policy in a Rapidly Changing World*, edited by S. C. Moser and M. T. Boykoff, 289–305. London: Routledge.

Moten, Fred. 2003. *In the Break: The Aesthetics of the Black Radical Tradition*. Minneapolis: University of Minnesota Press.

Moten, Fred. 2017. *Black and Blur*. Durham, NC: Duke University Press.

Muehlebach, Andrea. 2016. "Time of Monsters." *Society for Cultural Anthropology*, October 27. https://culanth.org/fieldsights/time-of-monsters.

Mufti, Nasser. 2017. *Civilizing War: Imperial Politics and the Poetics of National Rupture*. Evanston, IL: Northwestern University Press.

Mugglestone, Lynda. 1991. "The Fallacy of the Cockney Rhyme: From Keats and Earlier to Auden." *Review of English Studies* 17, no. 165: 57–66.

Natanson, Hannah, and Emmanuel Felton. 2024. "Business Titans Privately Urged NYC Mayor to Use Police on Columbia Protesters, Chats Show." *New York Times*, May 16. https://www.washingtonpost.com/nation/2024/05/16/business-leaders-chat-group-eric-adams-columbia-protesters/.

National Oceanic and Atmospheric Administration. 2023. "Greenhouse Gases Continued to Increase Rapidly in 2022." April 5. https://www.noaa.gov/news-release/greenhouse-gases-continued-to-increase-rapidly-in-2022.

Neeson, J. M. 1993. *Commoners: Common Right, Enclosure, and Social Change in England, 1700–1820*. Cambridge: Cambridge University Press.

Nelson, Louis P. 2016. *Architecture and Empire in Jamaica*. New Haven, CT: Yale University Press.

Nersessian, Anahid. 2015. *Utopia, Limited: Romanticism and Adjustment*. Cambridge, MA: Harvard University Press.

Nersessian, Anahid. 2020. *The Calamity Form: On Poetry and Social Life*. Chicago: University of Chicago Press.

Newman, Beth. 2007. "Introduction." In Emily Brontë, *Wuthering Heights*, edited by Beth Newman, 9–29. London: Broadview.

Newman, Rachel Grace. 2016. "Conjuring Cane: The Art of William Berryman and Caribbean Sugar Plantations." PhD diss., Stanford University. https://stacks.stanford.edu/file/druid:bd732xk1197/Newman,%20Rachel%20Conjuring%20Cane%20Full%20Text-augmented.pdf.

Ngai, Sianne. *Ugly Feelings*. 2005. Cambridge, MA: Harvard University Press.

Oak Taylor, Jesse. 2018. "Mourning Species: In Memoriam in an Age of Extinction." In *Ecological Form: System and Aesthetics in the Age of Empire*, edited by Nathan K. Hensley and Philip Steer, 42–62. New York: Fordham University Press.

Odum, Eugene. 1971. *The Fundamentals of Ecology*. 3rd ed. Philadelphia, PA: W. B. Saunders Company.

O'Gorman, Frances. 2010. "What Is Haunting Tennyson's 'Maud' (1855)?" *Victorian Poetry* 48, no. 3: 293–312. http://www.jstor.org/stable/27896681.

Oram, Richard W. 1994. "John Henry Wrenn." In *American Book-Collectors and Bibliographers: First Series*, edited by Joseph Rosenblum. *Dictionary of Literary Biography*, vol. 140. Detroit: Gale.

Otis, Laura. 2001. *Networking: Communicating with Bodies and Machines in the Nineteenth Century*. Ann Arbor: University of Michigan Press.

Owen, Bruce M., and Ronald Braetigam. 1978. *The Regulation Game: Strategic Use of the Administrative Process*. Cambridge, MA: Ballinger Press.

Palmer, D. J. 1973. *Tennyson: A Reader's Guide*. Columbus: Ohio University Press.

Parsard, Kaneesha. 2022. "Criticism as Proposition." *South Atlantic Quarterly* 121, no. 1 (January): 91–108.

Partington, Wilfred George. 1973. *Forging Ahead*. New York: Cooper Square.

Pateman, Carole. 1980. “Women and Consent.” *Political Theory* 8, no. 2 (May): 149–68. https://www.jstor.org/stable/190792.

Patmore, Coventry. (1857) 1961. *An Essay on English Metrical Law: A Critical Edition with Commentary*. Edited by Mary Augustine Roth. Washington, DC: Catholic University Press.

Patterson, Orlando. (1982) 2018. *Slavery and Social Death: A Comparative Study*. Cambridge, MA: Harvard University Press.

Phelan, Joseph. 2005. *The Nineteenth-Century Sonnet*. Basingstoke, UK: Palgrave Macmillan.

Pias, Claude. 2016. “The Age of Cybernetics.” In *Cybernetics: The Macy Conferences 1946–1953, Transactions*, edited by Claus Pias, 11–27. Zurich and Berlin: Diaphanes.

Pichon, Anne. 2013. “Chrome Yellow’s Darker Side.” *Nature Chemistry* 5: 897. https://doi.org/10.1038/nchem.1789.

Pinkus, Karen. 2018. “Afterword: They Would Have Ended by Burning Their Own Globe.” In *Ecological Form: System and Aesthetics in the Age of Empire*, edited by Nathan K. Hensley and Philip Steer, 241–48. New York: Fordham University Press.

Plesters, Joyce. 1966. “Ultramarine Blue, Natural and Artificial.” *Studies in Conservation* 11, no. 2 (May): 62–91. https://www.jstor.org/stable/1505446.

Plotz, John. 2018. *Semi-Detached: The Aesthetics of Virtual Experience since Dickens*. Princeton, NJ: Princeton University Press.

Poovey, Mary. 1988. *Uneven Developments: The Ideological Work of Gender in Mid-Victorian England*. Chicago: University of Chicago Press.

Poovey, Mary. 1998. *A History of the Modern Fact: Problems of Knowledge in the Sciences of Wealth and Society*. Chicago: University of Chicago Press.

Poovey, Mary. n.d. “Twenty Years of Feminist Criticism in the U.S.” Unpublished lecture, ca. 2000–2008. Mary Poovey papers, Ms.2017.001, Feminist Theory Archive/Pembroke Center Archives, Brown University Library, Providence, RI.

Popovich, Nadja, and Claire O’Neill. 2017. “A ‘500-Year Flood’ Could Happen Again Sooner Than You Think. Here’s Why.” *New York Times*, August 28. https://www.nytimes.com/interactive/2017/08/28/climate/500-year-flood-hurricane-harvey-houston.html.

Popovich, Nadja, Mira Rojanasakul, and Brad Plumer. 2022. “The Climate Impact of Your Neighborhood, Mapped.” *New York Times*, December 13. https://www.nytimes.com/interactive/2022/12/13/climate/climate-footprint-map-neighborhood.html.

Porter, Theodore. 2020. *The Rise of Statistical Thinking, 1820–1900*. Princeton, NJ: Princeton University Press.

Prins, Yopie. 2000. “Victorian Meters.” In *The Cambridge Companion to Victorian Poetry*, edited by Joseph Bristow, 89–113. New York: Cambridge University Press. https://doi.org/10.1017/CCOL0521641152.005.

Psomiades, Kathy A. 1997. *Beauty’s Body: Femininity and Representation in British Aestheticism*. Palo Alto, CA: Stanford University Press.

Psomiades, Kathy A. 2023. *Primitive Marriage: Victorian Anthropology, the Novel, and Sexual Modernity*. New York: Oxford University Press.

Puckett, Kent. 2014.“Caucus-Racing.” *Novel: A Forum on Fiction* 47, no. 1 (May): 11–23. https://www.jstor.org/stable/43829994.

Purser, Lara. n.d. "Kashmere Gardens after Harvey." Houston Flood Museum, *The Harvey Issue*. Accessed June 13, 2022. https://houstonfloodmuseum.org/category/hurricane-harvey/the-harvey-issue/.

Pykett, Lyn. 1989. *Emily Brontë*. Savage, MD: Barnes and Noble.

Pyne, Stephen. 2021. *The Pyrocene: How We Created an Age of Fire, and What Happens Next*. Berkeley: University of California Press.

Rada, Michelle. 2022. "Overdetermined: Psychoanalysis and Solidarity." *Differences* 33, no. 2–3 (December): 1–32. https://doi.org/10.1215/10407391-10124647.

Rajan, Balachandra. 1985. *The Form of the Unfinished: English Poetics from Spenser to Pound*. Princeton, NJ: Princeton University Press.

Ray, R. 2017. "Adverse Hematological Effects of Hexavalent Chromium: An Overview." *Interdisciplinary Toxicology* 9, no. 2 (May): 55–65. https://doi.org/10.1515/intox-2016-0007.

Rees, Ronald. 1982. "Constable, Turner, and Views of Nature in the Nineteenth Century." *Geographical Review* 72, no. 3 (July): 253–69. https://www.jstor.org/stable/214526.

Ricks, Christopher. 1972. *Tennyson*. New York: Collier Books, Macmillan.

Ricks, Christopher. 1989. Headnote to "Maud: A Monodrama." In *Tennyson: A Selected Edition*, edited by Christopher Ricks, 511–16. Berkeley: University of California Press.

Riding, Christine. 2013. "Introduction." In Christine Riding and Richard Johns, *Turner and the Sea*, 10–23. London: Thames and Hudson / National Maritime Museum.

Rooney, Ellen. 2007. "Foreword: An Aesthetics of Bad Objects." In Naomi Schor, *Reading in Detail: Aesthetics and the Feminine*, xiii–xlvii. New York: Routledge.

Roper, Derek. 1995. "Introduction." In Emily Brontë, *The Poems of Emily Brontë*, edited by Derek Roper with Edward Chitham, 1–29. Oxford: Oxford University Press.

Rosenberg, Aaron. 2023. *Scale, Crisis, and the Modern Novel*. New York: Cambridge University Press.

Rosenblum, Dolores. 1986. *Christina Rossetti: The Poetry of Endurance*. Carbondale: Southern Illinois University Press.

Rosenblum, Joseph. 1997. "Thomas James Wise." In *Nineteenth-Century British Book Collectors and Bibliographers*, edited by William Baker and Kenneth Womack. *Dictionary of Literary Biography*, vol. 184. Detroit: Gale.

Rossetti, Christina. 1870. "A Safe Investment." In *Commonplace, and Other Short Stories*, 241–56. London: F. S. Ellis. https://archive.org/details/cu31924073798906/page/n259/mode/2up?q=gasworks&view=theater.

Rossetti, Christina. 1885. *Time Flies: A Reading Diary*. London: Society for Promoting Christian Knowledge.

Rossetti, Christina. 1892. *The Face of the Deep: A Devotional Commentary on the Apocalypse*. London: Society for Promoting Christian Knowledge.

Rossetti, Christina. 1997. *The Letters of Christina Rossetti: 1843–1873*. Vol. 1 of *The Letters of Christina Rossetti*, edited by Antony H. Harrison. Charlottesville: University of Virginia Press, 1997.

Rossetti, Christina. 1999. *The Letters of Christina Rossetti: 1874–1881*. Vol. 2 of *The Letters of Christina Rossetti*, edited by Antony H. Harrison. Charlottesville: University of Virginia Press.

Rossetti, Christina. 2005. *The Complete Poems*. Edited by R. W. Crump and Betty S. Flowers. New York: Penguin Classics.

Rossetti, Frances Mary Livinia, ed. 1843. *Hodge-Podge; or Weekly Efforts*. The Rossetti Archive, edited by Jerome McGann. http://www.rossettiarchive.org/docs/5-1843.rad.html#5-1843.

Rossetti, William Michael. 1918. "Preface." In Christina Rossetti, *Poems of Christina Rossetti*, edited by William Michael Rossetti. London: Macmillan. https://babel.hathitrust.org/cgi/pt?id=uiug.30112088981300&view=1up&seq=14.

Rowlatt, Justin. 2023. "UAE Planned to Use COP28 Climate Talks to Make Oil Deals." *BBC*, November 27. https://www.bbc.com/news/science-environment-67508331.

Said, Edward. 1994. *Culture and Imperialism*. New York: Vintage.

Saintsbury, George. (1910) 1961. *A History of English Prosody*. New York: Russell and Russell.

Saito, Kohei. 2024. *Slow Down: The Degrowth Manifesto*. Translated by Brian Bergstrom. New York: Astra House.

Samalin, Zachary. 2019. "Introduction: A Map the Size of the Empire." *Criticism* 61, no. 4. https://digitalcommons.wayne.edu/criticism/vol61/iss4/1.

Samalin, Zachary. 2021. *The Masses Are Revolting: Victorian Culture and the Political Aesthetics of Disgust*. Ithaca, NY: Cornell University Press.

Samenow, Jason. 2017. "Harvey Is a 1,000-Year Flood Event Unprecedented in Scale." *Washington Post*, August 31, 2017.

Sanger, Charles Percy. 1926. *The Structure of Wuthering Heights*. London: Hogarth Press.

Saussure, Ferdinand de. 1969. *Course in General Linguistics*. Translated by Wade Baskin. Edited by Charles Bally and Albert Sechehaye. New York: Philosophical Library.

Scarborough, Camille. 2023. "Multifaceted Gift Supports Future Leaders in Global Business." Georgetown University Advancement, April 11. https://today.advancement.georgetown.edu/called_to_be/learning-discovery/2023/multifaceted-gift-supports-future-leaders-in-global-business/.

Scheffer, Marten. 2009. "Alternative Stable States and Regime Shifts in Ecosystems." In *The Princeton Guide to Ecology*, edited by Simon A. Levin, Stephen R. Carpenter, H. Charles J. Godfray, Ann P. Kinzig, Michel Loreau, Jonathan B. Losos, Brian Walker, and David S. Wilcove, 395–406. Princeton, NJ: Princeton University Press. https://doi.org/10.1515/9781400833023.395.

Schor, Naomi. 2007. *Reading in Detail: Aesthetics and the Feminine*. New York: Routledge.

Schuessler, Jennifer. 2021. "A Lost Brontë Library Surfaces." *New York Times*, May 25. https://www.nytimes.com/2021/05/25/arts/bronte-library-sothebys-auction.html.

Scott, Heidi. 2018. *Fuel: An Ecocritical History*. London: Bloomsbury.

Scott, James C. 1985. *Weapons of the Weak: Everyday Forms of Peasant Resistance*. New Haven, CT: Yale University Press.

Scott, James C. 1992. *Domination and the Arts of Resistance: Hidden Transcripts*. New Haven, CT: Yale University Press.

Scranton, Roy. 2013. "Learning How to Die in the Anthropocene." *New York Times*, November 13. https://opinionator.blogs.nytimes.com/2013/11/10/learning-how-to-die-in-the-anthropocene/.

Sedgwick, Eve Kosofsky. 1987. "A Poem Is Being Written." *Representations* 17 (January): 110–43. https://doi.org/10.2307/3043795.

Sedgwick, Eve Kosofsky. 1993. "Epidemics of the Will." In *Tendencies*, 130–42. Durham, NC: Duke University Press.

Sedgwick, Eve Kosofsky. 2002. *Touching Feeling: Affect, Pedagogy, Performativity*. Durham, NC: Duke University Press.

Sedgwick, Eve Kosofsky, and Adam Frank. 1995. "Shame in the Cybernetic Fold: Reading Silvan Tomkins." In *Shame and Its Sisters: A Silvan Tomkins Reader*, edited by Eve Kosofsky Sedgwick and Adam Frank, 1–28. Durham, NC: Duke University Press.

Shannon, Edgar F. 1953. "The Critical Reception of Tennyson's 'Maud.'" *PMLA* 68, no. 3 (June): 397–417. https://www.jstor.org/stable/459861.

Shannon, Edgar F. 1959. "Lockwood's Dreams and the Exegesis of Wuthering Heights." *Nineteenth-Century Fiction* 14, no. 2 (September): 95–109. https://www.jstor.org/stable/3044162.

Sharpe, William. 1904. *Literary Geography*. New York: Charles Scribner's Sons.

Shatz, Adam. 2024. *The Rebels Clinic: The Revolutionary Lives of Frantz Fanon*. New York: Farrar, Straus and Giroux.

Shaw, M. 1973. "Tennyson and His Public." In *Tennyson: A Reader's Guide*, edited by D. J. Palmer, 52–88. Columbus: Ohio University Press.

Shires, Linda. 1999. "Victorian Women's Poetry." *Victorian Literature and Culture* 27, no. 2: 601–9.

Shore, Daniel. 2018. *Cyberformalism: Histories of Linguistic Forms in the Digital Archive*. Baltimore: Johns Hopkins University Press.

Shore, Daniel. 2026. "The Limits of Worst in *Paradise Lost*." *Milton Studies* 68, no. 2 (forthcoming).

Shorter, Clement. 1908. "A Bibliographical Note." In Emily Brontë, *The Complete Works of Emily Brontë*, vol. 1, *Poems*, edited by Clement King Shorter. New York: Hodder and Stoughton.

Shuttleworth, Sally. 1987. *George Eliot and Nineteenth-Century Science: The Make-Believe of a Beginning*. Cambridge: Cambridge University Press.

Small, Helen. 2009. "Introduction." In Emily Brontë, *Wuthering Heights*, edited by Ian Jack and Helen Small, vii–xxi. New York: Oxford World's Classics.

Smiles, Sam. 2014. "Turner and Modern History." In *Late Turner: Painting Set Free*, edited by David Blayney Brown, Amy Concannon, and Sam Smiles, 144–75. London: Tate.

Smiles, Samuel. 1859. *Self-Help, with Illustrations of Character and Conduct*. London: John Murray.

Smith, Simon. 2006. *Slavery, Family, and Gentry Capitalism in the British Atlantic: The World of the Lascelles, 1648–1834*. Cambridge: Cambridge University Press.

Solnit, Rebecca. 2014. "Are We Missing the Big Picture on Climate Change?" *New York Times*, December 2. https://www.nytimes.com/2014/12/07/magazine/are-we-missing-the-big-picture-on-climate-change.html.

Solnit, Rebecca. (2014) 2016. *Hope in the Dark: Untold Stories, Wild Possibilities, Third Edition, with a New Foreword and Afterword*. Chicago: Haymarket Books.

Song, Min Hyoung. 2021. *Climate Lyricism*. Durham, NC: Duke University Press.

Spillers, Hortense J. 2018. "To the Bone: Some Speculations on Touch." Filmed March 2018 at Stedelijk Museum, Amsterdam. YouTube video, 51:38, at 18:30. https://www.youtube.com/watch?v=AvL4wUKIfpo&feature=youtu.be.

Spivak, Gayatri Chakravorty. 1985. "Three Women's Texts and a Critique of Imperialism." *"Race," Writing, and Difference*, special issue. *Critical Inquiry* 12, no. 1: 243–61.

Spivak, Gayatri Chakravorty. 1988. "Can the Subaltern Speak?" In *Marxism and the Interpretation of Culture*, edited by Cary Nelson and Lawrence Grossberg, 271–313. Basingstoke, UK: Macmillan Education.

Spivak, Gayatri Chakravorty, and Brad Evans. 2016. "When Law is Not Justice." *New York Times*, July 13. https://www.nytimes.com/2016/07/13/opinion/when-law-is-not-justice.html.

Stanford, Derek, and Muriel Spark. 1953. *Emily Brontë, Her Life and Work*. London: Peter Owen. https://archive.org/details/in.ernet.dli.2015.460383/page/n3/mode/2up?q=cardboard+sublime&view=theater.

Stern, Philip J. 2023. *Empire, Incorporated: The Corporations that Built British Colonialism*. Cambridge, MA: Harvard University Press.

Stewart, Susan. 2004. "The Ballad in *Wuthering Heights*." *Representations* 86, no. 1 (May): 175–97. https://doi.org/10.1525/rep.2004.86.1.175.

Stout, Daniel. 2017. *Corporate Romanticism: Liberalism, Justice, and the Novel*. New York: Fordham University Press.

Stuart, J. A. Erskine. 1888. *The Bronte Country: Its Topography, Antiquities, and History*. London: Longmans, Green, and Co.

Stwertka, Eve Marie. 1977. "The Web of Utterance: *Middlemarch*." *Texas Studies in Literature and Language* 19, no. 2: 179–87.

Suljević, Damir, Jasmina Sulejmanović, Muhamed Fočak, Erna Halilović, Džemila Pupalović, Azra Hasić, and Andi Alijagic. 2021. "Assessing Hexavalent Chromium Tissue-Specific Accumulation Patterns and Induced Physiological Responses to Probe Chromium Toxicity in *Coturnix Japonica* Quail." *Chemosphere* 266 (March): 129005. https://doi.org/10.1016/j.chemosphere.2020.129005.

Suvin, Darko. 1973. "'*The Time Machine* versus Utopia' as a Structural Model for Science Fiction." *Comparative Literature Studies* 10, no. 4 (December): 334–52.

Sweeney, John A. 2019. "Global Weirding." In *The Postnormal Times Reader*, edited by Ziauddin Sardar, 203–10. Herndon, VA: International Institute of Islamic Thought. http://www.jstor.org/stable/j.ctv10kmcqv.12.

Szeman, Imre, and Jennifer Wenzel. 2021. "What Do We Talk about When We Talk about Extractivism?" *Textual Practice* 35, no. 3 (February): 505–23. http://dx.doi.org/10.1080/0950236X.2021.1889829.

Taaffe, James G. 1963. "Circle Imagery in Tennyson's 'In Memoriam.'" *Victorian Poetry* 1, no. 2 (April): 123–31.

Tadiar, Neferti X. M. 2022. *Remaindered Life*. Durham, NC: Duke University Press.

Taylor, Charles. 1998. "Going Down (Review of Hans Blumenberg, *Shipwreck with Spectator: Paradigm of a Metaphor for Existence*)." *History of the Human Sciences* 11, no. 4 (November): 141–48.

Taylor, Christopher. 2018. *Empire of Neglect: The West Indies in the Wake of British Liberalism*. Durham, NC: Duke University Press.

Tennyson, Alfred. 1989. *Tennyson: A Selected Edition, Incorporating the Trinity College Manuscripts*, edited by Christopher Ricks. Berkeley: University of California Press.

Tennyson, Hallam. 1906. *Alfred, Lord Tennyson: A Memoir, by His Son*. London: Macmillan. https://archive.org/details/b22546656/.

Thomas, Deborah A. 2019. *Political Life in the Wake of the Plantation: Sovereignty, Witnessing, Repair*. Durham, NC: Duke University Press.

Thompson, Tosin. 2021. "Young People's Climate Anxiety Released in Landmark Survey." *Nature* 597 (September). https://media.nature.com/original/magazine-assets/d41586-021-02582-8/d41586-021-02582-8.pdf.

Thomson, James. (1748) 1751. "Ode on Aeolus's Harp." In *The Poetical Works of James Thomson. Containing The Seasons, Liberty, The Castle of Indolence, and Poems on Several Occasions*, 353–54. Dublin: J. Exshaw, R. James, and S. Price.

TOI Staff and AFP. 2023. "Gallant Tells Families 'All for All' Hostage Offer Phony, Pushes Military Pressure." *Times of Israel*, October 30. https://www.timesofisrael.com/gallant-tells-families-all-for-all-hostage-offer-phony-pushes-military-pressure/.

Tomkins, Silvan. 1962. *Affect Imagery Consciousness, Volume 1: The Positive Affects*. New York: Springer.

Tomkins, Silvan. 1995. "What Are Affects?" In *Shame and Its Sisters: A Sylvan Tomkins Reader*, edited by Eve Kosofsky Sedgwick and Adam Frank, 33–74. Durham, NC: Duke University Press.

Tondre, Michael. 2020. "Conrad's Carbon Imaginary: Oil, Imperialism, and the Victorian Petro-Archive." *Victorian Literature and Culture* 48, no. 1: 57–90. https://doi.org10.1017/S1060150319000536.

Tondre, Michael. 2022. "'On Fossil Finitude': Industrial Energy Systems and the 'Growing Good' in *Middlemarch*." *Dickens Studies Annual: Essays on Victorian Fiction* 53, no. 2: 283–321.

Tooze, Adam. 2021. "Ecological Leninism: Adam Tooze on Andreas Malm's Post-Pandemic Climate Politics." *London Review of Books* 43, no. 22. https://www.lrb.co.uk/the-paper/v43/n22/adam-tooze/ecological-leninism.

Townsend, Joyce H. 1993. "The Materials of J. M. W. Turner: Pigments." *Studies in Conservation* 38, no. 4 (November): 231–54. https://www.jstor.org/stable/1506368.

Townsend, Joyce H. 1993. *Turner's Painting Techniques*. London: Tate Gallery.

Townsend, Joyce H. 1994. "The Materials and Techniques of J. M. W. Turner: Primings and Supports." *Studies in Conservation* 39, no. 3 (August): 145–53.

Tucker, Herbert. 1988. *Tennyson and the Doom of Romanticism*. Cambridge, MA: Harvard University Press.

Tucker, Herbert. 2020. "Better Yet: Tennyson's Poetic Revisionism in the Harvard Manuscripts." In *Poetry in the Making: Creativity and Composition in Victorian Poetic Drafts*, edited by Daniel Tyler, 52–77. Oxford: Oxford University Press.

Turner, Fred. 2006. *From Counterculture to Cyberculture: Stewart Brand, the Whole Earth Network, and the Rise of Digital Utopianism*. Chicago: University of Chicago Press.

Turner, Fred. 2013. *The Democratic Surround: Multimedia and American Liberalism from World War II to the Psychedelic Sixties*. Chicago: University of Chicago Press.

Turner, Jenny. 2022. "Inside the Sausage Factory: Jenny Turner Reports from COP 26." *London Review of Books* 44, no. 1 (January). https://www.lrb.co.uk/the-paper/v44/n01/jenny-turner/inside-the-sausage-factory.

Uglow, Jenny. 2014. "Turner at Twilight." *New York Review of Books*, November 13. https://www.nybooks.com/online/2014/11/13/turner-at-twilight/.

Untitled photograph, Thornton-in-Lonsdale. n.d. Lancaster University Special Collections, SLA/5/2. Lancaster, UK.

van Brugen, Isabel. 2022. “Dallas Floods: Videos, Pictures Show Cars Submerged and Vehicles Abandoned.” *Newsweek*, August 22. https://www.newsweek.com/dallas-flash-floods-pictures-videos-rainfall-texas-rainfall-1735647.

van Ghent, Dorothy. 1952. “The Window-Figure and the Two-Children Figure in *Wuthering Heights*.” *Nineteenth-Century Fiction* 7, no. 3 (December): 189–97. https://www.jstor.org/stable/3044358.

Vernon, James. 2005. “Historians and the Victorian Studies Question: Response.” *Victorian Studies* 47, no. 2 (Winter): 272–79. https://muse.jhu.edu/article/185332.

Victorero, Lissette, Les Watling, Maria L. Deng Palomares, and Claire Nouvian. 2018. “Out of Sight, but within Reach: A Global History of Bottom-Trawled Deep-Sea Fisheries from >400 m Depth.” *Frontiers in Marine Science* 5 (April). https://www.frontiersin.org/articles/10.3389/fmars.2018.00098/full.

Vine, Steven. 1998. *Emily Brontë*. Woodbridge, CT: Twayne.

von Sneidern, Maja-Lisa. 1995. “*Wuthering Heights* and the Liverpool Slave Trade.” *ELH* 62, no. 1 (Spring): 171–96. https://doi.org/10.1353/elh.1995.0009.

Wallace-Wells, David. 2019. *The Uninhabitable Earth: Life After Warming*. New York: Tim Duggan Books.

Walsh, David. F. 1998. “Structure/Agency.” In *Core Sociological Dichotomies*, edited by Chris Jenks, 8–33. London: SAGE.

Ward, Nathaniel Blagshaw. (1842) 1852. *On the Growth of Plants in Closely Glazed Cases*. London: John Van Voorst.

Warner, Bernhard, and Rebecca F. Elliott. 2024. “ConocoPhillips to Acquire Marathon Oil in $22.5 Billion Deal.” *New York Times*, May 29. https://www.nytimes.com/2024/05/29/business/dealbook/marathon-oil-conocophillips-deal.html?smid=url-share.

Wells, H. G. 2005. *The Time Machine*. Edited by Patrick Parrinder. New York: Penguin.

Wenzel, Jennifer. 2017. “Turning Over a New Leaf: Fanonian Humanism and Environmental Justice.” In *The Routledge Companion to the Environmental Humanities*, edited by Ursula Heise, Jon Christensen, and Michelle Niemann, 165–73. London: Routledge.

Wenzel, Jennifer. 2020. *The Disposition of Nature: Environmental Crisis and World Literature*. New York: Fordham University Press.

“Western North American Extreme Heat Virtually Impossible without Human-Caused Climate Change.” 2021. *World Weather Attribution*, July 7. https://www.worldweatherattribution.org/western-north-american-extreme-heat-virtually-impossible-without-human-caused-climate-change/.

Wiener, Norbert. (1948) 1961. *Cybernetics, or Control and Communication in the Animal and the Machine*. Cambridge, MA: MIT Press.

Williams, Daniel. 2017. “Slow Fire: Serial Thinking and Hardy’s Genres of Induction.” *Genre* 50, no. 1: 19–38.

Williams, Eric. 1994. *Capitalism and Slavery*. Chapel Hill: University of North Carolina Press.

Williams, Raymond. 1973. *The Country and the City*. Oxford: Oxford University Press.

Williams, Raymond. 1977. *Marxism and Literature*. Oxford: Oxford University Press.

Williams, Raymond. (1980) 2005. *Culture and Materialism: Selected Essays*. London: Verso.

Williams, William Carlos. 1969. "Author's Introduction to *The Wedge*." In *Selected Essays of William Carlos Williams*, 255–58. New York: New Directions.

Wilson, Jennifer. 2022. "The Editor Who Moves Theory into the Mainstream." *New Yorker*, March 29. https://www.newyorker.com/culture/persons-of-interest/the-editor-who-moves-theory-into-the-mainstream.

Wilson, Tom, and Derek Brower. 2023. "What Big Oil's Bumper Profits Mean for the Energy Transition." *Financial Times*, February 10. https://www.ft.com/content/16f8800b-7300-42e0-a3c7-3400ed6c4fa5.

Wiltshire, Irene. 2013. "Speech in Wuthering Heights: Joseph's Dialect and Charlotte's Emendations." *Bronte Studies: The Journal of the Bronte Society* 30, no. 1 (July): 19–29. https://doi.org/10.1179/147489304x18821.

Winant, Gabriel. 2022. "Mike Davis's Specificities." *N+1*, November 16. https://www.nplusonemag.com/online-only/online-only/daviss-specificities/.

Wong, Sam. 2018. "When Humans Are Wiped from Earth, the Chicken Bones Will Remain." *New Scientist*, December 12. https://www.newscientist.com/article/2187838-when-humans-are-wiped-from-earth-the-chicken-bones-will-remain/.

Wood, John. 1872. *A Journey to the Source of the River Oxus*. London: John Murray.

Woods, Derek. 2019. "Scale in Ecological Science Writing." In *The Routledge Handbook of Ecocriticism and Environmental Communication*, edited by Scott Slovic, Swarnalatha Rangarajan, and Vidya Sarveswaran, 118–28. New York: Routledge.

Woods, Derek. 2023. "Genre at Earth Magnitude: A Theory of Climate Fiction." *New Literary History* 54, no. 2: 1143–67. https://doi.org/10.1353/nlh.2023.a907162.

Wordsworth, William. 2008. "Lines Written a Few Miles above Tintern Abbey." In *William Wordsworth: The Major Works*, edited by Stephen Gill, 132–35. New York: Oxford World's Classics.

"World Missing All Targets to Save Nature, UN Warns." 2020. *France 24*, September 15. https://www.france24.com/en/20200915-world-missing-all-targets-to-save-nature-un-warns.

Wright, Daniel. 2018. *Bad Logic: Reasoning about Desire in the Victorian Novel*. Baltimore: Johns Hopkins University Press.

Wright, Daniel. 2024. *The Grounds of the Novel*. Stanford, CA: Stanford University Press.

Wynter, Sylvia. (1992) 1994. "No Humans Involved: An Open Letter to My Colleagues." *Forum N.H.I. Knowledge for the 21st Century* 1, no. 1 (Fall): 42–71.

Zeavin, Hannah. 2022. "No Touching: Boundary Violation and Analytic Solidarity." *differences* 33, nos. 2–3 (December): 110–40. https://doi.org/10.1215/10407391-10124718.

Zierler, David. 2011. *The Invention of Ecocide: Agent Orange, Vietnam, and the Scientists Who Changed the Way We Think about the Environment*. Athens: University of Georgia Press.

Index